EVERYDAY GRACE

EVERYDAY GRACE

*Having Hope, Finding Forgiveness
and Making Miracles*

MARIANNE WILLIAMSON

BANTAM BOOKS

LONDON · NEW YORK · TORONTO · SYDNEY · AUCKLAND

EVERYDAY GRACE
A BANTAM BOOK : 0 553 81545 8

First publication in Great Britain

PRINTING HISTORY
Bantam edition published 2003

1 3 5 7 9 10 8 6 4 2

Set in 11/14pt Granjon by
Falcon Oast Graphic Art Ltd.

Bantam Books are published by Transworld Publishers,
61–63 Uxbridge Road, London W5 5SA,
a division of The Random House Group Ltd,
in Australia by Random House Australia (Pty) Ltd,
20 Alfred Street, Milsons Point, Sydney, NSW 2061, Australia,
in New Zealand by Random House New Zealand Ltd,
18 Poland Road, Glenfield, Auckland 10, New Zealand
and in South Africa by Random House (Pty) Ltd,
Endulini, 5a Jubilee Road, Parktown 2193, South Africa.

Printed and bound in Great Britain by
Clays Ltd, Bungay, Suffolk.

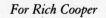

For Rich Cooper

CONTENTS

ACKNOWLEDGEMENTS

As I wrote this book, I was surrounded by three literary angels: Al Lowman, my literary agent for many years and once again my muse; Andrew Harvey, an extraordinary mystical author I am blessed to call my friend; and Wendy Carlton, the most dedicated editor I have ever known. All of them taught me not only how to make this a better book but, even more important, the true meaning of the word 'support.' If this book deserves any credit at all, then the credit belongs to them.

To Susan Petersen Kennedy, Riverhead's publisher, my thanks for both the inspiration and stalwart faith in my ability to deliver.

To Andrea Cagan, Alyse Martinelli, B. G. Dilworth, Charlette Manning, Matthew Albracht, Linda Puryear, Kathy Tomassi, Pam Rice, Suzannah Galland, and Christen Brown, with gratitude for help and encouragement.

To the many people who have supported my work at Renaissance Unity and throughout the world. I am surrounded in my dreams by your smiles and handshakes.

And to Emma, Mommy's darling. There really are no words.

A human being is a part of the whole called the 'universe,' a part limited in time and space. He experiences himself, his thoughts and feelings, as something separated from the rest, a kind of optical delusion of . . . consciousness. This delusion is a kind of prison for us, restricting us to our personal desires and to affection for a few persons nearest to us. Our task must be to free ourselves from this prison by widening our circle of compassion to embrace all living creatures and the whole of nature in all its beauty. Nobody is able to achieve this completely, but the striving for such achievement is in itself part of the liberation and a foundation for inner security.

ALBERT EINSTEIN

EVERYDAY GRACE

INTRODUCTION

Reclaiming Our Magic

My father used to speak of the Byzantine Rule, which is that nothing is as it appears to be. I have always had a sense that something is missing in this world – that at the very least there is something important we're not discussing.

I believe that hunger for a 'lost dimension' of experience is a natural yearning in all of us, and it doesn't go away just because we ignore it. It is evidenced among other places in the millions of children and adults who obsessively read the Harry Potter books. It is said that fiction is where someone gets to tell the truth. We *are* a bunch of silly Muggles, and we really *do* miss out on the magic of existence. There's a collective knowing that a dimension of reality exists beyond the material plane, and that sense of knowing is causing a mystical resurgence on the planet today. It's not just children who are looking for a missing piece. It is a very mature outlook to question the nature of our reality.

We are like birds who have forgotten we have wings, kings and queens who have forgotten our royal heritage. We feel enslaved by conditions that should have no power to bind us, and powerless before forces over which we have been given dominion. No wonder our children are drawn to reading about a world in which people live a more magical existence than the one we offer them here.

I have watched my daughter bury herself, like so many other children, heart and soul in the Harry Potter books. I remember that when I was her age I had a similar fascination with books like *A Wrinkle in Time, Half Magic*, and the Narnia series by C. S. Lewis. In a particularly passionate moment, my daughter once told me that the only time she was really happy was when she was reading *Harry Potter*. And, sadly, I understood what she meant. It was the only place she felt she could stay in touch with all the magic.

When I am honest with myself, I know that I cry deep inside, just as my daughter does, when I cannot find the magic. Emma has asked me several times, 'Mommy, are the Harry Potter books true?

Are there really magical places like that?' And I answer her as honestly as I can, which is to say that I answer 'yes.' But she is never satisfied when I talk about different realms of consciousness, when I tell her that the magic in Harry Potter is a magic that lives in all of us. She wants a simpler magic, which I understand. And I assume that one day she'll find her own path to the magic that lives and breathes inside her. No one can take the journey for anyone else – even parents for our children – as much as we might like to. But if and when my daughter makes her own mystical journey, she will learn that magic indeed is here in this world right now. It is literally all around us. Each of us has a mark on our forehead, just like Harry Potter, that speaks to the fact that all of us come from a very magical source.

Harry Potter is one boy in a long line of mythical heroes who have reminded the human race that we are so much more than we think we are, so much more powerful than we seem to know. Jesus said that we would someday do even greater works than He; should we not take Him at His word? And should not 'someday' be today? It's time for us to start working miracles, if indeed we have the capacity within us to do so.

This book is for those who seek to work miracles. The search for the Holy Grail of miraculous power

– humanity's instinctive understanding that we are meant to soar above the limitations of our physical world – has been going on for ages. Yet now the search has become a popular yearning not just among monks or adventurers in far-off places, but among many of us living very practical lives. We wish to cultivate the sacred in the midst of the great and small difficulties of our daily existence. We want spiritual principles to be more than beautiful abstractions; we want them to actually transform our lives.

'Heaven and earth shall be as one,' according to the Bible, meaning that one day we will live on the earth but think only the thoughts of heaven. The intersection between our material and spiritual existence is the mystical power represented visually in both the Christian Cross and the Jewish Star of David. It is the point where the axis of God meets the axis of humanity. The modern mystic is someone seeking to embody that point in his or her own experience.

In the words of author Manly P. Hall, mysticism is not a religion, but a 'conviction of the heart.' I realize now that the journey, which started in my childhood – beginning with books about magic, then moving on to philosophy classes, astrology, tarot, the *I Ching*, and ultimately more classical theological studies and *A Course in Miracles* (a self-study psychological training based on universal spiritual themes) – has been a fairly common version of my generation's spiritual journey. I was once someone – and in the 1960s and 1970s, there were many of us – who had moons and stars on the walls of every place I lived and encrusted in the jewellery of every outfit I wore. And we needn't discuss the Maxfield Parrish prints: the colour, the light, the hint of another reality . . .

I can see now what I was going for, however crudely, and I have compassion for the young woman I was, always thinking there was 'something more.' Now that I'm firmly planted in my middle years, I can see that the spiritual path has been the calling of my soul for a very long time, and I am ready to devote the rest of my life to walking it as best I can.

The seeker in us is always seeking more Truth, knowing that the search goes on forever. The mystic in us, on the other hand, is trying to practise what we've learned of it: right here, in this moment, whatever we are doing. The mystic is a spiritual practitioner, seeking not merely to understand the principles of spiritual awareness, but to embody them as best he or she can. We embrace the idea – advanced by both ancient philosophers and modern physicists – that the world is one. Everything connects to everything; therefore, as we change, the world cannot but change with us.

Modern mystics form a kind of spiritual underground in the world today, seeking to transform *everything*. We are everywhere, as mystics have always been everywhere; we come from every religion, as mystics have always come from every religion; and some of us relate to no religion at all. The mystical realm lies beyond all dogma and beyond the evidence of the physical senses. The mystic has been called to an inner journey, through the darkened entanglements of human existence to the radical love at the heart of God.

I have written this book as a travelling companion for the modern mystic, who goes through his day with the deepest desire to be in the world but not of the world – to be walking with her feet planted firmly on the ground, but thinking with her head soaring powerfully through the sky. To live solidly grounded, but from a spiritual foundation, integrating within ourselves the consciousness of earth and the consciousness of heaven – such is the mystic's longing. And that longing is not for ourselves alone. For as any one of us finds our wings, the entire world is lifted.

The mystical path is not always easy, and my

hope is that this book might be a bit of a map through some of its thorniest passages. I do not write as someone who has mastered the way, but as someone who has been walking it, though often clumsily, for several decades of my life. There are bits of information I've discovered on my way, pieces of knowledge and understanding that have made their way to me, as they've made their way to mystic travellers for generations. I have seen darkness, but I have glimpsed a little light as well.

May this book shed light on someone's path, and may all of us enter the illuminated door beyond which darkness is no more. May the darkened skies of the human heart be lit by the Light of Truth. May the mercy and the peace of God be upon us now and for all our days.

Amen.

PROLOGUE

PART I

THOUGHTS OF GRACE

The Mystical Wands

The first thing a mystic needs is his or her tools. When I was a little girl, every August my mother would take me to the store to buy school supplies. First there was the important decision to be made about my lunch box. Did I want Cinderella on the front of it, or ballet shoes, or Snow White, perhaps? And then, of course, there were the notebooks, pencils and pens, erasers, and myriad other accoutrements, such as index cards, markers, and notebook dividers. Only when I had all my supplies together was I prepared to go to school.

Ultimately I realized that tools are essential to almost any worthwhile endeavour. You don't go to school unprepared, you don't try to climb a mountain unprepared, and you don't walk the mystical path unprepared.

What are the mystic's supplies? They are spiritual principles, much like magical wands in their capacity to turn any situation into a crucible of miraculous transformation. They change the world by changing us. The mystic path is a journey of personal transformation, and while the goal of the journey is to become our true selves, we can only do this by letting go of who we are not. If we wish to experience the fullness of life, we must cut through layers of illusion that hide the truth of who we really are. The mystical path runs through a very deep forest – the forest of our own psyche – and we need our supplies in order to walk through it.

We meet monsters and demons on the inner path. We meet humiliation in order to grow to the point where our behaviour would not lead to humiliation; we meet rejection in order to grow to the point where our behaviour would not lead to the pain of rejection; we meet the pangs of deep regret in order to grow to the point where our behaviour would not lead to regret. We meet the monsters in order to slay them. The only way to rid ourselves of darkness is by bringing it to light.

Until we have met the monsters in ourselves, we keep trying to slay them in the outer world. And we find that we cannot. For all darkness in the world stems from darkness in the heart. And it is there that we must do our work. The universe is holographic, which means the whole is present in every piece. Therefore, as we address the shadow within us, we are addressing the shadow of the world. The mystic does not deny the darkness, in ourselves or in the world, but affirms a light that lies beyond it. And we have faith the light will prevail because we have faith that light is our true identity. Our task is to remember that. We invoke the light by actively acknowledging it is there, standing as Harry Potter stood on platform 9¾, knowing the door would reveal itself because of the nature of who we truly are. Being magic, Harry lives in a magical world. And, being magic, so do we.

The mystical realm arises from a different mode of perception than the one we are used to. The human race now stands on the brink of a historic transformation, with new eyes, new ears, new minds, and new hearts emerging from the cosmic drama of human evolution. As an embryo becomes a baby, we are becoming a new, more spiritualized version of ourselves. We are growing mystical wings as we evolve, as any species does, in the direction that supports our survival. We are moving now toward a universal compassion because, if we do not, we will cause our own extinction. To be a mystic is to choose rebirth, for ourselves and for the human race. We are participating in a collective quantum leap forward, in which our species will experience a fundamentally new chapter in our history.

Fundamental change is not a casual occurrence. We cannot casually commit to the process of spiritual transformation. It's not enough to say, 'Oh, I think I'll be a mystic this year.' Mysticism is not a trend. Our entire being is called to the task, for the journey from density to light involves every aspect of who we are. Whether we are angry at the dry cleaners because they've ruined our favourite sweater, upset with a friend who has broken a promise, or frightened at the diagnosis of cancer in the breast of a best friend; whether we're worried about the state of our marriage, looking for a new job, or anxious about nuclear bombs and terrorists in our midst, we see that everything we go through is a step along the path. We are taking the mystical journey as a way of transforming the world by transforming *ourselves*. Only by finding the love within us can we provide the love that will save the world.

Each of us carries, in the depths of our conscious-ness, a boxful of mystical tools. And central to our tool kit is the magical wand. A wand is not just silliness from children's literature. Fairy tales are rife with archetypal truths that teach not only children, but open-minded adults as well, deep and fundamental truths about the nature of our reality. A wand is a medium of power, not just for wizards, but also for you and me. A wand is essentially a principle, an intention, a focused thought. When focused thought is negative, it creates ill. And when focused thought is loving and enlightened, it creates miraculous breakthroughs. A mystical wand is the illuminated power that emanates from the mind when it is married to the heart.

Most of us love, to be sure. Yet far too often our love is passive; we must be pro-active in our love in order for it to change our lives. Spiritual laziness has no place on the path. First, we must outgrow the myth of neutrality. For in fact there is no neutral thought; all thought leads to love or to its absence. One who is not committed to love is surrendered to that which opposes it, opening up the door to fear as surely as one who consciously welcomes that fear.

There is so much love in the human heart, yet hatred threatens our planet. And why? Because hatred is currently more committed than love. In the words of philosopher Edmund Burke, 'The only thing necessary for evil to triumph is for enough good men to do nothing.' Indeed, the forces of fear in this world are more disciplined, more courageous in a perverse kind of way, than are the forces of love. For hatred, as we know all too well, has no problem announcing itself and its intentions to the world. Our response should not just be that we oppose hate; our response must be that we *love the world*. Then and only then will love truly triumph: when the children of God don't just *feel* our love, but *express* our love.

Our task then is to harness the energies of love – to actualize its enormous power in practical and meaningful ways. Love too must announce its intentions to the world, with all the passion born of a compassionate heart. We are a species that has everything, yet what we lack is what only we can give: conviction. It is the conviction to love that gives birth to miracles.

In the words of the French philosopher Teilhard de Chardin, 'One day, after we have mastered the winds and the waves, gravity and the tides, we will harness for God the energies of love. And then, for the second time in human history, mankind will have discovered fire.'

The mystic lives with that fire in our hearts. And that is why we use our wands, directing the power of their fiery glow to the darkened areas of human existence. Everything we encounter throughout the day is a spiritual opportunity, if we approach it with love. Every moment challenges us to rise to our highest: to choose strength over weakness, forgiveness over blame, faith over faithlessness, and love over fear. And when we can't, we ask God to help us. In choosing love, we are choosing to be healed from the forces that would hold us back. Love heals the world by healing our minds, for that which is healed on the level of consciousness is healed on the level of ultimate Cause.

The world will change when we change. We are living at a time when our technological power has so vastly outdistanced our spiritual progress that we are threatened by the prospect of global catastrophe. And yet there is within us the knowledge – etched on every human heart – that indeed there is a power beyond the mortal mind, which can do for us what we cannot do for ourselves. And if ever there was a time to humble ourselves, atoning for the arrogance of human conceit, it is now. There is a ripple of rising consciousness among the peoples of the earth today, as we consider the possibility that there might be a better way – a way the mechanical, rationalistic, technological left brain cannot access – which offers us hope that the mortal mind cannot.

There is another way of knowing, another way of living, and another way of loving on this earth. This 'other way' is a realm that is full of magic and miracles. It is a world more real than what we see around us. It is the realm from which we have come, and to which all of us long to return. 'As to me,' wrote Walt Whitman, 'I know of nothing else but miracles.' Everything but miracles, in time, will dissolve in the presence of love.

Our imagination is the womb out of which a new world will be born. Think of every situation in your life as being ripe for new birth. See luminous energy emerging from your heart, extending outward to touch all things. Cast the light over your childhood home. Cast it over your physical body. Cast it over warring nations. Cast it over the entire planet. Cast it over the people you love. Cast it over the people you judge. Feel now a bolt of energy coming over you as you extend this light. Avoid the temptation to invalidate this image. It's not an idle fantasy, for the light is real.

Now allow the light to flood your body, your blood, your bones. Allow it to illuminate your mind, your emotions, your relationships, your career. Congratulations. You have picked up your wand and begun to use it.

Our choice to stand within a field of infinite possibility is our miraculous authority in any situation. Changing our mental perspective is much like changing the lens on a camera. In the Bible it is written, 'Be still and know I am.' That moment of stillness is when our mental lens has a chance to refocus. And there, in a moment of sacred connection with all life, we know that only love is real. In the midst of war, we can quietly and powerfully know that peace is our natural state. In the midst of sickness, we can quietly and powerfully know that health is our natural state. To 'know I am' is to know, and affirm, that only God's universe is real. Everything is a veil of illusion brought about by our illusion of separation from Him. Our greatest power to change our world lies in our power to see beyond the veil. For we will invoke the world we choose to see. This may mean we repudiate the testimony of our physical senses, or even of our logical minds. This repudiation is a positive denial of the so-called realities of a darkened world. As we stand firmly within a point of light – though darkness might be all around us – the darkness begins to dissolve into the nothingness from whence it came.

The attention we pay to the nature of our thinking, therefore, is the most powerful attention we can pay. Our spiritual victory lies in rising above the mental forces of fear and limitation, using our wands to purify our thought forms, thus attaining the power to heal and be healed. We will think anew and see anew. Such is humanity's next step: our spiritual challenge, our power, and our destiny.

WAND 1

Miracles Happen

When I was a child, there was a well-known advertisement for V8 juice. Someone would drink something else and then realize, 'Wow, I coulda had a V8!' As an adult, I've realized many times, when situations have not turned out so well, 'Wow, I coulda had a miracle!'

I could have had a miracle . . . *except* . . . ! Except that I didn't think miracles were possible. I didn't think in a miraculous way. I didn't stand firmly on the principle that God can do anything. In the words of *A Course in Miracles*, 'There is no order of difficulty in miracles.' No problem is too hard for God to solve. This is a very important point to remember, as it's hard to have deep faith in a kinda-sorta-powerful God.

Faith in God, however, is inseparable from faith

in love. To say that there is nothing God cannot do is to say that there is nothing love cannot do. It does little good to ask God's help, if we ourselves remain unwilling to open our hearts in places where they are closed. It is not just God's love for us, but our love for each other, that paves the way for miracles.

If we fail to *express* God's love through faith or compassion or forgiveness, then the problem is not the absence of God's power but rather our failure to align our will with His. He cannot do for us what He cannot do through us. A house might be wired for electricity, but it still needs lamps if it's to be lit.

With every thought of miraculous possibility, the lamp is plugged in. A miracle is simply a shift in perception. The more we align ourselves with the principles of love, the more empowered we become. Children memorize the alphabet so they can learn how to read; we should memorize mystical principles so we can learn how to live most creatively. Each of us can live in the victory of spirit, claiming for ourselves the miraculous power that has been given to us as children of God. It is our *faith* that miracles are possible – that the very fabric of the universe is miraculous – which opens the mind, and thus the future, to unimaginable possibilities. 'Dear God, please send a miracle' is a powerful prayer for cosmic support. To pray is to take spiritual action.

This earth is dominated by thoughts of fear, and we are conditioned by those thoughts to forget the power of our Source. Having not been taught the grandeur of our heritage, we do not remember the grandeur of our mission. We forget that we have the extraordinary power to work miracles in the name of God. Illusion and fear tie up the Prometheus inside us. No, we cannot do this or that, because we don't have enough money, or enough talent, or enough intelligence. No, we cannot change the world, because it's been the way it's been too long. No one needs to hold us down if we believe we're down already. As long as there are walls inside our minds, we're bound to remain behind them. For if you think you can't, you can't. If you think you can, you might. And if you think *God* can, you're on your way to a life of spiritual triumph. You have claimed His power on your own behalf, *which is what He would have you do.* God is not stingy with His miracles; it's a pity we ask for so few.

It's neither arrogant nor overreaching to ask for a miracle. Miracles aren't possible because of anything we do; they are possible because of the nature of God. We do not *personally* work them; rather, they are worked *through* us as we open our hearts more deeply to love. The mystical heart is a loving one, and thus a conduit through which God naturally reveals Himself. We have a power in us, but not of us, that can miraculously heal the entire world.

Perhaps the miracle arrives in the form of an insight that unlocks a riddle in your life, a reconciliation with someone, or the opening of a door that had long remained closed. Try as you might, your efforts to break through using your talents, your power of rational analysis, or sheer force of will had remained fruitless. It was only when you put God first – when your heart softened, you stopped blaming, you stopped talking so much and started to truly listen – that some wall of resistance began to crumble. You had not done anything so much as you had released the energies of self-will. You had asked, in a way, that God's will be done. A miracle occurred not because you caused it but because you allowed it. In the words of writer Willa Cather, 'Where there is great love, there are always miracles.'

Mystical consciousness is humble but self-confident. We are not relying on our own strength, but on God's. Science, technology, economics, military force, and social prestige – all of which are seen by the mortal mind as sources of genuine might and strength – might have the power to affect situations significantly. But they cannot work miracles. They cannot transcend the time-space continuum. They cannot transform the human heart.

Only love has the power to alter the subtler vibrations of human energy, for love transforms events on the level of consciousness, and consciousness is the level of true cause. The world outside us is a world of effects, so to merely change things within that world is to ultimately change nothing. Spiritual principle addresses the true cause of every problem, because every problem is in essence a spiritual crisis. Every problem reflects an unforgiveness. In every situation, the consciousness of love either has revealed itself or remains hidden. The role of the mystic is to find the love, and reveal the love, that lies latent in every circumstance.

Terrorism, for instance, is not our deepest problem, but rather the effect of a deeper one. Hatred itself is our deepest problem. While military power might contain the terrorists, only love has the power to dismantle the hate from which terrorism emerges. There is no problem to which the love of God – manifest in our love for each other – is not the ultimate solution. Yet we must look for that love within *ourselves*. A nation that puts money before love must address that problem first if we wish miracles to bless and protect us. It's not the *word* God, but the *work* of God, that is necessary in order to call forth miracles.

If miracles are seen as merely some sort of metaphor, then they are likely to have the power of metaphor in our daily lives. And how much power is that? Rather, we can see miracles as sewn into the fabric of the universe, and when we do, our experience of the universe is altered. When we are open to the possibility that God's power is truly unlimited – that in the ultimate vastness of the cosmos, love prevails – then we are automatically transported to a realm of possibility in which miracles flow forth naturally.

Why should we so slavishly surrender to a fear-based worldview that purports to have the answers to everything and yet clearly has answers to very few questions of fundamental import? The mortal mind can design a gorgeous wedding, but it cannot weave two hearts together; it can invent medicine to keep us alive, but it cannot create the will to live; and it can manufacture an engine of war, but it cannot create deep peace. Isn't it time to leave behind us the limitations of a mortal perspective and embrace instead the spiritual freedom that emanates from the Mind of God? Is not the world in some way upside down? Does the mortal mind deserve the adoration it receives, and the Mind of God such weak allegiance?

I've been in many circumstances where it simply didn't occur to me to ask for a miracle. I would think, *This situation isn't about God; it's about money, or work, or relationships, or politics.* But *any* situation is about God because He is the ultimate ground of our being. We are either standing on the ground of our true Reality, or we have forgotten who we are, throwing the universe off kilter and making ourselves vulnerable to the forces of chaos. According to the ancient Egyptians, the purpose of our lives is to preserve order in the cosmos. And we do this by preserving order within ourselves. Each one of us is – quite literally, according to modern science – the centre of the universe.

Our relationship with God is our relationship with ourselves, for in no way are we separate from Him. Aligned with Him, we are firm within our own power; thinking ourselves separate from Him, we are cast into internal chaos and fear. To know that we are one with God is to know that we are infinite love. When we are not loving, we are literally not being ourselves. Infinite love is not an *attribute* of our being, but rather the essence of our being. Our only real problem is that we have forgotten who we are.

When we forget that we *are* love, we forget *to* love. And it is choice, not identity, that determines our experience. Should we wish to feel God's mercy, we must choose to be merciful. Should we wish to feel God's peace, we must extend God's peace. And should we wish to feel forgiven, then we must forgive.

It was not just the power of God, but the willingness of Moses to *receive* it, that caused the Red Sea to part. It was not just the grace of God, but the willingness of Jesus to *receive* it, that caused his resurrection. And it was not just the light of God, but the willingness of the Buddha to receive its illumination, that caused his enlightenment. It is in receiving God's love that we receive God's power.

When we want a miracle, we need simply to ask for one. In asking for a miracle, we are asking for a divine intercession, inviting the spirit of God to enter us and alter our perspective. It is useless to say, 'Dear God, I want You to work a miracle, but I don't want to have to change my mind about anything.' The Law of Cause and Effect is an immutable law of the universe. What we think is what we get, and God will not intervene between our thoughts and their effects.

When Cinderella's Fairy Godmother waved her wand – the Fairy Godmother representing the

Divine Intercessor, as does Mary in Christianity, Kuan Yin in Hinduism, and Tara in Buddhism – a shimmering energy of golden light surrounded the object of her attention. We can think of this as transcendent energy brought to bear on any situation illuminated by love. One attitude or perspective gives way to another, and the world is reborn. In the presence of the Fairy Godmother, mice turned into horses, a pumpkin turned into a carriage, and rags turned into a beautiful ball gown. Translated: people around us, *once we have shown more faith in them*, show up for us more powerfully than we had thought them capable; a job we had thought beneath us, *once we throw our creativity into it*, becomes the vehicle to a great success; our lack in some area, *once changed from a source of complaint to a source of thanksgiving for what we do have*, turns into a source of joy. Any situation can be redeemed. Overshadowed by the compassionate, faithful spirit of the divine, our lives become a space for miraculous new beginnings.

And new beginnings are possible anywhere, for there is nowhere God is not. Cinderella's Fairy Godmother worked with what was there: she didn't call a car service and order up a limo. She didn't call Saks Fifth Avenue and say 'Bring me over something gorgeous.' Rather, she surrounded what was already there with the illumination of divine understanding, and what already existed then miraculously transformed. Miracles change the world, though not always externally. They may or may not produce results as the logical mind defines them, but they always produce at least subtle breakthroughs in the energies at the heart of a situation.

The word 'discipline' comes from the same root as the word 'disciple,' and the mystic is a disciple of love. We are mentally disciplined to believe that there is no problem love cannot solve. Holiness is an internal state, a 'whole' way of seeing. When our minds are no longer fragmented by the illusion of our separation from each other, but healed by the truth of our oneness, we are awakened to a new dimension of compassion. Within the mantle of that love, there is literally nothing we cannot do. We have remembered who God is. We have remembered who we are. Finally, we are whole at last.

WAND 2

The Angels Are Waiting for Us

Every night before she goes to bed, my daughter says a prayer which I too said when I was her age: 'Four corners round my bed, four angels round my head. One to watch, two to pray, and one to chase bad things away.' It took me forty years to understand what a prayer like that is really saying.

Angels are the thoughts of God, and to ask for angels to gather near is to ask for God's thoughts to overshadow our own. To pray to an angel is to look to a level of pure thinking, divine thinking, and to ask that it replace our thoughts of fear. Such thoughts – of separation from others, as well as from God – are distortions of reality, mental 'miscreations,' and they lead us to conclusions and behaviour that are destructive to ourselves and the world around us.

'One to watch': May the Spirit of love tend my thoughts, guarding the holiness that alone should remain on the altar of my mind.

'Two to pray': May I remain in conscious contact with God, ever alert to the miracles in my midst.

'One to chase bad things away': May God's Spirit cast out of my thoughts, and my world, the things that are not of love.

When we pray to something higher than ourselves, we are not praying to something outside ourselves. Angels do not live 'somewhere else' – ultimately we realize that there is nowhere else – but simply in another realm of perception. They live within us as latent energies of divine power, potential but not yet actualized within most of humanity. In summoning angels, we're responding to the evolutionary lure of the angelic state. We're recognizing angels as spiritual mentors who can lift our thoughts to the heights of truth. And as we rise to meet them, we will ultimately become them.

With this second wand, we remember that it is our own responsibility, as best we can, to live up to the divine potential God has placed within each of us. We have our wings, should we choose to spread them. In almost any situation, if we're truly honest with ourselves, there are ways that we can fly higher, at fuller wingspan. There are ways to show greater honour and compassion to all life, to get over ourselves and serve something bigger. We are given as many opportunities to reconstruct the nature of our lives as there are moments in a day. We can think more insightfully, love more deeply, give more selflessly, and serve more faithfully the call of love. How many times have we regretted not having been kinder, or wiser, or more respectful to others? And how many times have we shown up lovingly for another person and been told, 'Thank you. You're such an angel.' Indeed.

Angel's wings are not just metaphorical, any more than a butterfly's are. Just because they don't materialize physically does not mean that they do not exist. They are an actual set of cosmic proba-bilities, increased in the presence of mystical awareness. They are higher thought forms through which we transcend limitations, flying above the earthly fears that would otherwise hold us down.

Humanity is now challenged as never before to actualize our divine potential, summoned by history to expand into the dimensions of mind and spirit that will divert us from a most destructive path. This is not a time to wait for angels, but to actively *become* them. Indeed, we are waiting for something that is waiting for us. The distance between the lives we are living now and lives of mystical enchantment – between lives of material bondage and lives of spiritual freedom – is no farther than a decision to think miraculously. Each time we consider a miracle impossible, or assume that we ourselves are not capable of working it, then we're choosing not to take flight. But that doesn't mean that we can't, or that we won't. We will emerge from our spiritual chrysalis into the light of a new state of being, when human consciousness has realized our capacity to do so.

We need not wait for the world to become more mystical; the world *is* mystical. Our problem is not that the world lacks magic; our problem is that we don't believe in its magic. We do not show up fully for life, and then wonder why life is not showing up more fully for us. I've seen so many people auditioning life, waiting for the *right* relationship, or the *right* job, or the *right* house, before deciding to live life to its fullest. People say, 'When I've met the right person, I will show up fully in a relationship . . . When I have the right job, I'll throw myself one hundred per cent into it . . . When I've lost the weight, I will try to look great . . .' Imagine a narcissistic angel.

The time to show up fully for life is *right now*, whatever the circumstances. The decision to be the divine attracts the divine. Life is a swirling pool of infinite potential at every single moment, and we ourselves either activate or refuse to activate the mystical fertility of the universe. The only way to achieve an exciting life is to be willing to be excited and exciting. The only way to achieve an excellent life is to be willing to be excellent. The only way to achieve love is to be willing to be more loving. Who and what we decide to be, in each and every moment, is reflected back to us in worldly forms. Situations that just 'seem' to happen are not necessarily random at all. With every thought, we ourselves decide whether to welcome God's reality and its miraculous prospects.

As we convert our thinking – much as one converts an electrical current – from identifying with the material realm to identifying with the spirit, then our spiritual wings take flight. We are lifted above the limitations of the past, for when we approach a situation from merely a material orientation, we remain at the effects of material factors. But if we approach it from a spiritual orientation, we are freed from the confines of material factors. We are heir to the laws of whichever world we believe in.

Knowing this, the mystic says, 'No, I am not buy-ing into the notion that wealth and position determine my destiny. As a child of God, I am bound by nothing'; 'No, I am not going to stop pursuing my dream because someone else doesn't see its value. As a child of God, I have the power to make dreams manifest'; 'No, I am not wallowing in the victimization of a youth that did not go my way. As a child of God, I am able to transcend the past'; 'No, I am not going to quiet my voice because other people are uncomfortable with my power. As a child of God, I am here to speak my truth.'

The path to a transcendent sensibility is neither even nor easy at times, but the difficulty of the journey sometimes turns out to be its blessing. Indeed, there are ways in which the pain we suffered yesterday increases our power to work miracles today. For challenges teach us humility and faith. Having experienced the pain of a broken wing, and having been healed by the mysterious mercy of God, we then fly again with a distinctive grace.

No matter what suffering has marked our lives, if we are open to a miracle now, then a miracle can happen. And there is no greater miracle than a person becoming all that he or she can be. We are healed as we begin to realize that we will be who we decide to be. And it's never what we are not getting so much as what we are not giving that can actually hold us back.

I once knew a woman who wanted very much to become a partner at her law firm. She was being groomed for the position. Yet, as time went on, her hunger for partnership overshadowed her performance, as though waiting in the background was simply not her thing. She did not perform at her best. And by not living fully in the present, she actually doomed herself to the background, for she wasn't showing up more powerfully before she made partner, so no partners in the firm could quite see how she had the stuff it takes to ultimately join their ranks. She would have been better off with a little less worldly ambition and a little more sense of service.

When we choose not to be an angel, the angels in our midst depart. People will tend to be to us what we have decided to be to them. Yet it can be difficult to shine on others when we do not honestly feel that there is light within us. There is a light in all of us because God put it there. We can look to those in the world who evolved to a higher level of consciousness during their lifetimes. They were not made of different stuff than we are so much as they made different decisions than we do. It was not easy for Abraham Lincoln to be the Abraham Lincoln we revere today; it was not easy to be Susan B. Anthony, or Mahatma Gandhi, or Martin Luther

King, Jr. They were born, as all of us are, with potential greatness. But the actualization of that greatness was not predetermined. They could have decided to do and be otherwise. Whatever spiritual force moved within their hearts, luring them toward a magnificent destiny, is a lure that exists in all of us. There is no rational formula for greatness, for greatness is not rational. On some mysterious level, despite whatever resistance they felt, the great are those who simply said yes at times when others would have said no. Fear did not deter them so much as it honed them. Something called to them from a higher place, and they responded to what they heard.

Are we not being called by history to become the greatness that lies in us? What happens to this Earth now is up to us. We can remain who we are and sink further into the troubled world we have already made, or we can allow our hearts to crack open like cosmic eggs, out of which will emerge transformed creatures – our own true selves.

Look at it closely, in yourself and others, and tell me that creature does not have wings.

Thoughts of Judgement Block the Light

When I was a little girl, anytime I would ask my mother something mundane – such as, 'Are we going to go out to dinner tonight?' or 'Are we meeting Daddy at the zoo?' – she would answer with a particular phrase: 'God willing.'

I never thought much of it when I was a child, but as I grew older it struck me how right she was. How often have people assumed this or that was going to happen, only to find themselves experiencing something very different indeed. You *think* you're going out to dinner tonight. But what's really true is that if something horrible like a car accident en route to the restaurant doesn't happen, *then* you're going out to dinner tonight. You *think* you're going to do this or that, but what you really mean is: If something out of my control doesn't interrupt my plans, then I'm going to do it. All of us are aware that God has to *agree* with our plans, or our plans will come to naught.

When my mother said 'God willing,' she was instinctively showing humility before the power of God. She knew it wasn't a good thing to assume that human will can totally control anything. And in saying 'God willing,' she was also praying that God *would* be willing – that God would bless our plans. I think she had all the bases covered.

In my parents' house, God was a given. I grew up to appreciate the meaning of the word 'awe,' as applied to the spirit of God. And that sense of awe has stayed with me all my life, only increasing as the years have passed. And I've moved from the realization that God is always present in my life to the realization that He is always *interested* in it as well. He's not a passive but an active force – and there is nowhere He is *not*. A God who created the world as one perceives it as one and loves it as one. That which *is* love cannot withhold love. His hand is in the tiniest details, whether they're a million miles away or right at the tip of my nose. His creation is a panoply of radiant genius reaching from the smallest wild flower to the mystery of quarks. The completely solid field of His presence, covering every aspect of existence, could not *not* include you and me.

Forget the idea that God has more important things to think about than you. This thought is not humble, but actually a thinly disguised arrogance. Could the Lord of the universe work at anything less than full capacity, surveying just some but not all of His creation? You will know that to God you are everything when He has become everything to you. God's infinite and imperturbable love is ever at work, creatively furthering the enhancement of good, everywhere and all the time. God has a plan for your life, and all life, which is perfect and un-assailable. There is only one thing that can keep it from finding its way to your door, and that is you.

As children of God, we've been given free will: we can think with Him, or not think with Him. But we cannot limit the creative power of our thoughts. When our thoughts are thoughts of love, then we are aligned with and receive His power. When our thoughts are judgemental, then we are choosing to turn our backs to God. We can no longer see the light He is shining on us when we stop shining it on others.

Cinderella's Fairy Godmother did not say to Cinderella, 'That stepmother of yours is such a bitch . . . We'll show her!' She could not have said those things, or even thought them, and retained her mystical power.

'But,' you might say, 'the stepmother was so *mean* to Cinderella, and the stepsisters were almost as awful! Doesn't the stepmother *deserve* to be judged?'

Notice that the Fairy Godmother obviously registered the fact that the stepmother was out of line, or she would not have stopped by in the first place. Clearly, she thought the situation needed to be rectified, or she wouldn't have brought her wand. But the Fairy Godmother was too wise to take sides. The archetypal wicked stepmother lives in all of us, as much as Cinderella does. The stepmother is not where we are bad; she is where we are wounded, divorced from our true nature. The Fairy Godmother came to heal, not to judge.

Cinderella's refusal to surrender to thoughts of retribution is part of what drew the Fairy Godmother to her in the first place. Hate can summon the powers of the world, but only love can summon the powers of God. It takes tremendous faith in the power of love to refuse to hate those who behave in hateful ways. Yet in that refusal lies our grace.

It can be very hard to love people who are not showing love to us. But God's love is a person's essential identity, regardless of how he or she acts. The miracle worker remembers a part of someone that they themselves have forgotten. People deserve love not because of what they do, but because of who they are. When someone has forgotten their love, they have fallen asleep to who they are; our mystical challenge, and our spiritual power, lies in choosing to remain awake.

No one was ever born to hate. God's love in our hearts cannot be destroyed but only temporarily put to sleep. We must know this and refuse to forget it, about ourselves and about one another. The perception of someone's innocence is a choice we make, based not on our opinion of them, but on our knowledge of God. The realm of personality, with all its good and bad, is not the realm of spiritual Truth. It is a 'fallen' realm. And we can escape it through the act of forgiveness.

While we can choose to remain focused on the realm of personality, it is not a realm of miracles. Focus on guilt will always breed fear, and focus on innocence will always breed love. Any time we project guilt onto someone else, we are fortifying the experience of guilt within ourselves. Like blood on Lady Macbeth's hands, we cannot remove our own guilty feelings as long as we are judging others.

Whenever you are angry, know you're hurting *yourself*. Ask for a healing. Ask to experience your own angelic nature, that you might see beyond someone else's behaviour to the angel, however wounded, within them. Given the unity of all minds, what we do to others, and what we think about others, boomerangs back to us. If we wish to feel peace, then we must wish peace for others. And whatever punishment we wish upon others, we subconsciously attract to ourselves.

Withholding judgement is a powerful wand, because often people show us what we invite them to show us: if I respond to your guilt, you will tend to show me more of it. If I approach you with a critical attitude, then I'm more likely to get a response from you that seems to prove my point. Yet if I respond to your innocence, you'll tend to show me that, as well. Our focus on the good in someone else, regardless of whether or not our ego thinks they 'deserve' it, casts a mystical light on any relationship.

This principle holds true whether we speak judgementally or even *think* judgementally. Sometimes we feel that if we clean up our behaviour ('If you can't say something nice about a person, then don't say anything at all!'), then that will be enough. But it is not. Our thoughts, not just our actions, create our experience. People telepathically register your real thoughts, regardless of whether you are consciously aware of them or not.

Also, we don't get points for having 'little' judge-ments rather than 'big' ones. Any diversion from love is a fundamental diversion from love. At the same time, we're human, of course. We are not asked to be perfect, but to be honest – to pray, 'Dear God, I have judgements about this person, but I am willing to see the situation differently. Please show me his innocence, so I will no longer focus on his guilt. Please make this a lesson in love and not fear. Amen.'

There is a way to affirm the divine perfection in a person, even while responding to their human flaws. And when we do – when we choose to affirm someone's basic goodness even when needing to share constructive criticism or complaint – we open doors to communication that otherwise remain closed. From an employer to an employee, for example, 'Excuse me, but this was not done correctly' is not a particularly miraculous communi-cation. On the other hand, something more along the line of 'I want you to know how valuable your work is, and how much of a contribution you are making here. Also, I would like to have you work on this particular project *this* way' is very different. It's a statement that affirms the heart and therefore opens the mind, providing the space for genuine communication untainted by resentment or fear.

If our goal is simply to 'get something done,' then we're often tempted by the delusion that our ego is the best guide to action; however, if we're interested in miracles, then we listen to the voice of Spirit, which would have us put the focus on a person's innocence before a focus on their guilt. This is sometimes easier said than done, but the ability to do so can make a tremendous difference.

When we realize our mission is to love and forgive, we realize that every situation is an opportunity to do so. What we might see as a problem is looked at differently when we recognize that every event is part of a divine curriculum, set up by God for our growth and healing. Sometimes our challenges in one area provide answers in another. A problem with a nasty neighbour becomes an opportunity to use our spiritual power, praying for someone as a way to resolve conflict. Dealing with a difficult employee becomes an opportunity to work on communicating compassionately, without compromising our truth. Having to make a difficult decision becomes an opportunity to surrender, learning how to ask God for guidance. Every situation is a lesson in becoming who we are capable of being.

Every situation is ultimately a lesson in forgiveness. Forgiveness is our decision to see the love that is real in all of us, despite whatever appearances to the contrary there are. Fear melts away when we refuse to affirm its ultimate reality. When we see *beyond* fear, it dissolves. I no longer blame you because I don't believe the part of you that acted out is who you really are. I relate instead to your innocence, to the angel within you, which remains, no matter what you do. That is the power of forgiveness: to call forth a higher reality by *acknowledging* a higher reality.

Think of the Israelis and the Palestinians. They are locked in war, but that is not who they are. They are one in spirit, as we all are, beyond the mortal plane. We will not find peace in the world by *fixing* the mortal plane, but by *transcending* it. Knowing that warring peoples in fact are one – holding to this mystical truth despite appearances to the contrary – establishes a womb for the rebirth of their relationship. While they are having such an understandably difficult time seeing the love in each other, all of us can help by seeing it for them.

Because all minds are joined, deep peace cultivated anywhere is a blessing on people everywhere. What we do on the level of consciousness affects what happens in the realm of bodies, far more than what we do in the realm of bodies affects the level of consciousness. Einstein said we would not solve the problems of the world from the level of thinking we were at when we created them. Situations such as the Middle East conflict are examples of both our challenge and our opportunity to move our awareness to a higher level.

Forgiveness is our mystical function, but it's often a gradual and quite painful process. Forgiveness doesn't mean that we pretend to like whom we do not like, or turn a blind eye to the evils of the world. Commitment to God's love doesn't destroy our capacity for discernment. But the way of divine compassion – though not an easy path, though often counterintuitive – is the next step in humanity's evolutionary journey. It's the only step that will enable us to survive the storm of hatred raging around the world.

Judgement is like an eclipse of the sun, which blocks its light. Spiritual light, it has often been said, is like the light of a thousand suns. We come from the light, and will return to the light, when light is all we choose to see. We will know that we are home in God when we are home in one another's hearts.

God commanded us to love one another as a way of removing from our midst all that is not love. Jesus did not say, 'Love each other, *but only under certain circumstances*.' His kingdom, He said, is not of this world. And neither is ours.

The End Is Inherent in the Means

When Mahatma Gandhi articulated his principles of political nonviolence, he stressed that, in all our doings, the end is inherent in the means. This concept reverses the common Western truism that 'the end *justifies* the means.' According to Gandhi, *how* we do something is as important as *what* we're trying to do, because ultimately whatever we do will be *determined* by how we do it. Who we are as we go through a process – whether we choose integrity, faith, and compassion or their opposites – affects the outcome of a situation more powerfully than the mortal mind admits. Love is a process as well as a goal.

As we concentrate on being the people that God would have us be, a path of light opens up before us to ease our way. Circumstances begin to fall into more harmonious patterns as we find more harmony within ourselves. We can tell when a situation is in the 'flow,' when we're no longer paddling upstream, when there is less stress involved in making something happen. The effort to align ourselves with the holy and good is our greatest power to affect external situations.

So it is that if we foster good cause, then good effects will ensue – not always immediately, but *ultimately*. In the words of Martin Luther King, Jr., 'The moral arc of the universe is long, but it bends toward justice.' There are laws of the universe that do not change. If we take care to honour the roots of a tree, then the trunk and the branches will take care of themselves. The mystic surrenders to the flow of God's love, knowing that it flows naturally in the direction of the highest good for all. There is a spiritual *beneficence* at the centre of the universe. And as we gain, through experience, more and more faith in that basic goodness, we learn to give up our efforts to control and instead begin to deeply trust. It is not human will or personality we are trusting, or human machinations of any kind; rather, we're placing our trust in the Law of Cause and Effect, or karma, which is God's blueprint for the spiritual workings of all creation.

The world is rife with human suffering. And yet

there is, behind the worldly veil of darkness and fear, another possibility, a truer reality than that which we are living now. Our capacity to reach beyond the veil does not emanate from what we do, but from whom we are audacious and devoted enough to now become. That is why entering deeply into the still waters of God's love is every bit as important as any external action we take if we are serious about trying to change the world.

Mental and emotional agitation are obstructions to the flow of God's love into the world, reflecting as they do our separation from the peace of God. In order for the world to heal, human beings must realign our hearts and minds with Him. For in that union of God and human – the esoteric meaning of the Christ mind – a wondrous cocreative power emerges, bringing with it a blessing on all the world. This power is a correction of all our mental miscreations, restoring harmony and order to every aspect of our lives. When our minds are healed, the world will be healed, and nothing that does not vibrate with love will long remain.

Love is literally the power of God alive on earth. It is a transformative, alchemical, miraculous *force*. And with that force, God is well aware of how to make this universe work perfectly for all of us. Yet often we do not allow it, however strongly we profess our belief in God's love as our salvation. For God's love is not just His love for us; it is, most important, the love we give the world. The highest commandment is that we love *one another*. And when we make the extension of that love our primary goal, no matter the circumstance, those circumstances are blessed.

We must take the actions that bring love to life, making it the organizing principle behind all our endeavours. Business should reflect it; politics should reflect it; education should reflect it; everything should reflect it. Love is more than sentiment, and writing in lights across the sky is not enough to bring it forth; we must sow its seeds in the ground beneath our feet. Sometimes we intend to love and yet remain unwilling to love.

Why do we consistently refuse to allow love to light our way? We resist the allure of love, while still longing for its comfort. And what is that resistance, really? First, it is resistance to the experience of a bigger life, in which our small and separate identity disappears. What is actually the birth of our spiritual identity feels to the ego like death. The ego, our small and separate sense of self, is an imposter personality. It is a false self. It resists our genuinely remembering God, because in the recognition of our oneness with

Him lies the death of the ego and the end of all fear.

Second, we resist love because it jams the rational mindset. The mortal mind cannot understand how miracles work, and for our entire lives we are taught to mistrust what cannot be rationally explained. Yet the fact that we cannot understand how miracles work does not mean that miracles don't happen. And while Western science argued for ages that the state of our inner being has little effect on the state of our world, even science today argues otherwise. Heisenberg's Uncertainty Principle reveals that as our perception of an object changes, the object itself will change. The relationship between our internal and external realities involves a quantum phenomenon inaccessible to the mind, yet accessible to the heart.

We can safely place our lives in the hands of God, as His Spirit knows far better than we do how to turn our earthly existence into streams of radiance. Yet the ego stands guard, lest we break free of our self-destructive patterns. The ego, after all, cannot live without them.

Think of the woman who is so intent on getting her boyfriend to marry her that she can't simply love him without an agenda. She feels the need to control the relationship in a way that's not possible if her only goal is the peace of God for her boyfriend and herself. Her neediness, of course, does not bring her love, but in fact repels it.

And think of the committed political activist who is so intent on fighting a wrong that he or she fails to honour the basic humanity of the opponent. Time and time again, the anger that feeds our political passions can be the very thing that invalidates us in the eyes of those we most wish to persuade.

The woman would best realize that the future of her relationship depends on the state of her being as she relates to her boyfriend now. The activist would best realize that there is no creating a loving world except through our willingness to *be* the love we wish to see. Sometimes it's less important to know how the world works than to know how *change* works. We cannot change anything unless we ourselves are willing to change, for whatever problem we see in the world is only there as a reflection of our own internal state.

We beat the Nazis, but the world is not yet rid of evil. We outlawed slavery, but our nation is not yet rid of racial tension. World War II could not end hatred, and the Emancipation Proclamation could not end racism. The deeper changes we are seeking to effect, in ourselves and in the world, are dependent on a level of inner transformation that no external force can dictate. Former generations did their part, and now we must do ours. We must work assiduously on the process of self-purification, for whatever we do to improve the world will be infused with the energy with which we do it.

We cannot *give* what we do not *have*: we cannot bring peace to the world if we ourselves are not peaceful. We cannot bring love to the world if we ourselves are not loving. Our true gift to ourselves and others lies not in what we have but in who we are.

I have noticed how different I am, depending on the way I begin my day. In the first scenario, my daughter goes to school, and I sit down with a good cup of coffee and *The New York Times*. I enjoy the coffee, the paper, and the morning time by myself. When I'm finished reading, I check my e-mail, dress, and go to work. This is fairly enjoyable and fairly productive. But I realize it's guaranteed to maintain the status quo in myself and those around me.

In the second scenario, I carve out at least twenty to thirty minutes each morning to spend quality time with God. It takes a little more self-discipline but offers an immeasurably greater gift to my life. For during this time, my mind is freed of mental patterns that would keep me tied to yesterday. I light a prayer candle and pray out loud, sharing with God my hopes and fears that day. I seek to atone for my own mistakes, and I seek to forgive others for theirs. Then I meditate silently, entering the deeper waters of the divine. I am a student of *A Course in Miracles*, as well as a Transcendental Meditator, but I don't think it matters what form our spiritual practice takes. What's very important to realize, however, is that the mind of someone who regularly practises prayer and meditation *is literally a different mind*. I know this is true of myself, simply from my own experience.

In what ways am I different? Certainly I am more serene, which affects all my interactions as I move through the day. Also, I think I'm *smarter*. I have greater insight, I view situations with greater depth, and my mind is not so cluttered with the meaningless preoccupations that bombard us each moment in this increasingly frantic world. My spiritual practice doesn't just make me *feel* better; I think it makes me a different woman than I am when I choose not to do it. Everything I'm involved with becomes infused with a peace I do not otherwise carry. It affects the reactions of people I meet and the outcome of situations I might not even know exist.

We don't need to push life so much as we need to

experience it more elegantly, to be motivated more by inspiration than by ambition. Sometimes we're so intent on moving up the ladder that we make compromises we know we shouldn't make while we're on the lower rungs. Yet faith is a ladder that leads to new heights. We are here to do what God would have us do; our prayer is to receive guidance not only as to what that is, but also how to do it in any situation. We can remain in the realm of divine understanding, for our depth of understanding is the key to the life we truly want.

When process matters most, we find that the deeper life is a mysterious river, leading us to places we would otherwise fail to go. The mortal mind says, 'I'm going to Boston for the week, to work on a new project.' The mystic realizes that every point in our journey is part of a mysterious unfolding. We would pray, 'Dear God, I surrender my trip to Boston and ask that it be used on Your behalf. I go to Boston in the service of the Light, that the love in my heart might be of use to someone. I am open to all the miraculous possibilities that could arise from this trip. I bless in advance everyone I will meet there. My goal is to experience the spirit of God in everyone I see, that I might receive the gifts that are in store for me. May I be, do, and say according to Your Will. Amen.' Just saying such a prayer automatically places us in a blessed space, and a greater life follows.

The normal business trip mentality might produce financial gain or a promotion, but it won't necessarily produce joy. The mystic's attitude is open to an abundance that is not of this world. And from that internal abundance flows good that the mortal mind can scarcely imagine, and not just for ourselves or for one particular circumstance. Any gift that is given by God is a gift that is meant for all of us. There is no end to the miraculous effects extending into the world when our minds are one with Him. Every prayer from the heart – be it for our career, or our family, or our nation – is a prayer for the world, whether we know it at the time or not.

'Dear God, please make me an instrument of your peace . . .' is one of the most famous lines of prayer. And there is good reason for that. We know it speaks to something profoundly practical and real that will, if we allow it to, overcome all the darkness and hatred in the world.

'Dear God, please make me whom you want me to be, and take me where you want me to go.' Such is the surrendered prayer of one who has figured it out, that all roads that lead away from God are roads that take us nowhere.

WAND 5

Sacred Silence Rights the Universe

In fairy tales like *Snow White* and *Sleeping Beauty*, an innocent maiden is walking through the woods with all the animals of the kingdom gathered around her, in harmony with one another and with her. Birds flock around her, as though to guide her, should she lose her way.

That image – of the sleeping beauty that lies within us all, snow white in its innocence and purity of spirit – is a subconscious message to children and adults as well, that when we're aligned with our own spiritual essence, the world is a safer place to be. Remaining serene within ourselves, we become magnets for harmony and peace in the world.

Yet the world is hardly ever a peaceful place, and you and I are not Sleeping Beauty. Inner peace is a real prize in these times; in the words of John

Lennon, 'I'd give you everything I've got, for a little peace of mind.' As difficult as it can be to find genuine inner calm, it is the key to creating peace in the world as we know it. The world will not change until we do, and there is nothing the world can deliver to us that will give us the peace we crave. Peace comes not from the world, but from God.

In any given moment when the world is too much with us, we can take a deep breath and travel home to the inner room inside our minds. There sits God on His radiant throne, always there to receive us in the sanctuary of the heart. He never abandons us, though we abandon Him so frequently. It is built into the design of creation that the Prodigal Son – whether we've been gone for ten minutes or ten years – can always return home, in any moment we choose.

The door to God swings open at the slightest knock. The portal that takes us from the hysteria of a fear-based world to the peace and love of God is any moment of pure and sacred silence. It only takes one moment, perhaps one good deep breath, in which we inhale the love of God and exhale the madness of the world. We wait in silence to receive His Spirit, willing to soften our heart, no matter how much we need His help to do so. It is a moment when we're willing to forgive anyone and everyone.

And it is a moment when we're willing to pray for a miracle, asking for a ray of light to break through whatever darkness is surrounding us at that moment.

I once saw a pseudo-Buddhist graffiti that read, 'Don't just do something – *sit* there!' It's humorous, but it's also a good spiritual directive. Where the ego would have us believe, 'I've got to do something! I've got to do something!' the spirit would have us remember, 'The best thing I could do would be to sit down and quietly seek the peace of God.'

The Western mind, particularly, is bent on the notion that we must do something all the time. However, when we remember that consciousness precedes matter, we recognize that serenity is more than a beautiful feeling. It's an essential strength. An agitated mind creates an agitated world, which then creates more agitated minds, which then create a more agitated world. But moments of sacred silence break the vicious cycle. And that is why the cultivation of such moments is one of our wands. It harmonizes everything.

Advertisements constantly hawk the latest pharmaceutical answers to our lack of inner peace. Yet all of us know, deep within, that psychic pain, like physical pain, is there for a reason. We don't heal a broken leg by numbing it, and we don't heal a broken heart that way, either. Ultimately, only the alchemical processes of spirit can actually disentangle the thought forms that cause our distress, guiding us to forgive one another and reconnect to God. When we're overshadowed by the Spirit of God, it's as though He's performing psychic surgery on our souls. We are literally transformed in heart and mind, as His peace comes upon us. It doesn't come in pill form, but it comes.

A moment of sacred silence is our cosmic reset button. My niece Meredith is a third-grade teacher, and she puts a moment of silence to great use when her students are beginning to spin out of control. 'Stop!' she says, putting a palm out in front of her like the Supremes singing, 'Stop, in the name of love!' Then she says, 'Take a deep breath,' and inhales. Then she taps the fingers of one hand to the side of her head, counting out loud to five. Then she slowly exhales. The kids inhale and exhale right along with her.

The first time I saw her do this, I thought, *Wow. I wish someone had taught me that when I was in the third grade. My whole life would be different!* I've remembered that technique, and I've used it a few times myself.

There are clearly times when quieting down and bringing our energy back into ourselves is a step toward inner peace. Yet the most powerful life is not one in which we bring ourselves back to our centre when we have spun away from it, but rather one in which we seek to live from that centre at all times.

One day I was sitting with my little girl on a bench in a public square, watching some college students play Frisbee in a field across the street. We were with several friends, chatting and making plans for the afternoon.

'You know, darling,' I said to my daughter, 'it seems, from a worldly perspective, that the people who are running around on that field are the ones who are moving energy, making things happen. And you and I sitting on this bench talking are not really doing anything.

'But, from a metaphysical perspective, you and I are moving energy, too. If you can really sit still at a moment like this, with your spine erect, deeply breathing in and out, and feeling love in your heart for everyone, then you're actually moving more energy around than someone who's playing Frisbee. When you learn to be really still, surrendering your mind to God, you are learning to summon energy from the furthest reaches of the universe. Your mind becomes like a magnet attracting the most positive things.

'The more still you become, the more the universe moves into powerful action on your behalf. Forces you will never be consciously aware of begin to move in your direction. The less still you are – the more emotionally and mentally fidgety you are – the more the universe stays stuck in old patterns of energy, reflecting the general chaos of your own psyche.'

As I relished the thought of my daughter as my spiritual apprentice, I also realized she was merely tolerating my metaphysical musings. But I continued, 'And that is because the tenor of your being, not your doing, is what establishes the pathways of energy that run through your life experience. Those pathways are real, and not just symbolic. They are the trains of thought, firing of mental synapses, and subconscious instincts to act and react that lie within each of us. Our goal is to purify that mental and emotional energy, so that the pathways of potentiality surrounding us are full of only love and creativity. It is fearful and destructive thoughts that set up fearful and destructive patterns in our lives.

'Okay? Do you get that?' I asked, hugging my daughter's shoulders close to me.

'Sure, Mom,' she answered sweetly, patting my hands as though she wanted to reassure me she'd be there to comfort me when they arrived to take me away. We both laughed. But I figured then, as I do now, that if I throw out seeds, who knows? We often hear things that make no sense when we hear them and then blossom in our consciousness years later.

I was no different when I was young. In my twenties, I read a lot of literature by Indian gurus. Their spiritual wisdom often went way above my head, and it seemed they would respond to just about any query with the same advice: 'Meditate.' In those days, I had little patience for such simplicity. *Who are these people, anyway?* I thought. *What do they know? They don't even date!*

But I hear that advice very differently now. I've realized that no matter what the problem, the single most powerful thing I can do is be quiet – go to the place of holiness in my own heart, release my attachments and unforgiveness, and surrender myself to God.

I've thought about what would happen if we were to be able, for one twenty-four-hour period, to get every single person on earth to remain totally quiet. And I believe that, were we able to do it, we would at the end of that one day have fundamentally altered the collective consciousness, and thus the destiny, of the human race. When enough of us learn how to become deeply, profoundly quiet, then the hysteria of the world will begin to subside.

Following my lectures, I usually hold a question-and-answer period. And I know from experience how different the questions are, both in quantity and in substance, depending on whether or not we meditate before the questions begin. That's because many of the questions we carry around with us have less to do with genuine issues, and more to do with the monkey mind itself. A trickling flow of hysteria pervades our day-to-day mental functioning, constantly influencing our thoughts and emotions. This subtle hysteria is our biggest problem, because it's the root of all others. When our minds are aligned with God's love and peace, two things are true. First, we don't create as many problems in our lives. And second, we have the spiritual strength to handle them powerfully and positively when we do.

Genuine quiet, however, is far more than a behavioural condition. I have seen 'quiet' people who were clearly seething with rage. Mystical quiet is achieved through the radical purification of prayer and meditation, combined with the consistent effort to love and forgive. You can be having a deep massage on the most beautiful beach in the world, on the most beautiful day of the year, but if you're harbouring judgement and resentment, then your mind is still agitated and you will not know peace. Our world is full of noise and violence, and it takes more than a house in a quiet neighbourhood to achieve a quiet mind. Whatever our meditation technique, what is important is that we meditate. Whatever or whomever we need to forgive, what's important is that we forgive. And whatever life presents us with in any given moment, what is most important is that we live in the temple of God. Our mind is His altar, and our heart is His sanctuary. The outside world is a realm of illusion, and its gifts, if we are attached to them, become the gifts of pain.

Staying within ourselves, feeling the centre of our own being, we allow the power of God to give us everything we need. Living there, we can always work miracles. Living outside, we will always be in need of them.

As we release our need to be 'seen,' to be clever, to achieve, or to perform, the way is made clear for our inner radiance to shine. In a noisy world, seek the silence in your heart. And through the power of silence, the energies of chaos will be brought back to harmony – not by you, but through you, as all miracles are.

When we visit that silence regularly, particularly in the morning, then the days of our lives become lit from above. Darkness and fear are cast from our midst, slowly at first, one moment at a time. Ultimately, all darkness will be gone from every heart. A deeper peace within your heart brings peace, in time, to everyone – for in truth, the world is one. Mystics are a spiritual underground providing the spiritual medicine that will heal the human race.

We have our wands now. We're prepared to begin.

Abracadabra

Spiritual mastery lies not just in understanding the wands, but in using them. It's like the difference between Cinderella's Fairy Godmother explaining how the light works and her actually taking out her wand and waving it around a few times. One describes the transformation of a pumpkin into a coach, while the other actually makes it happen. It's time for us to take out our own wands now and transform a few pumpkins of our own.

'Abracadabra and fiddle-dee-dee, my ego is outraged to see the new me . . . Abracadabra and hody-ho-ho, my former neuroses, where did they go?'

Every day we're confronted with a gap, often painfully wide, between the life we live now and a life of deep enchantment. As much as we might want to believe in the power of spiritual principles, we often feel like we don't know how to apply them. At times, they seem so far away from our practical realities. Yet, in fact, they are only as far away as our next perception, should that perception be filled with love. No matter what the circumstance, we can choose to infuse it with light.

In every hour of every day, dealing with small details or dealing with huge issues, the alchemical power of our spiritual wands provides a portal into another realm, a magic carpet ride above the turmoil of the world. This is not illusion, this is reality. From the time we awake to the time we go to sleep, heaven's light – the understanding of higher principles – is available to us, should we have the courage to bring it down.

We will not find true light in this world, for the thought forms that prevail here are guilt-ridden and fear-based. We will only find light in God, who gives it to us that we might extend it to every living thing. Every moment of every day, becoming more illuminated, we become the illuminators. Eventually darkness shall be no more.

Yet miracle-working is not a part-time job: we must bring to the table everything we are and all our experience. *Miracles happen*. It's one thing to know that, but another to apply it. *The angels are waiting for us.* It's one thing to know that, but another to apply it. *Thoughts of judgement block the light.* It's one thing to know that, but another to apply it. *The end is inherent in the means.* It's one thing to know that, but another to apply it. *Sacred silence rights the universe.* It's one thing to know that, but another to apply it.

And yet apply these principles we must, if we are to be serious agents of the sacred. And that is what comes next: bringing wisdom and grace from the abstract realm to the practical realm, where cars get rusty and our bodies grow old, where the news is so bad at times and life so sad. Hour by hour, day by day, we can find more light within ourselves, and the world will begin to shine.

PART II

A DAY OF GRACE

8:00 AM

Starting the Day

It's the beginning of your day. You awake and look around you, feeling perhaps a joyful expectation, or perhaps an awful dread. No matter which, remember this: God loves you with an infinite love . . .

At the beginning of the day, the mind is most open to receive new impressions. One of the most important things we can do is to take full responsibility for the power of the morning.

If you want to have a *non*miraculous day, I suggest that newspaper and caffeine form the crux of your morning regimen. Listen to the morning news while you're in the shower, read the headlines as you are walking out the door, make sure you're keeping tabs on everything: the wars, the economy, the gossip, the natural disasters ... But if you want the day ahead to be full of miracles, then spend some time each morning with God.

Most of us wouldn't think of beginning our day without washing the accumulated dirt from the day before off our bodies. Yet far too often we go out into the day without similarly cleansing our minds. And our minds carry more pollution than our bodies, for they carry not only our own toxicity but that of the entire world. We carry the fear, anxiety, stress, and pain not just of our own lives, but of our families, our nation, and millions all over the planet.

Our greatest weakness is the weakness of an undisciplined mind. We need not let fear steal the morning; we can consciously choose not to allow our minds to be programmed by the worldly viewpoint that dominates the earth. We can set our day upon another course. Each of us has an inner room where we can visit to be cleansed of fear-based thoughts and feelings. This room, the holy of holies, is a sanctuary of spiritual light. The light is not a metaphor, but rather an actual energy of mystical vibration. When we begin our morning within it, the mind receives a radiance that illuminates our thinking as we go through our day.

Imagine yourself sitting in a perfect, comfortable spot for meditation. It might be a chair in your bedroom or living room. It is a place of relative quiet and calm, where you go on a regular basis to find the peace that only God can give. You have come to realize that this time of rest, in its stillness and peace, is beneficent to both your mind and body.

Here you come to surrender to God, using a prayer or mantra to move beyond the frantic and overwhelming thoughts that stalk us night and day. You are making your daily pilgrimage home, where your life will be renewed.

While the power of such quiet time can be profoundly healing, we often resist it fiercely. We have scores of reasons why we don't have time to meditate: 'The kids have to get off to school . . . I have to go to work . . . My partner wants to be with me . . . I have early appointments . . .' and the list goes on. Yet none of those excuses would be used to avoid taking a shower or getting dressed. It would be ludicrous to say, 'I'm just too busy. I had to give up showers.' And yet 'busy-ness' is a common excuse for why we do not take the time, or give the time, to meet regularly with God.

Just think about it: we turn down the chance for a meeting with God. It's a meeting He is always available for, and perhaps that is why we fail to take full advantage of the opportunity. Perhaps it's hard for us to embrace what an astonishing gift is being offered. We figure if it's really that easy to do, then how could it be that powerful? That's how much we underestimate how important we are to God.

In choosing not to listen for Him, we are choosing not to hear Him. For God's voice is a whisper, not a shout. Legend has it that when the angels came to the Virgin Mary in the middle of the night, they told her to get out of bed and go up to the roof. There they would reveal the extraordinary destiny that was to be hers. She had to go on to the roof in order to receive their message, the roof symbolizing her higher mind. If they had merely told her to sit up in bed, her mind and body still close to sleep, then she would not have been able to hear them. We too must be in a heightened, awakened state if we wish to hear the voice of God. Certain insights come to us after five or ten or twenty minutes of meditation, which simply do not emerge from the shallow waters of normal waking consciousness. Setting our mental focus within deeper waters in the morning helps ensure that our mind will remain there throughout the day.

The story of Mary's annunciation is the beginning of the Christ story and, like all beginnings, sets the energy for what will come. Her deep surrender to the will of God was the original opening through which God revealed Himself. Whether it's the beginning of a life or the beginning of a day, energies become set and hardened then; once a pattern is off and running, it's more difficult to change.

Time spent in morning prayer and meditation

can save hours of tears shed later over something we have said or done. How many times have we said to ourselves, 'How could I have been so dumb?' The answer is that we are not dumb; we were simply at the mercy of a frantic mind, not centred on its own sublime power. We were focused on things that are ultimately unimportant, while the deeper issues of life were left mainly ignored. These are the things that are bound to happen when we do not take the time each day to purify our thoughts.

According to *A Course in Miracles*, five minutes spent with God's Spirit in the morning guarantees He will be in charge of our thought forms throughout the day. Each morning we can begin with spiritual confidence, surrendering to God's will and praying that our eyes be opened to the miracles He has planned for us. Each day can be a glorious canvas painted by the hand of God, and we pray for eyes with which to see it.

Every morning, visualize and pray for divine right order. If you are a teacher, for instance, bear witness with your inner eye to an angel, or Jesus, or Buddha, wrapping his arms around every child in your class, then allow your mind to hold that image for five minutes or more. See God's Light around your co-workers, your neighbours, your children, your spouse. Whatever it is you will be doing with your day – whatever your workplace or activity – consciously bless the people you'll meet, as well as those you don't even know. Remember to include those you don't like as well as those you do. Allow yourself to imagine, while in a prayerful, meditative state, the life you most long to experience. Then bless that image, and surround it with light.

Now you can leave the house smiling, because you've placed your future in the hands of God. You've helped set the universe on a harmonious trajectory. Every day we have a chance to re-create life, for ourselves and others, reshaping our energies with the thoughts we think, just as we reshape our bodies with physical exercise. Bless the house in which you wake, and the people who also sleep there. Bless your city and your country and your world. Bless everyone you will meet today. Bless everyone else who is driving along the roads with you. Ask that your mind be filled with light, that you might be a channel for God's love. You cannot do this regularly in a committed way and feel like your life has no purpose. When you give love you will feel love. That is Law.

Some days are harder than others, to be sure. Perhaps some of your mornings have gone like this: 'There is no way I can do this. I'm supposed to be on a business trip, and my daughter is having her dance recital tonight. If I can't get home on the three-o'clock flight, which I probably won't because my meeting isn't until one, then I will miss her recital and be a terrible parent.'

Now commit this truth to memory: there is no problem that holiness will not solve. No matter what the problem is, no matter how big or small, important or unimportant, you are entitled to a miracle because you are a child of God.

Using only our mortal minds, we have very little power to fix anything. The world is full of confusion, it is moving too fast, and the demands of parenthood, career, economics, and health are proving too stressful for almost everyone. But you're equipped with more than just your mortal mind. Within each of us there is a divine mind, the Mind of God. It is always there, with no exception, to work whatever miracle is necessary to lift us above the limitations of the world.

In *A Course in Miracles*, it is written, 'Prayer is the conduit of miracles.' There is no prayer too big or too small that we should withhold it from God.

So try this instead, on such a morning: 'Dear God, please give me a miracle. I don't know how I'm going to attend my meeting and still get back to my daughter's recital. This life is so full of stress, dear God. Please take my day and plan it for me. Take care of her, and take care of me. Thank you, God. Amen.'

Everything in the universe is of concern to God, since He loves everything as one. If you're too stressed, then you're not fully alive, and your problem is therefore very much God's business. If you're not fully alive, then you're not being who you were born to be or living the life you are meant to live. If you're not living the life you are meant to live, then you're not doing on this earth what you're intended to do – you're failing to take part in the unfolding drama of infinite good, which is the spirit of God. If you're not being the parent you are capable of being, then another child is set up to fail. Why wouldn't a loving God wish to correct that situation? We are told in *A Course in Miracles* that we do not ask God for too much, but for too little. Every need we have should be placed in His hands.

The moment a mistake – any deviation from love – occurs, a perfect, all-knowing God has already planned a correction. All we have to do is ask that it be revealed to us. 'Dear God, please show me a miracle.'

We take spiritual responsibility for our day when we pray that it be blessed. More than the way we look, more than the clothes in our closet, more than whether or not our papers are organized, this simple request – that our lives be reflections of an eternal love – releases us from the confines of yesterday and frees us to unlimited possibilities today. Every single morning we can receive from the universe an entirely new day, in every sense of the word. Our ego will screech, 'Denial!' should we have the audacity to consider the possibility of a radically new life today. Yet that's exactly what is available to us, and courage lies in claiming it.

Every morning, consider doing this: light a candle. Sit down. Close your eyes. Be with God.

There are many different prayer and meditation techniques, and they are all paths to God. It matters not which path we walk to Him, but only *that we walk it*. In whatever way suits you, talk to God.

> *Dear God,*
> *I give you this morning.*
> *Please take away*
> *My despair of yesterday.*
> *Help me to forgive the things*
> *That caused me pain*
> *And would keep me bound.*
> *Help me to begin again.*
> *Please bless my path*

And illuminate my mind.
I surrender to You
The day ahead.
Please bless every person
And situation
I will encounter.
Make me who You would have me be,
That I might do as You would have me do.
Please enter my heart
And remove all anger,
Fear and pain.
Renew my soul
And free my spirit.
Thank you, God,
For this day.
Amen.

Hearing the News

You read the paper or watch the news on TV. You learn about terrorist attacks, paedophile priests, corporate greed and irresponsibility, homicides, the destruction of our ecosystems, horrible injustices, lack of airline safety, and more, on any given day . . . Right, *you think to yourself.* So much for miracles . . .

It is a spiritual challenge to hear the news and still keep your faith.

Surrounded by terrible news, we are tempted to feel powerless before the strength of darkness. And yet we are *not* powerless, for we are children of an infinitely wealthy father who has shared with us the prosperity of His kingdom. Our primary task is to remember that it's ours. Through God, we have the power to use our spiritual resources to banish all darkness – to transform our world from a state of limitation and fear to a state of abundance and love. For the world is a reflection of humanity's collective consciousness, and each of us has access to the collective through the auspices of our own mind.

Viewing life through the eyes of the world, we learn about a world that is; viewing life through the eyes of spirit, we learn about a world that *could be*. It is a law of consciousness that what we think about expands: our focus amounts to a mental endorsement of the worldview that keeps the object of our focus in place. In order to change the world, we must change the mental lens through which we view it.

What is not love, according to *A Course in Miracles*, is a call for love. And according to the Jewish precept of *tikkun olam*, we are on this earth to heal the broken pieces of the world. The mystic views any problem as a chance to use his or her magic wands.

Think of the news as humanity's prayer list. How different the world would be if every day's newspaper reports were met with prayers for healing from its readers! And that will happen, when the modern mind realizes the power of spirit. Prayer itself will emerge from the constricting limitations of religious doctrine, to become a spontaneous call of the soul to the higher power from whence we came. Having claimed the dimension of power that spiritual wisdom provides, we will energetically engage in the process of creating a new civilization. We will no longer stand powerless before the so-called strength of illusion and fear; once we realize our spiritual power, we will assume it to its full degree. For through God, we have the power of the sun and the moon and the stars at our command.

Bless everyone mentioned in every news story, no matter where they stand or what they do. For what we bless is delivered to divine right order. Bless those who do harm as well as those who do good, for any judgement blocks the light and keeps miracles at bay. Becoming emotionally reactive when we are confronted with darkness only serves to keep the darkness alive. Reacting to fear with fear merely feeds the fear.

Instead, let us claim for ourselves the power of love. Read about war? Pray to be a peacemaker. Read about abused children? Pray to be an advocate for them. Read about corruption? Pray to be an active citizen who does his or her part to change that. Read about a reign of terror? Pray to see a loving world that exists in a realm beyond it, and for God to make you a significant part of the effort to bring it forth.

We invoke another world first by simply accepting that it is there. It's not something to be created, so much as something to be *recognized*. And that recognition is the miracle. Pure harmony *already* exists in the Mind of God, along with a blueprint for its emergence into the world. When our hearts and minds are realigned with His, then that world will naturally come forth. Regardless of what the news-papers or the television news might declare as the latest disaster, our job is to remain loyal to an emergent reality developing in the fertile ground of our passion and imagination. With faith in possi-bilities as yet unseen, we can *proclaim* the world we wish to see, and not take the ego's 'no' for an answer. It is a basic metaphysical truth that no lie can last forever.

The level of disaster now occurring throughout the world leaves us looking for answers that ordinary human consciousness cannot provide. A catastrophe can be a wake-up call to the human race; it's only when we have truly awakened to the limits of mortal consciousness that we awaken at long last to the miracles of God.

Transcendence is a universal spiritual theme, and no religion has a monopoly on the idea that in God we are lifted above the limits of the world. One does not have to be Christian, for instance, to embrace the concept of the resurrection of spirit. In claiming the resurrection as a universal reality, we realize that our lives too can be lifted into a death-less dimension above the consciousness of the mortal world.

Darkness penetrates the human experience, but our response need not be frightened or weak. Our task is not to avoid or deny the darkness of the world, but to lift it into the light. We certainly don't want to live in denial, but there is negative denial and positive denial. Negative denial is when we ignore the darkness, claiming that since only love is real and all else is illusion, we need not dwell on the problems in our midst. But positive denial is something else: we do look at the darkness, yet we deny its power over us. Our function is not to ignore the darkness, but to transform it *by becoming the light*. The spiritual activist doesn't dwell on what's wrong, but at the same time we must know what's wrong in order to surrender it. Our miraculous authority lies in *positive* denial: *denial of the power of darkness by knowing that only light is the ultimate Reality.*

We are born of an extraordinary light, and have within our hearts the tools we need to rise above this world, to transform our suffering and that of others. We can consciously and courageously claim a different experience for this planet. But only if we are ready to commit to change. Just as the alcoholic must come to accept that alcohol cannot be part of his or her life anymore, we must all come to accept that thought forms of separation and fear – with their inevitably violent results – have no place on this planet anymore; they are too dangerous to the survival of the species. When love and forgiveness replace blame and retribution, we will have begun construction on a new and better world.

Children starve by the tens of thousands on this planet every day. They starve not because they have to but because we allow them to, and decisions that each of us make every day affect their plight. People do not dwell in poverty for no reason; they are poor because of conditions over which all of us exert some control. And as long as love is not our top priority, we will continue to manifest a world of pain. Only when we make love the basis of all our institutions will the news begin to change. And *that* will be our miracle.

When I read or watch the news, my biggest temptation is to judge those who disagree with me. The prayer that often pops into my mind, after reading the newspaper or listening to a television news show, goes something like this: 'Dear God, please remove from my mind my sense that I'm right and other people are wrong, my temptation to feel contempt toward those I disagree with, and this feeling of complete and utter powerlessness with my sense that the world is falling apart. Help me to forgive. And use me, if possible, that I might help to make things better. Amen.'

When I read about corporations who wage

inappropriate influence on the government because of large campaign donations, I feel disgust. 'What do you *mean*, the Secretary of Energy met with ninety-six energy executives, and not one environmentalist group?!' I fly into a rage. And while my ego is fine with that, my heart knows better than to indulge my self-righteousness. I know that rage will never solve anything. My spirit seems to whisper to me, 'Fine. Fly off the handle if you want to. But be clear that it won't help the situation.'

I imagine a conversation between my ego and my heart:

'So what am I supposed to do? Just *forgive* all those people who are destroying the planet?'

'Actually, yes.'

'*Why?* They're ruining our country! They would destroy the environment, and they're destroying democracy.'

'I know this is difficult. Tell me what you're feeling right now.'

'Obviously, I'm angry.'

'And what is the feeling behind that feeling? What do you feel, in the deepest place within you?'

'I feel sad. I feel dreadfully, deeply sad. And I feel frightened.'

'Frightened of what?'

'Frightened that my daughter and her children

will only have polluted air to breathe, impure food to eat, and toxic water to swim in. I'm frightened that they won't even have a real democracy anymore, or enough rights to protect them should they choose to complain.'

'And that is the point, you see. At the deepest level, you're not angry; you are sad and afraid. *Feel that.*'

Feeling our sadness and fear is actually more difficult than exploding in anger, yet it's essential if we are to become the spiritual activists who can re-create the world. We must see with total clarity that what is not love is fear. And we must understand that every negative emotion therefore derives from fear. When we allow ourselves to feel the fear and sadness that lie behind our anger, our judgements undergo an extraordinary transformation, and our fury turns into compassion. This is an important issue if we really want to change the world. We have no morally persuasive power with people who can feel our underlying contempt. We cannot communicate in meaningful ways with those whom we approach with judgement or blame.

My heart asks, 'What do you think about those people now?'

'I think they don't know what they're doing. I don't think they're bad. They just don't see what they're doing.'

'And who are they to you?'

'They are my brothers. They are evolving spirits, and now I can see that they are my teachers. They are forcing me to open my heart and become bigger than my anger.'

'Good. You're glimpsing your spiritual victory. Before, you were self-indulgent – which is exactly what you thought of them. And that made you part of the problem, not part of the solution. Your job is to seek your own atonement.'

'Thanks for the guidance.' Busted.

How we react to news affects our power to influence it. Too often, those who are most sensitive to the injustices in our midst allow themselves to be whiny and angry, thus limiting their capacity to create meaningful change. It's important to realize how much our emotional state can negatively affect the quality of energy we express to those around us, regardless of how 'right' or 'wrong' we might be. Once again, the process is as important as the goal. Taking responsibility for our own internal state is key to working miracles.

I try to remember the wands as I read the paper or watch the news. I want to remember that miracles do happen, that we are becoming people in whose presence these problems will melt, that my judgements help no one, that I must be the change I wish to see happen, and that at any given moment I can stop and pray, inviting God's spirit to enter both my heart and my mind. Then I have done my part to change things, for prayer brings a blessing to everyone and everything. For myself, I am then ready to receive whatever instruction God might give me, that I might be of use to Him in His efforts to heal the world.

Often, we are guided to do something to make the world a better place. Often, we are inspired to pray without ceasing. Almost always, we are moved to do both.

10:00 AM

Working

You would rather be anywhere than going into this meeting. You think about being at the movies, being on the beach, being with your kids – being anywhere but here. The people waiting on the other side of that door don't know who you are or even seem to care. You don't have the feeling they really want you to succeed. You can't believe you work here. Welcome to your career . . .

Life today is centred on the workplace. The average adult spends more time each day with his or her employers or employees than with his or her partner, spouse, or children. Emotionally, our lives might centre on our families and friends, but in terms of sheer time and energy, we spend most of our resources trying to make it at work.

Work, for many of us, is full of tension, anxiety, and pressure – with a bit of boredom and frustration thrown in. The average workday is a less-than-sacred experience, to be sure. So how do we transform the area of work from a material-based focus – with all its psychological and emotional pain – to an experience of spiritual freedom and joy?

A mystic takes every circumstance back to its

spiritual foundation, asking fundamental questions about our higher identity and purpose. Who am I? Why am I here? What is the ultimate meaning of my life, my relationships, my work? If life is to have deeper meaning, can our work be something we merely do to make money? Or can work itself become sacred, a channel through which we shine our light and extend our love?

Ministry is not just for ministers: in the new spirituality, a minister is anyone who chooses to use our resources to tend to the wounded heart of the world. Anything we do can be a ministry, from menial labour to the highest professional endeavour. It is our ministry if it is an activity we use to spread peace and forgiveness and love.

We transform our work into a sacred experience by transforming our sense of its purpose – from that of serving our own needs as we define them to that of serving the work of God. This shift in purpose – from a focus on ourselves to a focus on God's love – activates a chain of miracles. For any-time we walk into a situation with a higher sense of why we are there, we are bringing down the light.

The decision to adjust our perspective on a situation, seeing as its only purpose the extension of love, automatically illuminates it. For a situation to be illuminated, our *thoughts* must become illuminated.

Within this light, our ideas are more insightful and wise, our personal energies radiate integrity, and circumstances around us unfold along a palpable path of divine right order. There is a 'flow' we can all feel when a situation is aligned with the peace of God.

We should not have to choose between being in the flow of God's love and having a successful career. Indeed, the former fosters the latter. Yet in our society, it's very easy to buy in to the ego's perspective on employment and career. The ego represents the belief in our own, small, separated self, and sustains its life by defending that belief. And this belief fosters fear, because it is not a belief that is natural to us. We then seek to overcome that fear by building up our own individual kingdoms of money or prestige or power. We are often faced with the temptation to build our own career wins on someone else's losses. But once we realize that we are not separate from others, that indeed what we do to others we are literally doing to ourselves, then our perspective changes.

When we remember who we *really* are, we embrace our interconnectedness with all of life and the infinitude of our powers. We aren't here just to bolster our individual kingdoms; we are here to glorify God's kingdom of love. As children of God, we are natural storehouses of talent and intelligence; creativity flows from us like mother's milk, when our consciousness is that of mother to a new world. Once we change our consciousness of work from self-centred ambition to love-centred service, we begin to experience the effortless flow of divine inspiration.

I was given a prayer candle by a girlfriend, with a prayer called 'The Goddess Within of Victories and Successes.' When I begin my writing day by lighting that candle, praying that the work I do be of use to God, then my nervous system responds with a sense of focus and clarity I do not otherwise have. If I begin my writing thinking about contracts, money, or bestseller status, then I'm trapped in the illusions of the ego, where my thoughts are fragmented and my focus limited. Only when I begin with a prayer that something I write might be of use to someone does a greater light infuse my thinking. My mind opens vibrantly to its natural talents, sprung free of its bondage to fear-based thought.

An attitude of giving will ultimately attract more material and spiritual wealth to us than will an attitude of getting. But it takes faith in the workings of the spiritual universe to trust that this is so. The voice of the ego is loud, but its message is a lie.

Pursuing success for nothing but personal gain will not and cannot lead to true joy, because it is a quest that is out of harmony with the ultimate reality of the universe.

In the movie *A Beautiful Mind*, the character John Nash makes a discovery that Adam Smith was not completely correct when he argued that capitalism works at its best when everyone does what is best for them. Rather, argued Nash, it works best when everyone does what is best for them *and* best for the group.

A business dynamic that puts short-term economic gain for corporate CEOs or their shareholders before the welfare of the people who work in the company and live on this planet is based on fear, not love. The proper role of business is to minister – not to exploit. Whether as an employee or an employer – and many of us are both – it is our job, as bearers of light, to transform an ethos of control, suppression, and competition into an ethos of sharing, creativity, and joy.

Remember, it's not just workers but souls who are gathered in the workplace; we're not just here to 'achieve' in a worldly sense, but to spiritually learn and grow. *That* is the purpose of work, because it is the ultimate purpose of everything. The ego's work drama is always centred on who does what, who works for whom, and how much money can be made. But beneath the ego's drama lies a deeper set of issues.

If we are the employer, then our spiritual lesson is that we learn to lead with compassion and respect for the output of others. If we are the employee, then our spiritual lesson is that we learn to serve and respect another's vision. And if spiritual transgression is no less significant when it occurs at work than anywhere else, then many values dominating the modern workplace are called into fundamental question.

The ego's bottom line in business is that as much money be made as possible this quarter, the project be finished by deadline, the sales of the department be increased, etc. Yet once we've taken on the mantle of mystic, we are committed to the furtherance of life and the revelation of spirit. This doesn't mean that we lower our standards of excellence; it means simply that we remember that the process is as important as our goal. *How* we do business is as important as the business we do. We are not just concerned with how business operates; we are concerned with how the universe operates. And we are not just concerned with what the market wants; we are concerned with what *God* wants. Love becomes our new bottom line.

Imagine how differently business would function were our faith in the power of goodness to replace our faith in the power of money. Huge industries would no longer make billions on activities that diminish the well-being and safety of our children, our health, and our environment, on the pretext that it's 'just business.' To put money before goodness is idolatry, and the laws of the universe ensure that in the end all idols will fall.

Within the workplace, we've known for years that money alone does not increase people's productivity. It's the feelings of respect, honour, and involvement that make people realize their highest potential. Both as an employer and as an employee, I've seen how very true this is. As an employer, it's obvious to me that work doesn't get done just because I say that it must be done. How I say something is critical; often, the energy behind my comment is even more important than what I say. Ultimately, it's only people who have done and continue to do their own inner work who can effectively lead a competent modern workplace. As an employee, it's equally obvious to me that I don't produce just because someone tells me to produce, but rather because positive reinforcement and encouragement help my creative juices flow. When I'm intimidated, it does not make me more productive; when I'm criticized, I shut down. The role of a leader is not to rule over other people, but to hold a space for their own genius.

Work goes better when we connect to our common humanity first and our common professional goals second. When it's the other way around, we are not aligned with spiritual truth, and therefore chaos rather than harmony prevails. We are always working alongside the children of God, and all of us contain within us the love of our divine source. When we spend five minutes every morning blessing everyone with whom we work, seeing them held in the arms of God, then our workplace cannot help but transform. When we pray before a business meeting – asking that it be graced by God's love and that we be instruments of His will – then the meeting will be blessed.

Still, both employees and employers often have very valid complaints: how can I work for someone who doesn't show me enough respect? And how can I respect an employee who has such a sense of entitlement and does mediocre work? Spirit does not suppress those questions, but creates a context in which they can be harmoniously and effectively addressed.

From a spiritual perspective, if we have a disrespectful employee *or* a disrespectful employer, the situation is there for a reason. If someone feels we aren't showing them enough respect, then probably, on some level, we are not. And if someone feels we're not performing at our best, then probably, on some level, we are not. It is our own thoughts – not someone else's – that hold the key to miraculous transformation. What am I not giving that needs to be given to my employer or my employee? What am I not seeing that needs to be seen in the effort of my employer or employee? And what am I not saying that needs to be said to my employer or my employee? Asking ourselves these questions can deeply affect the workplace. People who have not done their internal work – whose subconscious unresolved issues are projected constantly onto those around them – are difficult to deal with as employees and employers as well. But essentially we are all the same, with the same hopes and dreams. We wish to be both respected and honoured, and that is as true in the workplace as anywhere else.

Our modern culture has placed work and business in a dry and almost soulless context, where our deeper human needs are second to the needs of an economic machinery. Feeling no deeper acknowledgement of our own humanity, we can become insensitive to the humanity of those whose lives our businesses affect. Often no one, from the

CEO down, feels free to question the basic morality of a business decision. People sit with unspoken concerns about safety and ethics eating away at them, afraid to protest lest they endanger their jobs.

Can we really be all that amazed at the revelation of corruption in the Enron scandal? That particular drama is nothing more or less than the logical extension of the business values we've allowed to prevail over the last few decades. Many have lost their moral compass amidst the materialism and greed of our times. And can any of us honestly say that we ourselves have never been tempted to put first things second and second things first?

Let us stop and give ourselves time to re-envision our work and rethink its mission. The vast majority of people want to do good. We want to feel that we're contributing to something bigger than ourselves. Whether we are the CEO of a large company or the person who cleans the office building, we are made up of the same essential stuff. Compassion for each other and the world we are here to serve will open up new vistas of productivity and abundance for us all.

Compassion in the workplace does not mean we should lower our standards, acquiesce to the violation of boundaries, or indulge a sloppy performance. It does mean, however, recognizing that in God's world no one is above and no one is below. That does not mean that no one gets to be the boss or that leadership should not be respected. It simply means that the salute of one soul to another should be at the core of every relationship. We all get off the track at times; certainly I know that I do. But I also know that getting back on that track is essential if my spirit and my work are to thrive.

Shifting the workplace from a hierarchical structure of domination and competition to a new paradigm system of co-operation and partnership is a spiritual challenge for our generation. From more enlightened work relationships will emerge more enlightened goals; we will no longer abuse the planet when we no longer abuse one another. We will work to re-create society in the image of our better selves, and then we will know that the meaning of work, and the joy of work, lie in dedicating our work to God.

> *Dear God,*
> *I surrender to you my work.*
> *May I be who you would have me be,*
> *That I might do as you would have me do.*
> *May my relationships be blessed,*
> *With those for whom I work*
> *And with those who work for me.*

May Your light be upon us
As we do our work,
And may our work
Be Yours.
Amen.

11:00 AM

Needing Work

At first, the articles in the paper don't seem to apply to you. Sure, there are problems, but they don't seem to be hitting too hard around here. Then the rumours begin. . . . And the boss is looking the other way when you pass in the hall. You can feel it in your gut: 'This job is not as secure as I thought.' And then it happens, just as you feared it would. It's you. . . . It's your desk . . . It's your job. It's gone.

During the last months of 2001, the Ford Motor Company announced they would be laying off 35,000 North American workers, Enron collapsed in the largest corporate bankruptcy in American history, and the United States fell into a recession. Behind every statistic of a laid-off worker or an investor who had lost their life savings lay human anxiety, desperation, and fear. How many of us have lost our jobs, moved on from our jobs without knowing if the risk was worth it, or had a parent or partner who went through that experience?

Jobs are not mere statistics to the people who hold them. Our jobs are one of the means by which we contribute to society. They are the means by which we provide for our families. They are the means by which we pay our rent, and feed, clothe, and educate our children. When our jobs disappear, our self-esteem often disappears with them; when the money disappears, fear enters fast. For example, in the United States today – while things are very good for some – there are many for whom financial stress is a daily heartache.

The mystic's first recourse when we are stressed is to take a step back and view the situation from a cosmic perspective. How do we do this, when circumstances affect us in such significant ways? There is a kind of spiritual muscle we develop, which gives us the strength to visualize any situation surrounded by light and embraced in the arms of God. Our mystical power lies in knowing that any situation can be seen through different eyes, and that our choice to see a situation differently is an invitation for miracles to enter. God will do His part when we do ours. The work of resurrection is a continuous process, at work in all dimensions of time and space. Where there is lack, God's abundance is on the way. Hold on. Have faith. It's coming.

When we've lost a job, our mystical strength lies in not buying into the appearance of lack. Our emotions naturally run high, and it's important that we feel them. But spiritual victory lies in saying to any condition that does not reflect God's perfection,

'Get behind me. I know you're not real, even though it feels like you are.' From this conviction flows a miraculous elixir that alchemizes our emotions and brings them, in time, into alignment with God's reality. It takes time for one condition to transform into another, and during that time our consciousness is crucial. In denying the unreal, we call forth the Real.

The ego looks only to the externals: get a new résumé, call this person or that person, arrange for unemployment benefits, etc. All of that and more might be called for on the worldly plane. But it is a mistake to look to God as a last resort, second to more practical solutions. He is not, after all, a mere weak appendage to the really powerful things we can do to help ourselves. Our greatest power lies in asking God to light our way.

Do not pose for God, but rather be real: it is a good idea to present our pain to Him exactly as we feel it. We might pray, 'Dear God, I need a job. I give to You all of the emotions I feel about this . . . my grief . . . my fear . . . my humiliation. I know there were things I should have done differently. I am ashamed of myself; I don't know how to face my kids; I'm afraid no one will hire me, that I'm not good enough.' Whatever we actually feel should form the crux of our communication to God; He is, as Stevie Wonder sings, 'the only free psychiatrist that's known throughout the world.' We have to be honest with God, both about our pain and our shortcomings, in order for His spirit to enter us in the deepest places and transform us. According to *A Course in Miracles*, He cannot take from us what we will not release to Him.

We can lose a job and still know we have a career. We can lose money and still retain a consciousness of wealth. We can lose the things of this world, but the knowledge of our connection to God is something no one can take away. It's ours to remember if we choose to remember it. Place the shame, the humiliation, the fear in the hands of God. Literally pray it away. We can allow God's spirit to deliver us from the emotions that reflect our disappointment to the emotions that reflect our hope and joy.

Seekers are aware that in the mortal world, things come and go. And that's why we wish to keep our emotional centre of gravity elsewhere. We choose to remain in the House of the Lord – the energy of divine consciousness – both when the money and job are happening, and when the money and job are not happening. When money is here, it behoves us to remain humble, grateful, and devoted to service. When money is not here, remember that we live in God, work in God, lean on God, and will rise back up in God. Anything can increase our connection to Him if we allow it to, and often it is the situations that take us to our knees that take us home to Him.

From a spiritual perspective, while we can lose our earthly employment, we cannot lose the job God gave us. We are the permanent holders of a spiritual career, for it is what we are and not just what we do that represents our greatest work in the world. As long as we remain vigilant at building our internal abundance – an abundance of integrity, an abundance of forgiveness, an abundance of service, an abundance of love – then external lack is bound to be temporary.

So what's important is to remember that your first job on earth is to be a minister of God, whether you're employed or unemployed as the world defines it. We cannot be unemployed if we are employed by God Himself. We are on this earth to do a job for Him, to be about our Father's business, to become whom He would have us be, that through Him we might extend into the universe the love that will save the world. This is not a job that is given and then taken away. It is the opportunity inherent in every moment. As long as there are ways we can serve, then we have a job to do. Love and forgiveness form our mission on earth, and that is why they are key to our emotional well-being. In God's Reality, we cannot lose that job. God will not fire us, and His business cannot fail.

Appearances to the contrary exist only to challenge us, tempting us to place our faith in illusions. Having forgotten who we really are – suffering from illusions about our own identity – our perceptions of the world are doomed to be illusory as well. But as our sense of self is repaired, our illusions fall away. In remembering who we are in relation to God, we remember who we are in relation to each other and to the world around us. From the miracle of our realignment with God flows every other miracle we need. God's spirit is a heavenly consciousness of divine oneness, always beckoning you to remember that there is nothing you can do, nothing that can happen, that can ever lessen your eternal value in His eyes. You have tremendous gifts to give; God sent them with you when you came to this earth. And while you might forget them, or doubt that they exist, God does not forget and He will show them to you. As soon as your gifts are dedicated to His work, they will blossom. Chains that might have held you back for years will dissolve. And you will feel free. You will learn that your spirit is bigger than your circumstances, as soon as you put your spirit first.

If you have lost your job, then another situation, just as good or better, already exists in the Mind of God. It can be difficult to feel this way when stress is high, but our feelings are not always perfect indicators of reality. The infinite, unalterable power of God is such that whenever something contrary to His love is introduced into the universe, a miraculous alternative automatically develops. We pray that our eyes might be open, that we might see what has already happened. When we pray for God to illuminate our path, we are saying, 'Dear God, please show me the way. What thoughts do I need to think, to be able to navigate my life at this point? What perceptions do I need; what insights will guide me? Who do I need to forgive? What parts of my personality do I need to look at; what changes do I need to make? Please come upon me and heal my life. Amen.'

In God's world, there is only abundance, regardless of what we are experiencing within our human drama. The remembrance of our mystical identity will restore our confidence, reminding us that we're part of that abundance. Lack is a temporary condition, often reflecting a fractured sense of self: thinking we were small, we acted in a small way and now reap the effects of our self-limiting thoughts or behaviour. Material abundance will not restore a broken sense of self, but a restored sense of self will attract whatever abundance we need.

On a spiritual plane, 'having' and 'being' are synonymous. The greatest form of abundance is to remember who we are: that we are literally part of the abundance of the universe. Usually our experience of material lack reflects our failure to allow ourselves the hugeness of that realization. Our greatest need is for the hand of God to build a bridge over which we can cross from mortal perception to divine understanding. Our prayer is not simply, 'Dear God, please send me a better job,' but, 'Dear God, enable me to see this situation differently, that this area of apparent lack might be healed inside my mind.' There is only ever one problem: that we are separated somehow from the thinking of God.

Miracles can come from anything, anywhere, anytime. There is no situation that ties God's hands. He is bigger than layoffs, or recessions, or stock market losses. Every ending is a new beginning. Through the grace of God, we can always start again.

You have not been fired; you have been liberated. You might not feel that way, which is fine. Cry your tears, but remember this: the resurrected state already exists. It lives within us all as an eternal and operative principle. Claim your good, for it is on the way.

If you allow this situation to throw you more deeply into the arms of God, then the next time someone hires you – and they will – they will be hiring someone who is better at what they do because they are more fully who they are. Fear comes, but fear passes. Only the truth of who you are remains, to shine on everything. And that is your job, now and always: to shine and thus illuminate the world.

12:00 NOON

Being Happy

It was her third birthday, and we had the party in the garden. There were lots of children and lots of games, and Cinderella arrived just before we cut the cake. My daughter's jaw dropped open at the sight of Cinderella gliding across the grass. 'Mummy, you got her to come over to our house?' she exclaimed. Her eyes were wide and as sparkly as Cinderella's rhinestone tiara. Later she asked me in a whisper, 'Is Barbie here, too?'

I have learned from experience that happiness is an acquired skill. There is always something to complain about, even in the best of times. And there is always something to celebrate, even in the worst of times. Happiness is not an objective reality so much as a subjective decision. Chronic complainers miss the boat.

Many people are addicted to suffering and have a mental habit of pointing out the worst in people or situations. Not only are they robbing themselves of joy, but their failure to appreciate all the goodness that life has to offer actually diminishes that good. Both our blessing and our condemnation have power. Thinking that something is bad has the power to make it so in our experience.

Children are one of our greatest lessons in

happiness, constantly challenging us to enjoy the moment, as the next one will not be the same. There is no sense saying about a small child, 'Well, I'll enjoy watching her at the beach splashing around in the waves, but I'll do it later, next year or the next year.' Next year, she will not splash around in the same way. Two years old gives way to three and then four. And before you know it there is a teenager standing in front of you who won't even *want* to go to the beach with you. You'll wonder where all the years went, but they will be gone. No more watching her finger paint. She doesn't finger paint anymore.

I have lived large parts of my life in wonderful circumstances that I utterly failed to appreciate. Reasons to be happy were everywhere, but some-how I didn't connect with them. It was as though I was eating but couldn't taste the food. Finally, I've learned to celebrate the good while it's happening. I feel gratitude and praise today for what are some-times such simple pleasures. I have learned that happiness is not determined by circumstances. Happiness is not what happens when everything goes the way you think it should go; happiness is what happens when you decide to be happy.

There was a time a few years ago when several members of my family died in quick succession. It seemed as though all we did was go to funerals, gathering together to cry. Then, several years later, Hilary, the oldest of my late sister's daughters, got married. Finally, we were gathering not to grieve but to celebrate, and the gratitude everyone felt was palpable. Every living member of Hilary's family came to the wedding, from many places around the world, and all of us knew why. We would have loved her and celebrated her marriage even if her mother and her grandfather and her uncle had not recently died. But everyone knew that the circumstances of the last few years made this wedding, this *mitzvah*, even more important. The event was so infinitely sweet because it contrasted dramatically with the bitterness of the previous few years.

So those who have learned to be happy are often those who have suffered most. When simple pleasures have been taken away, such as someone's loving smile or encouraging word, then the next time such pleasures come around – and they do – we lift our cup of life to them. We sing God's praises in a way we had never done in the days when we took so much for granted.

Gratitude is essential to happiness. Developing a grateful attitude – knowing that every time we arrive somewhere safely, we have something to be happy about; every time our children rush up to us and smile, we have something to be happy about; every time we get out of bed and can take a deep breath and go out for a walk, we have something to be happy about – that is the essence of a happy existence. Happiness is a muscle we must use, or it will wither away.

Whatever we focus on is bound to expand. Where we see the negative, we call forth more negative. And where we see the positive, we call forth more positive. Having loved and lost, I now love more passionately. Having won and lost, I now win more soberly. Having tasted the bitter, I now savour the sweet.

Several years ago, a friend of mine lived with me during the final few months of her life. Not completely understanding the effects of her illness, I kept saying, 'Michelle, you must eat. You're getting too thin! Eat!' And after she died, I read in her journal about how 'Marianne takes it for granted that if you eat, you gain weight; if you want to go out somewhere, you can; and if you want to live past this year, it's a reasonable proposition.' She was someone who had so little to be happy about, but she taught me so much about happiness. During those months, right after the birth of my daughter, I would come home to find my dying friend with my baby snuggled next to her. There was a smile of bliss on both their faces that I will remember all my days.

1:00 PM

Feeling Jealous

You can't get a book contract, but someone else you know just had their first book hit number one on Amazon.com; you passed on taking shares in your friend's new company, and everyone who bought in is a millionaire now; you've just broken up with the love of your life, and everywhere you look there's an issue of Bride *magazine. Despite your best efforts, your skin is turning green . . .*

We're all a little ashamed to admit our own lovelessness when it comes to jealousy and envy. In a world that has constantly drilled into us a belief in scarcity, it seems that there are only so many pieces of the pie; if someone else gets a piece, we think there must be less for us.

But in God's universe, there is no scarcity. There is always 'enough,' because consciousness is endlessly creative. No one else's good fortune diminishes our own except when we choose to denigrate it. Only our own judgement can stop the flow of goodness to our door. Abundance is our spiritual birthright, which is ours to either receive or resist. Our blessing someone else's abundance only attracts abundance to us, just as judging those who have what we would like to have obstructs it.

None of us ever *wants* to feel jealous, of course. It's a feeling that comes over all of us despite our best intentions. We feel we can't help it at times, when someone else gets the promotion, or the credit, or the relationship, or the money . . . Their win can trigger primitive feelings of failure or loss, and the intellect has little or no power to assuage that pain. Mystics do not deny these negative emotions; we surrender them. We know we're feeling them for a reason, as they often represent the places in our psyche where we relive previous wounds within the context of current experience. The negative emotion we're feeling now – if we surrender it deeply and ask for God's healing – is our chance to transform the past and be free of its pain in the present.

While in the midst of our pain, we can reach for Truth – for the abstract principles by which we reinterpret our experiences in a more positive light. A tough mind is the greatest complement to a tender heart. Embracing God's Truth is a spiritual act: it alchemizes our emotions, providing the bridge from fear to love.

Think of the mystical 'three days' between the crucifixion and the resurrection as the time it takes for a situation to change, once spirit has infused our consciousness. As we come to look at an experience differently, in time it begins to transform. The choice to perceive any situation within a spiritual context cuts through our negativity. Where we place our faith is critical. For we *do* live in a limitlessly abundant universe. And even when we feel loss and limitation, our choice to affirm what we know to be true – that we are limited by nothing – brings the power of Truth to bear on any situation. We can have faith in a world of limitation, or we can have faith in a world of limitless good. But it shall be given to us according to our faith: what we have *faith* in is what we will experience on some level.

I once had a friend who was a struggling actor. I was always impressed by how genuinely happy he was when one of his friends got a break. Regardless of any pain or disappointment he might have been feeling about his own career, he was always sincere in his congratulations for others. When his big break did come, I wasn't surprised. By celebrating the success of others, he helped draw success toward himself. I wondered if I could've done as well.

Years ago, I noticed that several women who had started out by attending my lectures were now giving talks to audiences of their own, appearing on television at times in places where I no longer did. And I did feel a little jealous. I had to feel those feelings and not deny them; the only negative feelings that have the power to hurt us are those that haven't been processed and surrendered. It's only when we put our hurt feelings into the fire of transformation – allowing ourselves to feel them and continuing to surrender them – that they finally begin to burn away. I prayed for those women and their continued success and, as time went on, my own thoughts and feelings began to transform. I learned so much from this, gaining insight into how I might have appeared to others when I was younger, and about how best to gracefully fill the role I have now.

Those women were newer on the scene – a little hotter, a little younger. But once I gave them that – grieving the role that I can no longer play and passing that torch along to them – I received the blessing of another realization. I saw that now I'm an elder of sorts in my professional community. I have a role to play as someone who has been around a while, and my niche today is every bit as significant as the niche that now belongs to them. But I had to let go of what had been mine in the past in order to receive what is mine today.

For women, it can be particularly hard to deal with physical jealousy in our society, which is so geared toward youth and beauty. Many women of my generation are grappling with this phenomenon in our middle years, having so glorified our own youth and set the precedent for its overemphasis. Younger women, whose skin still glows with a voluptuousness we naively thought would be ours forever, can be particularly hard to love and bless!

Now, we tell ourselves, we are older and wiser: we're becoming the elders and we should honour that role, society needs its elders, etc. But often, what we're really thinking is, 'Yeah, I'm older and wiser, but I would rather look good. I know that society needs its elders, but I wish I wasn't one of them.' We try to paste on a more politically correct consciousness, yet still we need to feel our authentic feelings or our healing will not be authentic either.

Often we're confronted by people who have something we used to have, or have something we never had and still want. There are often things to grieve in life, whether they be youth or lost opportunities or people who have moved on. And grief is an important step along the spiritual path, because only when we have fully grieved over something can we completely let it go. Dreams often do die hard, and there is nothing negative about feeling their loss. Only when we have truly cried all our tears have we cleansed ourselves of the toxic barriers to the experience of genuine joy.

By surrendering to God's will, we receive so very much more than we would ever get by allowing jealousy to guide our thoughts and behaviour. From acceptance and surrender at last there comes an awe-filled grace. And with grace comes the opening of our eyes. We begin to see that every circumstance and every situation is just a corner of an infinite universe. No corner is really so good or bad, as it is simply a place the soul is in need of experiencing now. Whatever it is, it will not last. Whatever it is, it is leading to something better. And whatever it is, it is actually perfect.

2:00 PM

Making Decisions

Maybe I should let my daughter go to the school her friends are attending, or maybe I should send her to the other one; maybe I should take the job in the North, or maybe I should stay where I am; maybe I should keep fighting to make this relationship work, or maybe I should let it go. Making decisions is the worst thing in the world. Or maybe it's not; I can't decide . . .

Having to make decisions can be awful. We go round and round in our minds, not quite knowing which set of factors should be given greater weight. Sometimes reason competes with gut instinct, which only seems to make matters worse.

But what if we could place all our decisions in the hands of God? What if a decision surrendered to the divine was a decision surrendered to the highest level of intelligence, wisdom, and love?

We're not schooled by traditional modes of thinking to believe that such effortlessness is possible, and so we remain locked into the stress of making decisions about a future we cannot forecast. We stand before a bend in the road without knowing what's around the corner. Yet we are expected to make decisions about what *might* be there, decisions that could affect the rest of our lives.

Metaphysics is the study of the invisible forces that underlie our human experience. And God, according to metaphysical interpretations of religion, dwells in a realm that is separate from our human drama, in which the horrors and pain of this world do not exist. But He sends into this realm a divine ambassador, imbued with His power, to deliver us from fear to love. One of the names of that ambassador is the Holy Spirit.

Because the Holy Spirit is the part of our mind that remains in conscious contact with God, we can safely place all decisions in His hands. The mortal ego dwells in linear time and does not know the future; the Holy Spirit dwells in eternity and there-fore *does*. He knows not only what will happen in the future, *but also how every decision made will affect every living thing forever*. Imagine an infinitely complex computer that could reliably analyse any situation and give a readout, to the nth detail, of what would happen if this, this, or that were to occur. We don't get to see the readout, of course, but we are given simple instructions on how best to behave in order to support the highest outcome for ourselves and others. The instructions might come in a form as simple as an intuitive flash, or a complex process of growth and understanding that gradually unfolds within us.

There have been situations where I made what turned out to be a wrong decision, and I had to experience the remorse that comes when we realize we've acted against our own instincts and now regret it. Often we receive a kind of 'inner knowing' about something, yet we disregard that knowing because we can't rationally explain it. The more we pray, meditate, and take our spiritual practice seriously, the better listeners we become to the small, still voice of God. We come to understand that there are means of knowing beyond the rational. Now that I've fully realized how much smarter God is than I, and how willing He is to share what He knows, my life is much easier. It is not an abdication of responsibility, but rather the ultimate taking of responsibility, to ask God to do our thinking for us. He is not outside us, after all. He is the Mind of the realized Self.

Sometimes we'll wonder, 'Should I have that meeting on Thursday or Friday?' We look at our calendar and see that Thursday is the less busy day, therefore the most rational day to set up the meeting – but something inside keeps saying, 'Do it on Friday . . .' So many times in my life I've gone with Thursday, only to have something happen later that made Thursday very much the wrong day. And Friday, of course, would have been perfect.

Sometimes Spirit speaks loudly and directly. A friend of mine was once deciding whether or not to run for the office of mayor of his hometown. I knew he was going through a lot of questioning, trying to weigh all the various factors involved in making such a decision. One day he called to chat.

'So how is it going, Steve?' I asked him.

'Oh, it's such a whirlwind here,' he said. 'I don't know what to do. Bob Garner might run again for his Congressional seat, in which case I don't want to run against him. But he might not run because he might want to run for senator. The senator might not be running because he might want to come back here and run for governor. In the meantime, everyone keeps asking me to run for mayor, but I can't decide because I think maybe I should stay out of politics for another year or two and establish myself in the community first. Then again, I think maybe I should make the run for mayor, and I have to decide because the filing date is next week, but I keep going back and forth and it's driving me nuts.'

It was driving me nuts, too, just listening to him. My head was whirling. 'Steve,' I said. 'You're thinking about this in such a worldly way. Political strategizing tends to be very left brain and rationalistic. Have you considered making the decision about what to do from a spiritual perspective?'

'That would be great!' he said. 'But how do I do that?'

'Just ask God to decide for you,' I told him. 'You can't possibly know what the future holds. You can't know all the various factors going on behind the scenes. So just ask God if He wants you to be in politics – if that's the best way you can serve Him – and that if it is, please let you know whether to run for mayor in this next election.'

'That sounds great!' Steve said. And so we prayed. We placed his career, and this particular decision, in the hands of God.

'Thank you so much,' he said, when we had finished the prayer. 'I feel so much lighter.'

After that, we got off the phone, and about fifteen minutes later my phone rang again. It was Steve.

'You won't believe what happened!' he exclaimed. 'When I was talking to you, I was on the phone in my office, which is in a space behind my house. Right after we finished our call, I walked back into the house to get some coffee, and the minute I walked in, the phone rang. I picked it up, and it was the editor from our local newspaper. He was calling to tell me about an anonymous ad that was placed in his paper today, and that will be running in tomorrow's edition. It's a full page that simply says, "Run, Steve, Run." '

We giggled at the amazing serendipity, and after that, Steve certainly felt that he knew what he should do. I don't think he will ever forget that day, or doubt that God can answer his questions.

God's answers don't always come through as loudly or clearly as full-page newspaper ads, but they find their way to us nevertheless. Sometimes we don't hear an answer simply because we're not listening; we're not yet prayerful and meditative enough to have honed our spiritual 'hearing.' Sometimes we don't hear an answer because the answer lies in more fully living the question. And sometimes we hear exactly what God is telling us, but we are not yet prepared to own up to what we know. By cultivating a state of mind in which we place our decisions where they belong, in the hands of One who always knows what we should do, we draw on a mystical power no worldly means of decision-making can match. God will listen and God will answer, with a prescience and wisdom and intelligence and love for us and for everyone in the whole entire world.

Feeling Bored

You have been on the road for an hour and a half, and you are moving at perhaps twenty miles an hour. The smog is thick and the air is hot. This day is just the same old thing, with no variety or enchantment or joy. Will you be making this commute forever? Is this what you were born to do? You would have hoped your life was more important than this. . . .

Every day, millions of people commute long, boring hours to jobs they don't love and then go home to less than happy families. It's amazing how much time we spend on things that feel like wasted time.

The circumstances of our lives are not always exciting, yet they tend to change only when we do. The excitement we seek will not come from an external source, but only from an internal one. I have never known an exciting person who lived a really boring life. An exciting person makes a decision to live a more exciting way: to read substance instead of junk, to listen to books on tape instead of listening to bad radio, to engage in things that matter instead of frivolous pursuits.

Every moment, faithfully lived, is a chance to

practise the art of living. A life of magnitude does not just happen; it is consciously chosen. Living is an endlessly creative process in which we work on achieving the life we want through our willingness to be who we would like to be.

Spiritually, there is a lesson in every moment: when we are seemingly stuck in a boring routine, the miracle lies not so much in finding something else to do as in realizing how much we can do in any single moment – through the power of our own consciousness – to transform ourselves and the world around us. According to *A Course in Miracles*, only what we are not giving can be lacking in any situation.

How many times are we tempted to say, 'Well, this is just boring work, so I don't really need to show up for it fully. I don't need to be energetic, or excellent. It's really not an important job.'? Yet when we say our job is boring, often we are merely indicating our unwillingness to show up fully for it. Failing to be a giver, we feel ungiven to. Failing to show up fully for life, our life then seems to feel empty.

If we give it just a minute's thought, we realize our lives are usually far, far better than those of billions of people around the world. In any given moment, someone is tortured, someone is starving, someone is dying a painful death or grieving for his or her most beloved. If people can rise above such things – and miraculously they do – then we can pick up our mystical wands and rise above the frustration of being stuck in traffic.

The frustration of traffic is a good metaphor for the frustration of modern life. We want to get somewhere . . . But it's going too slow, and all these other people are in our way! If we wish to remain affected by traffic, or by anything else, then that's our choice. The day is hot, perhaps, and we have no air-conditioner, or the day is cold and we have no heater. We can think, *Poor me*. The drivers around us are acting nuts. We can think, *These people are total jerks*. We can think that way if we choose to, but we cannot diminish the power of our thoughts. Every thought of victimization or attack is an attack upon ourselves. When we think them, we are opening a door: enter stress, enter sickness, enter fear.

Using a mystical wand is a perceptual choice: in any given moment, we can reach for prayer the way some people reach for cigarettes or food. Prayer is a conscious decision to realign ourselves with divine right order, in the full awareness that without this realignment we are at the mercy of a chaotic world. And we need not be. The children of God are held back by nothing when we remember who we are.

And the only way to remember who we are is by also remembering who everyone else is. The drama of the material plane is an illusion that hides a truer Truth. The mystic has asked for new eyes, through which we see so much more than other people stuck in traffic with us, or on the subway with us, or in life with us. With mystical eyes, we see many other souls: hoping as we do, hurting as we do, trying their best from day to day just as we do. As we expand our understanding of their lives, we expand our experience of our own.

None of us, in our spiritual essence, is just a mortal creature, defined and limited by the material world. Rather, we are children of God who have been limited by nothing so much as the smallness of our story – the story we have told ourselves and believed when others have told us – that to be human is to be limited, powerless, or weak. It is not the transformation of our circumstances, but of our self-perception – from identifying with our limited bodies to our infinite spirits – that frees the world around us to sparkle with infinite possibilities.

You are free to experience life negatively or positively, and the choice you make determines whether you are at cause, or at effect, of the life you are living. You could be standing at your kitchen sink or sitting at your desk, sweeping your floor or painting a picture. It doesn't matter where you are or what you're doing; you could be in a castle by the sea, changing a baby's nappy, or living in a prison cell. Your mind is holy because you are a child of God, and now in this moment you have no higher purpose in life, nor will you ever, than to merely know that holiness, to be it, and to extend it outward to bless the world. As you do, you are initiating a spiritual propulsion more powerful than any worldly engine. And this generosity of the mystical mind reflects the fundamental nature of God. In reflecting God's love, we extend His love. And that which extends outward to bless others automatically extends inward as well. Your life will come to reflect your decision to use your mind for holy purposes.

Anything we do, anywhere we do it, is a chance to silently extend the blessing of our angelic spirit. We might be in line at the Post Office – every person in line is someone we can bless. We might be waiting in a doctor's office – is there not someone waiting with us who could use a kind remark, or a child who would like us to read to them? As long as our hearts are open, we can show up fully as the angels we are. Imagine an angel saying to God, 'Don't send me there, please. It's a boring town.'

There is no corner of the earth in which God's

love, expressed through you, is not desperately needed. And our most needed prayer, at times, is for the calming of our own impatient nature. We want an assignment from God, but we want it to be glamorous. However, if we look at our circumstances closely, we will usually see why they are perfect lessons for what we most need to learn, exactly as they are. Often we want to jump out of a situation and into another, when we have not yet truly mastered the lessons inherent in the first one. Only when we have done that will our lives transform. Otherwise, no matter where we go or what we do, we will subconsciously manufacture the same situation over and over again.

Remember that Cinderella's godmother didn't order a take-away, but rather transformed the pumpkins and the mice and the rags that were already there. Anything and everything is the raw stuff of miracles. We don't have to be somewhere else, doing something else, to use our power to serve the holy and the good. Every single part of reality is an aspect of the greater glory of God.

Often, when the modern mind experiences itself as bored, it's actually merely addicted to cheap stimulation, having been trained by television and so forth to constantly jump out of its centre. Learning how to slowly and purposefully arrange flowers in a vase, or how to enjoy ourselves while watching a small child play the same game over and over, can be a sign not of giving up but of growing up. We finally come to realize that there is not really a world out there at all, but merely a projection of all our private thought forms. Our capacity to behave powerfully in the outer world is increased by our ability to master the art of living serenely within the internal one.

And sometimes we are bored because the situation is asking us to do what we don't want to do, but would be better off if we did. When my child was very little, I lived in a small town for several years. While there, I didn't like it. I missed the action of a big city; I wanted the stimulation of late-night dinners at noisy restaurants. What other people considered calming and restful made me want to climb the walls.

And 'just being a mother' felt boring to me at times. I found it difficult to be with my daughter the way she wanted me to. I would grow bored at the park, watching her sliding down the same slide again and again or pushing her on the same swing for hours. Now I think it's the coolest thing in the world, being with a little child in the park, simply playing. I'm finally at a point where I can appreciate the beauty of just being somewhere;

my nervous system no longer revolts against it. I am no longer under the illusion that there's more exciting action somewhere else.

What I realized – unfortunately, after I had left that small town – was that my discomfort there was my detoxing from the overstimulation of the previous few years of my life. And the fact that I had very little to do while there besides being with my daughter was, in God's mind, precisely the point! I had been given those four years as a gift: the divine opportunity to deeply and mindfully concentrate on bonding with my daughter. But because I was so agitated, emotionally resisting my circumstances, I was blind to many miracles that were offered to me. According to the Danish philosopher Søren Kierkegaard, 'Life is lived forward but understood backward.' The mystic seeks to deeply understand life while it's happening.

Today, my only desire is to make the most of whatever experiences I am having at the moment. And whenever I am tempted to think that those experiences are boring – that the excitement of life would surely lie somewhere else – then I remember that I always have a choice: to experience the miracles of life as they come to me or blind myself to them, with the audacity to believe that God ever, ever, ever did not know what He was doing.

God *always* knows what He is doing – the question is, do we? The mystic, knowing there is nowhere where God is not, has realized His wisdom is unending. There is often hidden power in the times when nothing seems to be happening at all. The times when the material world takes less precedence are times when the holy has more chance to breathe. As I drive my daughter to school, we often use that time to pray for the day, to focus on what she would wish to have happen, and to surrender the day ahead to God. How could we consider it wasted time to have met with God and planned a new world?

Arguing

'I should never have trusted you,' he said, gazing out of the window and sipping his juice. 'You should never have trusted me?!' I jumped to my feet. 'Do you think this is my fault?' 'You should have called them on time.' 'You should have paid the instalment! I couldn't call them when the bill wasn't paid!' He looked at me with steely eyes. No love, no humour. I started to cry.

Sometimes it's not the all-out wars, but the common arguments that wreck relationships. Love is strong, but it's also fragile. Everyone wants to be treated tenderly, and it's easy to forget that when we strongly disagree.

The mystic doesn't seek to avoid a disagreement so much as infuse it with grace. A disagreement is like a cut on the skin. You need to treat it gently and not cut further. So it should be, when we see things differently, that the gentleness of spirit guides our speech. Emotional havoc usually comes not from the issues that divide us so much as from the things we say and do because of the issues that divide us. Indeed, it's often fairly simple things that we disagree about. Learning how to disagree with love is an important skill on the mystical path.

First of all, we need to acknowledge that people do disagree. Avoiding a disagreement on the misguided principle that spiritual people don't have them is as spiritually immature as it is psychologically unsound. A disagreement and an argument are two different things. Indeed, a disagreement need not become an argument when the people involved have the personal skills to hold to higher consciousness while on lower ground.

According to *A Course in Miracles*, our job is to tell someone they're right, even when they're wrong. That doesn't mean we're supposed to lie. It does mean, however, that it's always our mission to affirm someone's humanity, even when we're disagreeing with his or her perceptions. Our spiritual challenge in any situation is first to recognize a person's love and innocence, and then to speak from that perspective. For it is not our disagreements that wound; it's our criticism, attack and blame that wound. Until we know we're solidly on loving ground – past the temptation to even subtly blame – we had best be very careful with what we say and how we say it. Some words cut, while others heal.

But spirituality means a whole lot more than merely speaking in softer tones. Judgement can whisper, and it's still a judgement. Our spiritual task is to surrender the thought that we have the right, in any situation, to judge whom God would never judge, or to condemn whom God would never condemn. And that means everyone. God's perception is that each and every one of us is His beloved child in whom He is well pleased. And it is in learning to think as God thinks that we find mastery in life and love. So it is that when we disagree with someone, our prayer should not be that their eyes be opened to our point of view, but that our eyes be opened to theirs. According to *A Course in Miracles*, we try to understand someone in order to decide whether or not they're worthy of our love, but until we love them we cannot understand them.

Once we do – when we have allowed our hearts to soften into genuinely right relationship – the words with which we express ourselves in a disagreement become guided by a higher source. We remember to point out how much we appreciate someone before we point out what we perceive to be a problem. We are willing to express ourselves from a place of questioning rather than a place of blame. And we are able to see the difference between criticism, which tears people down, and honest disagreement, which can be a creative and even collaborative process.

When our basic humanity is affirmed, it's usually

not that hard to hear people say that they disagree with us. Sometimes it's even fun, like a mental fencing match. But no one wants to feel the sword in their side. And anyone who places it there has not learned the spiritual skills of communication.

The problem, of course, is that it's not always easy to see the innocence in someone, particularly when we disagree with him or her. Yet that work – the inner effort to achieve our own right-mindedness – is the work that God requires of us. He does not need us to police the universe. He did not send us to Earth to set other people straight. He sent us here to become perfect ourselves, which we're not doing by definition when we are pointing our finger at someone else.

And the truth is, it doesn't feel good to separate ourselves from others through judgement or blame. It behoves us to ask ourselves, as it says in *A Course in Miracles*, 'Do I prefer to be right or to be happy?'

When we disagree with someone, as much as we might be tempted to immediately express ourselves to them or to someone else about them, our best move is always to talk to God first. 'Dear God, please take away my temptation to judge. Please show me this person as You would see them. Please show me their innocence, that I might see mine. Amen.'

And then it is wise to hold our tongue until the hand of God has come upon us, readjusting our mental and emotional energies. The Holy Spirit needs time to work, like any kind of medicine, as it enters our psychic bloodstream. And when He does, He quickens the spirit within us. When that has occurred – when we are reconciled with our own divinity – we are automatically reconciled with others.

But until we are, we argue, and emotional danger looms. A small argument festers, and things are left unsaid. During the next encounter, someone makes a jab that is actually in reaction to what occurred before, and on and on, until grace breaks the chain. Finally, someone – and it need not be both parties – prays for help. 'Dear God, please help us find the love between us. I know it's there, and I am willing to change, that I might see it. Thank you, God. Amen.'

Listening to the ego – for whom separation is not a problem but a goal – we allow mental conflicts to separate our hearts. This divides us not only from one another, but also from the experience of God. For that place, where we feel we have been cast out of someone's heart, is our exile from the Garden of Eden. And in that exile, we are terrified. We then subconsciously respond from our terror – not at having been disagreed with, but at having been cast from the garden of God's love.

At such a moment, when we have been attacked, the mystic's prayer is to feel from God the love that has been denied us by someone else. We pray for the ability to send love to someone who has withheld it from us, that we not contribute to a wheel of suffering between us. Whether we are attacking someone or being attacked, our correction comes from the hand of God. It is our willingness to see things differently – our willingness to see that innocence beyond the veil of someone's personality – that opens our hearts to receive God's grace. And if that grace does not come immediately, that doesn't mean it isn't coming. There are layers of pain that we must burn through before we can recognize love in every situation. None of us can always do it, but our willingness confers upon us a mantle of light, and the light will penetrate the darkness of guilt. This penetration of darkness by the Light of God is a miracle in our hearts, and we will feel it when it comes.

Everything should be interpreted as love or as a call for love. When someone has not shown us their love, our power lies in knowing that they would have, had they known how. They are not wrong so much as they are wounded, and our role is not to judge them but to heal them. It is in cleaving to our own love that we awaken it in others.

In any situation where love does not rule, affirm that only love is real. Say it, repeat it, chant it like a mantra. Allow it to cast out all thoughts of blame and judgement and fear. Think of the mean-spiritedness of someone, then affirm that only love is real. Watch a horrible story on the TV news, then affirm that only love is real. Feel your own fears about this or that, then affirm that only love is real. This does not put you in a state of denial, but rather in a state of transcendence. You are not pretending that something is not really happening, but only that it is not Really happening. And just as the Wicked Witch of the West disappeared when Dorothy threw water on her, no manifestation of fear will long remain once humanity has risen to the understanding that only love is real.

If you've had a fight with someone, sit down and pray.

> *Dear God, I surrender this argument to you.*
> *Remove, Dear God, the walls between us.*
> *Send your Spirit here to remind us both*
>   *of our innocence and our love.*
> *May forgiveness reign.*
> *Dear God, may we begin again.*
> *Amen.*

And think about how many times we've had arguments with friends or family that seemed so intense when they occurred, but years later, it's so easy to forgive because no one completely remembers anymore who said or did what to whom. We go through the years and we learn from life, finding it easier at last to both apologize and forgive. Ultimately, everything but love burns away. The power of forgiveness lies in knowing that will happen, even when it hasn't yet. We can skip the despair and go straight for the love. Instead of trying to find common ground, we can claim common ground. And, in fact, it is only the ground we stand on together that is even real at all.

5:00 PM

Hoping Against Hope

'He said when he left that he might be back – that he needed some time to see this through – then maybe he'd come back to us. I saw my little boy cry but try to act like he wasn't, when I told him that Dad wasn't coming home tonight. The baby kept saying "Daddy" softly, as I put her to bed. And my oldest daughter said nothing. If he doesn't come back, I don't know how we'll live through this. Oh my God, I hope he will. I hope he will . . .'

Sometimes we hope against hope for a particular outcome: our estranged spouse will come back, the cancer will be cured, we will get that job. Yet there are often times when we do not get that for which we most fervently wish. Not everyone who hopes for something gets it.

In the words of Dr. Martin Luther King, Jr., 'If you lose hope, somehow you lose the vitality that keeps life moving; you lose that courage to be, that quality that helps you to go on in spite of all.' But how do we retain the spirit of hope when our circumstances seem almost hopeless?

Hope springs eternal not because of the nature of the world but because of the nature of God. The mystic knows that the light of Creation does not emanate from the material world, and so it is useless to seek it there. Nothing on the material plane is deeply stable. A house built on sand is vulnerable to weather, as Jesus said, while a house built on rock will stand. The material world is what the Buddha called *maya*, or illusion, testifying not to God's reality but to man's illusion of separation from God. It is not the true kingdom, and while it can *reflect* our good, it is a reflection only. It is not the *source* of our good because it is not the source of *us*.

It's best that we not place our hope in worldly satisfaction because, at the most fundamental level, there isn't any. Worldly satisfaction can bring temporary pleasure, which is certainly good. But nothing in the material world is deep enough to satisfy the true yearning of our souls. Our greatest hope is for the experience of joy, and often we are not as smart as we think we are when it comes to predicting what would bring us that joy. The mystic hopes not for a particular outcome, then, but for the *best* outcome for all concerned. And what that is can only be determined by God. Hope that is attached to a particular outcome is looking for pleasure but fishing for pain, because attachment itself is a source of pain. It is best to hope for an experience of life in all its fullness – a life that can embrace both joy and sorrow and still be at peace, because joy and sorrow are sure to come in this life. Our triumph over sorrow is not that we can avoid it but that we can endure it. And therein lies our hope: that in spirit we might become bigger than the problems we face.

Our problems in this world can surely be huge, but they are never as huge as God. The issue is never how bad things are, but *how good God is*. Hope lies in having more faith in the power of God to heal us than in the power of anything to hurt or destroy us. In realizing that as children of God we are bigger than our problems, we have the power at last to confront them. For all manifestation of fear is a reflection of the fact that humanity has forgotten its spiritual identity. In beginning to remember it, we put fear on notice that its days are numbered.

Where the ego analyses a problem, the spirit accepts that there is an ultimate answer that is the Answer to every problem. And that is why we place what we hope for in the hands of God. Our hope is that He will illuminate our hearts – that we will become the people He would have us be – for in the presence of an awakened spirit, all problems fall away.

We are the children of a loving God *for whom nothing is impossible*. As we remember that, we become as powerful as we are meant to be. We are not meant to cower before the darkness of the world; let it cower before us. Every problem is merely another opportunity to use the miraculous powers we've been given.

The suffering of the world is not the point of human existence; the point of human existence is that in God all suffering ends. Through God, we celebrate a happy ending to every situation, *convinced that it has already occurred.* And it's out of that conviction that miracles arise. The resurrection of Jesus, Buddha's enlightenment under the Bodhi tree, and the deliverance of the Israelites to the promised land are not fairy tales; they are messages from God. Their point is not what we should hope for, but rather what we should consider done, the miracles we can lean on because they were accomplished for all eternity. God has built into the structure of Creation that everything dark will turn light again.

True hope lies not in an illness cured or a marriage reconciled, but in a state of mind. The woman whose husband has left her should pray not that he comes home, but that God will carry her through this ordeal even if he doesn't. She should not pray, 'Dear God, please make my husband come back to me,' for she knows that God has given us all free will. But she prays, in spite of her tears, 'Dear God, I place this situation in your hands. May my husband find true happiness; may we all find true happiness. If his happiness lies here with me, then please touch his heart. And if it does not, then please heal mine. May Your will be done. Amen.'

The resurrective tendency of the universe is always at work in our personal trials and in our collective challenges. God, in His awesomeness and infinitude, has provided a solution to every problem the moment the problem occurs. The part that any of us can play in providing that solution is etched on our hearts. Even now, while the world is suffering the scourge of terror, our faith is to remember that God's harmony reigns supreme. God's light is not always our experience, but it can always be our faith. 'Blessed are those who have faith who cannot see.' For someone who is in prison, true hope lies not simply in an early release date, but in the knowledge that in God's world, there are no walls. The only walls that can hold us back are the walls that divide our hearts. Even within prison walls, we can cultivate a heavenly garden by fostering a beloved community. Our hope in God is not a hope for something to happen in the world, but for something to happen in us.

Essentially, our greatest hope has already been realized. Heaven is here and now, in our capacity to realize our oneness. Nothing can happen to make God not God, love not the only reality, or spirit not eternal. Our hope has already been met with a gigantic 'yes' from God. *We* are the ones who keep saying no.

Still, the offer to love instead of fear remains. We can choose again, at any moment. We can withdraw our faith in the thought forms that have guided us to where we are, realizing their complete inadequacy to guide us where we would like to go. To place our hope in God is to place our hope in love. We're not hoping that this or that will happen, but that we'll achieve a state of consciousness in which, whatever happens, we will not swerve from love or peace. Hope is simply an attitude, placing trust in the mystery of the universe before trust in the things of this world.

God has promised our return to the garden, but when we get there is entirely up to us. We may travel long and vicious lengths down the paths of fear. But someday, somewhere, we realize that our choice is either to live in fear or to learn to live another way. God is not our servant, but our deliverer. He enters where we invite Him, but an invitation not offered in love is not an invitation at all. Our hope is that, one day, He will have taught us how to love one another so completely that our world will become His garden.

In the meantime, our hope is born of participation

in hopeful solutions, for, ultimately, the only way to feel hope is to give hope to someone else. And then we see that it is all around us. The world should feel hopeful because *you* are here. You *are* the hope, because God is in you.

6:00 PM

Feeling Guilty

I was driving home. The stop sign was there — I had seen it before — but that day I was in a hurry. I don't remember hitting the car, but I remember seeing it fly across the intersection. I saw the car doors open and children started piling out, several of them, more than I would have thought possible for one car ... And then came the woman, holding a baby. I had no idea whether or not the child was alive. The woman looked at me and said, so soulfully, 'Why, Lady, why?'

Sometimes we feel we've made a mess of something important, and it seems there is nothing we can do to change it. We look back with remorse and wish to ourselves, 'If only I had said this,' or, 'If only I had done that.' We can spend years condemning ourselves for having failed to realize the wisdom of a course we chose not to take or the ridiculousness of one we did.

At such times we're apt to ask ourselves, 'What could I have been *thinking*?' Yet often we find that the problem was not what we were thinking, *but that we were not really thinking at all*. We were not deeply reflective, much less spiritually guided, in making a particular decision. We simply surrendered to the shallow thoughts that too often pass for real thinking today, following the path of least resistance (often the path of least nobility, virtue, and conscience). And now we are suffering accordingly.

Fortunately, from a metaphysical perspective, the past can always be reclaimed. In the words of *A Course in Miracles*, 'Nothing can be lost except in time, and time does not exist.' Even if we've chosen a path that was not illuminated, one that was not an expression of love or wisdom, then the possibility we chose not to manifest *still exists* as an abstract reality. It is like a computer file that exists but has not been downloaded. The loving reaction to any situation – regardless of whether or not it has been manifest – dwells as a possibility in the mind of God, and therefore awaits our decision to choose it.

Let's say Jennifer was unkind to you. She betrayed a confidence or lied about you to a co-worker, though now she has apologized. You might not have been forgiving toward her, though that certainly would have been the highest expression of your essential self. You might have understood the need for forgiveness, perhaps, but it was still too much of a stretch for you emotionally. The fact that you might have forgiven her – that in an enlightened state you *would* have forgiven her – means that the choice for forgiveness will be waiting for you until you're ready. You will now meet Jennifer, or someone just like her, no matter where you go. For forgiving the particular issue she represents in your life is the lesson your soul needs to learn. That issue will now be scripted into the curriculum of your life's journey, to motivate you to find your true self, your loving self that is aligned with the forgiveness of God. You will become more careful with your confidences and also less sensitive to other people's opinions. After encountering an issue and getting it wrong a few times, we become much more motivated to get it right. Praying for Jennifer, sending her light and love, is a mystical practice with far more power than anything the ego would have us do. It is the only thing that will make us invulnerable to the lovelessness of others.

In any given moment, with everything we think or say or do, it's as though we're pushing a button on a computer and bringing up a particular file. There is an infinite number of files in the universe, and one of them is named 'God's Will.' We click on this file by praying, 'May God's will be done.' Life is so much easier when we live by that thought, for it is a prayer for right-mindedness. It is a prayer that we create only the good. We might choose a file other than 'God's Will' – let's say 'Defensiveness,' 'Blame,' or 'Control' – but the file marked 'God's Will' still exists in the computer and can be downloaded at another time. It's the one file that can never, ever be deleted from the system.

You made a lot of money, but you weren't ready to stop self-sabotaging? You had a wonderful partner, but you failed to realize how lucky you were? You had wonderful kids, but you spent too little time with them and now you hardly know them? There are so many ways that a person can blow it. And while our guilt can sometimes feel overwhelming, remember there is nothing that God cannot do. There is no gap He cannot fill. There is no mistake too big for God to rectify.

Feeling guilty serves no one, but rather keeps us stuck in self-defeating patterns. Humility lies in atoning for our errors – becoming fully accountable for them in our own minds, and if necessary in our communication with others – and asking God to heal us. Only then can we begin again from a healed and holy place.

Whenever we have strayed from the light, thoughtlessly or recklessly ploughing ahead without God's guidance, we can always go back in our minds to the moment we made the mistake, humbly turn it over to God, and ask for the chance to begin again. The following prayer, from *A Course in Miracles*, is for just that moment. We are reminded by the Course, 'The Holy Spirit will respond fully to your slightest invitation.'

> *I must have decided wrongly, because I am not at peace.*
> *I made the decision myself, but I can also decide otherwise.*
> *I want to decide otherwise, because I want to be at peace.*
> *I do not feel guilty, because the Holy Spirit will undo all the consequences of my wrong decision if I will let Him.*
> *I choose to let Him, by allowing Him to decide for God for me.*

Once the pain of guilt begins to recede, the alchemical processes of transformation will begin. We can feel ourselves growing in spiritual maturity. Our thoughts and actions grow stronger and wiser. Through the grace of God, we become more spiritually aware in the area in which we made the mistake than we were even before we made it. When we have forgiven ourselves – 'Yep, I'm a human being and I make mistakes!' – and made appropriate amends, then God's spirit will offer us another chance at the fullness of life and love. Sometimes it's the same situation brought back around again, and we will be grateful in ways we were not grateful before, never again taking the miracles of life for granted. The next time we meet Jennifer on the road, there will be no need to experience anything but peace with her.

In our youth, we are tempted to think that nothing really matters. We have so much time, it doesn't matter; so much love, it doesn't matter; and so much of everything, it doesn't matter. But when we've lived enough – and made enough mistakes – we learn how very much things matter. We're often horrified at how carelessly we had lived before.

Yet God's compassion is with us at every step, not seeking to judge but to heal, that we might learn from life and then proceed differently. We've usually not done as much damage as we fear, and God is so infinitely powerful that He can transform and redeem whatever damage we did do. It is part of the miraculous mercy of God that He is there for us when we've made a mistake, as much as He is there for us when we've been our very best.

In the Bible, it was the returning Prodigal Son who received a great reception from his father, while the son who had not left home received no such fanfare. And we are an entire generation of Prodigal Sons. Our false ambitions, our idolatry, our breaches of integrity, our lack of ethics, our societal injustices – there is something for almost any conscious person to feel guilty about, for who among us has not been tainted by the corruptions of our time? But it is the darkest places that lead us to light when they lead us to the arms of God. Such is the infinite nature of His love, that there is nothing we can do to make Him turn His back on us, though we so often turn our backs on Him. To punish ourselves endlessly for our mistakes is to doubt His mercy. Do we need to make amends? Yes. Do we need to 'take a fearless moral inventory,' being honest about our weaknesses and willing to let them go? Absolutely. But do we need to live forever with the guilty feelings of a hopeless sinner? No, because the meaning of sin is that we missed the mark – we made a mistake. And God's desire is always to heal us, not punish us; to correct our thinking, not make us pay.

The mistakes I've made in my life have humbled me, helping me to become a person who may or may not have the same chances again to do the wonderful things I might have done before. But I know that the person I am today, honed in some way by the hours of remorse I've experienced, is better prepared to face the future. My mistakes have been my teachers, and my only job is to learn from them.

Sometimes the past is so painful to think about

that your only salvation lies in complete surrender
to the mercy of God. Only in Him are you given the
strength and courage it takes to keep on walking
when every step is hard. But, finally, after what can
seem like an endless journey into the darkness of
your own regret, you come upon the light again.
You have no doubt who has set you free, for only
One who is the author of forgiveness would give
you still another chance.

> *Dear God,*
> *Please take the past from me.*
> *I did ___, which I regret.*
> *I go back to that moment*
> *And I give it to You.*
> *Please, dear God,*
> *Make right my wrongs*
> *And take away my sorrow.*
> *Forgive me, please.*
> *May I begin again.*
> *Amen.*

Grieving

She was a teacher and she just kept working, through chemo and radiation and numerous hospital stays. For more than four years, she was such a trooper. But when her boss could no longer take the sight of her head scarf, she took away her classroom and broke my sister's heart. It was that – not the cancer – that killed her. When she lost her breast, she could take the pain. But when she lost her classroom, she was done . . .

Four or five days before my sister died of cancer, my brother and I sat with her in her bedroom. She was sitting up in bed, surrounded by the kind of halo-like aura that I have often seen around those who are nearing death. My brother and I were emotional, but my sister had already passed into that almost weird serenity that often accompanies one's final hours. I began to cry, saying through my tears that the three of us hadn't taken full advantage of the opportunity we'd been given to experience what it really meant to be siblings. We hadn't spent enough time together; we had moaned about each other as often as we had celebrated each other; we had loved each other, but passively, with sniping and complaining often drowning out our deeper feelings. And now I saw that we had utterly failed to embrace the miracle of our love for one another. In fact, we had had no idea that it was a miracle. My brother sadly nodded in agreement. But my sister said, 'Yes, but it's okay, because we get it now.'

And there, in that moment, we really did. All three of us did. We experienced a depth of connection that we had never known, between and among us, our entire lives. Yet the fact that we had experienced even that glimpse of genuine oneness proved that such a state is possible. Whenever I think of humanity's destiny, I think of that moment with my brother and sister, and I know in my heart where we are meant to be going. We're meant for that shimmering, radiant place where everything except what is most deeply true has melted away, and we can truly see.

We should not have to be at death's threshold to realize that everything but love is unimportant. Yet often it's the things that are most sad that remind us how much we have to be happy about. Tears of sorrow often pave the way for tears of joy. I will never take a relationship for granted again, the way I took for granted my relationship with my sister. For the rest of my life, I will try to squeeze every last bit of juice out of love. Losing a love that mattered to me taught me to love in a way I never would have known.

And I don't just grieve that I didn't know my sister longer; I grieve that I didn't know her better. Often we grieve most bitterly over things we had but did not allow ourselves fully to experience. Whatever is lived fully is easier to let go.

Tears have taught me a tremendous amount, and I know now that they often come bearing important gifts. There has emerged a half-baked spiritual myth that invalidates sadness, claiming it is beneath us if we are walking the path to true enlightenment. But surely one of the most powerful lines in the Bible is one of the simplest: 'Jesus wept.' There is nothing unenlightened about crying over the tragedy of human suffering; perhaps what is neurotic is how infrequently we do. There is an old Buddhist story about a monk who stood crying at the grave of his master. A traveller came by and saw his tears. 'Why would you cry? I thought you were enlightened!' The monk replied, 'Because I am sad.'

Our task is not to avoid painful emotion, but rather to transform it at its roots. And that we cannot do if we don't go through the emotion authentically. Sadness has to be experienced in order to be transcended. No situation can be transformed until it is accepted as it is.

Remember that when her stepmother and stepsisters drove away to the ball, Cinderella simply sat down and cried. They had quite literally left her in the dust, headed for all things fabulous while she had to stay at home. Surely Cinderella would have been justified had she run after their carriage shouting obscenities. But she didn't do that, for she is a being on the way to genuine awakening. Getting angry would not have helped, running after her stepmother and stepsisters would not have helped, and scheming to punish them would not have helped. Such behaviour might have satisfied her ego but not her soul. Cinderella, in tune with her emotional and spiritual essence, simply sat down and allowed herself to cry.

Cinderella was true to her feelings, remaining in grief as opposed to resisting the pain of it. She surrendered not to anger but to tears. And in that state of pure sorrow at having suffered so deeply the cruelty of the world, she magnetized the presence of a divine, illuminated being. There is a direct connection between Cinderella's emotional integrity and her fairy godmother's appearance. By aligning herself with a higher truth, Cinderella automatically called down the inspired intercession of otherworldly forces.

The key to finding the miracle inside sadness lies in learning how to allow ourselves to be sad. This is often harder than one would think. We live in a culture that mitigates genuine emotion of any kind, because it mitigates genuine *anything*. In a culture of denial, those who do not deny the depths of their feelings are often branded as fools or hysterics. Emotion not manipulated specifically for the purposes of selling something is seen as having little intrinsic value. Crying is often viewed as a waste of time or a sign of weakness. We no longer give deep cultural permission for the processes of grief; after all, it's an inconvenience to the speedy wheels of the status quo. Are you sad? Deal with it. Take this pill. Process it. And hurry. Someone once said to a friend of mine, 'Your mother's been dead a month already! Aren't you over it yet?'

But grief that is suppressed will force its way to expression – whether we want it to or not. It often emerges in dysfunctional ways when not allowed its proper place in the psychic and social scheme of things. There was a time when widows wore widow's weeds for a year, as past societies had a more sophisticated understanding of sadness and grief. They knew that both must be *allowed* in order for life to go on. The modern idea that we should move quickly through grief – because for some insane reason we should move quickly through *everything* – ensures that we will never move through anything in a very deep way. And then life actually does not go on at all, so much as it continually repeats itself.

So it is that the modern mystic, when experiencing the heartbreak of life, does not avoid the heartbreak nor try to distance from it in the name of spirituality, mental health, or anything else. Enlightenment does not consist of pretending to be where we are not; enlightenment means being in touch with where we are and being willing to learn what God would have us learn from it. Sometimes the purpose of a day is to merely feel our sadness, knowing that as we do we allow whole layers of grief, like old skin cells, to drop off us.

The wisdom that comes from having experienced heartbreak cannot be bequeathed; it can only be gained through experience. And having truly felt it, we are far more likely to have compassion for others. Anything that takes us closer to true compassion takes us closer to what will one day be an experience of even greater joy.

Life is often cruel. Yet I have found that there is a grief that is infused with the grace of God. At my sister's funeral, as I wept uncontrollably, my father, age eighty-five and nearing the end of his own life, leaned over to me, put his arms around me, and said, 'Littlest Sister, it's all a part of the mystery.' He was there, in the place where he could see that. I could see it in his eyes. And as I leaned my head upon his shoulder, continuing to cry, I knew I was on my way to the place where I would see it, too.

Learning Compassion

My sister was teaching severely disturbed children, and one day I went to assist her with her class. I met a little boy I will never forget, because it was as though he was a boy but he was not a boy. He did not seem fully human. As I tried to keep him from attacking a box of M&M's like an animal, I realized I was trying to reason with someone who wasn't there.

Completely shaken, I ran into the bathroom, crying. In a few minutes' time, my sister followed me. 'What are you doing?!' she scolded. 'Get back in there!'

'I can't stand it!' I cried. 'It's too hard! It's so sad!'

'Get back in there!' she commanded. 'He doesn't need your pity! He needs your help!'

One of the things I often wonder about is how I got so lucky. I constantly read about people whose lives are so much harder than mine. On one hand, I don't believe in luck; on the other hand, I'm certainly clear that living as a woman in a democratic society is a lot more fortunate than, let's say, living as a woman in Afghanistan under the Taliban. I have known sadness and grief, of course. But some people – far too many people – live lives of unending suffering, through no fault of their own. From children dying of AIDS in Africa, to young Israelis and Palestinians whose lives are put in danger by a hatred they did nothing to cause, to people in India and elsewhere living under conditions of crushing poverty, to people in our own country who are incarcerated unjustly – what is the mysterious force that seems to assign to some people such misery and to others such abundance and ease?

While many religions claim to answer that question, the fact remains that there are things we cannot know. Whatever is happening is simply happening. And, from a spiritual perspective, anything negative that happens has only one purpose: to foster compassion in the human heart. Anything can fuel the fires of compassion if our hearts are open wide enough. As it is written in the Bible, 'What man has intended for evil, God intends for good.' Even the most horrific situations can increase within us our capacity to love.

I have actually heard people say, about children dying of hunger or people living in war-torn regions, 'Well, that is their karma' – as though that somehow ends the conversation. What an astounding way to avoid the responsibility of bearing witness to human suffering. The night before he was crucified, Jesus sat awake in the garden of Gethsemane. When his disciples began to fall asleep around him, he said to them, 'What, can you not watch with me one hour?' Even when there is nothing we specifically can do to help our suffering neighbour, there is spiritual power in remaining awake with someone in the hour of his or her agony. In bearing witness to human suffering, we light a candle in the dark that illuminates the most painful night.

Just as some people have talent for art, and others for science, some seem to have a greater talent for compassion. Examples abound of humanitarian workers risking their lives for people living the ravages of war, of doctors giving of their talents and abilities to help those in poverty-stricken societies. But not every act of compassion is dramatic. All of us in our own way, just by being more tender and loving, can open our hearts and make a difference in someone's life. Compassion is not just emotion; it is *force*. It is an aspect of the infinite power of God. Humanity's next great leap in consciousness will be the realization that love is a *power to be applied* – no less than the power of steam, the power of electricity, or the power of the atom.

What if all of us dedicated ourselves to efforts of compassion for people we will never even know, and who will probably never know us? What an extraordinary burst of light would pervade the world, should a shift in consciousness from narcissism to compassion become a common miracle among us. At what point does the heart burst open and commit itself to doing something, *anything*, if it will possibly make a difference in easing the pain of someone else?

There were ages when people sat on great powers, yet did not know how to harness them for practical purposes. We knew there was an atom long before we knew how to split it. People enjoyed the beauty of Niagara Falls long before its hydroelectric power lit whole cities. Today, we know there is love in our hearts, but we have only begun to scratch the surface of how we can use it to restore and transform our world. It is the task of our generation to turn love into a social *force*. The most significant development of the twenty-first century will be the harnessing of the social potential of love.

Most of us don't lack compassion so much as we *avoid* it. Too often, we resist compassion with a peculiar hypocrisy, extolling the virtues of volunteerism, for instance, while making volunteerism more of a necessity by diminishing our budgetary commitments to the poor and powerless. In America, we take away housing for thousands, then build a hundred houses for Habitat for Humanity and everyone gets to feel good. Our primary response to human suffering appears to be making sure it occurs on the other side of town or the other side of the world.

In the Buddhist religion, the search for God is synonymous with the realization of our most compassionate self. The Buddha, like Jesus, lived a life that personified the path to divine Selfhood. The Buddha was born a wealthy prince named Siddhartha, whose father wished to protect him from the cruelty and the suffering of life. To this end, he built walls around his palace, only allowing in the pleasures of the material world. But the young Siddhartha instinctively knew that there was more to life than what he saw within the confines of his father's palace, and *he also knew he needed to experience those things in order to become truly human*. He left behind his beautiful wife and child, journeying beyond the walls of the palace to encounter human suffering for the first time. And, with that, his journey to enlightenment began.

Ultimately, the Buddha would reveal that untransformed human life is suffering, and out of that revelation would come enlightenment for millions. From his recognition that the palace walls we build around ourselves are merely holding the truth and meaning of human existence at bay came his exhortation to recognize the suffering of the world. We must open our hearts before suffering, he claimed, in order to become genuine channels for its transcendence. We live in a prison – not a palace – when our hearts have not yet cracked open.

But when the heart does crack open – when humanity's pain and suffering moves us to respond to it as passionately as we used to run away from it – then we are on our way to enlightenment at last. We realize our oneness with the angels, as we offer ourselves to help them. Every time we say a prayer for someone, serve a meal to a housebound person with AIDS, hold the hand of a dying patient as a hospice volunteer, give a deserving, struggling employee another chance to get it right, or lobby our elected officials for more compassionate policies, we are tending to our own evolution.

That which purports to be spiritual growth but does not involve an active compassion is not really growth at all. Whether we are seeking to heal ourselves or our planet, we must commit acts of compassion that go beyond the individual, beyond what is convenient, and beyond the confines of the status quo. Individual acts of kindness and compassion will not of themselves provide enough loving energy to transform our civilization. Rather, we must make love the centre of all our enterprises – collective, as well as individual. When harmlessness toward life becomes a personal, social, economic, and political imperative, we will be on our way at last to the restoration and regeneration of our civilization.

We have an opportunity at this time in history to completely change the course of human culture.

That opportunity is not simply an option anymore, it is a gauntlet thrown down by the forces of history, before a generation still not yet decided whether money and power or love and brotherhood should form the basis of our civilization. And we will decide, or life will decide for us. The human species *will* learn to become profoundly compassionate toward itself and toward all life. We will learn it through wisdom, or we will learn it through pain. But we will learn, because it's God's will that we become the people He has created us to be. It's not up to us where we are going – but how we get there, and when, is determined by every choice we make, every moment of every day.

PART III

A LIFE OF GRACE

Ritual

During the twentieth century, the Western mind fell into a materialistic stupor, so enamoured of visible, tangible complexities that invisible realities were shoved to the margins of our consciousness and our culture. Scientific truths were deemed real in an unassailable way, while spiritual truths were often thought to be superstitious relics of an age gone by.

Fortunately, the pendulum always swings back, and at last we are emerging from the rationalistic fog of an oversecularized worldview. We are collectively remembering that we are spiritual beings, the remembrance itself like Atlantis rising from a sea of ancient forgetfulness. It arises new, transformed, and cleansed of what it used to stand for, now recognized as key to both our mission and our joy. The material world can be a marvellous place, full of power and excitement, but it is not – even in its most intense manifestations – the world of ultimate truth. Only the truth of a radical, fundamental love is unalterable and eternal. Our own will may delay its expression, but love will always prevail. It's the truth we remember at the end of our lives, or perhaps at the end of the life of a loved one. It's the truth we see when the superficial preoccupations that compete for our attention and rob us of our life force begin at last to melt away.

This truth is reaffirmed by our participation in holy ritual. A sacred ceremony casts a spell on our hearts. It reminds us who we are, thus releasing us to become who we are capable of being. Rituals provide points of genuine connection with what is most authentically true – in ourselves, in each other, and in God. They are portals to divine radiance, and the light we receive through them remains with us.

Sacred ritual illuminates the meaning with which we have imbued a human experience, raising it to the realm of the divine. And it is in those places where we are most profoundly human that we are pregnant with divine possibilities: it's deeply human to give birth to a child, to grow into adolescence, to marry, to mature into our elder years, and to die. It's not an accident that traditional religious ceremonies take place in these moments; it's when we are most fully and vulnerably alive that our hearts cry out for an added dimension of soulfulness. It is when we are deeply touched by life that we most want to feel God's touch upon us. Holy ceremony marries the mortal and the immortal – the secular and the sacred – that from that point forward, the two shall be irrevocably connected within us.

When I was a child, I had a sense, as most children do, of the mysterious power of religious ritual. I loved being in synagogue, going to weddings, going to Bar Mitzvahs. I could feel the mystical energies they aroused within me. But as I grew older, I learned to forget the subtle vibrations of spiritual energy that emanate from moments of religious depth. Weddings became about bridal registries and pretty dresses, and baptisms became about baby gifts. I was not a child of God anymore so much as a child of American culture. The world we live in is too much with us; materialism bombards us relentlessly, and we surrender to its dominance at a terrible price. Consciousness attunes itself to one realm or another: we either vibrate with the world or we vibrate with spirit, and one casts out the other.

The mind cannot serve two masters, and

according to *A Course in Miracles*, we can be either 'host to God or hostage to the ego.' A mystic has made a choice for love, more than willing to sacrifice a materialistic perspective for a far richer, more varied, and more harmonious picture. That doesn't mean, of course, that baby gifts are not important or that brides shouldn't get the right serving forks. It doesn't mean we shouldn't live in lovely houses or enjoy beautiful things. It simply means that a mystical worldview puts the world in perspective, with eternal things in first place and everything else in second place. A fancy wedding does not guarantee marital bliss, no matter how beautiful it is. But a genuinely sacred marriage ceremony – be it Christian, Jewish, Muslim, Hindu, or our own spiritual hybrid – has the spiritual power to weave two hearts together.

When I was growing up, so many traditional rituals had become empty shells, performed perfunctorily by bored and boring officiants, with little power to genuinely uplift the spirit. In many cases my generation rejected them, seeking more modern relevance. Yet often we threw away the baby with the bathwater, desacralizing our sacraments in an effort to be more authentic, more 'real.' What we failed to realize is that the substance of sacred ritual is forever new and forever relevant. The problem, when there is one, lies not in rituals; the problem lies in the consciousness of those who perform them.

Rituals become empty when imbued with empty thoughts. Those who overemphasize the external world don't know how to meet ritual, to imbue it with the kind of meaning that emanates from a heart truly open and vulnerable before God. Today, people are recognizing anew that rituals can create cellular shifts within us. If someone commits in a sacred ceremony to the care and protection of another – whether as parent, godparent, or mate – then that commitment carries a spiritual, emotional weight that no legal transaction can ever match. Rituals evoke a commitment of the heart. When the shadow of the hand of God has come over us, lifting us to new purpose or binding our heart to someone else's, bringing comfort when a loved one has died or calling us to new magnificence and power, we know it. The Holy Spirit is not metaphor or symbol; it is a living, alchemical power that infuses our hearts with the glory of God.

I don't hear many people say anymore, 'Why get married? It's just a piece of paper.' For marriage, when placed within a sacred context, is not just a piece of paper. And more people today seem to realize that yes, you do go to the funeral, because it does make a difference. Prayers for the dead and prayers for their loved ones left on this earth create a field of blessing that is palpable, that is felt. It is not for nothing that the Holy Spirit is called 'the Comforter.' We are emotionally healed as we allow ourselves to surrender to the sanctity of a spirit-filled ceremony. We feel our souls have been bathed in light.

Many people, who might not have ever thought about it before, now want their babies blessed, and their adolescents to experience meaningful rituals marking this new stage of their lives. People are rediscovering the power of ritual both in traditional and non-traditional ways. We embrace rites of passage for adolescents and elders; we take vision quests and attend Native American sweat lodges; we perform solstice rituals and healing ceremonies for the Earth; we create birthday ceremonies and sacred New Year's Eve services, in which we surrender to God the disharmony of the year passing and ask for blessing on the year being born.

As an officiant, I have found that what people want from rituals is not that they be fancy, but that they be genuine. We do not need the specific words of a pre-written text so much as we need authenticity before God; we do not need an ordained officiant to perform our ritual so much as we need a spirit-filled consciousness; and we do not need external glamour, but rather internal simplicity before the throne of God.

As we participate in the miraculous process of holy ritual, we feel ourselves expand into the space of a mythical reality. In a coming-of-age ceremony, a mother named Carol is no longer just Carol bowing before her daughter Danielle as the young girl reaches puberty: she is every woman, honouring the emergence of every girl into adulthood. And from that point forward, Carol will not be the same, for something within her will have been altered. She has entered through a door that marks a greater fullness of her womanhood as mother, elder, and mentor to all young women. And Danielle will have been altered as well, as she is no longer a young girl, but is now rather a young woman. This will affect her relationship to herself, to others, and to everything around her. Her pysche will rearrange itself as her body already has.

The spirit needs constant care and nourishment, just like the body. And it is a process that must go on continually. For ages, religious ritual has been used as preventative medicine, keeping our lives infused with light that we might be less vulnerable to darkness. In this country, we're very good about praying once tragedy has struck. But if we prayed together more often, so much tragedy might not occur! A sacred ritual – even something as simple as lighting a prayer candle every morning – can make a tremendous difference in the quality of our lives.

From the oracles of Delphi to the Passover seder, from Midnight Mass on Christmas Eve to the beginning prayers of Ramadan, from chants on Buddha's birthday to the celebration of Krishna's triumphant presence, there are so many ways to elevate our relationship with God to the highest heights. We commune with Him, pour out our hearts to Him, receive Him, and are touched by Him. To the devoted heart, these are not just words. Whether saying a blessing or burying the dead, the moments when we reach out to God are the moments when our lives are graced with light.

Every time a flower blossoms, God demonstrates His grace. Every time a snowflake forms, God demonstrates His grace. Every time spring comes around again, God demonstrates His grace. Every time a baby is born, God demonstrates His grace. And every time someone takes their final breath, God demonstrates His grace as well.

We cannot match God's handiwork, but we can mirror His holiness. In every sacred ritual, we show Him our love and He shows us His. We are reminded of the constant presence of an all-loving, all-giving, all-merciful God. A holy ceremony is an act of spiritual intimacy, in which we connect deeply to our divine source. Having touched, however faintly, the Mind of God, our minds and even our bodies are blessed.

Having received a blessing of our deep humanity, we realize finally that we are more than human. We are creatures of fertile earth and endless sky, meant to embody their full integration. We are floating in the waters of an amniotic spirit, within a cosmic womb out of which we will emerge angelic and joyful. Praise and thanks and music and tears transform us. The time has come for us to be reborn.

The sacred moments of holy ritual are fragile and gentle, yet more powerful than the sea. And within the waters of that holy sea, we grow as our ancient ancestors grew. As they left the sea and climbed onto land, we reach beyond the land to find our wings and fly. In time, we shall soar through the mystical skies as easily as we now walk on land.

And life itself will be one long moment of gentle, unbroken grace.

Sabbath

The Fourth Commandment is 'Observe the Sabbath and keep it holy.' It's amazing, if you think about it, that observing the Sabbath is right up there with 'Thou shalt not steal' and 'Thou shalt not kill.' Why is it so important to God that we take one day out of every week and surrender it to Him?

The wording in the Bible is, 'Remember the Sabbath day, to keep it holy. Six days shalt thou labour, and do all thy work; but the seventh day is the Sabbath of the Lord thy God . . . For in six days the Lord made heaven and earth, the sea, and all that is in them, and rested the seventh day; wherefore the Lord blessed the Sabbath day, and hallowed it.' The Sabbath would be *His* day.

Having a relationship with God is in many ways like having a relationship with anyone else. In order for it to blossom, we must make time for it and tend to it with genuine attention. Observing the Sabbath is like having a steady date with God, setting aside time in our calendar of days to dedicate to our connection with Him. And in remembering who God is, we remember who we are. Knowing ourselves clearly in relationship to God, we are stronger in our relationship with everyone and everything.

As the leader of an interfaith spiritual fellowship, I have experienced the metaphysical power of a Sabbath service. For a Sabbath service is more than just bodies gathered in a room: it is a convening of hearts and minds in an internal as well as external sanctuary. The mind is our true altar and the heart our true sanctuary from the cruelty and limitations of the world. In Sabbath fellowship, we enter with others into the Inner Room. We go there to remember God, worship Him, and recommit our hearts to Him. We experience the stereophonic effect of amplified prayer emanating from the hearts of many. We participate in the creation of a devotional field of energy, which blesses its participants and remains with us when we leave the service.

Like taking a trip to a chiropractor's office to have our spine realigned, we attend a Sabbath service to have our mind and heart realigned. The power of God is not outside us but inside, and when the mind and heart are aligned with His spirit, then His will is accomplished within and without. Outside the blessing of that divine alignment, we are vulnerable to the machinations of the ego mind, where fear and chaos rule.

The Sabbath is a day when the ego takes a rest. We keep our minds on God's love – both His love for us and the love He would have us share with each other. And that strengthens us in ways that nothing else can do. Just as we recharge a computer or a mobile phone, on the Sabbath we recharge our souls. Day in and day out, most of us are pre-occupied with essentially meaningless things. We know this grind is not in keeping with our heart's deepest desire, yet we often feel trapped by our ego's demands. Our lives revolve around concerns that do not resonate with the grandeur of our spiritual identity, and yet, unchecked, those concerns devour our energy and time. The purpose of the Sabbath is to interrupt this pattern of superficial pre-occupations and return our minds to a path of holiness and peace. It is a day we invest in God in order to reinvest in ourselves.

There was a musical very popular in my child-hood called *Stop the World! I Want to Get Off!* Sabbath is a day when we simply get off the worldly merry-go-round and remember the truth of who we are. We are placed on this earth to love away the pain of the world, yet we cannot do that when we ourselves are living at the effect of it.

I had not expected, when I first took a pulpit, that the experience of a Sabbath service would be so different from any other spiritual lecture. Yet, in a subtle way, it is. There's something about people joining together specifically for a worship service on a holy day that makes the effect of prayer and prayerfulness particularly potent. Jews don't have to go to synagogue on Friday or Saturday; Christians don't have to go to church on Sunday morning. But when we do, we join in an experience of fellowship not only with other worshippers, but in a way with people all over the world, that we might receive the spirit of a living God.

Like boxers who go back to a corner when the bell rings, to be attended to by handlers, on the Sabbath we go back to our own corner to be ministered to by angels. For angels are the thoughts of God. Sabbath is a day to remember His thoughts: to forgive ourselves and others; to reconcile ourselves with Him; to study more deeply the principles of Truth; to pray for blessing and protection in the days ahead; and, most of all, to commune with the miraculous spirit of true life, as opposed to the spirit of shallowness and illusion that is in fact a living death.

One Sunday morning, when conflict in the Middle East was at a particularly high and violent point, I chose as the topic for my Sunday sharing: 'How we might spiritually help create peace between Israel and the Palestinians.' I asked if anyone in the audience was a native Palestinian or an Arab who felt strongly about the Palestinian cause. A man put his hand up. I asked if anyone in the audience was a native Israeli, or a Jew who felt strongly about Israel. A woman put her hand up. Then I asked both of them if they would be willing to participate in a healing ceremony. What followed was a prayerful apology, both by a Palestinian, on behalf of his people, for all violence and transgressions perpetrated against Israel and Israelis; and an apology by an Israeli, on behalf of her people, for all violence and transgressions perpetrated by Israelis against Palestinians.

In spiritual fellowship, our job is not to make a political stand for either Palestinians or Israelis, but rather to make a spiritual stand for both. Love makes a stand for eternal innocence, not worldly guilt, and we must stand on that love like a rock. On the Sabbath we articulate an alternative vision for life on Earth, that humanity might grow into it. In holding to our conviction that all souls are innocent, we're helping to create the space in which that innocence will shine forth.

The next evening, I participated in a peace circle along with several people who had been present at the Sabbath service the day before. One woman who had not been to that Sabbath service began to express her upset over the violence in the Middle East. As she spoke, it was obvious that she blamed one side more than the other, and as such her mind was still at the level of the problem, not the Answer. For the presumption of spiritual innocence is the only real answer. Those at whom we point fingers never represent our biggest problem: our biggest problem is that we point fingers at all. For those of us who had been at the Sabbath service and experienced the spiritual power of the apologies, guilt didn't overwhelm our perceptions. Our minds were oriented differently, not taking sides in the battle, but lifted by God above the battlefield. And I realized again why the Sabbath is so important, why it is so essential to gather together and ask, 'How would God view this?' Then for the rest of the week we can be conduits of a wisdom that we could only have received through His illumination. We observe the Sabbath not in order to give up worldly things, but in order to give up a worldly perspective.

Notice that the commandment reads, 'Observe the Sabbath.' In order to receive the blessing of the Sabbath, we must observe it. It's like the difference between knowing that the Super Bowl or Cup Final is on television today and actually sitting down to watch it; the idea and the experience are two different things. Bringing idea and experience together on the Sabbath, we recommit to our inner covenant with a living God. Then we are repaired and re-energized for the days ahead.

Yet how are we to celebrate the Sabbath if we don't feel tied to a particular religion? The realization of spiritual realities supersedes doctrinal direction, and the Sabbath is a concept that transcends religion. We can make our own Sabbath service with friends at home, lighting candles and saying prayers, reading aloud from sacred texts, sharing a meal in fellowship and communion. Observation of the Sabbath is a movement within the heart, more than an external attendance at a religious service. Some people might feel a desire to observe the Sabbath in solitude, allowing the day to be one of communion with God separate from fellowship or the experience of community. God is everywhere and He is in everything: Sabbath is important as the day we spend with Him, whatever that looks like and however it suits the individual.

Modern mysticism doesn't seek to dictate worldly form but to emphasize spiritual content.

Like everything else, life is as deep or as shallow as we wish to play it. A holy Sabbath is in the depths of the spiritual sea, where the soul swims as deep as we are ready to swim, as far as we are prepared to go, and as close to God as we dare to be. As we swim toward Him, we realize He swims toward us. In awe and in rapture, at last we become the sea.

Holidays

Holidays have become desanctified today. The fire wall separating the concerns of commerce from the concerns of God now seems to have crumbled, as we render unto Caesar what is Caesar's, and frequently render unto him what is God's as well.

Many of us know this and don't like it, yet the cultural undertow has been tugging at us for years. Like swimmers along the shore, we could have sworn we were far down the beach just a little while ago. We have no idea how we got where we are, having been pulled along by a force much more powerful than ourselves. Slowly and insidiously, the values of the marketplace have begun to dominate our entire culture.

In America, Presidents' Day has become less a

day to deeply honour great souls, such as Abraham Lincoln, and their contributions to the history of our nation than a day to take advantage of the Presidents' Day sales at malls across America. Memorial Day weekend has become less a day to deeply honour those who have died for our country than a weekend for barbecues, travel, and visiting friends. Martin Luther King, Jr.'s birthday? Great! The kids can get a day off school! And all over the world, Christmas has become so commercialized that the miraculous birth of Jesus gets practically swallowed up by the materialism surrounding it.

Days of honour thus become days of dishonour, as ego concerns take centre stage time and time again and the spirit of love, the spirit of God, is pushed aside. But those of us who wish for a deeper experience of the holidays should remember that we are responsible for our own thinking. We can embrace the deeper meaning of the holidays that matter to us, celebrating the days on which they occur from a place of serious wonder and awe. We don't need to go along with the pack; indeed, we can consciously repudiate the shallower thought forms that pervade it. Sometimes you can feel there's an undertow, but choose to try to swim across it with every bit of strength that you have.

Every year, weeks before Christmas and

Hanukkah, I say to people, 'Decide right now: are you going to give this season to God, or are you going to give this season to the ego?' These holidays are about the birth of God and the arrival of miracles. They are about personal transformation and the emergence of a new self. They are not about whose relatives we're going to be with, who we have to buy gifts for, and whether or not we have the money to pay for all of them. Such material considerations rob our energy and eat away at our soul. Yet such anxiety-ridden dynamics will prevail if we surrender to the endless nagging of our ego mind.

In surrendering a situation to God, we are asking Him to give us new thoughts and feelings about it. We are asking for His help in de-emphasizing things that don't ultimately matter and focusing on what does. We are asking that His thoughts replace our own, that we be lifted by His Spirit to a lighter consciousness and thus a lighter life. The spiritual life is one of mental discipline in which we cleave to higher thought forms because we know they are key to our happiness and peace. Only in Truth do we find a context for life that makes sense of our existence. And only deeper meaning assuages the suffering of the soul. When it comes to the temptation to make Christmas and Hanukkah more about the gifts of the catalogue than the gifts of the spirit, *just say no!*

One rarely hears a Christian say, 'I'm not going to Easter services this year, because I already know what happens.' One rarely hears a Jew say, 'I'm not going to Passover seder this year, because I already know what happens.' True, we know the stories intellectually. Jesus died on the cross, and then he rose. The Jews were in bondage, then Moses led them to the promised land. But religious stories are more than they appear: they are coded messages sent by God, heard by whatever part of our consciousness is open to receive them. If we meet the religious stories with shallow listening, they have shallow effects on our lives. The way we receive God's messages determines in large part what they are. Met superficially, the holidays are superficial. Met with genuine devotion, the holidays are transformative. They are as relevant to our lives as we allow them to be.

Why does the mystic celebrate Christmas? Because the birth of Jesus heralds the opportunity for new life on earth, not just for one man but for the entire human race. Christmas represents the spiritual possibility that we will leave behind who we used to be and become who we were created to be. Mary represents the soul, impregnated by the seed of God, giving birth to the highest possibility within us. We emerge as transformed beings, mothered by our humanity and fathered by God, risen at last to our true reality. The star of Christmas, the light that glowed in a darkened sky, is literally the realization that there lies within us such divine potential. Our mystical union with Mary and Jesus illuminates not only our understanding, but also the trajectory of our entire lives. It lifts us into the spiritual vortex of the truth their lives revealed.

Why does the mystic celebrate Hanukkah? Because the oil that the Jews were burning in their lamps was not enough to guarantee their survival, yet the oil continued to burn despite the laws of the physical universe. The Jew is reminded on Hanukkah that the God of our fathers is eternally there for us, aware of our suffering and committed to its end. He is the flame that casts out all darkness. For it is the light of God, not the light of the world, that nourishes and sustains us. To know this and remember it is to keep our living covenant with Him.

And why does the mystic celebrate Easter? Because Jesus' resurrection demonstrated a power that casts out fear, even unto death itself. 'Be of good cheer, for I have overcome the world.' The message was not that Jesus had *fixed* the world, but rather that he had *overcome* it. He had achieved a perfect love, which then made him invulnerable to the love-lessness of the world. His consciousness had risen so high that in his presence all lower thought forms were rendered null and void. Yes, it would take a symbolic three days, but love prevailed for him and will now prevail for us as well. No matter what has happened, if we should hold on for those 'three days' – standing on faith that love and forgiveness will work a miracle for us – then we too will experience a rising up as our hearts and our relationships receive new life. As long as we remain true to love, then love remains true to us. That is the resurrection of Christ.

Why does the mystic celebrate Passover? Because the slavery of the ancient Jews in Egypt is a slavery to which we can all relate. The pharaoh of our ego mind would bind us to the meaninglessness and pain of a life of fear. Yet God lifted up his servant Moses, as He lifts up hope in all of us. All of us feel the whip of Pharaoh, and all of us hear, if we listen well, the voice of Moses calling us out of bondage. Our bondage might be an addiction, a dysfunctional relationship, or a self-defeating pattern. And like the Israelites who initially resisted Moses, we fear the flight to freedom might be worse than our slavery. But, in the words of *A Course in Miracles*, 'God will outwit our self-hatred.' Finally, the Israelites were delivered, and we will be as well. Though God had to part the waters of the Red Sea to save the Jews from perishing, so He is willing to part the waters for us. In celebrating Passover, we remember that the God of Israel has been there for His people before and will be there always. God's love for us is so immense, we can scarcely recognize the dimensions of its mercy.

To celebrate these holidays is to do much more than buy presents, open them, cook dinner, show up for dinner, or make children happy. The joy is not just for children. It's for each and every one of us, when we realize the internal dimensions of the great religious holidays. The gift that needs to be unwrapped is the holiday itself. And one need not be Christian to experience the glory of the Christ, or Buddhist to experience the power of the sutras, or Jewish to experience the comfort of God's promises. The mystic responds to universal spiritual themes, all echoing in a different way a unified message from God: the potential of a divinely empowered consciousness lies in every one of us.

From Yom Kippur to Ramadan to solstice celebrations to Christmas to Shivaratri, the great religious holidays – as well as civil holidays celebrating noble civic principles – are ways in which humanity is reminded to keep faith with what is true. We appreciate the miraculous possibilities that the holidays provide: that on Christmas morning, for instance, millions of people consider the possibility of a perfect love; that on Passover, the Jewish people consider the possibility that God is here to deliver us even now; that on Easter morning, millions of people consider the possibility that through love we can transcend all limitations of the world – such is the power of the religious holidays, when we consider their invisible influence on hearts throughout the world.

And how do we participate in the mystical meaning of the holidays? Through prayer, quiet, spirit-filled ceremony or fellowship, reading, or any cultivation of deeper meaning that works for us. We might fast, meditate, sing, or build altars in our homes; we might read spiritual books with our families or create new rituals that deepen our experience of ageless truths. And, most important, we pray. For prayer, in the words of *A Course in Miracles*, is the 'conduit of miracles.' We need simply pray that God reveal to us, in our own life, the meaning of a holiday. And watch what happens. He will do the rest.

Once we recognize the real power of holidays, we

begin to approach them with deeper devotion. A holiday is a holy day, and holiness doesn't happen to us. Holiness is a choice we make, and holidays are portals of energy through which the experience of things that matter most is increased within us and in the world in which we live. Bear witness to what happened to someone else two thousand years ago or more, and you will enter the timeless dimension in which it is happening to you.

Relationships

French philosopher Jean Paul Sartre wrote that 'hell is other people.' People are heaven, too, of course, when relationships go well and people behave the way we wish. Either way, people are hard to get away from in this world, and our relationships with others go far toward determining our happiness or lack of it.

I remember that when my daughter was a baby, I kept wishing she could talk because I wanted to have a conversation with her. And now that she's talking as fast and as much as her mother, I remember how sweet it was when no matter what I said, she just looked up at me adoringly, giggling, never arguing! So if I want sweet and cuddly relationships with no disagreements, I might want to hang around infants. But if I want intelligent dialogue, I'd better get out my magic wands. People over the age of three have a way of saying what they actually think, which may or may not make your day.

The character of our relationships ranges from the heights of enlightenment to the depths of destruction, and most of us have been privy to both at some point in our lives. As with any other situation, the key to making and keeping relationships harmonious lies in placing them in the hands of God.

To place a situation in the hands of God, as we know, is to place our *thinking* in the hands of God. It means we're asking His Spirit to enter our minds and guide our perceptions. We're asking Him to help us remain focused on the divine essence in someone else and help them remain focused on the divine essence in us. We are asking that the possibilities of the present, not the mistakes of the past, guide our perceptions of each other and ourselves.

The key to right relationship – and every situation is, in some way, a relationship – is to allow each one, in every moment, to be lifted from the past. A relationship is reborn whenever we see someone as they are right now and don't hold them to who they were. Focus on the present, not the past, is essential to the experience of grace.

Relationships represent assignments made by Divine Intelligence, bringing together those who represent the greatest opportunities for learning from each other. In every relationship, there's an endless stream of potential healing, both for the people joined in the original encounter and for countless others they will each meet in turn. In *A Course in Miracles*, they are referred to as 'laboratories of the Holy Spirit.' Every relationship is a temple of God, blessed by love and innocence or desecrated by fear and guilt. Which it is, is up to us.

The mystic is always guarding his or her thoughts, seeking to drop the thoughts that condemn and extend the thoughts that bless. For there is no such thing as a thought that goes unnoticed by the universe. This is both exciting and horrifying when we think about it. For we can all be so judgemental at times, *even toward those we truly love*.

Yet our emotional reality is ultimately our own responsibility. We can *decide* to bless someone, even if we don't like his or her behaviour, and in doing so we're freed from the limited vision by which we judged him or her to begin with. It's our willingness to see the innocence in someone, even when they have shown us their guilt, that gives us the capacity to transform both their experience and our own.

While we are born with a perfect capacity to love, each of us is tempted by the realities of life to withhold our love and defend against pain. Compassion, defencelessness, and unconditional love are much easier to express before we become aware of how dangerous life and love can be. Only very small children – and saints – are really very good at it.

Yet our alternative to reaching for the angels is to slide down the slippery slope to hell. Hell is not a place we go after we die. Hell is right here on earth, and all of us have visited it at one time or another. It's the suffering of separation from those with whom we are already joined as one. Separation from others is a separation from God, and nothing hurts more, nor drives us more insane.

There is something to learn from every encounter. If someone is kind to us, the lesson is to be grateful, not to take kindness for granted, and, most important, to graciously return their kindness. If someone is not kind, the lesson is to rise above that, because reacting to them is like throwing petrol on a fire. Anger does nothing more than deplete our personal power. As Jacqueline Kennedy Onassis once said to a friend, 'Only amateurs stay mad.'

Someone who behaves in a non-loving way has simply forgotten who they are, and the role of the miracle worker is to remind them of the truth by remaining in touch with it ourselves. Our job is to remain awake to the eternal innocence at the heart of everyone, that in our presence other people might wake up to it as well. The light in our own mind will help dissolve the darkness in someone else's, but only if we refuse to judge or blame them for what we view as their errors. Our perception of someone's essential innocence as a child of God *is* the light, in a metaphysical sense, while our focus on someone's guilt *is* the darkness. To cast 'light' on something simply means to understand it more deeply.

If we are in serious conflict with someone, there are often limits to how much can actually be achieved by personal communication. On the level of personality, the walls that divide us can be too thick to tear down through mortal means alone. Phone calls, letter writing, or conversation are not always measures that would be received well.

Sometimes we say we have communicated with someone, when all we really did was share our own viewpoint. The word 'communication' has the same root as the word 'communion,' and where there is no communion there is no true communication. Only when we have taken responsibility for the heartspace between ourselves and another, practising humility and forgiveness as best we can, can we say true communication has occurred.

When the walls that divide us seem impenetrable, we can repair to our inner room, our holy sanctuary, to spiritually work out our differences with others. When we dedicate our relationship to God at its genesis, we are ministered to by angels as we progress within the relationship. And whether we have dedicated it or not, the key to healing relationships is to go back to God, asking for a miraculous shift in perception from guilt and fear to innocence and love. Sometimes both parties are willing to join in prayer and ask for this, and sometimes only one is willing. Yet one is enough. According to *A Course in Miracles*, 'whoever is saner at the time' can call on the Holy Spirit to enter a relationship. And no prayer goes unheard.

In the inner room, there *are* no differences between or among us. Whether an argument between friends or a war between nations, God does not choose sides. Rather, He removes the walls that divide us. Those walls primarily live in our minds, and it is God's love reaching beyond the level of human drama that has the power to dissolve them. It finds a way to remind us who we are. It delivers us from the drama of 'who did what to whom' and to the truth of our innocence regardless of who did what to whom. By looking to the sky instead of to the earth for answers, we spread our wings and fly above trials and tribulations that otherwise would keep us down. For it is only in looking beyond a problem that we have the power to resolve it. Everyone makes mistakes; we all have bad days, get in rotten moods, and say or do things we wish we hadn't. We would be much better off – and certainly our relationships would improve – were we to take every moment's word and deed less seriously and to trust in the deeper intentions of the heart.

I once heard something nasty someone said about me, and I shared my distress with a mutual friend. He said to me, 'Well, she might have said it, but that doesn't change the fact that I know she loves you.' When he said that, I remembered that I have made flip judgemental comments about people I love, and how horrified I would have been had they heard. It didn't really matter if my friend had said something unkind about me; it was up to me whether to attach meaning to it or release it as not important. On the spiritual mountaintop, we are kind to one another all the time. But in the meantime, we can stop taking it so seriously when we are not.

Even if someone doesn't like you, they love you whether they know it or not. And it's worth telling them that in meditation. 'I know you dislike me, but I refuse to dislike you. I hold to the Truth of our connection as God created it. I hold to the Truth of our inner oneness, and I invite the spirit of God to enter here and dissolve the walls between us. I forgive you and I ask that you please forgive me.'

Holiness surrounds a relationship with light, so that the darkness of blame and judgement has less chance of clouding our thoughts to begin with. That's why the beginning of a relationship is such a perfect time to surrender it to God, before the ego has a chance to claim it. Beginnings set the tone for what will follow.

> *Dear God,*
> *I place in Your hands*
> *My relationship with____.*
> *May our relationship serve You.*
> *May we see each other through the eyes of love,*
> *That only Light might enter here.*
> *Thank you, God.*
> *Amen.*

The more mindful and responsible we become, the fewer relationship disasters we will create in our lives. Yet none of us is perfect, and any deep and genuine relationship is bound to arouse temptations to fear instead of love. It's by being forced to recognize the times when we're not yet purely loving, surrendering them into the hands of God, that we grow into the angels we are capable of being.

Prayer will release us from our pain, if we're willing to humble ourselves. Sometimes it is very difficult to admit to ourselves, to God, and particularly to other people that we have been wrong and that we seek forgiveness. Yet it is only when we genuinely come clean with God that He can heal our lives.

While we instinctively understand the power of prayer when there is a problem, we tend to underestimate its power when there is not. We don't usually stop to say a prayer *before* the meeting, or *before* the date, or *before* the relationship gets going. We think, *Why should I say a prayer now? There's no problem!* But the sly and insidious ego is always on the alert for ways to separate the children of God, just as God is always on the alert for ways to reconnect our hearts. Prayer has a way of rendering the ego powerless, reminding the mind of our eternal innocence. And therein lies our salvation.

Relationships are where the ego seeks to do battle with the will of God. In reality, there is no battle, for those whom God hath joined together – and he has joined all of us to all of us – cannot be put asunder. It is only our thinking that we are separate from others that dooms us to conflict and struggle and pain.

Often, when someone criticizes us, the pain of their judgement makes it difficult for us to realize that some aspect of what they are saying might be correct. While the message may be delivered in words that seem unfair, there is often still a message worth hearing. The more spiritually mature mind burns through the pain of hearing important information from someone whom we would rather not hear from at all, asking, 'Is there some personality trait I've been carrying around for years that is possibly contributing to someone's dislike? Is it something I might surrender and transform?'

The work of the mystic is not so much to make ourselves better as to be honest about who we are right now. When we are candid with ourselves and with God, then we can release to Him the issues that we know need healing, and thus be purified by His spirit. Our best intentions to 'act better' don't mean all that much; our willingness to have Him make us better means everything.

It is not always our own darkness – indeed, sometimes it's the very fact that we have shone our light – that attracts other people's judgement. But then a profound lesson lies in realizing how threatening our own light can be. It's important to be conscious of that, lest we subconsciously dim our light in order to avoid offending anyone. We should pray for protection and humility as we shine in our world. For there's no dearth of light on this planet; there's just way too much of it that remains inside us, not shining at all. And that is part of the darkness of the world: how afraid we are to shine our own light. In asking God to help us shine, we're asking that His light shine through us.

> *Dear God,*
> *May Your light burst forth within me,*
> *To bathe my inner self*
> *and shine through me to bless*
> *all living things.*
> *Amen.*

We are on the earth to be joyful and to share our joy with others. The spirit looks to relationships as a place to share our happiness, while the ego looks to them to assuage our pain. Our fundamental loneliness, however, lies not in our separation from others but in our separation from self. To say that we are separated from God is not to say that we are separated from something outside ourselves, for

God does not lie outside ourselves. It is to say that we are fragmented inside, having experienced a profound split from our own essential nature. We have been lured away by the illusions of the world.

To look for the experience of 'home' in anything within the material world is to make the world a trap. For it is not our home. It's a fantastic hotel at best. The realm of physical things – the body included – is the realm of separation, not of true joining. Knowing that, making the focus of our attention the connection of spirits rather than the connection of bodies, gives us a fundamental, spiritual sanity that serves us well in relating to others.

Otherwise, we search the world for something to heal the pain that results from our being too attached to it already. Usually, we will look to *other people* to fix us. We are tempted to enter into relationships on a search for the lost self we cannot find. Yet outside ourselves we cannot find what only lies within. When we look to another to complete us, we doom the relationship because we are subconsciously looking to it to be what it is not. And every time I reach a place in our relationship where I am not in touch with myself, I will behave in a way that repels you. For if I am a yo-yo with myself, I will be a yo-yo with you. That is why healing our inner life is a prerequisite for relating successfully to others.

My family has often joked about the fact that when my mother was pregnant with me, she and my father both felt sure that I was a boy. My father wanted to name me Mordecai. My mother told him in no uncertain terms that I would not be named Mordecai, but it became a joke around the house nonetheless. He said Mordecai, she said Michael; and I have no doubt she would have prevailed, had she given birth to a boy. She did not, of course, yet when my mother brought me home from the hospital, we were greeted at the family apartment with signs all over the place that read, WELCOME HOME, LITTLE MORDECAI!

My mother and I still disagree about this decades later, but I swear to you I remember those signs. 'Great. They wanted somebody else . . .' And in many ways, as I went through my life, I would re-create that drama in my relationships with others. Feeling in various ways unreceived in my childhood, I desperately sought to be received by others in my later years. But I didn't know how to genuinely accept others into my life, because the pattern had not been modelled for me. So others would end up feeling unreceived by me, and the cycle would repeat itself.

It took a lot more than rational analysis to

interrupt that pattern. It could not be broken by finding another person who would finally, ultimately, accept me fully. That could not and would not happen until first I repaired my own underlying wound by learning to accept myself. I learned that I am received by God, and that my job is to help others feel as welcomed by me as we are welcomed by Him. Love is the miracle of a rewired heart, as our relationship with Him redeems our relationships with others.

A man once asked me if I knew any prayers for loneliness. I asked why he was looking for such a prayer; what was wrong in his relationships with others? He said he tried to get close to people but always ended up behaving in a way that was perceived as either needy or haughty. He just wanted a prayer to ease the pain. I understood. But just as we wouldn't pray to simply assuage the pain of a broken leg – we would pray that the leg be healed, as well – I suggested that he pray for God's healing of his neediness and haughtiness first. There was a place in his psyche where his spirit did not feel received, and so it went to sleep to avoid the pain. There, in that place, the hand of God, not the hand of man, has the capacity to heal us.

God does not wish for us to be lonely, and, in the fullness of ourselves, we are not. But God is not found outside our relationship with the rest of life – He is our relationship with the rest of life. When our desire to relate to life is a desire to share our joy, extending beyond thoughts that would separate us to thoughts that would bless and unite us with others, then loneliness fades. The key is not to build relationships; the key is to give up the many concepts that shroud us from this awesome fact: we are related already. We are one in spirit – how much more related can we be?

With every human encounter, God gives us the chance to re-create our world. We can extend beyond the boundaries of our isolated existence and bless the person, salute the angel, open our hearts to the similarly wounded one who stands before us. Or we can refuse to do those things, feeling the pain of having someone else withhold from us their bless-ing, their salute, their love. There is nothing and no one outside us, so much as there are mirrors every-where. Every person is a part of us, and we are a part of every person – sacred the chalice that holds us together, and painful the thoughts that would tear us apart. Both are within us. It is ours to choose.

And we do choose. Constantly.

May we choose the divine.

Community

It has been said that when the Buddha comes again, he will arrive not as a person but as a community. We will know that God is here on earth when we can see Him in one another.

Once, when I was in my early twenties, I lived in a house in San Francisco with several other people. In the dining room overlooking the city, there was a very long table at which there were always people drinking coffee and engaging in lively conversation at almost any time of the night or day. That was a period of my life in which I thought of my future as more important than my present – surely in my future I would find the secret to happiness. But now that I'm living what my younger self thought of as the future, I look back to that table and think, *That was it!* There at that table, I remember having my first and still one of my most potent experiences of community. My house today is nicer, to be sure. Like others of my generation, I 'graduated' into my own this, my own that. But also, like others of my generation, I sort of miss the old days when there was more connection and less competition, more community and less isolation, more conversation and less TV.

Today, when we think about people joining together, it's not always for such wonderful purposes. We know about 'terror cells,' made up of terrorists joined for the purpose of wreaking havoc on our world. We get chills as we realize the power of two or more terrorists joined together, exerting greater power than the sum of the individuals. Yet the power of joining together applies as much – in fact, much more – to those who love than to those who hate. For there is a cosmic propulsion behind love that is not behind hate. Our problem is not that hate is more powerful than love, because indeed it is not; our problem is that hatred today is more energetic and active than love. It's time for our generation to allow ourselves not only the satisfaction of deep love and community, but also the power of deep love and community. It is the greatest antidote to the darkness of our times.

Metaphysically speaking, God did not create us

individually, but as one; that is the esoteric meaning of 'only one begotten Son.' The awareness of our oneness, while foreign to the ego, is clear to the heart. And that's why unity is the key to our happiness. Spiritually, we do not exist in isolation. It is unnatural for us to perceive ourselves as separate; in fact, we're like sunbeams of the same sun and waves of the same ocean. Imagining ourselves as separate waves, we feel that we are tiny and powerless, when in fact we are integral to the immense power of the sea.

It's only when we transcend the illusion of separation, refusing the false testimony of our physical senses, that we will make the quantum leap forward into a joy-filled life. We will know peace when we learn to love as God loves, and God loves all of us as one. We were created as one and we remain as one. The Golden Rule is so fundamental because what we do to others, we literally are doing to ourselves.

The recognition of our unity is the healing of all our wounds. Yet how do we convert the consciousness of humanity to a perspective of spiritual oneness? And what would the world look like if we did? Every once in a while, we give ourselves a taste of what life on Earth could be like, were we to truly interact like brothers and glimpse a higher possibility for connection among us.

On the final day of the last millennium, as people geared up for New Year's Eve celebrations all over the world, television networks broadcast fireworks displays from London to Sydney, New York to Hong Kong. I remember a particular moment that day, when I was simply walking through my living room, becoming aware of the sense that the entire world was in love. I didn't have the feeling of being in love with a particular person, but of love as a feeling that filled the air, an all-pervasive sweetness such as I had never known. I felt everyone was capable of loving everyone. And in that moment, I thought, *This is how life is supposed to feel. It is how we will feel one day, when we've evolved to our divine potential.* Love did not feel like the exception – it felt like the rule that day. The air itself was peaceful in a way we do not ordinarily experience.

A friend who lives in New York City told me about her remarkable experience on day one of the year 2000, as she was on her way to work. She told me the subway was like one big party. Everyone was celebrating; everyone was kind to each other; people who didn't even know one another were talking and joking. Many of these same people had been riding to work together every day for months or even years, and yet what a difference a day made.

So what really happened on that day? Was there actually an external, objective shift of some sort – or rather, for one shining moment, did we not simply change our social contract? What spell of peace and goodwill came upon us, and why, like Cinderella at the stroke of midnight, did we feel compelled at day's end to go back to who we were before?

Just as Abraham Maslow asserted that studying psychologically well-adjusted people was more revealing, in the end, than studying those who were psychologically impaired, it behoves us to question what is really going on in those moments when we come together in peace. The truth is, nothing objectively occurred on New Year's Day as we entered this millennium. What did occur is that for the period of about one day, we gave ourselves per-mission to behave like brothers. We reached for a universal love that day, beyond the confines of a particular relationship to an individual or group. Our natural knowing superseded our ego, and we entered into a different, unspoken agreement with one another: this was not to be a day for com-petition, but for co-operation; not a day for war, but for peace; not a day for judgement, but for blessing; and not a day for unhappiness, but for celebration. Nothing more than a simple shift in how we saw life made the difference that day. It was an internal – not an external – power that tilted us toward the light. We simply changed our perspective.

From that shift in our thinking there arose, if only for a brief time, a different kind of world. For one day, the focus of our attention and genius was on the celebration of life. We saw the world we would want to see, because on that day it was what we *decided* to see. For that one day, we got it right. And if we could do it for a day, then isn't it reasonable to assume that we could do it for longer?

My point is surely idealistic. But what more is an ideal than a thought that has not yet descended from heaven to Earth, a thought that awaits the evolution of the human race to be accepted and made manifest? Wasn't the abolition of slavery once merely an ideal? Wasn't women's suffrage once merely an ideal? Wasn't the end of Britain's colonial rule in India once merely an ideal? Idealism, after all, is not a *neurosis*. What is neurotic is how little idealism we display anymore, how lacking in imagination we've become about anything beyond individual goals. Now is the time for collective goals and collective ideals, as our near-fanatical adherence to the belief in separation has reached such dangerous proportions. Realism is not particularly helpful when what is real is so painful to witness. What is idealism, after all, but a message from the Real to the real? It's the force that inspires us to improve the world with a deep inner knowing that something better is possible. An ideal is a pure idea that becomes miraculous when blended with human imagination and effort. Great ideas need not languish in the realm of abstract possibility; they are meant to be embodied. Through the willingness of people and the grace of God, they become part of our earthly experience whenever we choose.

Another example of a heightened state of group awareness occurs every two years at the Olympic games. While charges of corruption have soiled their reputation at times, the basic sensibility of the Olympics is one of enlightened, joy-filled competition. The unique talents and brilliance of all nations are on display in a stunning demonstration of human community. As the athletes march in for the opening ceremonies, our hearts thrill at the reminder of how things could be. We see nations of the world recognizing each other as fellow citizens of the planet, all created with special talents, expressing themselves fully and delighting in one another's magnificence. We get a glimpse of what's possible, and we can feel that the Olympic Torch symbolizes something much more than sportsmanship. There's a universal sanctity to its flame, as it clearly represents a light that shines in every person and every heart, calling us to wholeness of body, mind, and spirit.

Comparing the Olympics to the state of our world today, we are tempted to despair. It is hard to accept the simultaneous reality of such noble genius as Olympian athleticism and terrorist destruction. Yet both exist, and both are real within our experience. They arise from very different views of our purpose on this Earth, and one – not both – will ultimately prevail.

It's important for the spiritual activist to remember that things could be different in our world, that the moments we experience as magnificent exceptions could indeed become the rule. Robert F. Kennedy often quoted George Bernard Shaw in saying, 'Some people see things as they are and ask, "Why?" I think of how they could be, and I ask, "Why not?" '

Children holding flowers could greet us when we arrive in a new country, instead of customs agents and guards. People could live in abundance and peace, instead of poverty and war. Life could be a continuous dance of harmony for everyone, instead of a desperate struggle to survive for so many. Once we are ready to accept such a vision and consider it possible, because in God all things are possible, then our lives will become channels through which it will emerge. It's only a failure of imagination that keeps us stuck in patterns of limitation and fear.

There is a new peace movement emerging today among those who realize that our spiritual powers afford us tremendous opportunity to transform the world. We can imagine the world we want, we can become the people from whom that world would flow forth, and we can join with others in making it happen. There are millions among us who understand we are one. As we create deeper peace among any of us anywhere, the reality of peace becomes more probable everywhere. We can surround the world with a field of peace so powerful that hatred and fear will dissolve in its presence.

Scientists tell us we live in a holographic universe, which means that, on the level of energy, the whole is contained in every piece and every piece contains the whole. So it is that a healing between or among any of us literally helps to heal all of us. Any time walls that divide us melt, the world is brought closer to the reuniting of hearts, which is the mystical goal of human existence.

Peace is more than the absence of war; it's the presence of peace, a positive state of being that is predicated on brotherhood and justice and love. In its presence, injustice and hatred have little power to grow. That is why knowing the truth of our spiritual oneness and embracing it within our hearts is the ultimate answer to all the problems of the world. At the level of spiritual reality, none of us are separate. The body has differences; the spirit does not. Community arising from the realization of our oneness is community that goes beyond mere alliance or treaty. It stems from a knowing of the heart, which transforms the mind. Emerging from our depth, it touches others in the same place. And thus what was broken apart shall be mended.

The horrors of the world we live in today arise from spiritual ignorance. Until we reach that place in ourselves where we identify with one another beyond our differences, we will perpetuate the disharmony that results from spiritual immaturity. Technological and material progress, alas, is not necessarily accompanied by spiritual wisdom. Often, in fact, our material power is used by the ego as a way to resist the Truth. Yet the Truth remains and catches up with us in time: there's no material shield that our karma will not penetrate.

We cannot escape one another, and in our right minds we wouldn't want to. Spending extraordinary resources trying to protect ourselves from our fellow human beings, rather than on efforts to build righteous relationships, is a backward model of human interaction. And the fact that we don't quite know how to turn our civilization from a war machine into a peace machine is not a reason not to try. Perhaps all the problems on the earth today provide us an opportunity, a challenge to surrender to the Truth in our hearts. Perhaps the mortal mind has been pushed at last into the proverbial corner, where we'll admit to our inability to save ourselves – indeed, to our genius at destroying ourselves – and humbly ask God to do for us what we cannot do for ourselves. Man is very effective at waging war; God is most effective at waging peace.

Jesus told us to love our enemies and bless those who curse us. To pray for someone is to pray that they be returned to their right minds. What a thought, given the state of the world today. If every one of us took one minute a day to close our eyes and send the love of God to Al Qaeda, we would have far, far less to worry about. In your mind, surround any violent person with a diamond egg: no malevolence will be able to penetrate the hardness of the diamond, while its light will shine back on their hearts and heal their minds. With this mystical remedy, they are spiritually quarantined.

We will be brothers and sisters in peace – and not war – when that is what we decide to call forth. Until then, we will face the consequences of our not yet having chosen love as the organizing principle for human civilization. Building genuine connection and deep community among the peoples of the world is the historical task of our generation. Where our governments do not seem equal to that task – indeed, in some cases they clearly repudiate it – we ourselves must strive to accomplish it nevertheless. With love in our hearts, we can supersede all fear-based consciousness, no matter how much material power it might wield. We will forge a new field of human possibility in which war shall be no more.

In the meantime, we will continue to gravitate to long dining-room tables where friends await us; we will continue to fall in love on blessed, enchanted days; and we will continue to fervently love our children and watch their miraculous dance into adulthood. But there will be more. Now, in an extraordinary moment of global transformation, we will do more than just love: we will join our love and harness our love. We will pool our resources of forgiveness and imagination and grace, and in time we will collectively experience what physicists call 'phase lock,' a phenomenon in which individual oscillating rhythms – here, the beats of many, many hearts around the world – fall into a deep pattern of energetic resonance. We will form a community of consciousness – a collective love – that is humanity's next step on our evolutionary journey. Love is not meant to be alone. It reaches out to find itself at every opportunity.

Scientists tell us about 'phase lock' – not that it always happens, but that it is always *trying* to happen. No matter how much havoc fear and hatred wreak, God has a better plan that is incapable of failure. It lacks not power but adherents. It waits simply for us to say 'yes' to love as energetically as hatred says 'no.' Thus shall be the deliverance of the world, when we arise from our stupor and faithlessness and doubt, and create the world we were born to create. First we will do this in tiny increments, and at last in waves of huge significance. An awe-filled grace will fill the skies and flood our hearts, when we have remembered at last who we are to one another.

That we *are* one another.

Praise God.

Amen.

MARIANNE WILLIAMSON is the author of the No. 1 *New York Times* bestsellers *A Return to Love*, *A Woman's Worth*, *Healing the Soul of America*, *Enchanted Love*, and *Illuminata*. *Everyday Grace* was also a No. 1 *New York Times* bestseller. Her books have been translated into more than twenty languages. For more information, visit her website at www.marianne.com

Being an Adult

Lucy Tobin is an award-winning journalist, specialising in business and personal finance at the *Evening Standard*. She's also a regular in magazines and online media, including *Cosmopolitan*, *Marie Claire*, and the *Huffington Post*, writing on topics ranging from student life and uni to careers and parenting. Recently named Business Journalist of the Year at the Santander Media Awards, Lucy is the author of six books, including the Amazon-bestsellers *A Guide to Uni Life* and *Entrepreneur*. She can often be seen and heard commenting on news stories on TV (BBC Breakfast, News 24, Sky News) and radio (Radio 4's Broadcasting House and Woman's Hour, LBC). Lucy graduated from Oxford University with a first-class degree in English in 2008.

Kat Poole is editor of *Emerald Street*, the daily women's lifestyle email magazine from Shortlist Media. She started her career at *Stylist* magazine, and has written for *Empire*, *The Debrief*, and *Red*, specialising in lifestyle, culture, and entertainment. Kat graduated from the University of Warwick with a first-class degree in Film and Literature in 2011.

Thank you to my parents for setting me on my own wobbly path to being an adult; to Howard for being the grown-up so I can sometimes be a kid; and to Jamie for making me laugh and love every single day. To Toby, who grew into a tiny person during the nine months it took for this project to come to life, this book is for you, with all my love.

Lucy

James, thank you for showing me that it's far better to try than never to know. And for all the cups of tea.

Kat

Lucy Tobin
and Kat Poole

Being
an Adult

the ultimate guide
to moving out,
getting a job,
and getting your
act together

SCRIBE
Melbourne • London

Scribe Publications
18–20 Edward St, Brunswick, Victoria 3056, Australia
2 John St, Clerkenwell, London, WC1N 2ES, United Kingdom

Published by Scribe 2018

Typeset in Adobe Garamond by the publishers

Printed and bound in the UK by CPI Group (UK) Ltd, Croydon CR0 4YY

Scribe Publications is committed to the sustainable use of natural resources
and the use of paper products made responsibly from those resources.

9781911617327 (UK edition)
9781925693058 (e-book)

A CiP entry for this title is available from the British Library.

scribepublications.co.uk

Contents

Introduction

It wasn't just one moment that made us realise we had some-how crossed into territory known as 'being an adult': it crept up on us.

For most of her twenties, Lucy felt like she was still basi-cally a kid playing at being a grown-up. Evidence: she didn't (and still doesn't) like hot drinks. (Nope, not tea, not coffee, though she can slurp a hot chocolate, if it has marshmallows on top.) She still buys children's trainers (tax-free, a benefit of having size-tiny feet). She didn't go to the dentist from the age of 18, when her mum stopped making her, until the day when, aged 26, her face swelled up like an obese chipmunk due to a wisdom tooth infection and the choice was, go to the dentist, or spend the rest of her life in her bedroom.

See, she really wasn't an adult.

But then things started changing. She met a guy at a party who was a police inspector; then realised he was younger than her. She learned that one of her school friends was having a baby, ON PURPOSE.

She bought a pressure cooker and started talking, at

length, about the crazy benefits of this new kitchen gadget. (A casserole ready in just 15 minutes? You've got to get one!) She went to Homebase on a Saturday, spent a couple of happy hours perusing paint samples, and enjoyed it more than a night out.

Then there were the big milestones: getting married, applying to the bank for a mortgage. When a bank manager appears to believe you're mature enough to borrow what seems (especially when you ponder it sleeplessly at 3am) to be *a gazillion pounds*, even though your earnings were only £1.20 in pocket money until last week, that's seriously grown up.

For Kat, the realities of coping with adult life hit her when her dad became very ill, and suddenly becoming self-sufficient was her number one priority. She had graduated with one of those degrees with no obvious career path, and had planned to take her time 'working it all out' (a.k.a. living at home and doing work experience for pennies). Instead, she decided to move to London (and was very lonely), get a job (that she hated), and navigate employment contracts and rental agreements and a life budget (a what?) because she was suddenly responsible for herself.

Then she quit that job at 24 and started all over again, with the Big Dream of breaking into journalism — an industry where she knew no one, in which she wasn't very experienced, and with only a tiny pot of savings to see her through. She cracked it, and then had an actual CAREER to think of, and found herself negotiating her salary and managing a team.

Despite all that, she's still flummoxed in the face of a recipe involving more than three ingredients, and struggles to get up when her alarm goes off in the morning. (She had assumed

Jumping Out of Bed was a reflex that would naturally kick in after the age of 21. It didn't.)

In both of our lives, etiquette issues kept coming up — what are the right words to say to a mourner at a funeral? How much should you spend on a wedding present? We wondered if it was just us, or if everyone struggles with the whole 'adulting' thing. So we asked friends, all in their twenties and thirties, when they really felt like a grown-up.

When did you first realise you weren't a kid any more?

'When my dad — who I thought knew everything — started asking *me* for advice on interest rates.'

'When Topshop rejected my student discount card, and I complained, only to be told it had run out six months ago ...'

'When I bought a new lampshade and I completely fell in love with it.'

'When I drove past someone's house and thought, "Wow, that's a lovely lawn."'

'When I got my first proper job, including my own limitless supply of Post It notes, and a Sellotape dispenser and business cards.'

'When I wiped out a "friend" who'd always made me feel bad about myself. Okay, no killing was involved, but I stopped contact, deleted them from Facebook and Instagram, and moved on.'

'When I got into trouble, legally, and my parents said, "This is your mess", and I realised that was it, I had no one else to depend on.'

'When I started paying off my student loan.'

'When I decided to stop making the effort to see my old mates from school because I realised I had grown out of those friendships.'

'When I realised I'd rather go to bed at 10pm on a Friday night and sleep for 12 hours than go out boozing with colleagues.'

'When I became a parent.'

'When I suddenly got a workplace pension ... at 22. I thought retirement was a long way off!'

'When I joined the National Trust. In my twenties. Because I realised lifetime membership would be better value if I joined then.'

'When I began making a will.'

'When I had to sign a death certificate.'

'When I became someone else's boss.'

'When I found myself going to a parents' evening at my old school — now as a parent, but with a lot of the same teachers.'

It soon became clear that we could *all* do with a hand getting through the practical and emotional issues we face as we grow up. So this book is all about being an adult, with tips from real ones — who've also confessed their biggest mistakes so you can avoid them — to help us all navigate the big things in life.

Authors' note

All the websites, apps, articles, and other resources mentioned throughout the book can be found at the back, along with an index (very grown up!) ... so don't worry if you think you've missed something.

Food and scoffing

You know that time when, aged 17, you burst into tears over a crap date/ruined outfit/coursework fail and someone said, 'People your age are fighting for their country in war zones ...' And it didn't help at all? It's the same guilt-vs-nightmare feeling when you come home from work, hungry as hell, facing a fridge that's empty bar a mould-encrusted head of garlic (source: mushroom risotto-making circa six months ago), and someone helpfully points out you can't be that hungry, you ate three Pret sarnies and two brownies at 1pm, and don't you know there are starving children in the world?

Working out how to keep yourself well fed, your kitchen fully stocked, and enough food in the fridge so that you're never facing mouldy garlic for dinner is one of the most important life skills.

The good news is, keeping it simple and taking an afternoon to learn to cook some healthy, basic dishes is easy. (And, hey, you don't have to unleash your casserole on Instagram until you've honed the dish a few times and decoratively sprinkled some rosemary on top.) Here you'll also find recipes for a ridiculously-simple-but-looks-impressive cake, and the easiest anti-Pot Noodle meals for when you're totally knackered.

First up, though, if you've just moved into a new place and are getting used to your first time cooking in a non-parental kitchen, what do you actually need to own?

Kitchen essentials: how to avoid having seven pizza cutters but nothing to actually cook the margarita on

Obviously, it will depend partly on your ambitions. Working up to an 18-course taster menu dinner party for 12? You're well beyond the rest of us. Can we cadge an invite? But if you're just starting out, your kitchen should contain:

- A frying pan with lid, a saucepan (e.g. 3.5l), a baking tray, a roasting tin, and a cake tin
- Wooden spoons, a spatula, and a slice
- A vegetable peeler, grater, and tin opener
- Sharp knives — one chef's knife and one small vegetable knife
- Cutlery, crockery, and glasses
- Scales
- A chopping board
- A mixing bowl and measuring jug
- A colander
- Oven gloves
- A stick blender (invaluable for soups)

Store cupboard essentials: apart from penne (and 18 unused tins of sweetcorn), what necessities should actually be stocked in your kitchen?

The best way to cut waste and make sure you have enough food for a last-minute meal is to have a well-filled kitchen cupboard. According to the Love Food, Hate Waste campaign, 'The kitchen cupboard is the nerve centre of your kitchen. Keep it well stocked and you will save time dashing to the shops for that single ingredient and will always have a delicious meal at hand even when the fridge is looking bare.' Here are LFHW's top store-cupboard picks, as well as a few of our own:

- Balsamic vinegar
- Butter beans
- Caster sugar
- Chutney
- Coconut milk
- Chilli flakes
- Curry paste
- Herbs (we recommend rosemary, thyme, tarragon, and mixed herbs to start with)
- Honey
- Ketchup
- Pasta
- Plain and self-raising flour
- Marmite
- Mustard
- Noodles
- Olive oil

- Paprika
- Pepper
- Raisins
- Red wine vinegar
- Rice
- Salt
- Sardines
- Stir-fry sauce
- Sesame oil
- Soy sauce
- Stock cubes
- Sunflower oil
- Tabasco
- Tinned tomatoes
- Worcestershire sauce

How to shop for food on the cheap

When you pop down to your local supermarket and the bill racks up quicker than a rocket on its way to Mars, it can feel as if there's nothing you can do about it. You gotta eat, right?

But there are a few easy hacks to slash your supermarket bill, without resorting to existing solely on budget-range baked beans. First tip: try 'downgrading' a range. Some foods are worth paying more for, others just aren't. So try a few cheaper ranges and see what they're like: if the budget own-brand cornflakes aren't great, go back to the original after finishing the box. But the chances are, you won't even notice. The SupermarketOwnBrandGuide website is great for this — it helps you work out the best swaps using insider knowledge from food factory workers, shoppers, and supermarket staff, who share their tips on which store's own-brand products are the same as, or almost identical to, their pricier alternatives, and how they taste. Look out for yellow 'reduced' stickers, too — they can be especially good for meat, ready meals, and other things you can put in the freezer.

And always compare price per kg rather than the stickered price to see which item is actually better value — especially when different brands are selling the same thing. Checking the ingredients list is also a good idea if you're unsure why there is a significant price difference between similar products — sometimes the higher priced product will have superior ingredients, but not always.

Try shopping with a friend — not an extravagant one who'll sneak truffles into your trolley, but one with similar tastes (and budget) to you so you can make the most of buy one, get one free offers.

Don't be too wedded to supermarkets, though. Local markets, butchers, and bakers may all have cheaper — and nicer — produce. Some market stalls specialise in selling just-out-of-sell-by-date food, which usually tastes just as good but costs less. (BTW, 'use by dates' are about safety — foods can be eaten (and usually frozen) up until the use by date, but not after. By contrast, 'sell by dates' are not super important — it's about when foods will taste their best. So after the sell by date, the food might not taste as good, but it's not a safety issue). The website ApprovedFood does this too, alongside excess stock, discontinued lines, and food nearing its best before date, all at bargain prices. And if you're doing an online shop, use comparison site MySupermarket and deal-flagging websites FixtureFerrets and HotUKDeals to secure the cheapest offers. Buying online also means not having to walk past aisles of cheap chocolate and prosecco so you avoid impulse buys.

Try shopping your own cupboards now and then: when you think you've got nothing in the kitchen, reach to the back of that pile of tinned cans that you barely see when grabbing another tin of tomatoes and whip up a meal out of the contents. Also, working out what you've actually got in stock already will stop you re-buying the same stuff over and over. (Not doing this is why Lucy has about seven tins of sweetcorn at home right now.)

Lastly, meal planning — working out, say on a Sunday night, what you're going to eat for lunches and dinners all week — also means you only buy what you actually need, and can use the leftovers for work lunches which will also save money.

Top healthy meals for all occasions:

EATING WITH FRIENDS — BOLOGNESE SAUCE
Makes enough for four, leftovers can be frozen.

**1 onion, with all brown skin layers peeled off,
    finely chopped**
1 tablespoon of olive oil
2 cloves of garlic, peeled and finely chopped
500g minced beef

A pinch of salt and a twist of pepper
A shake of mixed herbs, or fresh basil if you prefer
3 carrots, peeled and grated
5 mushrooms, chopped
A dash of Worcester sauce
A dollop of tomato ketchup or puree
1 tin (about 400g) of chopped tomatoes
  or tomato passata

- Fry the onion and garlic with a little olive oil in a frying pan until soft and lightly browned. Stir in the minced beef and fry until browned.

- Add the salt, pepper, carrots, mushrooms, tomatoes, and sauces, and cook on a medium heat (bubbling lightly) until thickened — usually about 20 minutes — adding the herbs in the last five minutes of cooking.

- Serve with spaghetti, rice, couscous, tacos, wraps for fajitas ... the possibilities are endless!

SPEEDY MEAL — STIR-FRY ANYTHING
Makes enough for two.

2 tablespoons of sesame (or sunflower) oil
1 onion, with all brown skin layers peeled off, chopped
2 cloves of garlic, peeled and finely chopped
Stir-fry veg (Supermarkets sell these in a bag for about £1,

but selecting your own can mean more variety and fresher veg. Quantity-wise, you want 2–3 mugs filled with a mixture of vegetables — e.g. broccoli florets, peppers, mushrooms, peas, pak choi or other Chinese leaves, beansprouts, beans etc. — all chopped into small chunks.)

Protein (Either 2 chicken breasts, 500g beef sirloin, or a similar amount of tofu, tuna steak etc., chopped into bite-sized pieces.)

Stir-fry sauce (In a small bowl or mug, mix together: 2 tablespoons of soy sauce, 2 tablespoons of water, 1 tablespoon of red wine vinegar, 1 tablespoon of sesame oil, chilli flakes if desired, a 2p-sized amount of ginger, finely chopped, if desired.)

Noodles (2 sachets of the vacuum-packed, straight-to-wok variety will cost a bit more, but mean less washing up; 2 nests of dried noodles, boiled for 5 minutes, will also work.)

- Heat the oil in a large frying pan or wok until sizzling, then add the onion and garlic and fry for two minutes or until soft, stirring constantly. Add the veg in order of size (broccoli takes longer than beansprouts, for example, so add two minutes earlier). Make a hole in the centre and add the chicken breast/beef steak/protein.

- Wait for that to cook (the chicken should be white and not at all pink when cut through the centre, beef and other protein can be cooked to your liking). Then drizzle the stir-fry sauce on top, add the noodles, stir, and cook for another couple of minutes, then eat.

IMPRESSING THE FAMILY — ROAST CHICKEN

**A whole chicken (you want about 200–250g per person,
  less if you're making lots of side-dishes)**
2 cloves of garlic, crushed
1 onion, peeled
1 lemon, halved
50g soft butter
Salt and pepper

- Pre-heat the oven to 200 degrees Celsius (190 for a fan oven).
- Take the chicken out of any packaging (don't wash it, and keep any utensils that have touched raw chicken separate, to be washed in very hot water) and place on a roasting tray.
- Stuff half of the lemon, then the onion and garlic, then the other half of the lemon up its ~~bum~~ central cavity.
- Smear the butter all over the bird, then season with a few twists of salt and pepper.
- Place in the oven. After about 20 minutes, reduce the temperature to 190 (180 for a fan oven). The total amount of cooking time will depend on the chicken's size, but a good guide is 20 minutes per 450g, plus 15 minutes at the end. It's fully cooked when you can poke it with a knife and the juices that run out are clear, not pink.
- Let it rest for a few minutes once you take it out the oven. (come on, it's had a hard time ...) Serve with roasted potatoes and vegetables, or bread and salad, or whatever you like!

MAIN COURSE — SOUP DE PHILIPIO

Our go-to soup for Sunday lunches, when we're hungry, cold, or under the weather. Super-warming (pun intended), Lucy's dad invented this on a day when the fridge was bare, friends were coming for lunch, and he had to rely on the freezer and store cupboard for ingredients. Adapt it according to what you've got in stock, cut up some bread and cheese to go with it, and enjoy. Serves four.

1 tablespoon of olive oil
1 onion, peeled and chopped
1 clove of garlic, crushed
1 tin (about 400g) of chopped tomatoes
Mixed dried herbs, or fresh herbs if you have them
1 tin (about 415g) of baked beans
Extra veg (choose between 2 chopped carrots, a handful of frozen peas or sweetcorn, green beans, or any other veg)
150g pasta
A squirt each of ketchup and brown sauce
Salt and pepper

- Fry the onion and garlic until soft and starting to brown. Add 1 litre of boiling water, the tomatoes, a twist of salt and pepper, half the baked beans, and the herbs.
- Cook until bubbling, then use a stick blender to liquidise.
- Add the rest of the baked beans and your extra veg.
- When everything is cooked, add the pasta and the sauces.
- Once the pasta is fully cooked, serve. We like to grate parmesan over the top and dunk with crusty bread.

Weekend baking: awesome show-off (but shhhhh, pretty easy) bakes

VICTORIA SPONGE

Serves eight to ten, depending on appetite/greed

For the cake:
3 eggs
175g of softened butter
175g of caster sugar
175g of self-raising flour

For the filling:
142ml carton of double cream
5 tablespoons of strawberry or raspberry jam

Optional decoration:
Icing sugar and a few quartered fresh strawberries
**   or whole raspberries**

- Pre-heat the oven to 180 degrees Celsius (170 for a fan oven).
- Break the eggs into a large mixing bowl (or electric mixer) and stir in the butter, sugar, and flour until totally mixed and smooth. Split the mixture between two well-greased, 18cm, round cake tins (or do it in two goes if you only have one tin) and try to make the surface flat.
- Bake for 25 minutes — the cakes should have turned golden and almost doubled in height, and should spring

back when touched. Leave to cool for five minutes, then remove from the tins, and leave to cool completely.

- In the meantime, whip the double cream (with a fork if you don't have a whisk), and spread it on the base of your least-even cooled cake. Put the jam over the base of the other one.
- Sandwich the two cakes together, and sprinkle with icing sugar and fresh fruit to decorate if you like.

STICKY DATE BISCUITS

Because these are finished off with dark chocolate lines drizzled over white chocolate, they look Masterchef-*pro. Lucy was wowed when her relative Harriet first served them up. But when she shared the recipe, turns out the art skills required are more 'year one painting' than Monet, and they only take 10 minutes to make. Just don't tell anyone that. Makes 20–30 squares, depending on how generous a portion you opt for.*

250g of butter
250g of chopped dates
200g of caster sugar
2 eggs (beaten)
300g of digestive biscuits, crushed into crumbs
  and small chunks (excellent stress reliever)
300g of white chocolate
80g of dark chocolate

- Melt the butter and sugar, then slowly add the eggs. (If some of it goes into scrambled egg lumps, don't worry, but try to stir enough to avoid it.) Bring to the boil and add the dates. Cook until the mixture starts to thicken, then remove from the heat. Add the crushed biscuits and stir.
- Pour the mixture into a cake tin lined with parchment paper— ideally 20cm x 30cm (if you only have a bigger one, just fold up the paper to stop the mixture travelling too far). Leave in the fridge to set.
- Once the cake is set, remove from the fridge. Melt the white chocolate and pour onto the cake to cover it completely. Melt the dark chocolate and drizzle it in thin lines (just let it fall off a teaspoon and wiggle your wrist) for decoration.
- Chill in fridge; when cool, cut the block into small squares.

Avoiding kitchen nightmares

'Buying fast food isn't at all cheap. A kilo of pasta and some fresh veg will give you more than one meal, and cost less.'

'Always make sure there is a stock of wine at home ...'

'Learn to cook. Home-made meals taste so much better than microwave meals, and are way cheaper than eating out!'

'I have spent years learning how to cook cheaply ... My top tip is: lentils. They bulk out/replace the meat, and are full of protein and cheap as, errr, chips!"

'Get an allotment, or share one with friends or housemates, or just have a veggie patch or herb garden at home — you can have a herb collection even if all you have is a windowsill. Growing things is a great hobby and so cheap.'

'Meal planning comes in handy whether you're feeding yourself or your housemates. You save money by only buying what you need, and getting other people involved means that you all eat more varied meals.'

Cleaning

Once hunger is kept at bay (for now, at least), cleaning is the next step in the whole keeping-yourself-alive-and-healthy adult thing.

If you're anything like us, you spent two decades ignoring your parents' pleas to clean your room, only to insist that they use a coaster when they come round to your new pad for a cup of tea. Because everything's different when you've got your own place, and you're actually pretty proud of your Ikea furniture/charity shop boho decor.

But how do you go about keeping your home sparkling? What's worth doing, and, crucially, how can you do it as fast as possible, with the minimum fuss? Don't worry; cleaning a bathroom or kitchen is simple when you know how. This chapter covers what you need to do to get your whole flat/house spotless.

First up, ignore the daytime TV ads: you *don't* need a separate Mr Biceps Worktop Cleaner, Mrs Triceps Toilet Lid Cleaner, and Ms Glutes Tabletop Wiper. For most homes, your cleaning armoury need consist of just:

- All-purpose grease cleaner
- Furniture/wood cleaner (If you want to get posh with some polish and keep your surfaces clear of dust for longer.)
- Bathroom cleaner with bleach
- Washing-up liquid
- Baking soda (A brilliant all-purpose cleaner that is especially excellent at absorbing smells from carpets — just sprinkle on before hoovering — after parties/hung-over episodes.)
- Glass cleaner
- Broom and dustpan (Add a brush if feeling fancy!)
- Mop
- Toilet brush
- Duster(s)
- J-cloth(s)
- Hoover
- Rubber gloves
- Limescale remover
- Floor cleaner

How to clean your home in half an hour (because who wants to spend any longer when there's Netflix)

Obviously, you've got that all-day spring clean scrubathon in the diary for tomorrow. Definitely going to happen. But today, you've got your parents/poshest buddies/boss coming round in half an hour and you've spent so long cooking/outfit planning/Snapchatting that you, errr, kind of forgot about the judgemental eyes that will soon be following your dust-bunnies around the room. Here's your 30-minute cleaning regime. Go!

BATHROOM — 10 MINUTES

Clear all the crap from your sink/window sill/bath/shower, and hide it away until such a time as you can sort it out properly. Spray an all-purpose bathroom cleaner around the loo bowl, loo seat, bath/shower, and sink. Leave to do its work, while you wipe the mirror and taps with a j-cloth and glass cleaner. Hang up the towels, deal with any dirty clothes, and then hoover up all the skin cells, toothpaste, hair, and splatters of dried toiletries on the floor. (Lovely!)

Go back to the loo — use a toilet brush to scrub at the bowl, then flush it clean. Use another j-cloth to wipe the toilet seat and lid, then dump this in the wash. Use a new j-cloth or a sponge, plus the shower-head, to clean off the bath and shower.

If you have a tiled/vinyl/non-carpet floor, now fill your bucket with water and floor cleaner and mop it, starting in the far corner and finishing near the door. Bathroom complete! (Don't worry, the other rooms are quicker.)

BEDROOM — 5 MINUTES

Make the bed, and hide dirty clothes in the washing machine or laundry hamper. Either fold and put away clean clothes or, time allowing, stash them somewhere out of sight and come back to them later. Hoover the room, then take any dirty plates/glasses/cereal bowls to the kitchen.

KITCHEN — 10 MINUTES

Run the hot tap and fill up the sink with water and washing-up liquid. (You can skip this step if you have a dishwasher.) Clear the surfaces — dump any dirty crockery/cutlery/glasses/pans into your now bubbly, hot basin (or the dishwasher), and put food items back into the fridge/cupboards. Dash to the living room and check if there are any dirty dishes here — if so, bring them back to the kitchen to wash.

Throw away any rubbish, then wipe the now-clear kitchen counter and table with a cleaning spray. Do the washing up and put away the clean dishes.

LIVING ROOM — 5 MINUTES

Identify any dirty clothes or items that belong in other rooms; if the doorbell's ringing already (what, you were slow in other rooms?), shove them under the sofa for now. (Go deep, or they'll peep out when people are sitting down.) Otherwise, return them to their rightful places. Smack sofa cushions on the floor to fluff them up, arrange cushions/rugs/throws, put away remote controls, pile up old magazines/books/newspapers in an artful heap, and hoover the floor.

You're done! Now, try to look energetic and not like you've been sprinting around cleaning for half an hour, there's someone at the door ...

How to divide domestic chores without killing someone[1]

Sure, you fell in love with your flatmate/boyfriend/wife/the random dude you met on SpareRoom at first sight. And you both enjoy nothing more than a three-hour *Skins* marathon.

---

1   Your flatmate.

And occasionally you surprise each other with a gift of Wotsits — it's all so beautiful; living together was going so well. But then the cleaning wars began.

(Our friend's flatmates once had a three-day standoff over the toilet-cleaning rota that culminated in no loo roll (a shopping strike emerged) and people sneaking into the bathroom with cleansing wipes (the girls) or newspaper (the lads). It wasn't good news for the drains.)

One in three relationships/house-shares splits up because of the washing-up pile-up in the sink, according to research we totally made up, but could well be true. Plan ahead, though, and you can divide up those dull chores without turning into a passive-aggressive nightmare. Here's how …

1. HONESTLY TALK EXPECTATIONS

You've been obsessed with dust-free furniture, fleck-free worktops, and daily-hoovered carpets for the past 28 years? Then don't say, 'Oh, I'm easy' when the question of domestic jobs arises. You're fine with a monthly Big Clean, but reckon daily tidying is a waste of time? Say so early on. Being honest from the start cuts down on future arguments. You'll also need to recognise, if you're at the extreme end of the spectrum — either a clean freak or a messy pig — that you're going to have to compromise. Either do more work than others, or pick up the Cif a lot more frequently than you're used to.

2. SET OUT A LIST OF CHORES AND MAKE A CLEANING SCHEDULE THAT EVERYONE AGREES WITH

What's on your list will depend on the size of your pad,

and how much you want to do communally (the laundry is probably a solo job unless you're in a relationship). It might include communal shopping (toilet roll, cleaning products etc.), cleaning the bathroom(s), cleaning the kitchen, hoovering everywhere, dusting, mopping, cleaning the living room, tidying the garden (if you have one), putting the bins out, and checking smoke detectors and Carbon Monoxide alarms.

Make sure everyone agrees on the list, and then decide what tasks need to be done daily, weekly, or monthly, to devise a schedule of who is doing what, and when. It's a good idea to break down each room's tasks into a list — say, bathroom: bleach toilet, clean shower/bath and sink, mop floor, re-stock toilet roll etc. — again to avoid future bust-ups. With serious cleaning, like at the end of a tenancy agreement or a big spring clean, it's always a good idea to tackle the big jobs together.

3. PUT THE SCHEDULE SOMEWHERE EVERYONE CAN SEE

On the loo door or fridge. Make it somewhere everyone visits so no one can say, 'Oh, sorry, I forgot ...'

4. SPEAK UP IF YOU HAVE A PROBLEM

That flatmates' WhatsApp group is great for arranging nights out. It's less good for passive-aggressive missives such as: 'I'm not naming the person who made a big mess of the toilet at 3am, didn't clean it, and left it for me to discover while heading out on my 5am shift to work at the Samaritans, but can it NOT HAPPEN AGAIN, ADAM.' Discuss problems as they arise, or organise a monthly meeting, rather than resorting to social media or group chats.

How to split the cleaning with housemates without them wanting to kill you

Trying to keep your place in good nick can be more divisive than discussing who you voted for in the last election. Here's how other people managed their shared-house-shared-mess scenarios:

'I lived with three other female professionals when I first moved to London. We all had different schedules, but agreed that it was a group responsibility to keep the place nice, be that cleaning as you go, or one big clean at the weekend. Having said that, that kind of deal works when everyone pulls their weight — one housemate didn't, and it made for a really uncomfortable situation, especially when all efforts at constructive conversation failed.'

'I shared a place with two other professionals who, like me, just wanted to live somewhere nice and clean. We didn't feel like a rota was going to work for us, so — and it sounds boring — we just kept up a dialogue about it. If I saw them on a Friday, I'd mention that I was going to do some cleaning at the weekend and did they fancy chipping in. We'd usually just pick a few tasks each, and, by Sunday night, the place felt fresh again.'

'I've never had an issue with my house looking like it's lived in, but appreciate other people fall slightly on the cleanier side. It's important to set some agreed standards for the shared space — otherwise you'll constantly bicker over it — then you can be as messy as you like in your own space! I've also worked off the general rule you tidy up after yourself and don't leave dishes etc. out for days on end. I'd also suggest, if you think it'll be an issue, setting aside one day per month or so to do a good clean (or split the cost of a cleaner!).'

'I've learned, from years of different living situations, that being upfront is the only way that some people will do their share. Saying "The kitchen could use a good clean" is not the same as "Would you mind cleaning up after the party you had last night?". "The recycling bin is looking quite full" does not, for some people, translate to "Could you take out the eight pizza boxes that you've balanced on top of the bin, please?"'

'We accepted that there would be a cleaning boss, and she would tell others when/what they needed to do. And we always did our own mess!'

'An ex-boyfriend thought he deserved a medal every time he took the bins out (after I had spent the day scrubbing the kitchen, cleaning the bathroom, hoovering the whole flat, and unblocking the drain). There is a reason we are no longer together.'

'I'm a very clean guy and my girlfriend chips in when she's not working or struck down from the hangover plague. My other housemate isn't in the same league as me, but he still falls into the "clean and tidy" percentile, which makes for a happy flat.'

'Don't be the kind of person who'll put the washing machine on at 1am on a weeknight (or any night) and replace your housemate's damp clothes in the dryer with your own. There's literally no excuse that works in that situation.'

'If, like us, you have no organised weekly timetable, one of our favourites is the "when one starts the others join in" game. It only takes one person to begin the joy, and fingers crossed everyone else plays their part.'

Let's talk dirty (laundry, obviously)

When Lucy first went to uni, and the amazingly good (and free) Mum Express Washing Service came to a sudden end, new rules emerged. Jeans were washed only when they became so baggy another pair of legs could move in. Underwear — well, there was a really big Primark nearby and ~~quite often~~ occasionally she stocked up there rather than braving the university launderette.

But since then we've turned to the experts — i.e. an anonymous Reddit feed and some guidance from the Persil website (although we took this with a pinch of, errr, washing powder because they're obviously trying to sell more of the stuff). Obviously it will depend on your circumstances; if you've got a sweaty kind of bod or your work is messy, your daily clothes might require more washing. Anything that smells or looks soiled obviously needs to be washed ASAP. Those caveats aside, here's an overall lowdown on what to wash, when:

1   Every use: pants, socks, tights, shirts/blouses, t-shirts, cloths used to clean the toilet, gym clothes, swimwear
2   Every 2–3 uses: kitchen cloths, tea towels
3   Every 5–7 uses: pyjamas, dresses, jumpers, skirts, trousers
4   Every 2 weeks: towels, bath mats, bedding, jeans, bras (you might prefer to wash these more frequently, but it can damage the elasticity)

How do you actually wash stuff? (we *just* worked it out ...)

Yeah, it's the question you're too embarrassed to ask your mum because it shows you literally have never done the washing. But it's pretty easy. The main steps are:

1   Sort clothes according to a) your effort levels, and b) how much you love these particular clothes. Most clothes can be washed on the standard 30 or 40 degree cycle, but delicates like silk, wool, lace, suits etc. should be hand-washed, dry-cleaned, or washed solo, depending on their instructions and how much you're willing to gamble a machine wash. (See below for washing label decoding.) And, if you're not sure, washing clothes at a cool 30 degrees is better for the environment and will avoid most shrinking/colour disasters. Remove tissues, money (if you're lucky), and Cadbury Dairy Milk wrappers from pockets.

2   Separate coloured clothes from white ones, if you can. Bright red pants can turn an entire washing machine's worth of clothes marshmallow pink, and that's pretty devastating. If you're worried about a colour running (like with new indigo jeans), rinse in the sink to get any excess dye out first.

3   Put your washing powder/tablets into the machine — either directly in the drum (the massive hole where you shove all your clothes) or into a pull-out drawer; it will say on the container.

4   Don't overfill the machine — that time-saving idea might not work out if your clothes come out still dirty, more crumpled, and needing another wash.

5   Twizzle the washing machine's knobs to 'normal', at about 30 degrees.

6   Get on to the drying quickly.

How to go to war against stains (no fatigues needed)

The best way to tackle that globule of dirt on your favourite shirt obviously depends on what the dirt is — but even if you've no idea (or won't say out loud …), you can have a go at attacking most stains. If it's something really stubborn, or on a delicate fabric, it's best to take it to a dry cleaner.

1   **Protein stains (we're talking blood, vom, poo, meat, milk, grass, sweat):** pre-soak in warm water with detergent, then wash separately. To disinfect completely, add a washing-safe bleach or product like Napisan to the wash.

2   **Grease stains (oil, butter, mayo, make-up):** use a pre-wash stain remover (like Vanish) as soon as you can. Leave it for a

few minutes, then wash as normal. Repeat if necessary.

3 **Coffee/tea/juice/wine/chocolate:** scrape off excess, then mix 1 tablespoon clear liquid hand soap with 10 tablespoons of warm water, and apply to stain. Blot to remove, repeat if needed.

4 **Tomato sauce:** scrape off excess, apply the above soap mixture (1 tablespoon clear liquid hand soap with 10 tablespoons of warm water), blot off residue. If needed, apply some white vinegar and blot again. Wash as normal.

5 **Chewing gum:** rub it with ice to harden it and scrape off as much as you can. Use clear liquid hand soap if needed, rinse, then wash as normal.

6 **Nail varnish:** use nail varnish remover on the back of the stain with white kitchen roll. Keep changing the kitchen roll to remove the excess colour. Rinse, then wash.

7 **Yellowing underarm (from deodorant):** rub some white shampoo onto the stain before washing as normal. You can also find specialist cleaning products aimed at tackling this if the stain is ingrained — better than chucking a t-shirt away …

Drying clothes without a tumble dryer (and without that elephant-dung-like damp smell)

1 Use a high-spin cycle on the washing machine, so as much water as possible is removed from your clothes — although you'll need to be gentler if delicates are involved.

2 Act fast: the sooner you can get your clothes hanging, the better. Leaving them lingering in the machine = that damp

smell. So shove your washing basket somewhere you'll almost trip over it to remind yourself, or set an alarm. Just get to that washing machine door ASAP.

3   To dry effectively, clothes need the most amount of air to circulate as possible. An outside washing line is best, but if that's impossible, hang them well on a drying rack, indoors clothes line, and/or radiators, and rotate them halfway through drying to speed things up and avoid weird creases. Watch out for pockets, turn-ups, cuffs or underarm areas — if they don't get dry quickly they'll start smelling of damp — lay out your clothes as flat as possible to minimise creasing.

4   Watch out for your home, too — clothes on radiators can cause damp, so try to open a window or use a dehumidifier if you have one.

5   What about the towels? These can go a bit hard/scratchy when drying naturally, but adding a capful of white vinegar to the rinse cycle will help to get rid of any remaining soap and give you a fluffy, soft towel. Try drying them in an airing cupboard if you have one, or near the boiler.

6   If you NEED a particular top tonight and it's just come out of the wash, get it as dry as possible and then give it a blast with a hairdryer. Don't use the hottest setting — warm is good, it's about air-flow not heat. Rotate it frequently, and focus on pockets, sleeves, and collars.

How to defrost a freezer (one for a cold day)

This might be the ultimate grown-up task. Something your dad used to do on a winter Sunday, while you watched him dump all the food outside and painstakingly chisel off the ice from the freezer, and thought how pointless everything he was doing looked because the frost would be back tomorrow. But now you have your own freezer, and a thick layer of ice is making it impossible to open the drawer containing your emergency Ben & Jerry's stash. Plus, all that ice is making it less efficient, costing you more on your electricity bills, making ice cream less affordable. Something must be done. But what?

1   Turn the freezer off, and empty it. You'll need to work fast to stop food defrosting (or eat a delicious hybrid lunch of the entire contents); wrapping the food in towels or storing in a cool-box (placed outside if it's a cold day) will help.

2   Remove all drawers, trays, and shelves that you can (if stuck with ice, don't yank too hard as they might break).

3   Place old newspapers/towels around the base of the freezer to prevent the formation of a small swimming pool. (And don't underestimate how many you'll need, so keep a dry stack to one side.)

4   Now, defrosting time: you can place bowls or cups of hot water in the freezer and wait; you can use a hairdryer (just watch out for any puddles/water), or an ice scraper, or even a rag dipped into boiling water. A spatula or scraper will remove chunks of ice (but don't chip too hard, or you may cause damage to the freezer).

5   Once it's all clear, it's a good opportunity to clean the freezer — then always get it as dry as possible (with towels or cloths) before turning it back on — otherwise your old enemy ice will immediately return.

How to deal with mould ... the worst housemate EVER

Whether it's those gross black dots crawling up your wall, or furniture being 'eaten' up by spores, mould is gross, stinky, and can damage your health, especially if you are asthmatic. It's also a bit of a pain to get rid of — better at sticking around than your most persistent ex. If you're renting, put pressure on your landlord to tackle the problem, for health reasons. If not? You're going to have to get physical. Mould is caused by humidity — it can start growing on a surface once it's been wet for over 24 hours, and it's often a symptom of a bigger problem: damp. This can get so bad it can threaten whole buildings, so if you're seeing really serious amounts of mould, or if it's really prevalent in one area, which could be a sign that rain or moisture is getting through external walls or a leak, call in a damp-proofing expert for their opinion.

But if you've just got a bit of mould, what should you do?

First up, dress like a murder investigator: rubber gloves, plastic poncho, goggles, dust mask — you don't want to breathe mould in. Specialist cleaning spray HG Mould Spray works well, but mixing one part bleach to four parts water can also kill off mould. Scrub the cleaning solution on the mould until it's gone, then dry the whole area.

Prevention: mould likes to hang out in dark, damp spaces. So keep the room as light as possible during the day, dry any condensation on walls or windows as soon as you can, disinfect surfaces to get rid of spores, and use dehumidifiers (either run a machine and empty it when it's full of water, or buy moisture-sucking crystals that sit in pots and absorb water). Keep bathroom and kitchen doors closed, use extractor fans and/or open windows when cooking, and avoid drying your clothes in rooms with mould.

My mouldy nightmare — Lucy's story

'When the downstairs neighbours of my flat called one day to say that during their building work, they'd discovered some mould and thought it could be damp, I initially thought, "That's a shame for them ... but why are they telling me? It's not my problem." Well, it turned out it was — in fact they had dry rot, which had spread all over our flat, too. It was impossible to tell whose flat caused the issue, it was crazily expensive to fix and involved really disruptive building work. Often there's nothing you can do to prevent it (ours stemmed from a slow, hidden leak that we had no idea existed), but there are ways to lessen moisture in your home, and now I'm finally listening to my (chartered surveyor) dad's advice: use the kitchen's extractor fan whenever cooking, and dry washing outside if at all possible.'

Big house headaches — damp, subsidence, and rot

Damp and rot can be huge home headaches — making properties unhealthy to live in, as well as very difficult to sell on. A surveyor should flag up any issues before you buy, but if you're seeing signs of damp (like a musty smell, excessive condensation on windows, peeling wallpaper, or mould) in your own home, you'll need to tackle it. If the problem is simply due to a leak (like from a gutter or pipe), get that fixed ASAP. But you might need to call in a specialist for a damp survey to get to the root of the problem — and then shell out for a damp-proof course, which can cost anything from a few hundred pounds up to several thousand for a large house.

Subsidence is another serious — and fairly common — issue. It's when the ground under your house sinks or collapses, causing your home to 'move'. It can be caused by big trees nearby slurping up the moisture in the soil, or — very often — when a property is built on clay soil, which expands when wet and contracts when dry, without decent foundations. Signs of subsidence include major cracks in the walls — some cracks aren't significant, but any that are thicker than a 10p coin, diagonal, wider at the top than the bottom, or found near a new extension should be investigated by experts.

Rot is another big cause for concern — since most houses in the UK involve timber, the wood can be attacked by wet rot, dry rot, or insect infestations. The symptoms of wet rot are damp walls that feel soft and spongy, but don't panic, it's fairly easy for experts to fix. Dry rot is far more serious — one of our friends faced a £15,000 bill to sort out this problem in her flat. It is a fungus that loves moist, unventilated conditions and spreads like measles — experts have to cut out the affected timber and/or apply special chemical treatments. So if a surveyor's moisture meter spots dampness in walls or timber and it's dry rot, call in the pros.

House rules — tips on how to keep your home looking parental visit-ready

'Make sure everything has a place. Any stuff without a place in your house or flat will just lie about, and you'll end up with a mess, constantly wasting time looking for stuff. But if everything has a place, you'll know where it all goes and where to find everything. And if you can't find a place or work out what to do with something, bin it.'

'If you don't let mess and dirt build up, it's a lot easier to clean it — little and often!'

'Keep two plastic bags by the door. One for bits and bobs for charity and one for clothing to recycle. When they are full, move them on. One person's rubbish is another's treasure; if you don't love it or need it, pass it on.'

'Organise your paperwork so you can find it when you need it. Yes it's boring. But so is having to reapply for essential documents in a hurry, or not being able to prove you can work in the UK. It doesn't have to be indexed and cross-referenced in shiny folders, but having a box or drawer for important papers is an absolute must.'

'When moving out of home for the first time, start putting household items such as washing powder and toilet rolls etc. in a box. Buy them when they are on offer — this means that your first shop isn't really expensive.'

Physical and mental health

So, you've got a list of very adult priorities, including finding a job, getting paid, living somewhere sweet, and having a social life to rival the kind you see on sitcom reruns from the nineties. You're gradually getting your life in gear, but ... you don't feel great. You have no energy and you feel a creeping guilt every time you pass the gym by your house — or is that feeling actually a hangover from too many pints and the burger you devoured at 1am? Or a cold that's coming on?

You'd check in with your doctor, but you're still registered at your home practice, and that's a long round-trip when it's probably nothing.

There are two options: a) frantically Google every symptom, or b) ignore everything that feels out of the ordinary and hope it goes away. Right?

Wrong. Because there's actually a much better third option: getting your physical and mental health in check. And luckily, it doesn't have to be difficult.

How to find and register for a good GP and dentist

Once you've moved house and sorted out all the admin, maintaining your best life — with the help of medical professionals — is often forgotten about until you really need to see someone. (We know a 30-year-old who still has the same dentist as when he was a child, 80 miles away from where he now lives. With his wife. In the house he owns.)

The happy news is that finding a doctor or dentist is really easy. The NHS (our National Health Service) has a postcode tool that lets you see which practices are available to you. Literally just search 'Find a GP/dentist in my area' in your web browser, and it should be the first result. Like schools, each NHS doctor's surgery has a catchment area (dentists don't — you can choose a surgery that's convenient to you); if you fall within it, you should be able to register right away, as long as they're accepting new patients.

And if you're lucky enough to have a choice of surgeries, there are a few things you should consider before deciding who'll be handling your health:

- How easy is it to get there from where you live? In all likelihood, you'll be fitting appointments into your day-to-day schedule or commute.
- How do their other patients rate them on service and quality of care?
- Do they offer other services like online prescription ordering and appointment booking?

You can find all of this out on the same NHS website;

each surgery will be listed alongside a table of criteria to help you decide which one looks right for you.

If — argh — you can't see one you like the look of, don't sweat. Lots of surgeries are open to appeals from patients who are nearby, but not in the catchment area. Look up their appeals process (or call and woo a receptionist); usually this will just require a letter explaining why you want to join their list.

So far, so proactive. But what if you can't find a doctor or dentist who is accepting new patients and you're stuck on a waiting list instead of sitting in a waiting room? Now's the time to call NHS England's Customer Contact Centre for some assistance. If you don't have time and need to see a health professional right away, you can use one of the options listed below, or exercise your right to be seen for emergency treatment at any GP surgery for up to 14 days — this is also helpful if you are on holiday in the UK and need urgent help.

It's also worth remembering that, while it's free to see an NHS doctor, there are costs associated with dentistry. These start at around £20 for a standard or emergency appointment, and go up depending on what you need done. If you need a prescription for any kind of medical complaint, it'll cost you around £9 per item, but the NHS offers schemes to help with costs if, for example, you are on a low income. You can find all the details on their website.

How to win the GP appointment battle

This is where the fun begins. Doctors are busy, and those very same receptionists you were trying to woo earlier are often busier, gatekeeping time slots and dealing with lots of other people who want appointments. If you have the luxury of being able to take time out of work during the day for one of the less popular appointments (3pm on a Wednesday anyone?), book right in and be aware that most of your friends hate you.

But if flexibility is not on your side, how do you get seen quickly (and not end up settling for an appointment in three months' time with the locum)? Most surgeries offer same-day appointments that require you to ring up first thing in the morning. Here's how to get one:

1   First up, do your research. Find out when those phone-lines open and be poised to dial as soon as they do. You WILL be in a queue with lots of other people with the same idea, and you'll want to beat them to it.

2   Be prepared. Before you call, work out how late in the morning you could arrive at work, and how early you can leave. And make sure you're dressed; if you do get offered an appointment 30 minutes from calling, don't miss it because you thought it would be a good excuse for a lie-in and some daytime TV.

3   If all fails and you can't get seen, ring the surgery after lunch when the lines are much quieter, and ask for a telephone appointment with the on-call doctor. There are often slots free for patients who have a concern, but aren't sure how urgently they need to be seen. If the doctor you speak to thinks you'll need to go and see them in person, they'll book you in there and then. Job done.

Of course, you might have a problem that's a) more urgent than all that, or b) you're really not sure. The good news is, there are services available for that, too:

- **Out-of-hours doctor:** the surgery you're registered with will have a service you can call outside of their opening hours about complaints you don't think can wait until the next working day. You'll find those details listed on your surgery's website.
- **Pharmacists:** they're all trained professionals, so can help advise you on whether you need that doctor's appointment or if something over the counter will help sort you out.
- **NHS 111:** the free non-emergency number for the NHS, where you can speak with trained professional at all hours, every day of the year. This is for urgent problems that aren't life-threatening.
- **Walk-in centres and minor injuries units:** you can find your local centre on the NHS website; they deal with non-life-threatening illnesses and injuries.
- **Sexual health clinics:** same deal as above, but for the sexy (or rather, really unsexy) stuff. Again, you can use the postcode search tool on the NHS website to find the nearest clinic to you.
- **A&E:** there are departments up and down the country dealing with medical emergencies. If you're new to an area, it's a good idea to familiarise yourself with your nearest one, just in case.
- **999 and ambulance services:** these are the guys to call if you or someone you know is seriously injured, ill, or if a life is at risk.

How often do I need to have a check-up?

Everyone has a friend who'll boast about the fact that they haven't been to the dentist since they were 14 but still have great teeth. And while that's very nice for them, what might work for some isn't guaranteed to work for everyone. So how often should you be checking in on your own health?

1 **Doctor:** you should see your doctor if you feel unwell or have questions about your health. For specific tests (for example cervical screenings, which are available to women every three years once they turn 25), your doctor should write to you in advance when these are due, or let you know if you need to come back in. But don't always rely on the administrators — it's your responsibility to know when and how you should be getting test results, follow-up appointments, and the like. If you don't know, ask.

2 **Dentist:** if you have good oral health, it's recommended that you visit your dentist for a check-up once every one to two years, although others might need to visit more frequently. Get an appointment booked if you haven't had one in a while, and your dentist will then tell you when they want to see you again. Some surgeries will even text you a reminder when it's nearing time to book your next appointment. But again, if they haven't told you, then ask.

3 **Sexual health clinics:** sexual health charity the Terrence Higgins Trust recommends that you go for a check-up once every six months if you don't have a regular partner but are having casual sex; more often than every six months if you have lots of sexual partners; straight away

if you have symptoms of a sexually transmitted infection; and before starting a new sexual relationship (if you're thinking about not using condoms, HIV tests are also recommended). You can find more, in-depth information about sexual health and sexual health screenings on their website.

Health: the absolute basics

So now you know where you can get medical care if you need it. But with no one encouraging you to get enough vitamin C/ detach yourself from the sofa/stop at three bars of chocolate, how do you keep yourself out of the doctor's surgery in the first place? Here are some basics:

CALORIES!

You may vaguely remember hearing this term in a science class while you were busy setting fire to your notepad with a Bunsen burner. Now, you just see it on packets of food and think, 'That number looks small, I'll eat it!' So, here's a quick refresher. A calorie IS a number (short for kilocalorie, usually written as 'kcal'), and it measures how much energy a serving of food or drink has in it. We need to eat enough of these numbers every day to maintain our weight, energy levels, and health.

According to the current NHS guidelines, an average adult woman needs to eat around 2000 calories (kcal) a day to maintain her weight. For adult men, it's 2500 kcal a day. Helpfully, supermarkets label their food items so you know exactly how many calories are in what, and the NHS also has a free calorie counter on their website if you want to learn more about what you're putting in your mouth.

While it's not something to obsess over, if you are concerned about your diet or health, it is sometimes worth taking stock of your calorie consumption and making sure you aren't under-nourishing yourself, or consuming more than you need. Ultimately, what's right for each person will depend on a lot of things, like age, how much exercise you do, and your metabolism. But whatever that number is, it should come from chowing down on stuff that's healthy and balanced.

EXERCISE!

Just as important as *eating* calories is burning some off. And it's not just about staying in shape; it plays a huge part in keeping you in good health, too.

If you used to skip PE with the professional ability of an MI5 agent, or your main exercise was a kick-about in the park but you're put off by the teenagers who are running the place now, the thought of getting started again might be a bit daunting. The essential bit is that adults (anyone between 19 and 64 — yes, that means YOU) need to move their bodies in two ways each week: aerobic exercise and strength exercise. How frequently and how long you do these for depends on your personal lifestyle; there is a comprehensive breakdown of options on the NHS Live Well website.

But don't worry, we don't expect you to kit up in a brightly coloured leotard and take up Zumba. Aerobic exercise can be moderate or vigorous, and includes everything from walking and swimming, to volleyball and martial arts. Strength exercise is anything that makes your muscles stronger, like yoga or lifting weights. (Fun fact — aerobics actually counts as both at the same time.) You can find guidelines on how best to balance the two on the NHS website.

Feeling motivated now? There's also the free Couch to 5k app designed to get anyone, whatever level of fitness, from walking to running in nine weeks.

SLEEP!

If you've ever woken up on public transport seven stops past your house, with dribble running down your chin and your head resting on the stranger in the seat next to you, you'll know that sleep deprivation can be an absolute nightmare (and a nightmare would probably be preferable, to be honest).

And it's not something that's reserved for hung-over days or the aftermath of an epic Netflix binge; according to the Royal Society for Public Health, the UK public get just 6.8 hours of sleep a night compared to the 7.7 people think they need. It might not sound like much — but add those lost hours up and it means we're losing an entire night's sleep each week. It's exhausting to think about!

Actually, getting in those hours (a recommended 7–9 hours each night, according to the Sleep Council) can be pretty difficult when you're maintaining a social life, working long hours, enjoying ~~frequent~~ occasional late-night online shopping binges, or living with housemates who think playing the Disney back catalogue at full volume at 3am is acceptable.

So, how do you break the can't sleep/won't sleep cycle?

1   **Sort your room out:** are your clothes in a heap on the floor, is your bedside table working as a dumping ground, and are yesterday's dirty dishes in a corner by the door? Make sure your environment reflects the night's sleep you want to get (a.k.a. pleasant).

2   **Upgrade your threads:** having a bed you look forward to getting into each night is important. If you're renting, the chances are you can't do much about the frame, so buy yourself some good quality (or good-looking) bed linen and some stuff to make it feel cosy, like pillows or a throw.

3   **Get regular:** you probably have set times you do most other things (get up, eat lunch, go to the pub), and sleep shouldn't be any different. Even if you have a lifestyle that makes going to sleep at the same hour every day tricky, try to keep the hours you do hit the hay within manageable parameters. And aim for a before-bed routine. That could be anything from drinking a glass of milk (#adulting) to having a bath.

4   **Relax, don't do it:** exercise is great for tiring yourself out, but try to avoid doing anything really vigorous too close to sleep. The same goes for stimulants: drinking caffeine and smoking too close to bedtime will disrupt your sleep cycle.

5   **Put your phone down:** there have been numerous reports that suggest that the blue light emitted from phones and computers can disturb sleep. Science aside, does anyone really find scrolling through other people's social media updates relaxing in that half hour before shutting your eyes for the night? Try swapping your tech for a book, and see what a difference it makes.

6   **Get some assistance:** try Sleepio, an app that's designed
    to help adults with sleep problems and is available on the
    NHS and Apple's App Store.

First aid kit: making your own

As the saying goes, accidents happen. And everyone should
have a basic first aid kit in their home (and in their car, if you
have one) to help deal with them when they do. Here's what it
could include:

- Plasters, in various shapes and sizes
- Sterile pads, wound dressings, and eye dressings
- Triangular bandages (which can also be used as slings) and
  rolled bandages
- Safety pins, scissors, tweezers, and medical tape
- Disposable gloves and face shields (for giving rescue
  breaths if you have been trained in CPR)
- Alcohol-free cleansing wipes
- Thermometer
- Painkillers and antihistamine tablets (always read guidance
  on the packaging when administering medicines)
- Antiseptic cream and skin-rash cream
- Eye-wash and an eye bath

You can also buy ready-made first aid kits and first aid
guidance from high-street pharmacies or organisations such as
St John's Ambulance.

Feel better, in a month — from an actual doctor

So, you think you're living your best life (aside from a take-away now and again), but you still feel rubbish? There's some simple stuff you can do to improve your lifestyle, according to GP Dr Dan Bernstein:

1. CUT DOWN ON BOOZE

'People often use alcohol to disinhibit themselves or to cope with difficult stuff. When you're drunk, it causes a transient euphoria for most people — although not everyone — but it's actually a depressant. In my world, where we treat depression, giving people anti-depressants when they're frequently drinking alcohol usually doesn't work. So although alcohol might provide short-term euphoria, many people will become depressed because of it. It can certainly relax people who are tense or stressed, providing a temporary relief from anxiety, but there are lots of drugs that can provide temporary relief from anxiety that we don't recommend because of the side-effects, and alcohol is one of them.'

2. SLEEP, BETTER

'As important as cutting down on booze is making sure you get enough sleep. If you're going to bed while under the influence of alcohol, you're not going to get good quality sleep. You don't get regenerative sleep, so you'll wake up feeling rubbish and you may as well not have slept. Having insufficient, or poor quality, sleep on occasion might be manageable, especially if you've got time to go to bed early for the next couple of nights, but doing so regularly will not help you feel well.'

3. DO SOME EXERCISE

'A small amount of daily exercise is really important. I normally recommend that people try to make exercise part of their daily routine — treat it like you treat dinner; it's part of your day, you'll mostly have it, sometimes you'll skip it, because sometimes you skip dinner and that's okay.

But if your aim is that you'll go swimming on a Sunday morning and a Wednesday evening, you'll probably only end up going about five or six times a month. It's much more likely to be effective if you can make the lifestyle change to prioritise exercise. That might mean you decide to walk or cycle to work rather than get public transport. Or get off the bus a couple of stops earlier so you can walk home, or get up half an hour earlier and do some sit-ups in your room before you have a shower and get dressed, or go to the gym at lunchtime in the office.

It doesn't have to be a long session — 20–30 minutes a day is still great.'

4. DITCH THE CIGARETTES

'Anyone who knows anyone who has stopped smoking will know that the quitter feels better really quite quickly. In just a few weeks you'll notice the difference. People say, "I didn't realise I couldn't breathe properly" or "I didn't realise I couldn't taste my food, I didn't realise I couldn't smell the flowers." And of course, there's the cost difference it makes to your wallet — it could pay for your gym membership.'

5. TRY TO UNWIND

'Making time for yourself, and not feeling like you have to accept every party invitation or work demand or family commitment, is really important. This could mean playing sport or going to the pub with friends you don't see very often, but it might just be having an evening of pampering yourself. People who are stressed out get physically tense; they get headaches partly because they frown, they get shoulder and neck aches because they hunch their shoulders. Trying to think about physically relaxing your muscles is a really helpful thing to do. That includes improving your posture at your desk and how you carry your bag on the bus.'

Respecting your elders? You might want to listen to them, too

One fundamental element of the circle of life is that, no matter how old or far away their children are, parents will offer up sage and learned advice (drinking is bad for you, you'll regret that tattoo, wash your hands after EVERYTHING), and we, the children, will go straight ahead and ignore it. But is it worth taking notes once in a while? Over to Dr Bernstein to challenge some received wisdom:

SHOULD YOU ALWAYS LIFT FROM THE KNEES?

'Bending from the knees, definitely, and that incorporates lifting. I see people whose backs have gone from doing up a shoelace or picking up a pen. If you're bent forward and you stand up — not even lifting anything — you're still lifting two-thirds of your body from your lumbar spine, so doing that is going to be a big strain. If you're an 80kg bloke, you're going to be lifting 50kg — that's two and a half suitcases. So always bend your knees to do your shoelace up; it's a habit; once you get used to it, it's very easy.'

DON'T WORK FROM A LAPTOP IN BED?

'For long periods of time, laptops are a bad idea; being in bed probably accentuates the problem. Because the keys are all cramped together, you tend to have your shoulders hunched, your head down, and your wrist bent outwards in the direction of your little fingers. Doing that at your desk or on your lap is where a lot of people's repetitive strain injury (RSI) comes from. Everyone should have their keyboard at a height that doesn't involve them hunching their shoulders, and their screen at a different height that doesn't involve them bending their neck forward, which is why desktops are good. And most people should have some kind of wrist support, an inch or two off the desk, so their wrists don't have to be cocked upwards; they should be in a natural position.'

STRETCH BEFORE YOU EXERCISE?

'Absolutely, and more so as you get older. During their student years, most people get away with not really doing it very much, but when they try to take up five-aside football or netball when they're 30 and do themselves an injury, they don't understand why. Stretching and warming up are really important if you're going to do stressful stuff — if you're going to kick a ball, if you're going to change direction a lot. If you're going for a run, starting off with a gentle jog is enough.'

DON'T GO SWIMMING ON A FULL STOMACH?

'It's a physiological fact that after you eat your body wants to send blood to your gut to digest food. If you go swimming or running or anything like that, your body wants to send blood to your muscles to do the swimming or the running, so it can't really do the digestion very well. It's not dangerous — you're not going to drown — you just might not digest your food very well.'

DON'T SIT TOO CLOSE TO THE SCREEN?

'I think the myth was that this would make you need glasses. It certainly can cause eye-strain, particularly for adults. To be focusing on something very close up for a long time causes eye-strain and headaches. But it won't make your vision go.'

SCRATCH YOUR SKIN WITH YOUR PALM, NOT YOUR NAILS?

'Definitely. Rubbing or perhaps slapping an itch is better than scratching it. When you scratch your skin, you release more of the chemicals which cause the itch, so it often creates a vicious cycle.'

SQUEEZING SPOTS WILL MAKE THEM SCAR?

'It's certainly true that acne can scar, but I don't think it's because people are squeezing them. Some people who really aggressively squeeze spots can of course cause more damage to their skin with their fingernails, and that can increase the risk of scarring.'

WILL WEARING A VEST HELP PREVENT ME CATCHING A COLD?

'Short answer: No.

Long and more interesting answer: It's known that colds are more common in cold weather, but the reasons why aren't entirely clear. To get a cold, your nose has to be exposed to a virus that has to reproduce enough to take a hold before your immune system defeats it. In cold weather, we're more likely to spend time in enclosed places with sneezers and coughers, all exposing us to the virus. And we know that rhinoviruses (the main cold virus) replicate better in a mouse's nose cells if the nose cells themselves are colder, possibly because of changes in the way the immune system works in the nose cells when they're cold. This hasn't been proven in humans as far as I know, and unless your vest is warming up your nose, it's not going to help.

The vest just makes it a bit easier to maintain your normal body temperature. If you're chronically cold (e.g. you can't afford heating), then a vest is definitely a good idea.'

TILT YOUR HEAD BACK AND SQUEEZE TO STOP A NOSEBLEED?

'Definitely squeeze, but tilting is less important. You squeeze just below the bony bit, and it should be firm enough to be a bit uncomfortable, and hold it there for a good 10–20 minutes until it properly clots — don't keep checking if it is still bleeding because the whole process will have to start again!'

How do you actually know when you're ill enough to stay home?

When you were younger, there was always a grown-up who could tell you whether you were ill enough to stay on the sofa all day drinking hot chocolate and watching *ThunderCats* on VHS — and write you a sick-note to prove it. Now, that grown-up is you. Congratulations! But how do you know when you're actually ill enough to call in sick?

Your body is a smart machine. If you're feeling so under the weather that you can't do your job properly, there's no point having a pity party at your desk while everyone else avoids you, annoyed that you've brought your delightful germs into the office. Still not sure when yuck is yucky enough? Here's a different kind of note from Dr Bernstein:

'It depends on what you do and your physical environment. If you're a builder and you're climbing up some scaffolding, it really matters if you're a bit dizzy. But if you do marketing and you can work on your computer from home, then it might matter less. If you're travelling around a lot between meetings, that might influence how much you can cope with illness, but if you're sat in your office that might be fine.

As a rule of thumb, if you can't do your job 100% you have to think about what percentage is acceptable. If you have a critical job, or if making a misjudgement might lose your company a million quid, then going into work probably isn't smart. But if your job isn't quite so critical, then 90% is fine.

If you actually have a temperature — and people should

really have a thermometer at home if they can afford one — you shouldn't be going to work. If you have really important stuff to do and you can do it at home, just do the really important stuff and not the full day's work — log off again and set your out-of-office.

If you're coming down with something, you might find that you are really low on energy. Even if it is "just a virus", it can be temporarily quite disabling and come with some significant symptoms. Sometimes you've just got a cold, and you feel okay, you've just got a bit of a bunged-up head. But sometimes, even if it's "just a virus", you can be achy all over or really run down or tired; that's okay, it's legitimate.

You have to recognise that when your body is trying to get over an illness, it needs more energy than it does the rest of the time. So, you definitely should be making sure you cut out smoking and alcohol, which will impair your immune system's function, and you should be getting enough sleep, because you've got a lot less reserve to cope with little sleep. For many people, part of that is going to be not going to work.'

And if you *do* need to call in sick, do it properly. Most companies write this stuff into your contract and you need to stick to policy — usually, that means letting your line manager know by telephone that you aren't well enough to be there shortly after the working day begins. (So, if you are — *shhhh* — pulling a sicky, you're going to need to practise that snotty-nose impression before you start dialling.)

Do I still get paid when I'm off sick?

As with most employment questions (aside from whether you actually have to do any work — that's always a yes), this depends on individual company policy and the type of work you do.

In most cases, you can be off sick for up to seven days in a row (including weekends) without being asked to prove that you're medically unfit for work. You may be asked to fill in a form when you return (known as self-certification) to confirm that you've been absent due to illness. If you are very unwell and you need more than those seven days away, you'll likely be asked for a 'fit note' (or Statement of Fitness for Work) which can be signed by your GP — or, if you've been treated in hospital, your doctor there.

The level of pay you then receive will depend on your contractual arrangements. At a basic level, most workers are entitled to statutory sick pay (SSP), around £90 a week for up to 28 weeks. You'll get this if:

- You've already started your job (i.e. your contract has begun)
- Your weekly earnings are above the threshold specified on the gov.uk website
- You've been sick for four or more days in a row
- You're eligible to receive SSP — a list of criteria can be found on the gov.uk website
- You follow those important company guidelines we just talked about

Some employers will actually pay more than the SSP (legally they cannot pay any less), depending on their own policy. And if you're an agency worker or on a zero hours contract, you should be entitled to SSP, too. Speak to your employer — if they say no, ask them to explain why, or talk to your union if you are in one.

What kind of illness should I actually worry about? (Because the internet says everything!)

In this magnificent digital age, it's as quick and easy to find out the late-night opening hours of your local corner shop or how closely related you are to Kevin Bacon as it is to ask the internet why the tickly cough you've had for weeks won't shift. And, if you believe what you read at the top of those search results, it's even easier to fly into a blind panic because your time is QUITE OBVIOUSLY UP.

The thing is, it's very important to pay attention to your health, and there are some things you need to take seriously. Dr Bernstein says:

'Don't necessarily worry, but seek advice, if you experience any of the following:

- Breathing becoming fast, difficult, or painful
- Unintentional weight loss
- Bleeding from almost anywhere you shouldn't be
- Double vision, loss of vision, sudden blurring of vision, eye pain (as opposed to discomfort)
- Any symptom that is getting progressively worse — an increasing headache, a growing lump

- Chest pain brought on by physical exertion
- Unexplained, persistent vomiting
- Weakness on one side of the body or face
- A mole that is changing in appearance or sensation
- Confusion or disorientation
- Drowsiness (more than just being tired — drowsiness is finding it hard to stay awake, or being unrousable)
- Hallucinations
- Feeling suicidal or thinking about harming yourself
- Pain that wakes you from sleep

While all of the above can be caused by serious conditions, they can often be explained by non-serious conditions, too. Conversely, other common symptoms (such as pain, itching, numbness, coughing, fatigue, fever) are usually not down to anything serious — but if they are persistent, or if they are severe enough to be affecting your work or social life, they too warrant a chat with your GP.'

This is by no means an exhaustive list, and if you're worried about anything to do with your health or wellbeing, you should check with a professional medical practitioner or call NHS 111 for the right way to proceed.

How to manage your workload/time/obligations around appointments

So, you've waited two hours (or two months) to get an appointment and finally, you're in! But the only thing they can offer you is 2pm on a Tuesday afternoon which is, of course, right in the middle of the working day and the same time as your weekly team meeting. How do you react?

A) NOT A CHANCE

Don't give up! Ask if there are any alternative appointments. If not, find out what the waiting time is for a more convenient time slot. If you're on a waiting list (i.e. to see a specialist) you won't have to join the waiting list again, but you might have to hold on for a little while longer.

B) DEFINITELY MAYBE

If you think it's doable but aren't sure, now's the time to speak to your boss. Place that appointment time on hold, if you can, and come up with a plan to work around taking time out of the office. Can you come in an hour early or work late? Is there anything you can do from home?

C) I'LL TAKE IT!

There's absolutely nothing wrong with telling your boss that there's a time in the week that you need to be out of office, or a regular appointment you need to attend. But it's helpful to go into this with a plan on how you can work around it together. Full disclosure: Kat was so nervous about telling her then-boss about her first round of cognitive behavioural therapy that she lied and said she was going to physiotherapy appointments. The next time, she told her new boss where she was actually going. Both reacted the same way — with understanding. She thinks the latter actually hugged her.

How to get mental-health support if you think you need it

Managing your mental health — Kat's story

'In my early twenties, I landed what should have been my dream first job. For the first time, I was finally able to live off my wages instead of other people's kindness, pay rent on a small room in a small flat, and occasionally buy lunch instead of packing it the night before. I should have lived and loved every minute of that little success. Instead, I found myself unexpectedly under a deep and disastrous black cloud, which chucked down anxiety, obsessive compulsive disorder, and depression in one torrid and unrelenting storm.

Only I didn't know my diagnosis then, so rather than explaining things to my bosses and asking for help, I stuck out my job until I simply couldn't any longer — convinced I wasn't cut out for it, and sure I'd made all the wrong decisions.

I quit, and tried two other jobs, both abandoned in the space of three months. I went freelance, with no plan, and finally my family and friends intervened. First, to get me to talk to a doctor, and then into the process of seeking professional help.

What I learned then was that mental-health problems can be so severe that they'll throw your life into disarray. But they're also more common than you might think, and, if you're suffering, there is help — excellent, accessible help — out there.'

Imagine you want to go on holiday. You know where (let's say Lisbon — lovely!), and you've got a good idea what kind of time you want to have (relaxing, lots of wine and custard tarts). But before you arrive and start making the most of it, you need to decide who you're going with, find the dates, book the time off work, choose a hotel, get some cheap flights, buy your travel insurance, pack ... the process sounds exhausting. Still, it's worth it though, right?

While seeking mental-health support is clearly not a holiday, it is so, so worth the effort. Getting to your first appointment doesn't have to be daunting; here are the two simplest routes to getting help:

THROUGH THE NHS

Depending on what your mental-health condition is and where you live, there will be different routes to getting yourself referred for help. In Scotland, Wales, and Northern Ireland, you are advised to make a visit to your GP the first port of call. In England, you'll either need a referral from your GP or in some cases you can fill in a self-referral form yourself without needing to see a doctor first.

To find out which applies to you, you can use the NHS postcode tool (if you live in England) — this time for mental-health services — which will direct you to services in your area and explain how to access them. Alternatively, you can ring your GP surgery and ask the receptionist about local organisations, and if you will require a doctor to refer you.

Once you are referred to a service, in many cases, you will receive a phone call from a trained professional to establish what help you require. This is essentially triage (that bit in A&E before you see a doctor) and it can take a while to talk through all their questions, so if you've scheduled the call during your work day, it's worth making sure you have somewhere quiet and private you can go and sit for half an hour or so.

Once they've established what help you need and how urgently you need it, you'll be put on a waiting list. As with most NHS services, the more flexible you can be on appointment time and location, the more chance you'll have of moving up that list quickly. Remember to ask how long they expect you'll be waiting to see someone — if this is, say, two months, make a note in your diary to call them back two months from then if they haven't yet been in touch.

GOING PRIVATE

There are plenty of reasons seeking private healthcare could be a good idea: you want complete control over who, how, and where you get help; you want to get seen quickly; or maybe you'd just prefer to visit a private clinic. But there's also one big reason why it might not be right for you — the cost. However, if you do have the funds or are covered by health insurance (more on that later), here's how to get help this way:

1   **Find a service in your area:** you can pay a visit to
      your NHS GP and ask them for their own private
      recommendations; or, for private therapy and counselling,
      the British Association of Counselling and Psychotherapy
      have a simple search tool which organises therapists by area,
      your reason for seeking help, and their kind of approach.

2 **Decide which options seem right for you:** look at price
   lists. Some therapists will have a sliding pay scale dependent
   on circumstances (if you earn a low wage, for example), and
   it's worth asking if that might apply to you.

3 **Contact a few who seem like a good fit:** they may have a
   form for you to fill out, or you might need to drop them an
   email to briefly explain why you're getting in touch.

4 **Schedule some initial meetings:** it's important that
   whoever you're engaging in helping you is the right fit, and
   that might not be the first person you meet. There may be a
   fee for an introductory session, so ask about costs upfront.

Different types of psychological (IAPT) therapies: a glossary

Depending on your mental-health diagnosis, there are
different types of help available. Common NHS-approved
therapies include:

Brief dynamic interpersonal therapy (DIT): a short
face-to-face therapy designed to explore things that have
happened in the past and may still be having an effect on
you today.

Cognitive behavioural therapy (CBT): a talking therapy
commonly used to treat anxiety, depression, obsessive
compulsive disorder, and eating disorders (amongst
others), it targets unhelpful behavioural or thinking patterns.

Counselling for depression: talking therapy either in
person, in a group, on the phone, by email, or online, to help

people to process their thoughts, feelings, and emotions.

Eye movement desensitisation and reprocessing therapy (EMDR): a therapy for people suffering from traumas, designed to change the emotions involved with disturbing memories or feelings.

Interpersonal psychotherapy (IPT): this therapy focuses on how relationships affect us and our mental health, and how they too can be affected by mental health.

WHO CAN YOU GO TO IF YOU'RE NOT READY TO TALK TO FRIENDS OR FAMILY?

Let's be honest, talking to your nearest and dearest about serious things (money, whose turn it is to do the washing up) can be uncomfortable at the best of times. If you're not ready to add 'mental health' to that list just yet, no sweat. There are other ways you can begin to share and understand what you're going through.

MIND, the mental-health charity, is a good place to start. Their online resources include a 'What do I need help with right now?' section, designed to help you understand what you're going through and how to help yourself cope, with stories about what other people have been through.

The Samaritans are a charity with free phonelines open 24/7, 365 days a year (just call 116 123 from any phone, in England, Scotland, Wales, and Ireland). Speaking to them is confidential, and they are there to help anyone struggling. You can also email or write to them, or visit a branch.

The NHS offers access to some online resources for mental-health therapy (usually through a referral or with a subscription), including SilverCloud, Big White Wall, Fear Fighter, and Ieso Digital Health.

If you need to speak to a doctor urgently, here's how:

1 **Emergency Services:** the NHS treat mental-health emergencies in the same way as physical ones. Depending on how quickly you require help, you can call 999 (an emergency), NHS 111 (urgent care), or visit your local A&E.

2 **Your GP:** just as you would book an emergency doctor's appointment for physical care, you can do this for your mental health, too.

... AND HOW TO EXPLAIN TO THEM WHAT YOU'RE GOING THROUGH WHEN YOU ARE

Kat's story continued ...

'In my case, my mum gently told me that she and my dad were worried that I was sad all the time. That was enough to trigger me sobbing on her for an hour (in a cafe ... during my lunch break) while trying to explain how I was feeling. She was my ally, helping me explain things to my brother, who took me to my GP the next week, and travelling up to London to hold my hand as I told my two closest friends what I was going through. They were understanding, too — and, although they may not admit it, I think a bit relieved.'

But there's never going to be a simple, one-size-fits-all answer. Here are how some other people have opened up:

Talking about mental health

'People around me had noticed something was wrong, but I shut myself off and refused to talk about it until a close friend trapped me in an Indian restaurant, stuffed me with cocktails, and refused to take "Stop asking. I'm fine." for an answer. We worked out an action plan together, and it was only after that evening that I told my partner I had decided I needed to see a therapist. I still haven't told my parents and I'm not sure I will just yet — they have a military background, and mental health isn't an easy topic at home. Maybe when I'm further along with my sessions and have the strength to face it.'

'I was coming to the end of one round of counselling and cognitive behavioural therapy when I met my boyfriend, and after a few weeks of "Oh, I can't have a late one tonight because I have an early 'meeting' in the morning", I knew I needed to explain where I was actually going at 7.30am on Wednesdays. I was petrified that he'd judge me or fancy me less, and ended up telling him as we were about to go to sleep one night, in a pitch-black room, so he couldn't see me. But he was brilliantly supportive, and has been ever since.'

'It was easier for me to speak about than I am sure it is for most, as both my mother and sister had also gone through something similar. Me and my sister both started to go to therapy at around the same time, and she got hers through her work, which I thought was really great.'

'The biggest mistake I made was to try and pretend to myself that the internal struggles I was facing were something I could deal with on my own, despite not understanding what it was I was dealing with or why. Telling my family and best friends, and going to see a doctor, were the best decisions I have ever made. I realised I wasn't abnormal, and didn't need to try to get by on my own, or hide things to stop people seeing that something was wrong. Mental health isn't anything to be ashamed of and it affects most people in some shape or form. Understanding why you feel the way you do, and your significant others understanding that too, is hugely empowering, and was the first step to me taking control back over my life.'

NAVIGATING MENTAL HEALTH AT WORK (OR HOW THE HELL DO YOU TELL YOUR BOSS?)

Even if you have a friendly and honest relationship with your line manager about most things (sleeping through your alarm, hangovers, needing a tampon), you may still find talking to them about the inner workings of your mind that bit too tricky.

There's nothing to say you have to speak to someone within your company, but if you feel like your mental health is affecting your work life and do want to have that conversation, here are some things to think about beforehand:

1 **What's the company approach:** more and more organisations are beginning to actively address their own

policies around employee mental health, which you'll be able to find in your HR resources at work. Reading this should give you a good steer on how you can ask your manager to support you.

2 **What you need from them:** if you can pinpoint areas of your role that are making your mental health worse and what your company could do to make these more manageable, jot down some practical solutions. (MIND have Wellness Action Plans that you can fill out and take in as a guide.) If you're not sure, ask your boss what they think they could do to help you.

3 **What you want to say, and to whom:** your manager might be the obvious person to speak to, but if that's not an option you're comfortable with, speak to someone in HR. You can tell them as much or little as you like; it's your choice. It's also your choice who they share the information with.

4 **When you want to talk:** if you have regular one-to-ones with your boss in a private setting, think about raising your concerns during that time together. If you are speaking to HR instead, ask for a meeting in a space out of the way from your colleagues (darn those glass-walled meeting rooms!) so you have some breathing space.

NB: Some mental-health issues are treated as disabilities under the 2010 Equality Act, which means that you can't be discriminated against for any 'physical or mental impairment that has a "substantial" and "long-term" negative effect on your ability to do normal daily activities'. You can find out more about the conditions that might be treated as a disability on the Citizen's Advice website.

HEALTH INSURANCE: WHAT'S THE DEAL?

If you have health insurance through work, now's the time to look into it. Read the policy (if you don't have it to hand *because who actually keeps this stuff*, ask the HR department for a copy); you may find that it will cover the cost of therapy sessions or mental-health appointments.

If you don't get health insurance through work, your company may have an Employee Assistance Programme. These are schemes that can offer employees access to free and confidential care. Again, you'll need to ask, if you haven't already been made aware that something like this is in place.

If there's no such scheme at your workplace, you might want to consider taking out health insurance yourself. The main reason many people don't is funds, or lack thereof — depending on what you want your health insurance to cover, you could find yourself looking at big premiums (how much you'll pay for the policy). And for all its benefits (you'll likely get seen quicker if you're covered privately, you may be entitled to extra health checks), there's still the risk that you won't be covered for pre-existing or longer-term conditions — which, under the NHS, you can be seen for. Of course, if you do decide to go for it, you should use the same comparison tactics as outlined in the Finance section of this book like the savvy adult you are.

HOW TO PRACTICE SELF-CARE

Beyond therapy, there are now more ways than ever to help you take care of your mental health in daily life. This could include practising mindfulness and meditation through classes or apps, reading self-help books, unwinding with colouring books, making time for activities that make you feel calmer — whether it's keeping a journal or spending some time with someone you trust. Whatever works for you.

DIY SOS

Nothing makes you feel more like a five-year-old pretending to be a grown-up than something Going Wrong At Home. You sleepily turn on the hot tap to wash your face and the water is Arctic. There's suddenly a leak in the roof. You use the loo and it refuses to flush ... Or maybe you impulse buy a bunch of assorted tat, get home, realise you have no shelves to put them on, and suddenly you're thinking that you should really have paid more attention to DT classes in school.

Sure, if you're renting you can call out the landlord, and some things will require a specialist. But landlords tend to take their sweet time, specialists are expensive, and some basic problems are easy to fix yourself. Here, expert plumber Ben Margulies of London firm BeeXpress Plumbing and Heating explains how:

'Before we start, you'll need the following equipment in your DIY toolkit:

- A long flat-head (where the tip is just one straight line) and cross-head (where the tip is X-shaped) screwdriver

(a handy tip for screwdriving: to tighten or loosen
remember the rhyme, "righty tighty, lefty loosey")

- A very thin, short screwdriver (think tightening up
  a pair of glasses)
- A radiator vent key
- A plunger
- Bucket
- Pliers
- Gloves (plunging can get messy …)
- WD-40 lubricant
- Spirit level
- Hammer
- Drill (for advanced DIYers)

You should find everything at a local household store
(those ones on the high street with buckets, stools, and
wrapping papers spilling out onto the pavement), or a super-
store like Homebase or B&Q.'

BEN'S TIPS ON HOW TO:

**Unblock a toilet (because it's nice to start with the sexy
jobs):** 'You'll need to push a plunger into the loo, making
sure it's made a seal all around the drain opening. Pump
the plunger handle gently up and down for a few goes;
a not-too-serious blockage should come clear. Don't be
rough, or you could literally be in the shit. If that doesn't
work, you might need to use a chemical drain cleaner,
which you can pick up in any supermarket. Check it's
okay with the material your toilet is made of (some aren't

compatible with porcelain, for example), and flush lots of times afterwards to check all is well.'

Unblock a sink: 'You could first have a go at sticking an unwound coat hanger down the plug-hole in case a hairball or something similar is blocking the sink — but please be careful as you don't want to get the hanger caught down the plug-hole. If that doesn't work, put a plunger over the drain and block off the overflow (that's the hole above the drain that excess water can flow into) by holding a damp towel over it. Gently push up and down on the handle of the plunger about five times to release the blockage. If all is well, the sink should drain. Run hot water through it for a few minutes to clear it entirely. If that doesn't work, try pouring a few teaspoons of baking soda down the plug-hole, followed by a cup of white vinegar. Or you could try a chemical drain cleaner, which you can get at the supermarket. If none of that works, you might need to remove the U-bend — see below.'

Recover lost jewellery dropped down the sink: 'Turn off the taps ASAP to stop the valuable being pushed further along. If you can't see it anywhere near the plug, or caught in the sink apparatus, you'll need to tackle the U-bend, which is the U-shaped pipe under the sink — in some cases, this might be at the back of a cupboard. This is officially called the 'trap' because it traps water to stop the smells coming back from the sewers — call it a trap when speaking to the plumber and he'll think you know what you're on about. Put a bucket under the U-bend, use a pair of pliers to loosen the nuts (large plastic rings) attaching it to the pipes on either side, and gently pull it down into the bucket (watch out, it'll be chocka with dirty water). Hopefully you'll find your lost treasure in this grimy water — gloves are recommended. Then re-fix the U-bend by hand and/or with the pliers. Be careful while you're doing this — make sure you don't 'cross thread' the nuts — this is when you screw something at a slight angle and the parts aren't lined up. You'll know you're doing this if it feels really tight even though you've not completed one turn of the nut, and you also might see bits of plastic shredding off the U-bend. You also need to make sure the 'washers' are in position — these are the flat rings placed between two joining surfaces like a nut and a bolt. Once you've finished, make sure that the nuts are watertight, but not so tight that they'll crack the pipes.'

Turn the water off at the mains: 'This can be a good starting-point when you have a suspected leak. The inside stop valve is usually under the kitchen sink, but if it's not there, check in an airing cupboard or under the floorboards near the front door. The valve looks like a metal tap, usually made of brass. Turning it clockwise will close it, first slowing the amount of water passing through the pipes, then stopping it altogether after a few minutes. If the valve is stuck, try spraying some WD-40 on it. To turn your water back on, just turn the valve anti-clockwise.'

Repair a leaky tap: 'Dripping taps could mean one of two things: 1) You need to replace the cartridge — the filter inside the tap, or 2) You need to replace the washers.

To do either, turn off the water, either from the water mains or the isolation valves that are often under the taps. (Isolation valves are small silver tubes, with what looks like a line-indented screw at the end. If the line is parallel with the arrow on the valve, then water will flow through the pipe, so turning the line 90 degrees with a flathead screwdriver so that it's perpendicular to the arrow will turn off the water). Turn the taps on to drain any water lingering in the pipes.

Next, you need to access the screw inside the tap handle. It might be obvious, or could be hidden under a cover. Unscrew the tap head to reveal the valve.

Taps generally have either washers or ceramic disc cartridges — and the main problems depend on the type of tap. If you can turn the tap and rotate the handle through one or more turns, it is most likely a rubber washer design. In this case, the old washer can be easily removed — flick off the old one with a screwdriver, make sure the new washers are the right size, slide one on, and then reassemble the tap.

If the tap handle only rotates through a quarter of a turn, it will be a ceramic disc cartridge. Pull out the cartridge — the gold mechanism with one thin end — using pliers. Then take it into a DIY store to buy an exact replacement.

Turn the water back on and put the tap on, slowly, to check there are no more leaks.' (See our notes at the back of the book for more advice.)

Tighten up a loose toilet seat: 'Pop the chrome cap that's under the seat (usually at the back) off, get a screwdriver and tighten the screws up, then replace the cap.'

Bleeding a radiator: 'If your radiator is hot at the top and cold at the bottom, it's probably due to the dreaded sludge — you'll need to call a plumber. But if the bottom of the radiator is hot and the top is cold, it's likely that air is stuck in the radiator, which you can tackle by bleeding (or 'venting') it. Venting a radiator can be easy. You need to turn off the heating, then grab an old rag and a vent key. First, find the vent point, which will be at the top on either the right- or left-hand side of the radiator — usually either a slot for a screwdriver or a square or triangular hole. You'll need a vent key from a DIY store (or a screwdriver if applicable) which fits the hole snugly. Hold the rag next to the vent point. Turn the key slightly, until you can hear air whistling through, then don't turn it any further. Once water starts bubbling out onto the cleverly positioned rag, turn the key in the other direction to close the vent. If you have a pressurised system like a combi boiler or a system boiler you will need to top up the pressure again — try YouTube or your boiler manual for instructions on how to do this.'

Protect yourself from Carbon Monoxide poisoning:
'Carbon Monoxide is an odourless, colourless gas — it's likely that you won't know if there's a CO leak, as the symptoms of poisoning are similar to the flu, and unnoticeable if you're asleep. You might have a headache and

feel tired, go to bed, and then simply not wake up the next morning. So you can understand why it's important that you get yourself a CO alarm — and definitely not one of the (rubbish) ones that stick on the wall and change colour — you need a loud alarm. You can get a good quality one for around £35 — I recommend Honeywell. Put the alarm in the same room as your boiler or gas fire. A few years ago, I did a boiler service and insisted they bought a Carbon Monoxide detector. About six months later I received this text from the homeowner: "Ben I just wanted to call you quickly to say thanks. Without you insisting that we get a Carbon Monoxide detector the fire brigade has said we wouldn't have woken up this morning. So thanks for saving me, my wife, my 2 boys and my baby daughter.'"

And some more DIY ideas ... How to:

PAINT A ROOM

Start by getting hold of a large paintbrush, a roller, a pole for rolling paint onto the ceiling, a paint tray, and a small brush for detailed work.

Make sure you've bought enough paint — look at the manufacturer's guidelines on the back of the pot for how many metres it will cover. Buying enough paint to decorate an average-sized living room, including the ceiling, shouldn't cost much more than £40. You can also get a good set of paintbrushes for £10–15.

Remove as much furniture as you can, and cover up anything you can't take out using dustsheets or old bedsheets.

Fill any holes in the walls with filler, sand down any bumps or imperfections. It can be a good idea to clean the walls using sugar soap — which removes old paint and marks. If there has been a leak on the walls in the past, or smokers lived in the property and the smoke has left stains, consider also using a stain-blocker before painting. Without this treatment stains will bleed through most paints however many layers you slap on.

If painting the whole room, start with the ceiling, then move on to the walls. Next up are doors, skirting, and windows — these woodwork areas will need a different kind of paint, so choose between a gloss, eggshell, or satinwood. If possible, try to tackle the windows at the start of a day, so that they can be left open to dry thoroughly without sticking, before closing them at night. Don't forget the radiators — left unpainted, they often end up looking grubby in a freshly painted room — and will need a specialist radiator or metal paint.

For the ceiling, use a roller on an extension pole dipped into a tray full of paint, but don't overload the roller. Finish the edges using a brush, overlapped onto the wall if they are being painted the same colour.

Next, use a roller to vertically paint all walls, finishing off the corners with a brush.

When painting skirting boards or woodwork, use the brush slowly to create as straight and smooth an edge as possible.

Lightly sand down window-sills then thoroughly wipe them to remove all dust before painting. You'll get the neatest finish on windows if you first temporarily remove any parts — handles etc. — before you start to paint, but that depends on how exacting you're being. It's a good idea to use masking tape on the glass to avoid painting that — unless you're an extremely accurate paint handler! Paint the edges closest to the glass first, then work outwards towards the frame of the window.

For doors, again removing handles first makes it easier. Paint from the top down, and paint the edge of a door according to which room it faces when the door is open. Don't close until totally dry or it might stick!

PUT UP A SHELF

You'll need your shelf, brackets, a pencil, a spirit level, a hammer, a screwdriver, screws, and possibly rawl plugs (a plastic insert to help use a screw in a brittle material) and a drill.

The first step is to work out where you want your shelf to go by holding it, with the brackets, against the wall — you might need two people for this bit.

Make sure the shelf is horizontal using a spirit level.

Mark where the screw-holes on the brackets are on the wall with a pencil.

A very small shelf might only require a hammer and nails, but most will need you to drill a hole, plug it with a rawl plug, then screw in the brackets — you'll need to be aware of what the wall is made of so you can buy the correct rawl plugs.

Once both brackets are fitted, lay the shelf on top and secure it with screws from underneath.

READ YOUR METERS

Meters are used to measure how much power your household is using so that your providers know how much to bill you for. Most gas and electricity meters are now digital, so you just write down the numbers from left to right, ignoring any numbers in red.

If a meter is older and has dials, watch out, as each dial turns in the opposite direction to the one before it. Before you read a dial meter, check the direction of the dials so you know which arrows are looking where. Then read the dials from left to right. If the pointer is between two numbers, always take the lower number. And don't read the last dial on the right.

SORT OUT SQUEAKY FLOORBOARDS

Unless you've a resident mouse, a squeaky floorboard is generally caused by boards that have come loose over time and started rubbing against each other.

Often just shaking some talcum powder through the cracks is enough.

If that doesn't work, you may need to screw the boards down more securely using a drill or screwdriver.

FIX A TRIPPED FUSE

Find your main fuse box, which will be next to your electricity meter, usually in the main hallway of a house, often in a purpose-built cupboard.

Open the cover on the fuse box (also known as a consumer unit) to see which switches have tripped to the 'off' position, and flip them back to the 'on' position. There may be more than one switch, if so flip them all. If it happens again, it is probably being caused by a faulty appliance or circuit, so you'll either need to safely investigate further, or call in an expert.

DIY disasters — Lucy's story

'It can take time to work out how to do DIY jobs, so my advice is to practise on something other than your flat or house's walls before you start … I was really enthusiastic about trying DIY in my first flat. My dad's great at it, so I figured I would be too. I'd put up pictures all over the place, and sometimes the plaster was too weak and those nail holes would turn into, errr, rather larger chasms that I'd hide behind paintings. When I took them all down when moving out, some walls looked a bit like they'd been used as punchbags …'

How to build flatpack furniture and stay (mostly) sane

Even if you have zero DIY skills, flatpack furniture building is actually pretty easy — think of it as a giant grown-up jigsaw; take your time, study the instructions really carefully, and have a pint waiting at the end.

Having spent the past year assembling most of the items Ikea sells (yeah, we have really unique-looking homes), here's what we've learned:

1   Open the box, take everything out, and put all the screws and parts that are the same in little piles. Make sure you've got everything you need and only dump the packaging after you've checked, in case you need to take it back.

2   A £20 electric screwdriver with replaceable bits will be the best money you've ever spent. The freebie tools Ikea et al

provide often require the strength of a wrestler. An electric screwdriver will do this all for you. Avoid using a proper drill, as it can damage MDF.

3   Stare at each instruction panel for five whole minutes before proceeding. Look for the little details you might not notice until you've put a cupboard door on inside out. That tiny screw-hole casually visible in the right-hand corner? You need to pay attention to that.

4   If you are planning to customise your flatpack furniture (there are some great ideas for how to do this on the web), you will probably need to make any alterations — e.g. painting, adding colour slabs, before building.

DIY disasters that make us feel better about our own shortcomings

'When we did our first home DIY project — the kitchen — I hired a (distant) friend. I should have known it was a bad idea when he crashed his work van into a tree the night before work was to start ... He had to stay with us through the duration of the project, during which he became increasingly drunk, even getting a reputation at our local for being off his head ... His workmanship seemed to reflect his state of mind, and my unwillingness to assert myself meant he laid the floor marginally uneven. We've had years of tiles cracking every few months as a result.'

'There was a leak in my flat and, after weeks of trying to get the landlord to fix it, they finally said they would send someone out that day. Determined to educate myself on the source of the problem, I went up onto the roof to see if I could work out what was going on ... only to have a huge gust of wind blow the giant metal safety door off. And then one problem very swiftly became two ...'

Don't Google that emergency ... when should you really call a professional?

You might have mastered YouTube-led home repairs, and your flatmate's agreed to do all the cooking for the next three years after you successfully followed the above steps and retrieved her engagement ring from the U-bend ... But sometimes you really will need to call out an expert. Electricity and plumbing work can be dangerous, and 'having a go' at a serious job could both be risky and cost more in the long run. So when should you ask for help? The people who really know about that are the insurers — who are called in to deal with DIY disasters all the time. Anne Kirk from insurance firm Swinton Group has checked through their files of nightmare claims to warn about four jobs you should always leave to the pros. These are tasks that are a simple fix for a qualified professional, but which could be dangerous for an amateur to tackle, and could even invalidate your home insurance if you do. Over to Anne:

DON'T FIX A GAS LEAK

'If you smell gas in the house, don't try to handle the leak yourself. Turn off the gas at the meter if it's safe to do so — this will be a metal valve with a key-like shape sticking up at the top. Turn the handle so the lever is at 90 degrees to the upright gas pipe. Call the 24-hour Gas Emergency Services line on 0800 111 999. An operator will talk you through the next steps and send someone to you.

If it's safe, try to open any doors and windows to help the gas escape, and don't turn any lights off or on — using a light switch could spark an explosion.'

DON'T REMOVE ASBESTOS

'Any home built or renovated before 2000 will most likely have asbestos. Asbestos used to be put in place for insulating and fireproofing buildings, but can release dangerous fibres if disturbed or damaged — these can cause serious diseases if they're inhaled.

If you think there's asbestos in your home, you don't necessarily need to remove it, but you should check its condition from time to time to make sure it hasn't been damaged or started deteriorating. If you're planning to do any renovations, make sure you call someone trained in asbestos removal so this can be done safely and legally disposed of — it's classed as hazardous waste.

You can also ring the Environmental Health department at your local council for more advice.'

DON'T FIT A NEW BATH

'Jobs like fitting a new bath or shower are complex plumbing jobs and should be left to a qualified plumber. If you're not careful, you could be fined for breaking Water Regulations and could even be disconnected from the water supply if approved fittings aren't used. Save yourself the worry and get the professionals in.'

DON'T KNOCK DOWN ANY WALLS

'The idea of an open-plan living space is great, but there are a few things to consider before taking a sledgehammer to any walls around your house.

First of all, seek the advice of a structural engineer. If the wall you want to get rid of is load-bearing, which means it supports the upper level of your house, your home could be at risk of collapse if you knock it down. Load-bearing walls also often contain electrical wiring and plumbing within them which will need re-routing before you do anything.

Getting a qualified professional in to do a job like this is the best option, as it's their responsibility to make sure the work complies with all regulations. You'll also need to speak to your local council before starting any substantial building work like this — you might need to get Building Control's approval.'

Other times to ask an expert include:

If you've got low water pressure throughout the house, or you keep having to top up the boiler and you don't know why — call a plumber. You might have an obstruction in a pipe, or a hidden leak; ignoring the problem will just make the damage worse, and it can be really hard for an amateur to identify where an issue has started. Plus, one drip per second can waste as much as 3000 gallons of water a year.

If you have frozen pipes, you can try turning off the mains water and attempting to thaw the pipes yourself with a hairdryer, but if any have burst or cracked, you're going to need a plumber to replace that section. You'll also need to get a plumber in pronto if the toilet's blocked and the plunger isn't helping. This one is pretty urgent, as it might indicate a problem with the sewage line.

If circuit-breakers or fuses are often tripping, there could be a dangerous electrical fault or your circuits are overstretched — call an electrician.

If plug outlets, switches or other electrical-system surfaces feel warm, are blackening or rusting, or if a switch or outlet often gives a mild shock, you also need to call in an electrician.

And finally, if you've got an electricity problem anywhere wet like the kitchen or bathroom, definitely don't try to handle it yourself. GCSE physics dictates this one isn't worth the risk …

So, you need a good handyman/plumber/electrician…

… but you're worried about getting ripped off because they'll realise you're clueless when you don't know where your fuse box is. (Obviously, do work out where your fuse box is — see above for help.) But unless you're renting and have a responsible, hands-on landlord or managing agent, it's important to have some household gurus that you can trust. Here's how to find a great one:

1   Make a list of the jobs you want tackled. There are usually a few things once you think about it, and you'll get better

value hiring one pro for three hours than asking them to come back on several occasions to do lots of 20-minute jobs.

2 Try to find a personal recommendation. Ask local friends, neighbours, and family; or put a post on a community group on Facebook.

3 If that doesn't yield results, look up online reviews on sites like Yelp. Or check apps like TaskRabbit or Fantastic Services — you can see other people's reviews and pick, for example, between a cheaper, less experienced tradesman or a pricier pro.

4 Quiz a few to check they are adroit at all the tasks you want; then ask them for quotes.

5 Request references from clients who have hired them before, and ask about their qualifications — certain trades, such as electricians, need to meet minimum standards.

6 Watch out for scams. Never pay upfront: reputable firms will ask only for a deposit to pay for supplies; and avoid anyone who just knocks on your door or makes unsolicited phone calls.

7 Particularly for a bigger job, you'll want to get a full quote in writing. You should have an agreement setting out the details of the job and a timescale too.

8 Ask for a guarantee. A lot of tradesmen will guarantee their work, usually for one year, and they should also leave you with paperwork if any parts came with a warranty.

9 Inspect the finished work before paying to make sure that you are happy with it and that they have done everything you agreed on.

Planes, trains, and automobiles

A major realisation as to exactly how much of their lives your parents gave up for you comes at the point when you move out and their amazing chauffeuring services come to an end. Maybe Dad was always willing to collect you from late parties as a teen. Maybe Mum would always pick you up from uni at the end of term. Maybe they were always in charge of buying your train or plane tickets, and you didn't have to navigate the more-complicated-than-GCSEs minefield of apparently random timetables and fares. But now you're meant to be an adult. How do you easily, cheaply, safely get from A to B?

How to learn to drive

Red L-plates used to be the accessory everyone wanted for their seventeenth birthday. But packed roads, city living, environmental concerns, and the cost means a lot of us are postponing getting our licence — government figures for 2017 show the number of teenagers learning to drive fell by nearly 30% in a decade — until something like a new job, or having a baby demands you take sole control behind the wheel of two tons of metal. So how do you actually learn to drive nowadays?

First, there's admin. Say cheese at an unflatteringly lit photo-booth: you'll need a photo to apply for a provisional licence, which you can do up to three months before your seventeenth birthday, or any time after. Alongside the provisional licence application form, (available online and from some Post Offices), you'll need to send off the photo, along with ID (like your passport), details of your residential address(es) for the past three years, and your National Insurance number, to the government's licensing body, the DVLA. (Quick note on the photo front: instead of pricey and annoying photobooths, you can actually get photos for official purposes, such as your driving licence or passport, for a fiver just by uploading your own photo online at Paspic.)

Once you've got that provisional licence, you're allowed to hit the road — but only supervised by someone aged 21 or over who has held a full driving licence for at least three years, with L-plates and full insurance. (You have to have motor insurance to drive any car, except a professional instructor's.) You'll almost certainly want some professional lessons, at least at first. (And if you don't, you're insane! A car is a potential killing machine and will Matt from downstairs really be as good a teacher as a pro with a dual-control car?) Lessons cost about £25 an hour (more in central London, less in rural areas). The government recommends about 40 hours of lessons before you attempt the practical driving test, so you'll need about £1000 for tuition alone — but practising driving with a parent or friend will help you gain confidence.

Then there's the tests — yup, two parts: one theory-based, which you have to pass before you can book the second, practical test. The theory test is all based around the Highway Code — so the best way to pass it is to learn the Code and revise using online tests. During the test, you sit at a computer for a multiple-choice questionnaire lasting about an hour. Then there's the 'hazard perception' test — a bit like *Gran Turismo*, but you definitely want to approach it in a more measured way. You're shown a series of 14 clips of everyday roads and have to click the mouse when you spot a 'developing hazard'.

Once you've passed both parts of your theory test, the practical test looms. It kicks off with an eye check ('Can you read that number plate over there?'), then there are some vehicle safety questions, and finally there's a 40-minute drive where the examiner will ask you to do at least one of the classic manoeuvres, the 'reverse around a corner' (which you'll never do after passing), turning in the road, or parking.

And then what?

If you've passed your test, congratulations. But remember that new drivers are still far more likely to have accidents than experienced drivers. Road charity Brake points out that drivers aged 17–19 only make up 1.5% of UK licence holders, but are involved in 9% of fatal and serious crashes where they are the driver.

So, after you have passed your test, how can you actually become a good driver? Here's the lowdown from Richard Gladman, head of driving standards at the Institute of Advanced Motorists:

'Remember we have speed limits, not targets — in busy traffic, 20 mph (miles per hour) is often plenty. Slow down around schools and in residential areas. This may not be rocket science, but it's easily forgotten while running late on the morning commute. A 50-mile journey at 80 mph will save you at most six minutes compared to the same distance at 70 mph. Is it worth the stress and the extra fuel?

Dazzle from low sun is a factor in more crashes than dazzle from headlights. Keep your windscreen clean and don't put those sunglasses away just yet.

It is legal for motorcyclists to filter through traffic, so give them space and never try to deliberately block them. Check carefully for all types of cyclists before changing lanes.

When driving at night, familiar routes can pose totally different challenges, so make sure you are wide awake and looking out for pedestrians and cyclists in the gloom. Per mile driven, the risk of a crash is actually higher at night despite the quieter roads. Check your car lights: do a daily walk around to check all lights are working, and use a wall or garage door to check the rear lights if you are on your own. Changing a bulb on a modern car is often a garage-only job, so get it done before the police stop you and issue a ticket or repair notice.

One of the biggest night-time hazards is the dazzle caused by the bright light from oncoming motors. Dip your headlight when you meet other vehicles.

Carry a basic emergency kit — tools, torch, map, and a first aid kit, plus a fully charged mobile phone with the details of your breakdown cover.

Most crashes actually happen close to home, so ensure familiarity does not breed contempt by keeping your focus. Glancing away from the road ahead even for a few seconds can make you miss that vital clue of a dangerous situation developing.

Multi-tasking is a myth — even the shortest phone call or text is taking your attention away from the road, so talking on the phone while driving is a big "no". Even though you may have devices in place such as Bluetooth headsets or hands-free, these can be very distracting — if you can't stop yourself using the smartphone, put it in the boot!'

How to buy a car (without getting ripped off)

As you stand at the bus stop watching hundreds of toasty drivers roaring past, radio blaring, chocolate raisins quite probably sitting in their glove box, car ownership looks tempting. But be aware, cars swallow cash faster than a hipster sinks craft ale. There are alternative options to owning your own ride — car-club services like ZipCar and Enterprise Car Club, or lift-share sites like BlaBlaCar and Liftshare. Because buying the car is just the start, owning a motor means stumping up for:

1 **Car insurance:** a legal necessity. The average annual price is nearly £500 in the UK, according to the Association of British Insurers, but the younger and/or less experienced you are, the more you'll pay.
2 **Car tax:** this is free for very low-emission vehicles, then there are another 12 bands ranging from £10 a year to

£2000 for big gas-guzzlers. When you buy a car, the tax isn't transferred with the vehicle, so you have to tax it before you can use it.

3   **MOT:** the annual, obligatory-by-law test for all cars over three years old. The standard cost is around £55, and on top of that you'll have to pay for any repairs needed to pass.

4   **Fuel:** the bill obviously depends on how much you drive — and oil prices, and tax. But as a rough guide, a driver with an annual mileage of 12,500 will spend about £2300 a year on fuel. (Quick money-saving tip: use the PetrolPrices website or app to find the cheapest nearby fuel — on average, users of the website who fill up weekly save £240 a year.) Other regular costs might include parking permits if they apply where you live.

5   **Maintenance:** the RAC estimates that it's around £420 to service and repair a used car for a year.

6   **Breakdown cover:** not a legal requirement, but would you want to be stuck on the side of a motorway with no way to get home? Options stretch from budget £25-a-year deals which will tow your car to a nearby garage, to £150+ cover that will have your car picked up anywhere in Europe with a courtesy car to get you home. Use a comparison site to get the best deal.

HOW TO NAVIGATE THE CAR BUYING PROCESS

Walking into the average high-street showroom, it can feel like you've stepped into a tank of unfed sharks stuffed into Nylon suits. So be prepared. The first step is to research what you want from a car. Cost will probably be the biggest factor (unless you're after a Bugatti — the luxury brand recently revealed that their average customer has 42 other cars. WHAAT?). While it sounds obvious, note that second-hand cars are always MUCH cheaper than new cars — even if they're only a few months old. The average new car is advertised for £28,500, while a one-year-old motor with 10,000 miles on the clock is £21,000, according to MoneySavingExpert.

Don't focus only on the upfront price — also compare the running costs of different models (you'll find lists in magazines like *What Car?* and websites like Cap HPI). The running costs take into account fuel economy, tax, and insurance. Surveys of the cheapest cars to run in the UK flag up those like the Toyota Aygo, Peugeot 108, and Citroen C1 — basically, small cars with small engines. And when you're ready to look into nitty gritty details, there are motor reviews on sites like Carbuyer, Honest John, Top Gear, and Parkers.

Found the one you want? Once you've done the research, taken a test-drive (organised via a local dealership), and picked your top specifications (for Lucy, this was the colour; you're probably much savvier and know the eco-rating, engine type, and mileage you're after), it's time to blitz the phone.

Car buying is still pretty old-school; your objective is to ask as many dealers as you can for their lowest price for the exact car that you want. It's worth calling dealerships everywhere — including Aberdeen, even if you live in Penzance — because they'll often bring a car to you, or local ones might match their price. Unless you need a car for a set date, like to start a new job, aim to buy at the end of March, June, September, or December — when dealers are facing the end of the quarter and trying to hit their bonus target.

That obviously won't affect you if you're buying from a private seller — which can be cheaper, but riskier. Dealers may offer guarantees like 'approved used', where the car's history has been checked and it comes with a warranty, while going for a private sale is more of a shot in the dark. If you do go to see private cars for sale, always go with a friend or family member, be wary if a seller wants to meet in a car park or station, rather than their home, to view the car, and opt for a £20 HPI check which will reveal if a car has ever been stolen, listed as an insurance write-off, has outstanding finance, or has been 'clocked' on mileage — when fraudsters tinker with a car's computers to reduce the recorded mileage, making it seem a better deal for potential buyers.

SEVEN OTHER CHECKS TO MAKE BEFORE BUYING

1   Ask to see the V5C registration document — you need this to tax it, and the seller should be listed as its registered keeper. If not, investigate.

2   Make sure the mileage, age, and appearance of the car all look consistent — double-check recorded mileage on service records and MOT certificates.

3   Look for any small signs of damage — like gaps between panels or mismatched colours — they could be hiding extensive repairs.

4   Check that the tyres, seatbelts, lights, warning lights, and windscreen wipers all work.

5   Are the brakes effective and even? Any weird noises from them or from the engine?

6   Do all the locks, including central locking and remote
    control, and windows work properly?
7   Have you got all the right keys? The handbook should
    state which keys were provided when the car was new (new
    'master' keys can cost hundreds ...).

FOUR ROUTES TO CHEAPER DRIVING AND PARKING

If you rely on your car to get to and from work, the costs can
add up. But here are four ways to save on parking and petrol:

1   Try to share the cost — if a co-worker lives nearby, go
    together and share the costs of fuel and parking.
2   If there's a car-club in your area, work out if membership
    might be cheaper than the daily costs of parking, petrol,
    and insurance.
3   Look up alternatives to pricey multi-storey carparks or on-
    the-street bays. Sites like Parkopedia list parking fees across
    the UK, so you can find free or cheaper options, while at
    JustPark you can pay individuals to park in their driveways,
    office spaces etc.; this can be especially economical if you
    need to park near to a big event (like a concert).
4   If you're looking for parking near to an airport or train
    station, book ahead, and consider 'off site' or 'meet and
    greet' parking — your motor will be stored in a car park
    miles from where you want to be, but you'll get a shuttle ride
    or have someone drive your car there for you. You'll need
    to allow more time, but it'll be much cheaper. (Look up
    reviews online first, as some suspect companies are around.)
    Shop around on comparison sites like Holiday Extras.

How to maintain a car — Lucy's story

Until recently, nothing made me feel more like I was walking around with a PLEASE ROB ME forehead tattoo more than a trip to my local garage. The leery blokes; the fact that I could never remember my number plate details; the bit where I'd hand over my keys and just wait for the Call of Doom saying the motor needs £5473-worth of work. I was so clueless about cars that any time there was a problem I reverted to kid-mode and called my dad.

After getting hit by a particularly huge (and dubious) bill from a mechanic and then going on to turn my car over on the motorway a few months later, writing the whole thing off, I figured it was time to sort this issue out. No need for anything as embarrassing as a car maintenance course — instead, I watched a few good YouTube videos (DIYautotech and eHowAuto, AutoMD and Expert Village are the simplest) and learned the basics. Then, instead of going back to that greasy garage, I asked for recommendations on a local Facebook group and double-checked on mechanic comparison site Honest John to find a garage that I was happier with.

Some other things we've learned about cars — so you don't have to make the same mistakes we did!

If a garage calls and says you need a new part, it's pretty easy to price-check their quote: phone local rivals to compare costs, or view the second-hand parts prices on a site like

AutoPartsTrader. Some garages let you buy parts yourself, and just pay them for the labour.

In general, independents are cheaper than main dealers for garage work, while for MOTs, especially on newer cars, you should save your cash by going to a council-run test centre. These charge the fee set by the government and since they only do tests, not repairs, they have no incentive to fail you.

Always get a written quote, and check whether VAT is included, before agreeing to any major works.

While they may look like crazy complicated machines designed to suck you in, cover you in oil, and spit you out feeling sheepish, cars are, in fact, a bit like Lego: follow the instructions, stick the right bits in the right holes, and a lot of maintenance tasks that would easily swallow £50 at a garage are fairly doable. Especially with YouTube.

The most common car jobs that you can DIY include:

CHECKING THE OIL

- Switch off the engine and let it cool.
- Open the bonnet and you'll see four tanks. One will be marked for oil (your car's instruction manual should help you locate it if you're unsure).
- Pull out the dipstick — the rod for measuring oil, it usually has a yellow handle that sticks out, with 'engine oil' written on it — and wipe it with an old rag before putting it back.
- Then pull out the dipstick again and see where the level is. If it's below the minimum mark, refill it.

TOPPING UP THE SCREENWASH

- Open the marked cap under the bonnet, and if it needs a refill, use a funnel to pour fluid up to the maximum mark.

CHECKING TYRE TREAD

- Take a close look at the tyres (not forgetting the spare one in the boot) to see where the tread is worn. Uneven wear can be a sign of steering faults.
- Then check the tread — place a 20p piece (it's the correct size!) flat in one of the grooves of the tread: if you can see some of the outer edge of the coin, then your tyres may be illegal and could have a dangerous braking distance. Test on all tyres.

CHECKING TYRE PRESSURE

- Use the air pumps at petrol stations.
- Park up, check the pressure (the requisite tyre pressure number should be listed in your car's instruction manual).
- Unscrew your tyre caps, insert the air nozzle, and wait for a reading: if it's low, start the hisser.

How to rent a car (and stay solvent)

The car rental industry is where you stroll up to a counter with a set price for hiring a car, only to face a monotone teenager warning you that if you so much as drive over a marshmallow the wheel damage charge will be £4.2 million. After gagging, you sign an insurance waiver form and then spend four times the price you were originally quoted. So how can you avoid this? Start by looking online, but before booking, you need to check:

1   **The age limit:** this varies across different companies and countries, so check before you book.
2   **Which documents you'll need:** such as both parts of your driving licence, a credit card, your passport, or another form of ID.
3   **The price:** comparison sites like CarRentals let you search a huge number of sites in one place. Book as early as you can to make the biggest savings.
4   **The opening times:** if you've booked a Ryanair flight that arrives at 5.20am, will someone be at the rental desk waiting for you?
5   **What's included:** full tank of fuel to get you to your destination (or at least enough to reach the nearest petrol station)? Comprehensive insurance?
6   **Damage waiver:** most rental firms impose a hefty excess on their insurance policy (think £1000 for a single scratch) thereby enticing you to buy their 'excess waiver'. But you can get annual policies for this for about £25 online, so do your research first.

When you first receive the car, check it carefully for any damage. Really carefully. As in, look at each panel of the car closer than you've ever looked at any potential life partner. Make a note of any scuff, scratch, or dirt, and ask the rental company to sign a form to confirm that they've also seen it. Take photos on your phone, too. Then when you return the car, you avoid being unfairly charged for pre-existing damage.

Make sure to return the car with the fuel required — usually either a full tank, or the amount in the car when you hired it. The charges car rental firms impose for taking a car to a petrol station to refuel can be ridiculously high.

What is insurance excess?

It's the set amount that you have to pay out if you make a claim. So if your excess is £150 and you make a £1000 claim, your insurance provider will keep the first £150 and give you the remaining £850. If a claim is deemed to be someone else's fault, the insurer usually waives the excess, but it depends on each policy's terms. Some insurers offer 'voluntary excess' on top of the compulsory excess. Increasing this figure is one way to lower the cost of insurance — you can choose to 'top up' the excess to, say £250 (the above £150 excess plus a £100 voluntary excess) which would lower the insurance premium, but obviously mean you'd have to pay out more (both the compulsory and the voluntary excess) in the event of a claim.

Train tickets — seven tips on how to buy them for less than the price of a three-bedroom home

… and without spending three-quarters of a weekend working out what an 'apex non-pronto express direct-indirect leisure fare' really is.

1 Time it right. Generally, the earlier you book, the cheaper the fare — cheap tickets are released 12 weeks before travel, so if you know about a trip in advance, buy a ticket ASAP. That's true even if you're travelling tomorrow — booking even 24 hours in advance is usually cheaper than doing so when you've just turned up the station. (If you know about a trip reallllly far in advance, TheTrainLine's ticket alert email will ping you as soon as your desired ticket goes on sale.)

2 Visit National Rail's cheapest fare finder. Unlike the websites of train operators, National Rail shows the lowest-possible fare for all UK train operators on all routes — so use it, but …

3 Also check the operators' websites (and others like TheTrainLine and RedSpottedHanky too) just in case they're running special online discount codes that will save you money. Sometimes they offer £1 fares, or special deals because a certain journey is looking empty.

4 Avoid automated ticket machines — even if you have to buy a ticket for an imminent train at the station, and there's a snaking queue for the kiosk, join that queue. Most ticket machines don't advertise discounted or group tickets.

5 Use any railcard discounts you can. The day you can no longer use the 16–25 Young Person's Railcard is indeed the sad end of your youth (though note, this £30-a-year card is valid up to your twenty-sixth birthday) — but there's a new 26–30 railcard to soften the blow, extending the discounted years. Railcards are generally worthwhile if you spend £100 or more on off-peak train travel each year.

A £30 Two-Together railcard will get you and a friend/ partner a third off your journey, but you can only use it when you travel together. In London and the southeast of England, a Network Railcard gives the same discount and covers up to four adults who travel after 10am on weekdays or at any time on weekends, plus up to four children who get an even bigger discount. The £20 Disabled Persons Railcard gives a third off both the holder's fare plus that of an adult companion.

6   Split it. The confusing train ticket booking system means it can be cheaper to book several tickets for one journey rather than just one — while still arriving in the same place. So a ticket from Portsmouth to London and then one from London to Edinburgh is often cheaper than just booking one journey from Portsmouth to Edinburgh. The website TrainSplit will do the work for you — just remember the train has to stop at each of the stations you've bought tickets to travel from.

7   Join a cashback site. See below.

Cashback sites – legitimate free money (f'real)

The concept might sound dodgy, but cashback sites give you free money back on shopping you were already doing. The biggest are TopCashback and Quidco — and they work by paying you back the referral fee from shops or websites. So where Google, for example, might receive money if you clicked a link on its site then bought a train ticket, this way, you keep the referral cash. Both sites often offer extra vouchers for train travel, such as £10 towards bookings at TheTrainLine.

Bum deals on bikes

Two wheels are one of the cheapest ways to get around — and there are schemes you can use that make it even more economical, such as the government's Cyclescheme which lets you buy a bike tax-free, and pay off the cost gradually from your wages, from 2000 bike shops and online. The only catch is that your employer needs to be a member of the scheme — but you can help them sign up if they're not.

You'll have to think about maintenance costs too — when a bike breaks down and you're in the middle of nowhere in a rainstorm, a bit of bike know-how won't go amiss. The Evans Cycles chain run £15 bike maintenance classes twice a month, teaching pre-ride safety checks, how to change an inner tube, cleaning and re-lubing chains, and brake and gear adjustment. Make friends (a.k.a. buy a bike/accessories) from your local cycle shop and they might offer the same for less or even free. And YouTube is also good for basic bike maintenance lessons.

How to book a flight and ensure you've paid less than everyone else on the plane

Think of cheap flights as contraception — because the key to bargain plane journeys is not being bound by the school holidays. Start your flight search on Kayak, Skyscanner,

Momondo, or another comparison site (but always use incognito browser mode, as cookies in your computer tell sites when you've looked at a journey multiple times and so might force you to stump up more for the trip). Most comparison sites bring up a graph revealing the cheapest days, months, and times to fly to your chosen destination, which is the best route to a cheap deal if you're not fixed to a set date. Research shows that flying out and back on a Tuesday is usually the best way to bag the least expensive ticket, while Momondo analysis also claims it's cheapest to book exactly 60 days before the date of the flight (so if you're booking well in advance, count back from your departure date), and to fly after 6pm (it's especially important to avoid early mornings, when you're competing with expense-account — a.k.a. flush — business travellers).

It totally contradicts the Tuesday-to-Tuesday theory, but travel experts say that going away for 4, 6, or 9 days rather than the usual 7, 10, or 14 can cut flight prices, so play around on comparison sites. If you're looking for flights to a popular destination, check for availability on charter flights — the likes of Thomas Cook sell off unreserved seats when their holiday packages haven't sold out — via CharterFlights, FlightsDirect, and TravelSupermarket.

If you have fixed dates (such as you or your partner work in a school, so you have to fly in the set school holidays), Skyscanner's 'Fly Me Anywhere' option will tell you the cheapest places to fly for your dates — it can open up new destinations you haven't thought of, as well as flagging up bargains.

For long-haul journeys, look into code-share offers, where airlines in the same alliance sometimes offer the exact same flights, on the same plane, at different prices. British Airways and Iberia are owned by the same company, for example, but a friend secured a bargain flight to Brazil by booking with Iberia not BA. These flights *should* show up on comparison sites, but, if you've found a set flight that you want to take, it's worth checking the airline's code-share chums' direct websites to see if one sells it cheaper.

If you've got more time than money, consider an indirect flight — stopovers are almost always cheaper, but they do obviously take longer, and you might need to factor in overnight accommodation. Whatever you book, try to use a credit card if at all possible — it means if the airline was to go bust, and you spent over £100, the card company has to refund your money.

Work

For one small word, 'work' sure takes up a lot of our time. And we mean that literally. Deciding how you want to earn money for the rest of your life can be tricky; working towards a career can be a long, unrewarding, and sometimes expensive process; and persuading someone to hire you and pay you actual money can be even harder. Yeah, working out how work, errr, works (see what we mean?) is a minefield.

Take it from Kat. She graduated with a degree in Film and Literature, then took a job as a personal assistant because she was a) skint, and b) too scared to pursue a career in writing. She finally left her job and begged magazines for work experience, temping in offices to keep her afloat, and when, at last, she did get the job of her dreams, she left a year and a half later under a cloud of self-doubt and anxiety. She tried another line of industry (a hard no), then became a freelancer, and eventually returned to full-time employment in an office and got promoted very quickly. On paper, she's a career mess. She is, however, happy.

How to work out what you want to do

Our parents might have hoped we'd be able to walk into a 'job for life' (or at least for a minimum of five years or so), but times have changed. The workplace has become less stable, with freelancing and temporary contracts more common than ever, which can sound a bit scary. But the upside? Workers have become more open-minded and, in some cases, more likely to walk away from a job that doesn't feel right. These days, you're unlikely to commit to the first thing you think of, so it makes sense to see what's around before pledging your allegiance to a career. Even the chosen few who struck life goal gold at 15 and knew exactly what they wanted to do and how to get there might change their mind somewhere along the line. So how the hell do you work it out? Some key points to think about:

1   **What fulfils you:** it can be hard to know what's going to make you happy in the workplace if you're looking for your first job — but try to have a think about it. Even if you have years of steady employment under your belt and want a change, considering why you might want to get up and go to work every day is a pretty crucial first step.

2   **Money:** for lots of people, this is the most important part of the package. Ask yourself whether you'd be happy earning a basic wage and growing that over time, or if you want to absolutely rake it in immediately. Think hard about the lifestyle you are aiming for (be realistic, this isn't an episode of *Cribs*), and do some research into what it's going to take for you to live it. If you're not out there to make the big bucks, but you have concerns about how

much certain career paths would allow you to earn, there are online search tools which will give you the average salary for specific jobs based on their data. Total Jobs' salary calculator and Glassdoor's compensation checker both do a similar thing.

3 **Creativity:** this one doesn't necessarily go hand in hand with money. But if you really value your own creative fulfilment, it's worth thinking about whether that's more important than a big pay-cheque, or the time it might take you to get one.

4 **Location:** specific industries are often based in certain parts of the UK, or beyond. If you see your future working in a theatre, you'll more likely be drawn to London than if you're interested in agriculture — which usually requires a bit more open space than the capital has to offer.

5 **Flexibility:** in happy news, there's been a recent push across industries to allow employees more options to work flexibly — and all employees are legally allowed to request it, though not all companies will grant it. That could mean dictating your working hours, or spending some time doing your job remotely. This can be better for costs (train fares and fuel prices aren't coming down), or it might mean you can free up some time to pursue other interests. Many companies will offer flexible arrangements for their staff who have decided to raise a family — for example, through compressed or annualised working hours. Every workplace is different, so it's worth asking about flexible working arrangements early on if this is a priority for you.

6 **Power! (or being in charge):** some people are born great,

some people achieve greatness, and some ... well, they just want to be the CEO. If you see yourself as a leader, look at the industries you're interested in, but also the entry positions that could take you through that path to the top.

7   **Passion:** it might be that none of that motivates you, and you're looking to spend your days fulfilling another passion. That could be helping other people, being part of a start-up ... Whatever it is, make a list and keep referring back to it during your job search.

Congratulations! You now have a vague idea of what your priorities are, but what specific careers will match up with your list of must-haves? Now it's time to ...

DO YOUR RESEARCH

If you're in college or university, you'll probably be familiar with the careers advisor tasked with getting you on the right track (or any track, frankly). But there are plenty of other places to find jobs inspiration:

1   **Ask around:** one of the best ways to find out what jobs exist and what they're like is by talking to the people doing them. That might mean starting a conversation with a friend of your parents at that usually boring Christmas drinks party, or asking a friend of a friend on Facebook for a quick chat about what it is they do, exactly. It's amazing how many people will be happy to talk about their work over a drink or a coffee — they were inexperienced young job-hunters too, once.

2   **Social media:** of course, relying on people you already know can be tricky if your network is small or restricted to certain industries, but there are various other ways to try to get an insight into different careers. Twitter and Instagram are great for peeking into what people actually get up to every day, especially in creative jobs. If you have an inkling of which organisations appeal to you, seek out their key players online to get an insight into how they work.

3   **Career taster events:** look for job fairs and schemes that help young people get access and information to different careers. Prospects have a thorough list of events across the UK on their website; TheJobFairs website lists events designed to connect jobseekers with recruiting companies in their local area, all over the UK. There are also organisations like Creative Access that hold events and help provide opportunities to support young people from BAME backgrounds get into full-time employment in the creative industries.

4   **Do the reading:** admit it, sometimes the hardest part of thinking about your career is understanding what certain jobs titles actually mean. 'Solutions architect', anyone? Prospects is great for this — they not only have a pretty exhaustive list of job profiles which go into detail (responsibilities, salary, qualifications, skills) and explain what work experience or additional courses might be beneficial, they also have a Career Planner and a Job Match tool which aim to match you to roles you'd be suited to. UCAS, too, has a brilliant 'Explore Jobs' portal that lets you discover roles that you might never have thought

about, by searching by job family, subject, or skill. If you want an actual book to read, try Lucy's *Book of Jobs*: *Exclusive Careers Guidance from Insiders*.

GET EXPERIENCE

The only reason you know what you enjoy is because you've tried it. This goes for jobs as much as anything else. If you're seriously considering a particular career, it's helpful to get some kind of experience under your belt so you can see whether you'd actually like it. It's important to remember that there is always a difference between how a job looks, and how it feels to do it. Things like a swishy central London office, top-of-the-range work phone, or a ping pong table in the 'break out room' might look cool, but if the nature of the work itself or the culture of the industry isn't a good fit for you, you aren't going to enjoy your job very much. By contrast, you might find that you love doing something that looks glamour-free but gives you other rewards, like a sense of autonomy, the possibility for rapid advancement, or the satisfaction of working in a tight-knit team.

Here's how other people found what they wanted to do

'I only worked it out in the last couple of years — and I'm 28. I took a Modern Languages degree at university, and after graduation I worked in a couple of sales and admin-based roles, which I didn't find fulfilling. Thankfully, I was given an opportunity to take a business-focused marketing qualification through my company at the time. It opened my eyes to a whole new field that I was fascinated by — consumer psychology, digital technology, brand management — and I excelled. I wanted to read the giant course textbooks from cover to cover and spend hours watching TED talks by marketing professionals. I knew I needed to pursue marketing as a career.'

'I still haven't! I think it's great when people have that underlying passion from a young age and go and have a career in something, but for those of us who don't, we can have a fun journey all the same. I still have no idea what I really want to do at 30 years old, but I'm happy enough trying to figure it out. Plus, most research shows the days of one-job careers are over, and we'll all have numerous different careers before we retire anyway.'

'I went to sixth form, mostly because I didn't know what to do after GCSEs — but had no idea what job to do after that. I ended up working in a supermarket for a year, but realised I had no future in it and went back to college so I could apply to university — I couldn't afford to move out of home, so I thought this would give me three years to be independent. University didn't go well, so I left and ended up doing jobs that offered no progression and low pay. I moved to Berlin with an ex and then back to London, but was unable to find work and was on benefits for eight months. Eventually, I got a job working in the stock room at a high-street shoe retailer and did this for two years. I became known for hard work and then successfully applied to an entry-level role in head office. From that point I learned more and with some luck became manager of my department. I turn 37 this year, so it shows that these things can take a long time!'

'I was lucky enough to work out that being a ballet teacher was what I wanted to do from the age of 13. It helped that I had an inspirational teacher and she helped me achieve my goals and encouraged me to audition for the Royal Academy of Dance. All my A-Level options were chosen based on what I thought would help me if I got a place on a dance degree and what might be useful as a ballet teacher.'

'When I was younger, I didn't really know what I wanted to do. Nothing really jumped out at me. When I left school, I started a college course in childcare, but quickly realised that it just wasn't for me. Rather than see it through, I left the course and started looking for an opportunity that really excited me. Fortunately, I walked into a photographic shop on the high-street and they offered me some work experience. That work experience turned into a job and now, years later, I'm still here doing something that I really love.'

'When I graduated with a degree in literature, my dream was to work with books, and I've been lucky enough to achieve it. But while I was imagining sitting alone in a room editing for days on end, the career I've ended up with has been focused very much on working directly with people and with the media, as I specialise in book publicity, marketing, and sales — things which seemed completely daunting to me as a student. Through my work, I've broadened my understanding of what I enjoy, and realised that sometimes you don't know you will find something fulfilling until you try it.'

'I'm 27, I still don't really know, and I think that's okay. I have a type of job that I like, but I make sure I'm always learning and that my skills are adaptable.'

'My mum worked with young and special needs children, so when I left school I wanted to go into childcare myself. I chose to go to college and completed a BTEC National Diploma, Level 3 in children's care, learning, and development, and worked in four different placements. When I finished my two-year college course, I got a job working in a children's holiday club which was attached to a school, where I later became a teaching assistant. After a few years, I moved to the younger ages and worked in nurseries, and I recently became a baby-room senior. I love watching them grow each day and reach their milestones and next steps.'

'All the way through my GCSEs and A-Levels I knew I wanted to do something related to art and design, but I struggled to put my finger on exactly what. I took an Art and Design Foundation course at college in the hope that it would help me discover what I really wanted to do. As the course got nearer and nearer to the end, it looked increasingly likely that I would go down the path of becoming a graphic designer, even though I really didn't want to (and knowing that I don't take instruction/orders very well). I explained to my tutor the predicament that I was in and how I was the one that wanted to be giving the orders. It was at that moment that my tutor replied, "Have you thought about advertising?" and the rest is history.'

How to get a job

Even when you've decided what you *want* to do, getting to the bit where you *actually do it* can feel a bit like everyone else was given a secret password for a hidden door labelled EMPLOYMENT and you can't find it. But there are ways to streamline the way you get there, without spending ages knocking on the wrong ones.

1 **Work experience and internships:** not every industry will require prospective employees to have on-the-job experience (Prospects has a very comprehensive list of job profiles and what's usually needed to get them). But it looks good on your CV and — even if you're only helping out with the filing — can give you an unfiltered insight into what it's like to work somewhere. You can usually find work experience or internships listed on company websites, and websites like Milkround, StudentJob and RateMyPlacement have huge pools of opportunities and guidance on getting them.

2   **Traineeships:** these are schemes for young people aged 16–24 who don't quite have the skills or experience to get a job or an internship yet. They run for six months, and offer training, on-the-job experience, and English and maths lessons if needed. They aren't usually paid (although travel and lunch expenses often are), and they're offered across all sorts of industries, from fashion to IT. You can find further details on the government's website.

3   **Apprenticeships:** this is essentially the next step up from a traineeship. Apprenticeships are placements paid at a rate of just over half of the minimum wage per hour (and you are also entitled to holiday pay) with companies who offer hands-on experience alongside their staff, where you can learn the skills to get onto the career ladder. Some might even earn you a diploma. Again, details are on the government's website.

4   **Networking:** sticking on a name badge and introducing yourself to ~~total strangers~~ potential employers might make you feel seasick, but networking is a great way to show yourself off before you even get to the job application stage — and to find out about the roles that aren't advertised. Websites like EventBrite and MeetUp list various events, or you can search by industry. If you don't want to face a room full of strangers on your own, take a friend looking to get into the same line of work.

5   **Word of mouth:** how many times have you heard someone talk about 'being in the right place at the right time'? This doesn't have to mean waiting in the doorway of the company you want to work for until someone has a job

to fill. But keeping in touch with contacts you've made from work experience, internships, or networking will go a long way to making sure you're top of the list when they're thinking of someone to fill it. Maybe don't call them every week, but a brief friendly email now and again won't hurt.

CLIMBING THE ENDLESS MOUNTAIN OF JOB APPLICATIONS

So you've got some experience and you're ready to go full steam on the job hunt train (which, if it was real, would probably have a three-hour delay followed by a long and jerky journey through torrential rain). In short, it can feel relentless. But break it up into bits:

1 **Whittle down the list**: applying for jobs isn't necessarily a numbers game. Work out exactly which roles you a) have the experience for, and b) actually want. If you can't show that you have the skills and passion in your application, the recruiter will probably see that.

2 **Write a cracking CV**: make it look good, too. You're going to want yours to stand out in a pile, so add a bit of colour or use a font that's a bit different (not too different though — it needs to be professional and legible). Remember to spell-check it and, if you can, ask someone to read it over in case you've missed any mistakes.

3 **Do what they ask**: some adverts will ask for just your CV, others may require more, like a cover letter and/or a task. Make sure you've done all of it, or the employer will likely put your application aside (after all, they'll probably be looking for someone who can follow basic instructions).

4   **Tailor your covering letter:** even if you've only been asked for a CV, it's good practice to sell yourself, as well as your relevant experience. A cover letter should never be any longer than a page (remember how many applications the hiring manager will be going through), and it's a good idea to have someone read it through and give you feedback — that might be a parent, an older sibling, or, if you're a student, a helpful tutor.

5   **Consider using a recruiter:** you might have seen headhunters on TV shows and thought they were only for people in important jobs with big salaries. But actually, recruiters can be great at any stage of your career — even in the very beginning. These are people who are paid to match your skill-set to certain jobs; they'll help work out where your experience will get you, help improve your CV, and get you to the interview stage. Many focus on particular job sectors (finance, for example), while others will recruit for job types (i.e. administration). Usually, you simply need to send across your CV (they'll provide that information on their website) and you'll be invited in for a chat if they think they can help you in your job search. However, it's worth remembering that recruiters don't work for you, they work for their clients. So while they can be a great way to get a job, you need to be a bit wary as they are looking to do the deal and earn their commission — they are not necessarily interested in finding the right fit for you.

How to nail the interview stage

DO ...

Your research: read about the company, their competitors, and the person (or people) who are interviewing you, so you don't have to answer any questions with 'I'm not sure.'

Dress smartly: whether you're interviewing to work in a bank or a high-street shop, you should look like you've taken care over your appearance. Choose something that reflects the attributes you want to put across; that could mean creativity, an attention to detail, or a sensible attitude. It will never mean sloppiness.

Be curious: at the end of the interview you'll be given the opportunity to ask questions, so have some in mind. These could be along the lines of what the company culture is like, or where your interviewer sees the company developing in the next five years.

DON'T...

Be late: prepare well in advance and give yourself plenty of time to allow for traffic or delays. But it doesn't pay to turn up too early, either, even if that means sitting in a coffee shop for half an hour while you wait.

Rush your answers: if you're faced with a question you're really unsure of, give yourself a minute to reply by saying, 'That's a really interesting question, I need a moment to think about it', or turning it back to the employer, 'I'm interested in why you ask that, is XXX important to the company?'

Ask about money: if you're not sure what the salary is, that shouldn't be the last impression you make when you leave the interview. There will be an opportunity to ask if your application is progressed.

How to know when to stop working for free

First things first — no one should feel they have to work for free, and many people can't afford to. But unpaid arrangements are legal, and it's important to understand where you stand.

Whether or not you are entitled to be paid by the organisation providing your internship depends on the nature of your relationship with them — just saying you are there as an 'intern' or a 'volunteer' isn't enough. Either you are truly a 'volunteer' — which means you're doing work on a purely voluntary basis, can come and go as you please, and are not being remunerated in any way other than expenses for things like travel or lunch — or you're a 'worker' — and you are likely to be entitled to the National Minimum Wage (NMW) and other employment rights. There are some conditions under which 'interns' or students undertaking work experience aren't due the NMW; if it is part of a course of further or higher education, if they are school-aged, if they are taking part in workplace shadowing.

It's important to understand your rights, so head to the government website for a full outline, or ask an advisor at your school, college, or university before agreeing to any arrangements you're unsure of. Don't be afraid of raising anything that makes you feel uncomfortable with the organisation offering you work experience, or of asking to be paid the appropriate amount. If a company is breaking the law by offering a long-term unpaid placement, you have the right to call them out on it and see how they respond.

Still, depending on the field you want to work in, these kinds of placements can be valuable, so how do you know when to stop giving your services for free, and start earning money for your hard work?

1   **When you've got some experience:** call it stating the obvious, but the reason anyone applies for work placements in the first place is to get experience under their belt and onto their CV. Got some? Great — start applying for paid jobs. When a future employer is looking at your CV, they won't look at your month-long stint at a competitor and think 'Oh, what a shame they didn't stay for six!'

2   **When you can't afford it:** no one can afford to work for nothing forever (and even if they could, why should they?). Before you even take up unpaid work, figure out how long you can sustain that for. Are you using savings to fund yourself, or couch-hopping? Are you working for free during the day and at a bar in the evenings just to pay your rent? Set an end date and work to it.

3   **When your responsibilities and obligations are those of a 'worker'** (see above)

4   **When you're asked to stay on, or promised future work:** by law, any promise of future work means you would be entitled to NMW for the whole period you had worked for an organisation. The government website outlines these scenarios in greater detail.

What to look for in an employment contract

Although your employer is not legally obliged to provide you with a written contract to start working, you'll usually receive your terms of employment within about two months of starting a job. These should include:

1 **Your employment status:** if you are classed as a 'worker' (with basic rights), an 'employee' (entitled to more rights, and obliged to give notice if you want to leave), or 'self-employed'.

2 **Your employment pattern:** for example, if your role is fixed-term, zero hours, part-time, casual, or temporary.

3 **Details on automatic enrolment:** since April 2017, companies have been required by law to enrol eligible employees in a pension scheme. This means some of your salary will go into your pension pot, instead of your bank account, but you can opt out at any time.

4 **Express terms:** these are parts of your employment agreement that are specifically highlighted, and can include: your wage (and bonus and overtime pay, if any), your holiday entitlement, sick pay arrangements, and hours of work, including overtime.

5 **Implied terms:** these aren't actually written into contracts, but are things that you can take as being 'implied' — for example, not stealing from your employer, or that you won't share confidential information.

6 **Probationary periods:** some employers will require you to pass probation (usually this is anything from a month to six months) before they decide to keep you in their

employment. During this time you may have fewer rights and a different notice period than after the period ends.

7 **Entitlement to any other benefits:** this could include things like: medical insurance, a company car or phone, subsidised gym membership, a company pension scheme, enhanced maternity or paternity pay, travel assistance, or eye health vouchers.

How to do office chat (and when to stop ... a.k.a. not telling your boss about your raging hangover)

You spend almost all day, every day at work, and it's natural that in that time you're going to want to cut loose and be yourself sometimes — you're not a robot, after all. But at the same time, think carefully about the impression you want to create in the workplace. The key to having a solid professional image without losing your soul is to keep different levels of chat reserved for different colleagues ...

THE RANDOM FROM THE DEPARTMENT NEXT DOOR

You're standing in the communal kitchen at work, waiting for a kettle to take approximately 13 minutes to boil, when Kevin from accounts strolls in. Ah yes, there you are Kevin. This is the most basic level of office small talk — the person you know, but not really. Perhaps you've been in the loo at the same time on a couple of occasions? Stick to entry-level chats like the weather, how much milk there is in the fridge, or where they got their tie/shoes/skirt from.

THE RECEPTIONIST

This is simple: a) keep your small talk to asking about them because receptionists are brilliant people who deal with other people's endless shit all day, and b) don't tell them that the huge parcel you need them to frank and put in the post is actually something you've sold on eBay.

YOUR TEAM-MATE

You work with this person every day, but you're not sure how close your relationship is destined to be. Abide by the top-line info rule here: talk about your partner, but keep it light; don't mention that time your ex cheated on you. Chat about the workload, but avoid stating JUST how much you dislike Sue from marketing. Wait and see how the relationship develops — you can always bond more in the future, but you can never take back the time you had one too many and accidentally told them those hilarious but humiliating sexual anecdotes ...

YOUR AWKWARD BOSS, WHO PUZZLES AND TERRIFIES YOU IN EQUAL MEASURE

You know the one. The boss who asks you questions which are either designed to make you feel uncomfortable, or a sign that they have never, ever learned how to make casual small talk with their employees and could do with reading this, too. Stick to the facts — the weather, the news, their dog.

YOUR OTHER BOSS, WHO SITS NEXT TO YOU AND YOU ENJOY A DRINK WITH OCCASIONALLY

It's lovely that you can have a friendship with the person who is also responsible for giving you pay rises and performance reviews. Just avoid talking about things that would put them in a difficult position, like when you start applying for new jobs, or the day you called in sick because you'd been out until 5am on a Tuesday night. And while you might be bonding, bear in mind that the difference in work status might mean you don't want to divulge quite as much as you would to a friend who was your equal, unlike ...

YOUR WORK WIFE/HUSBAND

This is your closest work friend, someone you bond with and bitch with freely. There's no point telling you what's off-limits here, because when you meet The One at work you wouldn't listen anyway. But, unless this person works in a very different team with a very different job, don't talk about your salaries, unless either of you enjoy slowly simmering resentment. And although you might love to share every detail of your inner lives, be careful about how you communicate — try to keep office gossip for your face-to-face lunchtime escapes, and avoid leaving a trail of work emails or Slack messages behind that rubbish your colleagues. In short: keep your cathartic but brutally frank convos off the server.

YOUR INTERN/ASSISTANT/JUNIOR COLLEAGUE

Think navigating small talk with your boss is tricky? It can be even harder to handle when it's with someone more junior than you. What you're aiming for here is something between pleasant professional colleague and a supportive older sibling. Do: give them valuable advice and help them with tricky situations if you can. Don't: overshare, talk in any great detail about your private life or gossip about other colleagues. And if you're giving instructions, it's ok to be firm, but don't be power-mad or rude. You were junior once, too.

How to get a pay rise

Hello, and welcome to the workplace Dreaded Question. If you're British, you'll already be aware of your utter inability to talk about money, so asking for more of it (ARE YOU KID-DING?) is as awkward as telling your boss you've seen them naked. For the record, of the two options, asking them for more money is a lot less awful.

How I learned to ask for more money — Kat's story

'I used to be really, really bad at this. In the early stages of my career, when my rent was going up faster than my salary (which wasn't going up at all), I asked my then-boss if we could talk about my remuneration because ... well, the rest is a blur, because at that point I burst into tears, muttered something about "progression", and that was that. No more money for me.

It was only when I went freelance and realised that my work was *worth* something that I became confident that I could ask for a bit more. The worst that ever happened was that they said no, but they'd look at their budgets next time.

And when I went back into full-time employment, I started asking for more money all the time! I'm joking — but I have managed to demonstrate my worth and negotiate.'

So, you need a pay rise, you think you deserve it, but how, exactly, do you ask for it?

KNOW WHY YOU'RE ASKING

Unfortunately, just wanting a pay rise isn't enough of a reason to get one. Sorry. You're going to need to know why you deserve more money and be able to explain that to your line manager effectively. (If you're not sure if your line manager is the right person to ask, check with your company's HR department.) The good news is, the 'why' could be any one of these things: your role has changed, you have additional responsibilities, you've delivered on projects and can show the positive impact that's had, you've met some big objectives or made some big client wins. You might even have been head-hunted by a recruiter or successfully applied for a role elsewhere, but would prefer to stay put and get a raise. Don't aim for sympathy though — telling them that you need more money because you've just rented an expensive flat says nothing about why you deserve a raise, and more about your inability to budget.

Do some research into how other jobs at your level are being salaried. Look on job sites like LinkedIn, Glassdoor, and Indeed and work out the average for a role like yours, with your responsibilities. If you have a friend in a similar industry (though best to steer clear of the same company), ask them about what their job entails and for a rough idea of their salary.

MAKE LISTS

Whenever a friend of ours asks for a pay rise, she gets the job description she had when she started the role, and then rewrites it to include all of the other responsibilities she's taken on since. It makes her feel more confident in her own experience, but it's also something her line manager can take away with them.

Whether your request is based on your experience or your performance, listing your achievements is a good idea. Arm yourself with the evidence to back that up (and that'll differ between industries — it could be figures or client feedback, or however else your department measures success) and examples of where you've achieved, and take those in with you.

PRACTISE ASKING

Even if you're the sort of person who loves interviews or talking to strangers on public transport (really?), straight up asking for more money can be daunting. So, practise how you're going to lead in to it ('While I have you, there's something I wanted to speak to you about — do you have time?'), and then the actual question. 'I'd like to talk to you about my current responsibilities' is going to be more palatable than 'I think you should pay me more money.'

FIND THE RIGHT TIME

There will never be a perfect moment to ask your boss for more money, so don't look for one. Instead, work out when they might be more open to discussing your salary with you (i.e. probably not when they've come out of a three-hour board meeting). If you have a regular one-to-one with your line manager, can you use that time to add this on to the agenda? Likewise, if you're working somewhere that has annual or bi-annual employee reviews, these are designed to discuss your progression.

But there are other things you can take into consideration. Do you have an annual company-wide pay review period? Some people swear by avoiding this time by about three months either side. Ask just before, and you could be told that it'll come up in your pay review. Great. Ask after, and you'll have probably just got an incremental pay rise and they won't be prepared to give you another one.

It's also worth noting if your line manager is recruiting anyone else to work in your team. It's always good (and a bit sneaky, but hey ho) to get a pay rise request in before they have to negotiate with a new member of staff.

Have a back-up plan

Worst-case scenario: your boss says they can't give you any more money at this point. Obviously that sucks, but don't see it as all being lost. If they haven't explained to you why that is, take this opportunity to ask them. Then see if you can work together to turn that into solid objectives, with a timescale, so you can review your progress — and your salary — together at a set time in the future. And make sure you do get something firm out of them — whether that is a yes, a no, or an 'I'll let you know', agree a date that they'll give you an update — and follow up if they don't.

Some advice from others who have been there, tried that

'I was honest. I told my boss that I felt undervalued and underpaid. If they didn't give me a view of where my career was going, and when my salary would increase, I would start looking elsewhere.'

'I've always timed asking for a pay rise to just before the beginning of the financial year, or halfway through it, when budgets are being set. That's always seemed like the most sensible time to ask.'

'I've just moved jobs as a way of getting a lot more money than I would asking for a pay rise.'

'I've asked, and not always had the answer I've wanted. If the answer is no, I've asked for constructive advice on what I can do to achieve a salary increase, gone away and done it, and come back and asked again, with proof of my achievements.'

'My year's contract came to an end recently, and I was asked to stay on permanently. I'd previously been nervous about asking for more money, but my bosses obviously didn't want me to leave. I said I wanted a new salary that reflected my responsibilities and experience, and while I was at it, I asked for a more senior job title. And got both.'

'I've never been comfortable with this, but recently had a situation at work where it reached tipping point and I couldn't see where any progression was coming from. I voiced my concerns in a constructive way and, because I've been loyal and cooperative down the years, I did get a pay rise and progression. My advice would be to make a clear case around it — you're asking because you deserve it, not just because it'd be nice or because so-and-so got one. Don't be afraid to ruffle feathers.'

'As a freelancer, I've put my rates up annually, at the beginning of every financial year. It's an easy way to justify giving myself a pay rise — not to mention less awkward, as the conversation is usually through email.'

How to know when to leave a crappy job

Kat has stayed in roles that weren't right for every kind of reason: because she thought she should 'be there a year', because she was scared she'd 'never get another one', because she really liked her colleagues but absolutely hated the job itself. So how do you know when it's time to go? First, work out why your job feels crappy in the first place. That could be any, or many, reasons, including:

1   **The pay is rubbish:** see all of the above. If money is a
     motivator in this decision, but you've had no joy asking for
     a pay rise, or even the hint of a glint of a future one, that
     will probably make your mind up for you.

2   **You feel demoralised:** it could be your peers being
    promoted around you, a boss that doesn't give you praise or
    credit, or you feel like you're doing thankless tasks all day.

3   **There's no room for professional growth:** if your
    current job doesn't offer you any room for training or
    development, you might be considering how you progress
    your responsibilities.

4   **You don't like the company culture:** without fast-tracking
    your career path to CEO, this one is quite tricky to change.
    If it's your department, though, it might be something you
    can flag with your line manager.

5   **You're really, really bored:** if there's no spark of excitement
    left in you, that's enough said.

Once you've worked out what it is that's making you want
to get out of there, have a think about if there's anything that
could change and would persuade you to stay. If there is, it
may be worth having a frank chat with your line manager.
If there's not, the very least you have is knowledge of what's
important to you going into your next job.

Here's when other people knew they had to go

'When my mood caused by work started impacting my
relationships outside work.'

'It wasn't so much the case that the job was crappy and
more that my boss was crappy! Over three and a half

years, she'd criticised me and taken credit for my ideas, had been rude and condescending, and made me doubt my own worth and my abilities. The penny finally dropped when I discovered that she'd given herself access to my emails. I deserved better than this.'

'I left a job when it took a toll on my mental health. I had reached breaking point — low salary, unprofessional boss, overwhelming workload — and couldn't see any of those things changing.'

'When my old boss told me to "stop being so English and be more German" — yes, really. At that point I realised I would have to significantly change myself to fit into the company, and I didn't want to do that.'

'When I started to not care about the outcome of something I'd been tasked with.'

'The crappiest job I ever had wasn't actually that crappy, I just didn't want to do it any more. I realised that I'd started on the wrong career path, and it wasn't making me happy. I didn't even have a plan when I left, but it felt great to get out of there.'

... and how to do the resigning bit

Yeah, we all have dreams of marching up to our boss, bellowing, 'Here's your report — oh, and by the way, I QUIT,' before flouncing out of that office and never looking back. But the reality is that most people have a notice period to work out (awkward) and need money coming in. So, get an action plan together. It's worth thinking about:

1 **Looking for another job:** in an ideal world, you'd start job-hunting before you hand in your notice, so you don't have any fallow months eating up your savings (yeah, we do mean that £52 you were keeping aside for a rainy day). But if it's taking a long time to find something and you can't stand your job any longer, it might be worth considering …

2 **Lining up some freelance work or temping:** if you can't find a new permanent role that's right for you, start putting the feelers out for freelance or contract work that can tide you over. Contact old colleagues. Get in touch with employment agencies who deal with temporary positions. Get a couple of months' worth of work ready to go, and take the pressure off finding a full-time position right away.

3 **Selling all your belongings:** just kidding! Kind of. But if you've thrown in the towel and don't know how you're going to pay the next council tax bill, see if there's anything you don't use/wear/want any more, and start selling it on eBay. It might not make you a millionaire, but it will help in the short term.

When it comes to handing in your notice, regardless of your circumstances, keep it professional. You don't want to be remembered as that guy who resigned after sinking two pints during a lunchtime pub visit, or the girl who quit two days before taking all of her annual leave in one go. Why? Because your employer might be called on to give you a reference in the future.

Book a meeting with your boss, and type up a formal resignation letter in advance. Address it to them, and include:

- Your terms of notice, and when your last day in your job will be. Make sure to check your annual leave allowance in advance — if you have any pro rata days owed to you, you may be asked to take them during your notice period.
- A thank you to your employer for the opportunity to work with them.
- A note to say you hope you can rely on them for references in the future.

And that is it. You might be required to do an exit interview with someone from HR before your last day, where you can go into more detail about why you've decided to leave the company. How honest you are is an entirely personal thing; you are entitled to bring up issues that you feel must be addressed (though stick to the facts, rather than using it as an opportunity to offload), or you can choose to avoid re-treading the ground you're about to leave.

What to do if you lose your job

As fun as it might be to daydream about the moment you finally get to hand in your notice to the boss you can't stand, the same can't be said for finding out you have lost your job. Unfortunately, in the working world we live in now, fewer roles are becoming the stable, 20-year-plan jobs our parents had, so it's good to be prepared, just in case. Here's what you should do if you're asked to leave:

1 **Firstly, ask why:** if one day you had a job and the next you don't, it's important to understand what led to that decision. You might not want to hear it, but ask your line manager for constructive feedback on what went wrong, and what you could do differently in the future so you can learn from any mistakes.

2 **Look into your rights:** it's important that you fully understand the circumstances in which you have lost your job. If you have been working in an organisation for over two years and you're not on a fixed contract, there must be a lawful reason to fire you and a procedure will need to have been followed; if not, this may be an unfair dismissal. And if you are made redundant after being employed by an organisation for two years or more, you have certain rights, too — like redundancy pay. The WorkSmart website is an excellent resource for finding out what your rights are.

3 **Get in touch with your network:** now's the time to contact all the people you met networking to find your current job and let them know you're looking for new work.

4 **But don't be too honest:** it might not be the right moment to be explicit about being fired; tell people what they need to know, and then move the conversation on. 'It wasn't working out' or 'it wasn't the right fit' imply enough. It's also not the time to bad-mouth your previous employer, particularly not in interviews.

5 **Get your finances in check:** find out when you can expect your final pay-cheque, and what it will be for. Cut back on expenses like taxis and takeaways, and work out what you can realistically afford while you search for new employment.

6 **Find a short-term gig:** while job-hunting, you might want to think about signing up with a temping agency, where you'll be allocated short-term positions (often a few days to a few weeks long) that match your skill-set.

7 **Look into Jobseekers' Allowance:** you may be entitled to receive this from the government while you look for work. You can use the benefits calculator on their website to find out.

What is a union and should I join one?

Many industries have associated bodies called trade unions — these are organisations that help to safeguard workers' rights, get you a better deal on pay and conditions, and provide support through unfair treatment. If you're a member of a union, you will pay a subscription ('subs') which funds the work that organisation does.

Employers can't discriminate against you if you choose to join one, and many have recognised unions that they choose to work with. It's worth checking your employee handbook to find out if your workplace has a union representative.

The Trade Union Congress (TUC) have a full list of unions in England and Wales on their WorkSmart website.

How to get on with colleagues you can't stand

They say you can't choose your family, but at some point in your working life you will find yourself wishing it was your meddling Aunty Mildred working next to you, instead of your actual desk-mate. Sadly, you don't get much say over them either; so how do you make the most of a grating situation?

1 **Dig out the headphones:** yes, yes, other people might call this ignoring the problem. But if your issues are noise-related (they talk too much, they eat too loudly, they *breathe*) and you work in the kind of office where headphones at your desk are allowed, just put them on and listen to your own thing. Obviously, this isn't going to work the whole time (and if you're a more junior member of staff, it might drive your boss mad), but think of them as an emergency service.

2 **Have a word:** if you have a genuine grievance with someone — they loudly make sexist comments, or steal your ideas in meetings, for example — you are perfectly entitled to take them to one side and ask if they'd mind not doing that, because you don't agree with them and it's making you feel uncomfortable. If they don't cooperate, speak to your boss.

3 **Keep the talk small:** some people are naturally nosy. They'll want to know everything that you got up to in minute detail and then ask you about it very loudly again when other people are around. Set yourself a challenge: come up with the most nondescript answers humanly possible, so they have nothing to work with. This is an incredibly satisfying exercise.

4   **Don't rise to it:** if you find it hard to be quiet when someone says something you fundamentally disagree with … try to learn how. If their views are pushing you to boiling point and you don't want to start a verbal punch-up in the office, just ignore them and wait until they run out of steam. They'll soon move on.

5   **Ask for a change of scenery:** this is a more extreme solution, sure. But be crafty: offices are ALWAYS moving their staff around. If you get a whiff of that in the pipeline, offer to help with the planning because you have 'some ideas on productivity'. It'll mean brownie points from the poor sod tasked to do it in the first place, and (hopefully) a more peaceful environment for you.

The practical skills you'll need to get on in an office

One of the most important things you'll ever need to know in an office is how to do actual office-y things. We're not talking about those CV-friendly catchphrases like 'adept at balancing budgets'; no, you're going to need to pick up a few key skills that'll mean you can get on, day to day, without asking your boss how to fix the photocopier. Whether you work in marketing or banking or a theatre, these are the basics — told to us by other real-life workers — that'll see you through:

'Being friendly, open, and making the effort to know

people. I find people are much more willing to do stuff you ask if they know who you are and like you.'

'Timekeeping. Show up on time, or be five minutes early, and always have a pen and a notepad.'

'Learn to touch type. You're going to spend untold years of your life doing it, so do it properly!'

'Tea/coffee is a must. I recently got called into an emergency situation in the kitchen by a friend at work — it turned out an external guest had asked for a black coffee and she had no idea how to make it!'

'It's always good to have sound computer skills — you'd be surprised how many people don't. Even if you're not sure how to fix a tech problem, just having the wherewithal to Google it or look it up on YouTube puts you ahead of a lot of people who simply give up in despair.'

'The soft skills are really important — being open, social, and a good communicator is key.'

'I can't speak for all offices, but knowing how to fix a paper jam in the photocopier has helped me get ahead in mine. And having a secret stash of chocolate biscuits that you're ready to crack open in case of emergency can be a life-saver!'

'Over- rather than under-communicate, and never promise to deliver something at a time you know you can't meet.'

'Remembering faces/names. If in doubt, do a small floor plan sketch in the back of a notebook till you learn who everyone is and where they sit.'

'Get your head around Excel and PowerPoint. Even if you work in a job where you never have to use them, at some point you'll hear someone shout "Does anyone know how to work a spreadsheet?" from the other side of the office. And it always pays to help people out.'

'Basic politeness and decency towards the person working on reception, or cleaning your office, or working in the post room. Firstly — it's nice to be nice. And secondly, you never know when they might be able to help you out, or what role they might end up in one day.'

How to have a 'working wardrobe' — and knowing what's right for which job

Working out what to wear in an age that is long past power-suits and shoulder-pads can be pretty tricky. Not all corporate companies have a dress-code, and places that you'd think would have a more relaxed vibe can be pretty strict.

So how do you work out what to wear? You can prep for this before you even get the job. If you go into the office for an interview and have time to wait, look at the people working there and make a mental note of their get-ups. And if you get the job, make the dress-code one of the things you ask about when you're checking about working hours and other fundamentals.

If you're starting from scratch, the key thing here is not to buy everything at once, but add stuff to your wardrobe slowly, depending on what your workplace is like. If it's a corporate vibe, that might mean a couple of suits and three new shirts, plus some shiny new shoes. If it's more casual, don't just rock up in your old jeans and a jumper — add in a few work-only tops or dresses.

And even though this whole 'working wardrobe' thing doesn't sound too sexy, it does make sense. Literally separate what you would only wear to work from what you'd only wear outside of it in your wardrobe — it'll make your decisions easier in the morning, you'll always know when you need to put a wash on, and it'll also mean you can switch off that little bit more at the weekends, when you've got your 'home' clothes on.

Shopping for a working wardrobe — Kat's story

'One of my Adult Gateway moments was going shopping for a new wardrobe for my first job after university. My mum came too, because she IS an adult and I wasn't one YET (I didn't own a suit). I ended up with smart tailored trousers, neat shirts, some hideous clingy-yet-appropriate tops in autumnal shades, and a blazer. I spent a lot of money crafting this sharp look (for it was an entire LOOK), but when I started my job — as an executive assistant — I felt so unlike myself that I started all over again.'

Here's what other people wear to work

'I'm in insurance, but I wear very casual clothes.'

'I recently changed jobs from being in a small interior design school to a mid-level marketing professional in a global property company. The effect that this has had on my work wardrobe has been profound! I used to rock up in skinny jeans and a plaid shirt most days, maybe adding a blazer for external meetings. It was a creative atmosphere and the dress-code was "fluid". In my new role, it's corporate power-dressing all the way. The other day they updated the dress-code to include no leather skirts. I gulped and looked down at my leather pencil skirt in dismay — there goes one of my wardrobe staples! *frantically loads the ASOS app*'

'I work in public affairs/stakeholder management and I've settled on chinos and a shirt. I always have a nice pair of shoes and a suit in the office for when it's needed, but the rest of the time smart casual is fine by me — as long as you're not so scruffy people take notice then there's no problem. I've accepted the descent into middle-age now too, so I go for the comfort of trainers on my commute.'

'I work for a magazine, which isn't half as glamorous as you'd think. I'll throw on comfy stuff if all I have on for the day is writing at my desk, but I'll put on something more put-together when I'm in meetings where I play a key part. It's for my own benefit — it makes me feel like I know what I'm doing.'

'I'm a creative resource manager. I'm pretty lucky and can get away with most things; usually jeans and a top, and trainers or flats. If I know I am in a lot of meetings or a meeting with a specific person (usually senior management or external) I try to dress a little smarter.'

'I work for a small and relaxed company, but over the years I've bought myself a range of smart tops that I classify as work-only attire — things like silk shirts from vintage stores. I wear these when I have meetings, and because I never wear them on the weekends they create a bit of a division between my "work" clothes and what I wear on my own time. I like keeping a distinction.'

'I work in banking. That's a suit and an optional tie — unless I'm seeing clients.'

'I work in the creative industries. The dress-code is quite relaxed and casual — unless of course, you have a client meeting and then you're expected to dress a bit smarter. Shirt, brogues, wash behind your ears … you get the idea.'

'I'm a primary school teacher — that means no cleavage, nothing too tight, not too much leg, no denim. Wear heels at your own personal peril! Where does this leave me?! Luckily, in a school there's no need to make a fashion statement; kids don't judge and teachers tend not to either. Feeling good is still important though. Clothes are relaxed but smart.'

How to recognise and deal with workplace bullying

Thought you'd left nasty bullies back in your school days? We're very sorry to inform you that they do actually exist as adults, too. And if you encounter one in the wild, this is basically Bullying 2.0, because you can't tell your parents when you go home, and these are people who are messing with your damn career.

Bullying at work isn't illegal, even though *harassment* is (under the 2010 Equality Act), but your employer also has a duty of care to make sure bullying doesn't happen in the workplace. So how do you spot if it's happening to you? Here's what to look out for:

1   **Overt criticism:** if someone is constantly putting you or your performance down. Maybe they do have a problem with your work, maybe they're just an arsehole. Either way.

2   **Aggression:** if someone is using anger or threats against you, this is a problem.

3   **Exclusion:** this is the office, not a house party, so not getting an invitation to a meeting or a project that you should be in is NOT OKAY. This might not even be

a formal scenario — the same applies if a colleague is purposefully trying to exclude you from ad hoc conversations or planning sessions that are to do with your job.

4   **Rumours:** because apparently not everyone has moved on from taking tips from teen movies, malicious rumours can be rife in the workplace. If you find yourself at the centre of one started by a colleague, this is bullying.

5   **Being picked on:** this could be anything from being the constant butt of someone's jokes to someone rubbishing your ideas in meetings.

IF YOU WANT TO DEAL WITH IT YOURSELF

If you genuinely feel that it'll do more harm than good to escalate the problem at this stage, you don't have to pretend it's not happening. There are things you can do to try to stop the bully yourself, first.

1   **Be really, really nice:** yes, it kills to be an arse-kisser. But see if you can keep your frustrations in check for a few days and be exhaustively nice to whoever isn't being nice to you. It might just defuse someone's crappy attitude.

2   **Screw those rumours:** you know what's as bad as being the butt of a rumour? Spreading them yourself. It can be SO tempting to get one over a nasty colleague by telling your workmates about their awful breath/ill-fitting jeans/fling with Rachel from HR, but you know what? It won't help. Avoid getting involved.

3   **Have a quiet word:** if you feel you can, take the person you have a problem with aside and calmly explain that the way

they've been speaking to you has made you a bit uneasy, and is there a problem, because you'd like to be able to resolve it and move on. Often, asking someone to identify their issue is enough to make them realise they don't have one.

... AND IF YOU DEFINITELY DON'T

If this isn't something you feel comfortable handling on your own (and why should you have to?), here's how to take the next step:

1 **Keep a paper trail:** you might never need to use them, but keep notes of any correspondence that you've had which you've deemed inappropriate, or jot down the details of any unsettling verbal conversations and what they were about. That way you've got some first examples to refer back to, should you need to.

2 **Tell someone:** this might be your line manager, another manager, or someone from HR. Ask them for a meeting and explain that you are being bullied or harassed at work. Now's the time to also ask them for the company's policy, and work out a plan together to try to put a stop to it.

3 **Look for an informal resolution:** there's nothing to say you can't still sort out the problem in an informal way. Ask HR to facilitate a meeting between you and the bully, and try to come to an agreement together. At the very least, it's a gesture of goodwill that you're not trying to blot someone's employment record.

4 **Formalise things, if you have to:** in an ideal world, you'll be able to resolve things without having to do more than

a quick chat. But then again, in an ideal world we'd each get a bonus for getting up in the morning. If you've exhausted all your options, call the ACAS (The Advisory, Conciliation and Arbitration Service) helpline and ask how you can escalate the situation.

Want more suggestions? MIND the charity have a comprehensive list of recommendations and advice on their website.

How to network

Baulking at that word before you've even got going? Yeah, networking might seem uncomfortable, old school, and more than a touch dry, but it's actually a bloody good idea to do it. 'BUT WHY?', you're screaming at us internally. Because, reader, it's a good way to put a firework up your career's bum — and all you have to do is be friendly to people you meet who work in your field. So, here's how to network and not want to cry:

1 **Start somewhere:** a good way of finding out about the events in your industry is to ask your boss. The chances are, they've had to network too (and are still doing it) and will know what's worth your time and what you should steer clear of. If you don't want to go on your own, find a colleague or a friend in the same industry who would a) provide moral support, and b) actually benefit from it too, and work the room together.

2 **Do some research:** if you're going to an event with a panel or speakers, read up on them before you go. Even if you

don't want to ask them a question personally, it'll be handy small talk when you're working the room.

3 **Take names:** if you speak to anyone interesting, make a note of their name and company (and anything else they've told you) in your phone, or ask for a business card. The next day (not that night, keeno!), find them on LinkedIn or send a quick email saying how nice it was to meet them and you hope to speak to them again in the future. And add them to your personal contacts with a note to say when and where you met them.

4 **Find a mentor:** one of the nicest ways to have doors thrown open for you (or even just winched ajar) is to have a mentor. This is someone, usually in your industry, who draws on their own experience to give guidance, make valuable introductions, and help with your career progression. Look for schemes within your industry or, if you've met someone you look up to, ask them outright if they'll mentor you. It doesn't have to be a formal set-up, but it's good to establish some rules around how often you'll meet and what you'll cover.

5 **Stop looking up:** networking isn't all about you working your way UP the ladder, it's also about giving a hand to people a few rungs below you. Aside from the fact that the office intern might one day be running a company, drawing on your own experience and contacts to give someone you believe in a better chance of succeeding is a blooming nice thing to do.

So you want to be an entrepreneur?

Setting up shop on your own is becoming an increasingly popular option, but be warned; it comes with a paperwork curse. Not deterred by spreadsheets? Read on.

HOW TO GO SELF-EMPLOYED

You probably know at least one person who works for themselves. Industries like journalism, construction, contract work, plumbing and maintenance, web development, project management, and social media all rely on a steady stream of freelancers, and there are benefits to going self-employed; it can mean setting your own rates and hours, choosing your clients, sacking off the commute, and spending a lot of time in your joggers. But — here's the buzz kill — it can *also* mean an uncertain cash flow, working unsociable hours, losing out on holiday and sick pay, and a fair bit of admin.

Before you take the plunge, a few things to consider are:

1 **Your current financial situation:** pretend you are your parents, and have THAT conversation with yourself. Do you have an overdraft the size of a Hollywood inheritance? Are you currently on your third credit card? Do you have any savings tucked away for a rainy day? If your numbers are teetering on perilous, consider what you'd like your bank statement to look like before deciding whether to ditch your steady pay-cheque.

2 **What your rates would be:** work out what money you expect to make. If you pay rent and bills each month, winging it isn't going to work. Figure out the minimum

you need to earn each month, then how many days/projects/work assignments you need to achieve that. If it translates as working non-stop, even on the weekends, think about adjusting those rates.

3   **If you're looking to get a mortgage soon**: when anyone buys a house, their mortgage lender will want to see proof of their income through payslips and bank statements. If you're self-employed, you'll probably be asked to show two to three years of these. It's worth speaking to a mortgage broker to understand the implications of going freelance.

4   **Your current home set-up**: if you'd be doing most of your work from your house, look around you: do you live in a freezing flat with five other people and no room for a desk? Not even a kitchen table? Is there a local cafe with free Wi-Fi you can sit in all day? Or do you need to go the shared office-space route, and — importantly — what would that cost you?

SETTING UP A COMPANY, OR NOT

Please fetch your Business Hat. We're on to the even-more-practical-than-the-other-stuff bit. If you decide to go self-employed, the two most common routes are:

- Registering as a sole trader
- Becoming a Limited Company

And here's how they're different:

SOLE TRADER

If you're working for yourself and have paying clients, you're a sole trader. That means:

- You own your business, and can have all of its profits after tax
- You can do business under your own name, or come up with a new one (as long as it's not trademarked … and ideally isn't something you thought up after too many glasses of wine)
- You're responsible for any losses the business incurs
- You need to register with HMRC for self-assessment and Class 2 National Insurance, and file a tax return each year (and then pay it, on time)
- You need to keep a record of all the business you've done and the expenses you've incurred
- You must register for VAT if your income exceeds £85,000 each year
- You may be eligible for self-employed housing benefit, self-employed grants or self-employed tax credits

LIMITED COMPANY

Anyone self-employed can set up a Limited Company. In some industries, going down this route won't matter. In others, being a company is par for the course. That means:

- Finding a name that you want and is available, then forming a company by, as a minimum, registering with Companies House online (or getting set up properly by an accountant for £100 to £150 plus VAT)

- Any financial losses are incurred by the company, not you, its director
- You will pay corporation tax and income tax (which, with a bit of planning, actually works out slightly cheaper than the tax on all your profits as a sole trader)
- You need to set up a separate business bank account
- You must do that darned self-assessment as well as your company's taxes

Side note: if you're employed and also work a day job for a company, you can be self-employed and work for yourself outside of those hours. And you can then also refer to yourself as having a side-hustle.

FINDING A GOOD ACCOUNTANT

You don't have to employ someone to do your paperwork for you, but if having an accountant means fewer receipts, maths, and filing, it's a tempting option. If your basic records are decent, it should generally cost a few hundred pounds a year plus VAT if you're a sole trader, and double that for a small limited company. Whatever your business structure, the more you ask your accountant to do for you, the more it will cost you.

A good way to go about finding one is to ask your friends or other freelancers in your industry for recommendations. It's also worth checking if your parents have any friends who are accountants; you might get a better rate that way. If not, the website Unbiased will help match you to one who fits your bill.

INVOICING

If you ever want to see money in your account, read on. Invoicing is how you get paid for the work you do, so you'll want to do it properly.

First, set up a way to record all the money you are owed, and when it is supposed to come in; a basic spreadsheet will do the trick. For each piece of billable work you've done, you'll need to record:

- The date you did the work
- The company you did it for
- The fee agreed
- The date you invoiced
- The date you expect payment (in line with your terms — see below)
- The date you received the payment
- Any other notes

Now on to the fun bit — telling people to SHOW YOU THE MONEY! Before you invoice, ask whoever has hired you where you need to send their bill. This might be a finance or accounts department, or it might be them, but not getting it right could lead to delays in payment. Each invoice should include:

- Your name/company name and address
- Your invoice number
- Their purchase order number (if they've given you one)
- A brief description of the service you completed

- The agreed fee
- The bank details where the money should be paid
- Your terms of payment (each industry will have its own standards, but 30 days from the date of the invoice is a good ballpark)
- If you are a company, your registered company number and business address

Simply send that on to the right person, and wait to be paid …

HOW TO FOLLOW UP LATE PAYMENTS

… which might be a while. According to Zurich Insider, in 2016, more than half of SMEs experienced problems with late payments; and that could mean you find yourself with terms of payment that have passed, and not a penny added to your bank account.

You're entitled to chase the client — but to begin with, try not to piss them off too much. The softly-softly approach sounds counterintuitive, but if it's a genuine mistake, you don't want to put them off giving you repeat business. Here's a guideline for chasing:

Send a simple email to the person you sent your invoice to; there might be a reasonable explanation. Ask them for a timescale for payment.

Contact the accounts department and ask them the same questions. Stay calm and polite and you may be able to get them to rush yours through.

If you have no luck down either of those routes, you can

take things up a level. The law says that — if terms haven't been agreed — a payment is late after 30 days from the date the customer gets the invoice, or the date you provide the service (if that's later). So, if you're still waiting on payment, you can charge 'statutory interest' — currently 8% — AND the Bank of England base rate for business-to-business transactions. You can outline these new terms in an email to the client, and wait for their (probably speedy) response before deciding whether to invoice for the new amount.

SAVE, SAVE, SAVE

Now you've got the money coming in, it's time to get spendy, right?! No, I'm sorry, that's wrong. Really, really wrong. Because no matter how much you earn, you still need to put a big lump of this away in your savings. The big, essential bits of that equation to account for are:

1 **Tax and National Insurance:** how much you'll pay depends on how much you've earned during that financial year (the government's self-assessment ready reckoner is a good way of estimating this if you're newly self-employed). Save each time you get paid, and you won't even notice it.

2 **Student loan:** if you've ever taken out a student loan, you'll — surprise! — need to pay it back. Standard employees on a company payroll have these contributions deducted at source — i.e. their employer will take it out before it gets anywhere near your monthly salary. But if you're self-employed, you'll need to include it in your self-assessment (if you have an accountant, they'll work out your student

loan liability for you). Your deduction will be based on 9% of your total income above the threshold of your loan plan (1 or 2). There's a good explainer on the government website.

3 **The emergency pot:** you may have periods where work is thin on the ground or payments are late. Think about how much you'll need in savings to tide you over; it might be something you build up incrementally, but it will mean you don't find yourself in a pickle later down the line.

4 **Fun money:** now's also the time to also think about putting money aside to cover any holiday you intend to take or things you know you'll end up spending on, like Christmas presents.

A note on payment dates from Kat's dad, chartered accountant David Poole:

'If you're **self-employed**, your business profits will be declared on your self-assessment tax return covering the tax year from 6 April to 5 April. Your tax and National Insurance will be payable by 31 January the following year — 9 months after the end of the tax year.

In the first two years, the rules can appear a little complicated, but after that everything settles down.

So, if you started trading on 1 August 2018, your profits for the 8 months to 5 April 2019 will be included in your tax return for the year to 5 April 2019, and tax will be payable by 31 January 2020.

In your second year, profits for the year 1 August 2018 to 31 July 2019 go in your tax return for the year ending 5 April 2020. Tax will be payable by 31 January 2021 — a long time after your accounts year-end, but remember to put money away each month to cover the liability.

If your total liability is more than £1000 you have to pay an equivalent amount 'on account' of the next tax year, in two instalments; 31 January, on top of your actual liability, and the following 31 July. It's painful the first year it happens, but after that it balances itself out.

If you operate through a **limited company**, the corporation tax on company profits is due nine months after the end of its accounting year. If a company is set up in February, it's accounts year will run to the end of February next year, and the corporation tax liability will be payable nine months later, by the end of November that year.

If you draw a salary or take dividends as income from your company, you will be liable to pay income tax in the tax year in which your salary is paid or dividends are declared, irrespective of the company's year-end.'

EXPENSES

You didn't think we'd end on a financial low-point, did you? Happily, you can chalk a fair bit of expenditure down to running costs, and offset these against the tax you owe at the end of the financial year. You need to keep receipts for all of them, and a record of when you paid out and what it was for. But you can claim money back on all of these lovely things:

- Travel necessary for your work (train tickets, petrol costs at 45p per business mile)
- Stationery, phone bills, and other office costs
- Clothing, if you wear a uniform (no, buying designer kit because you work in fashion doesn't count)
- Banking or insurance charges
- Website and advertising costs
- Accountants' fees

If you work from home, you can also claim back on costs like electricity and rent; the government website has a 'simplified expenses' calculator to help work that out, but generally accountants put through a charge of say £5 per week for 'use of home as office'.

Writing a business plan

If you're comfortable with being self-employed, have a genius idea, and want to run a business of your own, it doesn't have to be as daunting as *Dragons' Den*. The Prince's Trust charity have free downloadable business plan packs and templates available on their website, which will guide you through writing up the start of your success story.

Life admin
(a.k.a. THAT DRAWER)

'I'm so excited to ignore that house party invite tonight, switch off Netflix, and make a date with *that* drawer full of unopened letters, out-of-date passports, energy company demands, and something about a final deadline,' said no one, ever.

One of the worst things about becoming an adult (up there with having to force yourself to go to the dentist) is how much time gets sapped up by organising dull stuff like insurance, appointments, banking, zzzzzzzzz. It's especially annoying when you're at a computer all week long at work, and come the weekend, you just want to relax or go out, not tackle more paperwork and dull demands.

But staying on top of your life admin is important — just ask Alex, who endlessly shoved paperwork into a drawer 'to deal with later' and … accidentally bought a car. Seriously.

How I accidentally bought a car — Alex's story

She's a corporate high-flier, whose name is a pseudonym because 'no one can find out — it would ruin my reputation at work and my family wouldn't stop laughing at me', but Alex explains:

'One thing that always seemed Mysterious and Boring and Expensive to me was the world of cars. So at my old job, I jumped at the chance to choose a company car over a pay rise. The shiny car was so nice I almost forgot I hated the job. And if a light on the dash came on — no problem — it would be fixed. When I got another job, I had to give the car back, and then I went on holiday, leaving me with one weekend to find a new car before I started my new job.

I ended up at one of those massive car supermarkets, with a bored salesman who had no time or inclination to explain anything to me. I landed a car that was about a year old, taking out something called a PCP (Personal Contract Purchase), where you lease a car monthly and then pay a "balloon payment" if you want to keep it at the end. I never wanted to keep it, so I completely ignored this waffle, confidently knowing I would swap it for another car in a year or so.

Three years later (and one house move on), I was still the owner of the same car. All the paperwork for it had been stuffed into various cupboards, or lost. I meant to go and swap it again, but I hadn't the faintest idea how to do it. Did I have to go to the same awful garage? Was it mine? Was it theirs? Where on earth was the damn paperwork? I pushed it aside.

One morning, I was buying toilet roll from Sainsbury's and my card was declined, strangely. I nipped outside to check my balance on the ATM. FOUR AND A HALF THOUSAND POUNDS HAD DISAPPEARED FROM MY BANK ACCOUNT. Panicked, I went on my online banking app and saw those awful words on the screen that meant I'd accidentally bought the bloody car. I called the car place, but they said it was nothing to do with them, it was the finance company. Eventually, I sort of realised that I had bought a shit car, by mistake, and for way more than it was worth. They had probably sent me letters, but I had moved house ... So I had a cry. I left the stupid car on its own for three months and got the train to work instead.'

To avoid expensive mistakes like Alex's, start by creating A System. When Lucy bought a flat, got married, and switched jobs in the same year, and her life admin started piling up, she set hers up like this:

Buy five box files, labelling each one for a set subject, like 'house stuff — energy, insurance, mortgage'; 'banking'; 'work stuff — pension, pay slips etc.' 'personal docs' etc.

Set aside a drawer or pile (based somewhere that you won't ignore it) for interim 'filing' — e.g. when letters arrive that need Something To Be Done, either do it immediately (pay a bill, write on it 'paid', file in box file) or put it in the drawer to deal with swiftly.

Tackle the drawer once a week to make sure nothing serious escapes your attention (e.g. accidentally buying a car).

What do I actually need to keep and what can be thrown away?

Things you can recycle pronto (after ripping up or shredding any sensitive details):

- Receipts (not ones for work-related expenses) and ATM records, once you've checked the transaction via online banking or a statement
- Bank deposit slips, once the funds appear in your account
- Credit card and bank statements, once you've checked them over (long-term records are all online — so consider switching to paperless and just being sure to regularly check payments there)

Things you can throw away once a year:

- Insurance policies that are now out of date (though keep a record of who your insurer was)
- Any retained bank statements, unless needed for tax purposes
- Lingering receipts/bills for bigger purchases/services, unless required for a warranty
- Utility bills, unless you need them for tax reasons (you have a home office, are self-employed, etc.)

Things you should keep for longer:

- Rent statements: these may be required if you're renting a new place and need proof you're a timely payer, or for mortgage applications

- Supporting documents needed to complete your tax return (e.g. pay slips, expense receipts etc.) should be kept for at least 22 months after the end of the tax year (which ends on 5 April) the tax return is for, according to HMRC. (So if you submitted your 2017–18 tax return online by 31 January 2019, keep your records until at least the end of January 2020.) It's longer for self-employed people, though, where HMRC demands records are kept for at least 5 years after the 31 January submission deadline of the relevant tax year.

Things you should keep forever:

- Tax returns, with proof that you filed and paid
- Other important tax documents like your P45, P60, P11D, and any information about redundancy terms or pay
- Work contracts (if nothing else, they're useful points of comparison if you're looking at a new employer's offering)
- Pension statements
- Mortgage documents
- Receipts for large purchases, for insurance purposes
- Investment details

How to go paperless (a.k.a. shoving everything on the 'cloud' to get a cupboard back)

While you need most of the above documents, in many cases you don't actually need them clogging up your space — you can often just scan and upload to a secure location, then rip up and recycle the original.

A caveat — with some VIP documents, listed below, you should always keep the original somewhere safe, and make back-up copies just in case, too. They are:

- Birth certificates
- Citizenship papers
- Custody agreements
- Debt repayment records
- Deeds and titles
- Divorce certificates
- Investment documents
- Loan/mortgage paperwork
- Marriage licences
- Passports
- Powers of attorney
- Wills and living wills

But as for the rest? You don't need paper copies. Back-up anything you want to keep a record of by shoving it on a cloud[2] service, like Dropbox or Google Drive. (Watch out, as experts warn there's no way to ever be completely sure your data will remain secure once you've moved it to the cloud. Most of us choose to bury our heads in the sand about this because it's really convenient. But you can look into heavy encryption and security if it's a worry.) On a phone, most data is automatically backed up online (in Apple's iCloud, for

---

2 After grilling three developer friends about WTF the cloud actually is, it turns out it is composed of servers connected to the internet. They're the things that allow you to upload files from your laptop/phone/any device that's online to store in this mystical place, and then access the same files from anywhere.

example) but make sure it's up to date.

And be aware that online banking, insurance, mortgages etc. mean our computers basically know more about us than our best friends. So regular back-ups are key, and, if you're selling or binning a phone, tablet, or laptop, you need to follow up a back-up with these steps to protect your data:

1 'Deauthorise' any software that comes with licences or similar — iTunes purchases made with an Apple ID, for example, can only be 'authorised' on up to five devices, so click on the Store menu in iTunes and select 'Deauthorise This Computer'.

2 For a computer, wipe the hard drive, following the instructions given by 'data destroying' software such as DBAN. Newer computers have in-built ways to wipe a drive, found in the control panel. You can also remove the hard drive and physically destroy it — drilling holes in it should do the trick, making it unreadable.

3 On a smartphone or tablet, use the 'factory reset' or 'erase all content and settings' option in Settings.

You'll miss that inbox if it's gone …

When Dani's email got hacked, at first he thought it was annoying, but that he'd be back in the account soon. Days later, still hammering at the virtual door of an unhelpful email host, unable to access his messages, he realised it was more than just annoying … He'd stored a bunch of important documents on email alone; he was waiting to hear back from a few job interviews, and he couldn't check if the firms had sent him a message; plus the admin that basically ruled his life — the reminders about appointments, the real-life addresses of friends and family — was all tied into his email.

Since hackings are getting more common, working out ways to keep your data as safe as possible is becoming even more important. And yeah, the first thing is passwords. We all know it's a pain in the bum (and fingers, and brain) to remember 18 different online passwords, especially when none of them is allowed to be 'Password1' (and apparently '123456' isn't the best idea either). But using a solid password could be the difference between being hacked or staying tech secure. So, don't reuse passwords, and don't make them predictable — involving your name, birthday, popular dictionary words etc. There are password generator tools to help you conjure up a hard-to-crack letter-number-symbol combo. Even so, you should still change your passwords regularly to keep cyber-criminals at bay.

It's hard when you're tapping out a deep 'n' meaningful tome to a uni friend who moved to Australia, or just dashing out a 'Pls can you pay this bill? Here are my banking details' missive to your housemate — but, according to one secretive cyber crime expert whose main job is stopping A-listers getting hacked, even us ordinary people need to start thinking of email as more like a postcard to a friend than a top-secret recorded delivery letter.

Why? Because phishing scams have become far more complex than the old 'Hello Friend, I've WON the Loteri, if yoo send me YUR BANC deetales I will share wiv you?' Fraudsters are now honing in on people after tracking them on social media ('Congrats on your engagement, click this link we've sent you a present …'). So be aware, and never share sensitive information like account details or personal tax info via an email or in a public domain. If a company contacts you via email to ask for information that could be easily compromised, contact them by phone (or on their website, but **not** after clicking on an emailed link) to check they are legit.

Sign up to 'login notifications' on your email and most-used social media so that if someone logs in from a new computer or device, you're told by email or text. It's sometimes annoying when you get an alert just because you've used a friend's phone to check your Twitter, but it's worth it to be notified on any unusual activity ('Account sign-in in Ulaanbaatar' when you're in Slough might ring alarm bells) and you can quickly change your password.

Lastly, make sure your virus scanner and operating system is up to date. Pretty annoying when your phone's latest OS update takes up approximately 2.4 million gigs worth of data, but it's one of the best ways to avoid falling victim to a scam. Use all of the security features on social media sites like Facebook, Snapchat, Twitter, and Instagram, too — and be careful of what personal information you share online.

The best apps to organise your life

- **Evernote:** basically an epic to-do list that lets you take notes and make lists (including images, audio clips, newspaper clippings etc.), syncs across your devices (although you can only sync two in the free version of

the app), and allows you to share them with partners/
housemates/siblings who might need reminding of the
cleaning rota!

- **Loyalive:** you know when you go to the coffee shop for the
  fifth time in a fortnight, but realise you've forgotten your
  loyalty card, and it's devastating because you were ONLY
  ONE STAMP AWAY FROM A FREE LATTE? Or you
  forget to stuff your Ikea Family card into your wallet, but
  stop by after work one day and would have saved £40 with
  it …? This is why you need the free Loyalive app: it works
  with hundreds of loyalty programmes, from Tesco Clubcard
  to Topshop and Nectar, stores your card details and points,
  and even tells you when you've reached a reward.
- **IFTTT:** this stands for 'If This, Then That', and allows
  you to create actions that make things happen in set
  circumstances. So you might set up an alert to get a text
  reading 'Remember umbrella!' each morning at 7am IF
  rain is in that day's forecast, or set your music to start
  playing when you get home, or tweet your Instagram
  pictures as native photos in Twitter, or mute your Android
  at bedtime etc.
- **Unroll.me:** this free app brings up a list of every mailing
  list you're subscribed to, so you can quickly remove any
  you don't want, and then combines all the newsletters that
  you do want into one digest email, instead of receiving
  loads of interruptions during the day.
- **Citymapper:** combines the convenience of Google Maps
  with live travel information for buses, Tubes, train, ferry,
  tram, and cycling dock stations in most major cities.

- **RedLaser:** turns your phone's camera into a barcode scanner so you can beep through a product in a shop and the app will give you a list of places that you can buy it for less.
- **Good Budget:** a free budgeting app that tracks your spending, makes graphs highlighting where your cash goes each month, reminds you to pay bills, helps you calculate if you can afford a splurge, and warns when you're overspending.
- **Calm:** our phones make us stressed and crazy most of the time, according to endless reports, but this meditation app is all about relaxing, boosting your mood, and helping you sleep. Sessions range from 2 to 10 minutes, depending on how long you can afford to be ... calm.

How to ... fit something feel-good into your life

Fitting in work, exercise, cooking, life admin, freelancing to save up to become a homeowner one day, seeing friends and family, AND keeping up to date with Netflix and iPlayer to ensure you have something to talk about when you do see them into the average day might make you feel as if your life couldn't be any fuller.

And then, a few hours after telling someone at work how you're SO CRAZY BUSY THERE'S NO TIME FOR ANYTHING, you realise you've just spent 90 minutes browsing through the wedding (and honeymoon, and first child) Facebook photos of someone you once met during Fresher's Week — and all this after you only initially clicked on them to remind yourself who they actually were.

Basically, if most of us try to cram in one do-good thing a

week, or a month, or even sporadically, we'll probably find we actually do have the time after all. And it might make you feel a little bit good too. Here's some inspo:

- **Good Gym:** multi-tasking at its best, this mainly London-based community of runners combines getting fit with doing good. You might find your group of runners helping older people with tasks like gardening or maintenance work, or planting trees for community gardens. With group sessions, you'll be back in 90 minutes, and starter sessions have a shorter run and easier task. Other national groups are springing up, or start your own with friends and a local charity.
- **Casserole Club:** volunteers share extra portions of home-cooked food with older or ill people in their area who aren't always able to cook for themselves. They share once a week, once a month, or whenever works best for them.
- **Befriend a local elderly person:** loneliness is a huge problem for older people — over 5 million are affected, but it doesn't have to be that way. Charities big (like Age UK) and small (Friends of the Elderly) organise willing volunteers to pop into an isolated older person's home, or pick up some shopping, or just join them for a cup of tea in a cafe.
- **Be a school governor:** this might sound surprising if you don't have a tot in your household, but most of us had a helping hand up the ladder of life from our schools, and now a lot of primary and secondary are desperate for help from people with a range of skills. Your tech/financial/

policy etc. know-how could be invaluable for them — and volunteering is great for your CV. Free matchmaking website Inspiring Governance can help would-be volunteer governors find a school in need.

- **Volunteer positions:** there are thousands of other volunteer positions available via networks like Do It, V Inspired or NCVO, which help match your interests and skills with charities' needs — posts include sports-related roles, outside volunteering, festival volunteering, careers-related volunteering, and more.

Etiquette and emotional intelligence

We can talk about mortgages and defrosting freezers and asking for a pay rise until we've grown new wrinkles, but ultimately, nothing says 'I do not know how to be an adult' like dealing with ACTUAL LIFE THINGS you've never encountered before. Like when the first of your friends has a baby. Or when someone younger than you loses both their parents. What about when you have to buy a wedding present for the first time, or when you need to end a proper relationship but you've got shared bank accounts and, worse, TV subscriptions? Feeling overwhelmed yet?

You don't need to be. It might look like everyone around you knows how to behave in situations where you honestly don't have a clue, but trust us: they are all winging it. Because there's a lot more than practicality involved, there's those damn emotions too. We can't give you a definitive answer on how to behave in life, but for some guidance, think of this as City-Mapper for your personal life.

What to do/say/buy when someone gets divorced or goes through a break-up

They say romance isn't dead, but according to the Office for National Statistics, an estimated 42% of marriages end in divorce, with around half of these splits occurring in the first 10 years. So that's … nice. The chances are, you'll know someone who won't stay with their partner whether they're married or not, so what can you do to make things easier for them?

1 **Don't sugar-coat things:** Kat broke up with someone she lived with after seven years, and the best thing anyone said to her was, 'It's totally shit. It will probably get worse,' closely followed by, 'You'll get there, eventually.' Obviously, you don't want to kick a mate while they're down, but telling them that you understand that they're going through something awful is actually pretty helpful.

2 **Get practical:** shoulders to cry on and bottles of wine are great, but so is practical thinking. In these situations, you're going to be the one with a straight head, not your friend who hasn't slept in a week and is treating cheese as a major food group. So, if they need to move, offer a day to help them pack up their stuff. Source the packing boxes. Find an affordable storage company to stash their belongings if they don't have room for them all (or offer your own attic/spare cupboard if you have one).

3 **Offer to help:** think about what you'd want if you were going through the same thing. Top of your list would probably be: a place to stay that isn't with your now ex-partner, and not having to tell everyone you know that

you're going through a break-up. If you can, give them a place to stay for a while and suggest that you quietly spread the word amongst your mutual friends.

And if you're not that close, but still want to let them know you're thinking of them? Then do. Send them a message saying you heard the news, you're thinking of them, and you hope they're holding up okay. Simple.

What should you say to someone in mourning?

They say dying is the only thing we can count on, but we'd like to add 'being speechless when someone dies' to that list. Death and mourning are near-impossible situations to prepare for because everyone copes in different ways. So where do you start?

It might not be a break-up, but showing an honest understanding, offering to help in practical ways, and acknowledging that you've heard their news and are there should your friend/family member/colleague need you is a good place to begin. Sending flowers and a condolence card might be tradition, but try thinking outside the box: could they use a cleaner for a few weeks, or some home-cooked meals?

And if you're attending a funeral, you can of course tell the mourner that you're sorry for their loss. But imagine if it was you — what would you want to hear? Perhaps someone else's fond memories of your loved one, or how much they made you smile. Don't keep it formal if you don't have to — if telling them you always remember that time down the pub where you ended up dancing on tables together feels right, then do.

The one thing to avoid at all costs is clamming up out of awkwardness and failing to even acknowledge their loss. Even if you're not sure how it will be received, saying something simple like, 'I'm so sorry', or sending a brief condolence card is always better than simply ignoring it. They may not thank you now, but they will remember that you showed you cared. Conversely, silence can end up creating a rift.

How are you meant to show you care when someone gets married or has a baby?

There comes a time in everyone's life where your social media feeds will stream endless pictures of engagements and new babies and weddings and slightly older babies. And even if you've reached your love limit (it happens), some of these exciting things will probably be happening to people you're close to, and you'll need to show that you are a nice person and you care. Here's how:

ENGAGEMENTS

This one's pretty easy because not many people expect an engagement present. But best practice (and we really mean *practise* because you'll be doing this A LOT) is to send a card to the couple with a nice message. If your friendship group goes big on gifts, get them something they can enjoy together, like a bottle of champagne, but the real gifting happens when they actually get married.

MARRIAGES

Knowing when to buy a gift for someone getting married is pretty straightforward — if you aren't invited to the wedding, you only need to say congratulations. Luckily, most almost-weds will give you some direction on what they expect as a present — if anything. Some will make a gift list with big shops like John Lewis. (Tip: get on that as soon as you can, so you can choose a gift in your budget and don't end up staring at a list of one really expensive milk jug and a sofa.) Others will ask for money towards their honeymoon fund, and some won't ask for anything at all. (But, to confuse things, it's still customary to put something in an envelope and give it to them on the day.)

So how do you know how much to actually spend? Well, you don't. It'll vary depending on how well you know the couple, how much you like them, and what your own budget it. But here's what actual adults we know have to say on the matter:

How much should you spend on a wedding present?

'It depends on who it is for. For a very close friend, I'd spend a lot more than for someone I wasn't as close to. I'd say for someone I didn't know so well, it would be about £20 or so, but try to make the item look more expensive.'

'It depends how well you know them and how often you see them, but anywhere from £20–£60. It also depends on your disposable income and how much you are spending to attend the wedding. If the wedding is abroad then you may spend a little less on the wedding gift to compensate.'

'If you have the money, £100, and if you don't, you can't go wrong with a bottle of something!'

'I personally always opt for something you could actually see yourself buying the happy couple as a gift … I wouldn't buy someone one pillow, a towel, or a glass for a present, and not vouchers if possible. Spending £30 on something is fine if you know they'll enjoy it — but always try and sort the present early or you'll be scrounging around their wedding list looking for something decent!'

'It depends on how much you're spending on the wedding — if you're travelling from far away and are having to shell out on a hotel and other stuff, people appreciate that and wouldn't expect a lavish gift.'

'I've had to go to quite a few weddings on my own, and decided that I'd spend a standard £25–£30 on each of the couples. And now I'm in a long-term relationship, my partner and I agreed that we'd spend about £50–£60 on each and split that evenly between us, regardless of whose side of friends/family the couple is on.'

'The first question I ask myself here is "How much do I like the people getting married?"'

'I'm married and this provided me with a very useful tip — keep note of what people spend on you and then you're able to spend the same on that person if you're buying them a wedding gift.'

'If the gift list is down to a set of teaspoons and a toilet brush, and you don't want to give money or generic vouchers as it's too impersonal, I like to get the couple a voucher for their favourite restaurant. They will probably be skint after paying for their wedding, and this will enable them to have a date while they are still paying off a zillion pounds of wedding debt. You can look on the restaurant's website to work out how much the voucher will need to be for them to have a slap-up meal. You can also buy vouchers for hotels and flights from places like HotelGift and FlightGift if you are feeling extravagant!'

A NEW BABY

Again, this depends on how close you are to the people who made that new human. If it's a friend you don't see much, a message to say congratulations or a card is a nice gesture, and a small gift if you feel it's appropriate. If it's anyone in your life more important than that, a card and a present is the norm. But try to think outside of the box — there's plenty of stuff more useful (and interesting) than a massive bouquet of flowers:

- A glow-light for when they're up doing night feeds
- A supermarket shop, home-cooked meals (or something

ready-made, but nutritious), or vouchers for an online ordering service

- A subscription service like Don't Buy Her Flowers or Birchbox (because babies are cool, but their parents are probably feeling really, really tired)
- A voucher for a cleaner
- A pledge to babysit so they can enjoy an hour off (or night out)

How to navigate the marriage minefield

Sounds so fun, doesn't it? The truth is — because we want to prepare you — that weddings will take up a lot of your time and money. So, let's get started.

ARE STAGS AND HEN DOS OPTIONAL?

Nowadays, those last nights of freedom aren't just a few-too-many pints in the pub and someone getting tied to a lamppost. They can be expensive, last longer than a weekend, and leave you out of pocket and recovering for a couple of weeks. They can also be really fun. So, you need to work out whether it's worth going to every single one you're invited to.

Think of this as a sliding scale of social obligations — the closer you are to someone, the more important it is to turn up to their do.

1   **Bridesmaid/groomsman:** the chances are you've organised the thing, so unless you're heavily pregnant or out of the country for properly legit reasons, you need to be there.

2   **Close family:** I'm talking brothers, sisters, your mum, in-laws … yes, you need to go. Unless you haven't been invited, in which case this isn't the place for advice.

3   **Not-so-close family:** Kat didn't go to her cousin's hen do because a) she was broke (it was a long weekend away), and b) she didn't know anyone else. She explained, and her cousin was okay with it. Some people won't be, so take it on a case-by-case basis.

4   **Close friend:** these events are mainly for close friends, so the obvious answer is yes. But if this is three days in Las Vegas that will send you into debt for the next two years, speak to them and explain your situation. Another way to save money is to only join for part of the day/event if possible.

5   **Generic mate:** you know, the one who you spend time with, but wouldn't call up and cry to if you'd smashed a tile in your bathroom. This is your call — everything is optional, you just need a good enough reason not to attend.

6   **Colleagues:** same as above. Your workmates *might* be inviting you because they think it would be awkward if they didn't. Only you'll know the depth of your co-worker friendship.

7   **Someone who hasn't invited you to the actual wedding:** absolutely not.

Still not sure? Here's what other people had to say:

'I'm self-employed, so it depends on work commitments

— if it was someone I'm not in frequent contact with, then I would be more inclined to decline the offer.'

'You shouldn't put your life on hold to attend these things. Only do it if you want to and it doesn't break the bank.'

'In my limited experience of stag dos, I'd say they only time that you really must go is if you're a member of the wedding party.'

'I honestly don't really enjoy hen dos very much. The low-key ones are great, but I find some levels of organised fun exhausting! If it's not being held for someone I'm really close to, and it's something that involves a stay overnight and parting with a lot of cash, I usually politely decline and go out for dinner or drinks with the bride separately.'

'Everything is optional! Although I would say if someone has invited you on a stag/hen and therefore ranked you as one of their closest friends, generally there should be a good reason for you not to go unless they've massively overestimated your friendship!'

'If it's a close friend I would 100% try to attend unless I really couldn't afford it or wasn't around on the dates. For someone not so close, I'd try to attend if it wasn't too expensive. If I can't go, I always make sure I sound extra thankful that I was invited.'

WHAT DO YOU DO IF YOU REALLY CAN'T AFFORD IT?

Work out how much you *can* afford. If you can stretch to the wedding, but not the stag/hen, speak to the bride/groom and tell them that, as much as you'd like to be there, you can't find the budget. If you really don't like talking about money, no one will sue you for making a believable and reasonable excuse, like a party for your grandma.

If it's the wedding that is the problem (maybe it's abroad, or in the middle of nowhere, or you're going solo and the hotel room is too expensive), explain your circumstances. They might be able to introduce you to other guests who need to buddy-up, or who could give you a lift. But really, no one should sacrifice the money they need to live off just because someone they know fancied getting married in the Med.[3]

THE PLUS-ONE DILEMMA

Lots of couples don't invite partners of guests to their weddings if they aren't married, in a long-term relationship, or if they haven't met them before. And there's usually a decent reason — it might be financial, or simply because they don't want people they aren't close to at the most important day of their lives.

So how do you make riding solo less daunting?

Tell the couple that you understand why [insert name] wasn't invited, but that they'll be more than happy to step in if they end up with some free seats.

Team up with another mate, and share a hotel room if you

---

3   Maybe tell them in nicer terms than that.

need to stay overnight. You can also share the cost of a wedding gift with them.

If you're worried that you won't know anyone else at the wedding, ask whoever is getting married if they can introduce you to a couple of their nicest friends over drinks, or by text, and arrange to meet up with them on your way to the wedding.

Ask the bride/groom if they wouldn't mind sitting you on a table with your other friends or people you've met before.

How and where to find new (adult) friends once you've left the framework of school/university

As you get older, everyone will tell you that you'll meet your friends for life at senior school, at college, at uni ... And the truth is, it might not be like that. You might find them in a flat-share, in a football team, through your partner, or in the kitchen at work.

But, as charming as that sounds, without the handy frameworks that come with studying, extra-curricular clubs, and hanging out in the same halls, it can be legitimately nerve-wracking to go out there and find new mates when you're grown (ok, grow*ing*) up. Here's how to start:

1   **Hobbies:** one of the easiest ways to meet people who
    you'll have at least one thing in common with is to join a
    group that's all about that one thing. It could be knitting,
    archery, taxidermy, am-dram, or board games; you can
    guarantee you'll find a club that's all about that in your
    area. And if there's anything you really want to learn —

like Spanish, or how to make screen prints — find a class you can go to after work or at the weekend. MeetUp is a huge website that lists social gatherings and trips by topic or interest.

2 **Sports:** okay, sports are hobbies too. But usually they come with in-built camaraderie, so if you're going to play football or netball or whatever it is, you're most likely signing yourself up to after-match drinks too. And if you find a couple of people in that group that you get along particularly well with, don't be afraid to ask them out separately.

3 **Apps:** if you can get a boyfriend/girlfriend/takeaway/ manicure through an app, you can bet you can find friends on one, too. If you don't feel comfortable seeking people out in big group situations, this could be a good way to go. Bumble BFF is a big one, but (cue parental warning ringing in your ears), you should still treat this the same way you would if you were going on a date. Make sure someone (your flatmate, your mum) knows where you are and who you're spending time with. There's also the City Socializer app across UK cities including London, Manchester, Bristol, and Leeds, which helps you join up with local people into the same kind of stuff as you.

4 **Work:** almost no one starts a new job because of the exciting social life it offers, but when you're spending day in, day out with a group of people, you'll probably find a few you really get along with. If it's not inappropriate (you're the intern and they're the CEO), ask someone if they fancy going to grab some lunch together, or make

the most of after-work drinks. And things like office messenger (yeah, they're meant to be a place for work chat, but sure are a good way to get chatting to people outside of meetings or group events).

5   **And bonus points for:** saying yes to things! House parties with a bunch of strangers might not be up your street, but try saying yes to those things where you only know a couple of people, like birthday parties or Sunday afternoons down the pub. You may hate it, you may meet some future best mates. But you won't know until you try!

How to deal with your parents (or how to be a nice child, without them realising it)

Everyone's relationship with their parents is different. You might be joined at the hip, or have moved far, far away. You might really like one of them, but can't stand the other. You might only have one. They might not be your biological parents. Or you might love them dearly, but can't think of anything you have in common aside from your DNA.

Establishing a more balanced and mature relationship with your parents over time will make you feel more confident — in some ways, it's the psychological final frontier of Being An Adult. It's attractive, too — no one is impressed by seeing their girlfriend/boyfriend interact with their family as though they are still 12 years old.

There's no one-size-fits-all for learning how to help that relationship as you (and they) get older, but there are some things that might make it a little bit easier:

1 **Be supportive:** parents tend to be very good at bottling things up around their kids, but now you're growing up you can ask them about things like work (How is it going? Do they have any retirement plans? What is their team like?), their friends (How is so-and-so from their book club? Who are they playing tennis with these days? Did they ever resolve that problem with the neighbour?), or how their health is. They might be going through anything from problems with their boss to illness, and showing that you're interested and supportive will mean a lot.

2 **... And be useful:** if you know what's going on in their lives, that's the first step to helping them out when they might need you to. Do they need taking to a hospital appointment? Book a day off. It won't be fun, but it'll probably be hugely reassuring for them. Even if you're not dealing with anything serious, you might still be able to help with practical things. What about those boxes of old photos your mum keeps mentioning to you? Or the fence they've been trying to fix? If you have some time or you can make some, find out what you can do to help them out.

3 **Let them help you:** if your parents have looked after you for 18+ years, they aren't just going to switch that off now you've got a job and your bank statements get sent to a different address. Sure, that can be annoying sometimes ('Yes, Mum, I am getting enough sleep,' 'No, Dad, I promise I won't get too drunk') but you know what? Who *doesn't* want someone to care about their wellbeing? If you feel like that's verging on interfering, though, divert their attention to things you could actually use a hand with,

like choosing a good travel insurance policy or digging out some old family recipes so you can start making more home-cooked meals. Giving them a concrete task to help with can soak up that energy.

4   **Ask about them:** when you're the one starting a new job or moving house or going on really, really terrible dates, it can be easy to forget to have a two-way conversation with your mum or dad. But if they're willing to listen to you bang on about how much you hate your new boss, it's not hard to ask how their day was, too. You can ask them bigger things; like if they're reaching retirement age, what they would actually like in that next stage of their lives. They might have some really cool goals like taking up beekeeping or doing the Inca Trail. At the very least, it'll probably mean they give you a heads-up on any major plans and don't just sell up and flee to Spain to 'Enjoy themselves, finally.'

5   **Don't just take:** if you're making money now — even if it's just a bit — this is your chance to show your parents that you appreciate what they've done for you financially growing up. Lots of people have to support their parents, sometimes from a young age, but if you're lucky enough not to be one of them you can still make a contribution. You don't need to splurge, but offer to buy them a meal once in a while. And it's not just about money. If you go home to visit, clean up after yourself. Offer to hang out the washing. Unload the dishwasher. It's easy to revert to being looked after, but you're grown up enough to know that's not cool any more.

6   **Be the one to make the effort:** this one's easy. Instead of waiting for them to call you, or organise a visit, give them

a ring every now again. (Got a 10-minute walk to the office in the morning? Use it to ring home and keep them in the loop about your life.) Don't wait for them to ask you to visit or invite themselves to stay with you — find a free weekend in your diary and suggest it yourself. It's a small thing, but showing you care enough to make the effort will go a long way.

7   **Finally … how to manage a toxic relationship with your parents:** not everyone has the kind of family dynamic you see on adverts for breakfast cereal. If your relationship with one or both parents is bad or toxic, you don't have to manage alone. Website MyHorridParent has a useful list of resources that can help you cope when your relationship is distant, or if things get really bad.

How to eat at a formal dinner (so much cutlery!)

No matter how much you like street food and pub grub, you live in the UK. Which means one day you'll probably find yourself at a proper dinner with no idea how to behave because tradition is a weird thing and somewhere, a long time ago, some genius thought it would be a good idea to eat with seven different kinds of fork.

Still, we are where we are. Here's the absolute minimum you need to know:

- Use cutlery from the outside in; you'll have a different set of tools for each course.
- If you're eating bread, use the butter knives provided —

they're usually smaller and blunter, and sit on top of your side plate. Your side plate sits to the left of your place setting; with glasses and cups and saucers to the right.

- Your soup spoon sits to the right of your plate. Your dessert (not pudding) spoon is up top, with another fork, and you're meant to use both.
- You'll have different spoons for condiments, so don't use the soup or dessert spoons (or, god forbid, a knife) for those.
- When you've finished a course, place the cutlery together, the ends curving upwards, in a 6.30pm position on your plate.
- If in doubt, don't dive into your food before you've slyly glanced around the table to see what everyone else is doing. Get it wrong? Don't panic. At the end of the day, these are knives and forks we're talking about.

Some other general advice:

- Always arrive on time; being late or far too early will be considered rude.
- Don't cancel at the last minute if you can help it. Formal dinners have carefully thought out seating plans, and you'll be part of that equation.
- Keep your elbows off the table, and if you're in between courses with fidgety hands, put them in your lap.
- Read the dress-code: you probably won't be expected to wear full black tie, but make sure you don't turn up in jeans if everyone else is there looking the business.
- Put your phone away.

Tips for keeping old friendships strong:

Remember how easy it was when you were younger and you'd see friends in the classroom, other mates at lunchtime, and literally everyone else you knew online on MSN Messenger after school? It's unlikely that you have that many opportunities to be social now you're older and busier (and MSN Messenger, alas, is no more). Here are some ways to make sure you keep in touch with the friends who count:

1 **Remember why you like spending time together:** if you bonded over the theatre, make that the thing you do every few months.

2 **Manage expectations:** there are some friends who you don't need to see more than once every few months, or even less, so talk about that. Explain that you 'love how whenever you see each other, you can pick up where you left off' and remove the pressure.

3 **Make it work around work:** even if a friend lives on the other side of a city to you, they might work close by. Find out where their office is, and if it's convenient, go for lunch every now and again.

4 **Show them you're thinking about them:** texts are great, but if you see something in a shop that reminds you of them (even if it's a cheap bit of tat), put it in the post. Or take a photo or a screenshot of something funny/poignant and send it on with a message that just says 'I saw this and thought of you'.

5 **Pick up the phone:** so you can't get time face-to-face? Ring them. A half-hour chat on the phone is way more personal than a text that someone can forget to reply to.

6   **Remember their birthdays:** one way of knowing for certain that a friendship is doomed is when you stop congratulating each other on getting older. Write it in your diary, set a reminder, whatever. But don't be the mate that forgot.

... and knowing when and how to say goodbye to ones you've outgrown

In economics, there's something called the Sunk Cost Fallacy. This happens when you've incurred a cost that you won't be able to get back and which then distorts your thinking. It can mean that you end up making decisions based on how much you've invested in something — whether it's an object or a relationship — rather than its actual value to you today. The Sunk Cost Fallacy makes it very hard to let things go, even when they no longer give you what you want.

It's the same with people. If you've been mates with someone for a decade and grown apart, it's easy to think that the friendship is a 'good' one, and it'll carry on for the next 40 years. But if, deep down, you know it's not, it's time to call it quits. If a friendship is no longer making you happy, or it's actually making you sad, or if you simply don't have anything in common with that person any more, it's okay to let it go. Here's how you can do that, the nice way:

1   **Let it fizzle out naturally:** this happens to everyone; you try over a few months to get a date in to hang out, and it never happens. One of you tries again a few months later, but you never set a date. Leave it here. If one day, you start

chatting again, then great. Don't, however, ghost them by not replying to their texts until they get the point.

2   **Make the excuse:** okay, okay, excuses are never nice. But if you genuinely don't want to hurt someone's feelings, you can go down the route of 'I'm really busy at work. It would be lovely to see you, but I just don't have a lot of time at the moment.'

3   **Tell them, straight up:** if something has happened that's made you rethink that person and your friendship with them — and excuses and fizzling out won't work — then let them know. That's not to say you can't be kind, but explaining to someone that you don't think the two of you hanging out is a great idea because of x, y, or z, is fair enough.

Why — and how — other people have ended friendships:

'I find it happens when you both keep making plans, but when they don't happen you don't feel that bothered. And then you keep making them and they never happen! That's usually a fairly obvious sign. That, and when you have conversations and more things they say you disagree with/ don't interest you.'

'If someone doesn't actually support you or bring you happiness, it's time to move on.'

'I had to walk away when the divide between a particular friendship and other areas of my life was becoming too big, and conflict was slowly rearing its head. I wanted to try to fix the problem, even if at heart I wasn't sure how or what it was. I think changes in our personal situations played a part — moving away, new friends, new relationships. It was a long process, made up of subtle changes. Small remarks or feelings of awkwardness. Eventually it reached a point of no return; it was so hard to finally admit that no more good could come from that friendship for either of us, but it's important to be honest with yourself. Even if you've had a great past together, it doesn't always equal a great future — that's the worst bit.'

'I've never done anything as drastic as end a friendship — in my view, this only ever happens after a fallout — but I've definitely had friendships where we drifted apart. It's a case of realising your lives are going in separate directions, and if you haven't had that urge to meet up, there's probably a reason. That being said, I have friends I might only see once a year but I'd still class them amongst my best and oldest.'

'When conversation doesn't flow like it used to. When spending time with that friend feels awkward rather than awesome. When the jokes that used to make you LOL now make your eyes roll.'

How to do small talk (and end a conversation politely)

Another way to describe adulthood is as a series of semi-awkward situations where you're introduced to new people and have to talk to them. Whether you're at the pub or a dinner party, here's how to start small talk and end it when it dries up:

CONVERSATION STARTERS

- What they do for a job — closely followed by what that job involves and if they always knew they wanted to be a lawyer/farmer/tap dancer.
- The situation you're in — were there the most awful train delays? Where did they travel in from? How long have they lived there for?
- How they know your mutual friend — was it from University? Did they meet them at 3am in a club one night? There has to be a story in it.
- What's happening in the news — the ins and outs of Brexit might be a bit much, but anything both moderately interesting and bland enough that it won't get offensive should do.
- Sport — who's winning, who's losing, which transfers were off the charts.
- Anything eye-catching that they're wearing (as long as it's because you like it, not laughing at it).

If you want to get past the bare bones of small talk, crank it up a notch by asking open-ended questions like 'How has your day been?', and offering a few details from your own day. If they mention a film they've seen, a place they've been, or other titbits, follow up and ask them a few questions — it sounds blindingly obvious, but being curious and asking questions, gently, really is the key to getting a good exchange going. When you meet someone new, it's easy to spend so much time worrying about what you'll say next that you don't really pay that much attention to what they're on about. Simply listening and following up on their cues is the way to get past any awkwardness.

CONVERSATION ENDERS:

- 'That reminds me, I keep meaning to ask Sam about his dog — excuse me, I'm going to grab him before he goes.'
- 'Right, I owe someone a drink. I'm sure I'll see you around later.'
- 'I've just remembered, I need to give my housemate/mum/ brother a quick call.'
- 'Well in that case, I must introduce you to [insert name of unwitting friend]!'
- 'It's been lovely chatting to you; I hope you don't mind, but I've just seen an old friend who I really ought to catch up with.'

You don't need to keep a conversation going forever — if you're ending it because it's drying up anyway, your conversation buddy will probably be as happy as you are to move on.

Five things you should know about your partner before Getting Serious

It's all sweetness and light until you find out they can't sleep without their nightlight on and they want to name their first child after a *Star Wars* character. Actually, those things are probably manageable. These are The Big Things that you should probably find out about before thinking about sharing a life with someone:

1 **Where they see themselves settling:** you might have met in the city, but is that something either of you want later down the line? Do they want to move abroad? Or have they got dreams of moving back home to be near to their family?

2 **If they see children in their future:** it seems obvious, but a lot of people avoid talking about whether or not they'd like children because it's something that screams 'commitment' and 'future'. Yeah, and? If you genuinely think someone might be *drumroll* The One, this will likely be one of the most important conversations you have. Once you've leapt that hurdle, find out how they picture themselves raising children, if they want them. Are you a staunch atheist but they want to go to church every week? What about childcare — is it a nanny all the way, or is one of you going to be expected to stay at home with the kids? Don't make assumptions and end up fighting it out later down the line.

3 **Their goals:** it's important to understand what someone sees on the cards for themselves. Do they want to travel? Do they see themselves committing to their career for

another 15 years before they even think about their home life? This is anything big that may leave you on two different paths later down the line.

4   **Their vices:** if it's important to you, find out their views on drugs, smoking, drinking, or anything else you might have concerns about. You might enjoy all of the above, but you might also hate it, and it's important to understand where that person stands.

5   **Anything big they haven't told you:** this could be anything from their previous dating history to if they are in debt, or if they've experienced any major run-ins with bad health. (Or, you know, the law.) Ask them if there's anything important they think you ought to know, and offer the same information to them.

How to have a frank conversation without it turning into an argument

Hands up who's bottled something up so tightly that when it's come to finally addressing it with another person, you bubble up and say things everywhere and at once and turn into an absolute mess, like a bottle of Coke that's been shaken up way too hard? There is another way:

1   **Work out what's behind the problem:** let's say, for example, your partner has had friends round on a Saturday night and left a massive mess in the kitchen, and not cleared it up by Sunday afternoon. You're entitled to be annoyed, but what's driving that annoyance? Is it that they

don't pull their weight around the house? That they had people round without asking you?

2 **Find the right time to talk about it:** that messy flat might be your top concern when you've had a long week at work and all you want to do is relax, but having a go first thing at someone who is partly responsible for those 10 empty bottles of wine is probably bad timing. Find a moment when they're not already feeling sorry for themselves.

3 **Don't go in all guns blazing:** even if you're angry, shouting at someone will either upset them or make them defensive. Find a way to bring things up calmly: 'Can I talk to you about something that's been on my mind?' is a decent enough way in. Explain the situation, and remember to ask for their thoughts, too.

4 **Watch your language:** try to avoid labelling them by saying things like 'You're being lazy' or 'I think it's really selfish what you're doing'. Instead, try to name your own feelings: 'When I went into the kitchen, I felt really frustrated', 'I want to relax in my own space, but the mess makes the house feel chaotic'.

5 **Listen to what they have to say:** you might not like to hear it, but you may be at fault somewhere along the line, too. Don't let them turn the fight onto you, but if they're making valid points, promise to take them on board.

6 **Decide how to move forward:** and do that together. There might be a simple answer (like your partner should have tidied up, and didn't). But if the solution you're looking for needs a bit of leg-work (they did all the cleaning last weekend, and didn't want to do it again), have a calm

conversation about what will work for both of you, so this doesn't become an ongoing problem.

7 **See if they change their behaviour next time:** and if they do, show that you noticed and that you appreciate it! Positive reinforcement can be more effective than any argument.

How to fix arguments when they happen

Sure, some of us can be persuaded into forgiveness with a bag of chocolate buttons, but if an argument blows up and you need to sort it out — and want to make it to the pub together afterwards — there's no one-size-fits-all way to do it. But here's what other people in actual relationships recommend:

'Take 15 minutes to yourself to reflect on who's really in the wrong. If it's you, just admit it.'

'Apologise for your part in the argument as soon as possible and move on. Be the bigger person.'

'Turn the TV off. Phones screen down. Look into each other's eyes. Remember that no one has died (hopefully).'

'Remember to be kind and try to understand, even if for that brief moment you're wondering what on earth is going through their brain! Kindness goes a long way.'

'For all the times I believe my partner is being irrational, I think of those times when he took the brunt of the "Why didn't you remember the avocado?!" debates and remember that we all have our moments. You've got to try and meet each other halfway.'

'We often find our arguments are caused by not spending enough time/quality time with each other — cooking together is always our go-to for remedying that.'

'Never, ever say anything you'll regret afterwards. It can be so easy to shoot from the hip when you're angry, but you can't take back nasty comments.'

... and know when they're not worth fixing

Ultimately, you can't fix everything. Not every relationship will be a confetti-shower of success, and you're entitled to leave at any time. If any of this stuff is going on, it's time you start thinking about it:

- If you're fighting about the same thing over and over again
- If one or either of you has promised to change, but can't (or won't)
- If that person makes you feel crappy
- If that person makes you feel uncomfortable
- If they put you down in front of other people
- If you find yourself saying more bad things than good about them

- If you don't find them, or their personality, attractive any more
- If they're no longer making you happier than you would be on your own

The point is, you don't need a million reasons, or even one huge one, to end a relationship. If it no longer feels right, and you don't see that changing, then leave.

How to perfect the polite dump

And now, the fun bit! Okay, joking; dumping someone is one of the most singularly awful things you can do in life, so follow these simple steps to emotional untangling:

1 **Meet somewhere convenient:** unless you want to tell them at their house (then run away) or your house (then kick them out), you need to choose a spot that's not going to humiliate them, but also gives you different routes home. A park is good (also, it's public, so you can guarantee less of a scene), or a coffee shop if you want more people around. (Note: If you live together, have somewhere you can stay prepared because you can be sure that it's you who'll be leaving. Unless it's your house, of course.)

2 **Be certain:** you want to know that as soon as you tell someone it's over, they're not going to persuade you back into the relationship that was making you so unhappy.

3 **Don't give them excuses:** everyone who's ever been broken up with knows that being told 'It's not you, it's me'

translates to 'It absolutely is you, but I don't know what else to say'. If it's not working, be honest, and call it. 'This isn't working for me any more' or 'We don't make each other happy enough' are both legitimate reasons, so feel free to use them.

4 **Handle the friends:** if you share a group of mates, the person you've just dumped probably won't want to shout about it. So, tell your close friends you ended things, if you must; everyone else, just explain that it wasn't working, and ended. That's it.

If, however, you need to leave an abusive relationship, the above rules won't apply and it's important to stay safe. Refuge offer practical advice and support and their freephone national domestic violence helpline is open 24 hours on 0808 2000 247, run in conjunction with Women's Aid. You can find more information, get help with coming up with a safety plan in order to protect yourself (and your children, if you have any), and think about how to increase your safety in the relationship whether you decide to stay or leave, on the Women's Aid website. If you are worried about your safety, contact the police right away.

How to split everything up if you're ending a relationship

As liberating/satisfying/petrifying [delete as appropriate] as it may be to put an end to something that's not working for you any more, there's a pyramid of practicality that you'll have to scale depending on how long you've been a couple, and how much of your lives are tied up together. The key is to make this as painless as possible so you can both start moving on (no matter how much you'd like to squabble over unpaid gas and electric bills).

Finances: let's start with the big one, shall we? Say you're living together in a rented property and splitting everything down the middle, here's what you need to do:

1   If you have a joint savings account, move everything you've put into it (and nothing more) back into your personal bank account. Even if you trust each other, it's better to eliminate any financial casualties now. You can also call the bank and get the account frozen, so that nobody can take out any money until you have both agreed on how to split it.

2   Decide if either of you is going to stay living in your property. Yes? Work out when the other needs to move out and stop paying rent. No? Serve notice on the property and find out, right away, what fees — if any — you'll be liable for.

3   Create a spreadsheet of your current utility outgoings, then decide who is going to deal with which accounts. While you're doing that, record what is left to pay for each, if you're getting any refunds, and any additional fees (like if you need to buy yourself out of a TV package). Add the amount of rent that's left to pay, and anything on top of that — like a fee for a deep clean of your property when you leave. Split that figure fairly, and agree to pay your share by a certain date.

4   Bought furniture you want to sell? Great. List it now so
    neither of you needs to cart it around when you move out,
    and split the profits.
5   Agree on whose account your flat/house deposit is going
    back into, and a timescale for that being transferred from one
    of you to the other. If you know you're losing any of it, also
    agree who is getting what percentage of what comes back.

    NB: You may feel, given your particular circumstances,
    that one of you should pay some sort of financial penalty
    for heartbreak. That's up to you. But usually it takes
    two people to cause the problems, so don't go beating
    your wallet up. Unless you've cheated or done something
    similar. In which case, you might need to be the bigger
    (poorer) person.

Belongings: don't let a four-day stalemate over a three-year-old
half-melted spatula be the straw that lost you the TV. You need
to get practical, then get packed, so write a list of everything
you bought with your own money, and everything you split
between you. Decide if there's anything you really, genuinely
want out of this break-up (or — sneaky! — what you can get
the most money for), and present those as your 'Honestly, I
don't mind what you take, but I'd really appreciate it if I could
keep hold of the x, y, and z' side of the bargain. Haggle a bit if
you have to, but know where to stop.

Pets: if you were with someone long enough to buy a pet with
them, then there's probably a lot more emotional heavy lifting

to do here. But that animal has got to live somewhere, and it's going to need to be with the person who ~~loves them the most~~ can genuinely look after it. If that's not you, make peace with it. You can't take a house rabbit to the office.

Joint accounts: this includes stuff like gym memberships, Netflix, cinema cards, and supermarket points accounts. These are very low on the pyramid of practicality, so don't make it a priority. But it is, actually, quite important to your general wellbeing. Kat was once unceremoniously chucked off a joint Netflix account halfway through an episode of *Suits*, and it was one of the more tragic things that happened to her that month. Don't let that be you.

Friends: the general rule of fairness is that if you brought your friends into the relationship, you should get to leave with them in tow, too. Easier said than done? Sure. So, make some ground rules. Make it clear whether you're okay with your ex seeing your mates, but not coming to group meet-ups; or if you're okay to have them there; or if you don't want them involved with your friends at all. And pass that information on to your friends, too. You might not be able to stop a blossoming bromance, but you can ask that people respect your feelings. Remember: don't involve other people in a tug of war; it's not fair on anyone.

Money, money, money

The thing about tackling financial stuff is that it can seem incredibly boring, overwhelming, and complicated, all at once. So you put it on your to-do list ('Sort money stuff') and then you notice there's a new infomercial on hypoallergenic pillows, hamster wheels, or dusters on QVC so you watch that, or do frankly ANYTHING else in the world. Because it's better than having to work out what your pay slip actually says, or doing some maths to figure out whether your weekly sushi habit means you'll never be able to afford a mortgage, or opening those thick big envelopes containing gobbledegook from a pensions company that you think might relate to a job that you had four years ago.

Obviously, the TV pillow advert is a whole lot more fun. But think about it in incentive terms: spending a half-day working on your outgoings (energy bills, insurance costs, aforementioned sushi habit etc.) and making a budget could be the equivalent of giving yourself a multi-thousand-pound annual pay rise. (And you could buy a LOT of those amazing pillows for that. Or a holiday. Or put it towards a flat deposit.)

Staying on top of complicated-looking documents like pay slips, tax demands, and loan agreements will save you a whole lot of time, cash, and stress in the long term. Here, the 'money stuff' is broken down into chunks — and you might want to do the same, especially if you haven't thought about it for a while. Tackle one element each day for a month, and you'll be sorted by payday!

The pay slip — what do all the numbers mean?

It's a piece of paper — or, more likely, a PDF on a screen — which summarises your earnings, and any deductions for tax or other things, that your employer will provide either once a week, twice a month, or once a month, depending on how often you get paid. It'll be made up of a bunch of numbers and words, including:

1 **Payroll number:** this you don't need to worry about. It's just HR's way of distinguishing between each member of staff. If you work in a big company, you might need it if you're raising a question with HR.

2 **Gross pay:** this is your full pay (including bonuses and commission) before any tax or National Insurance has been taken off. It is definitely NOT how much money you'll get in your bank account (that's coming up).

3 **Variable deductions:** money that's removed from your total pay, but which might differ each payday, such as tax and National Insurance.

4 **Fixed deductions:** money taken from your pay that doesn't

change from payday to payday. Might include union fees and paid-for perks.

5 **Total take-home pay:** what you'll actually be paid.

6 **Your tax code:** the rate you're taxed at. You're given this code by HMRC, and it will look like a bunch of random numbers and letters. But different people have different tax codes, depending on their circumstances, and your code is HMRC's way of telling your employer how much tax-free allowance you should get before they should start taxing your earnings. If the code is wrong, you could end up paying too much or too little tax, but all you need to do is check the code on your pay slip matches your latest tax code notice, which will have been sent to you by HMRC.

7 **Expenses:** if you're owed any expenses from work (like travel costs, meals etc.), these will be displayed here.

8 **Pension:** if you're paying towards a workplace pension, the amount you're contributing will be shown.

9 **Student loan:** repayments will be shown on your pay slip if you're making them.

10 **Workplace benefits:** things like health insurance or a company car will also be listed on your pay slip.

Tell me about my tax (without putting me to sleep)

Okay, grab a coffee and read on. You'll already know that tax goes towards keeping the country running (the NHS, police, the street lights, the biscuits at the council meetings etc.), but there are more ways than you might have realised that you could be paying for all of these things:

1   **Income tax:** it's a biggie. You pay this on anything
    you earn (whether you have an employer or you're self-
    employed), plus on pensions, benefits, savings, and any
    income from investments or anyone paying you rent.
    You get a tax-free chunk called an 'allowance' each year,
    currently hovering around £11,000 — anything you earn
    above that gets taxed.

2   **National Insurance:** a second tax that's paid on your
    income (or if you're self-employed, from your business's
    profits). Paying a certain amount of NI is obligatory for
    access to some state benefits, like the basic state pension,
    Employment Support Allowance, and bereavement
    benefits. Everyone who earns above a certain amount
    (which changes each year) has to pay National Insurance as
    well as income tax.

3   **VAT:** already built into a lot of the things you buy, both
    goods (those new jeans) and services (the plumber's visit),
    it's currently 20%. Not charged on books, children's clothes
    (which is why Lucy's size 3 feet are ALWAYS in kids'
    trainers), and most food. Fuel and power are taxed at 5%.

4   **Stamp duty:** paid when you buy a flat or house that costs
    more than £125,000 (cue Londoners' search for mouse
    holes that cost less than this, then laughing at the futility).
    It's only paid if the property is going to be your main home
    (buy-to-let or second homes face different taxes) and it
    starts at 2% for properties worth between £125,001 and
    £250,000, rises to 5% on the portion between £250,001
    and £925,000, then keeps on going up after that. From
    2017, though, the rules are different for first-time buyers,

who will pay no stamp duty on the first £300,000 of any home costing up to £500,000 (and only 5% on any proportion between £300,000–£500,000).

5 **Excise duty:** the 'sin' tax on tobacco and alcohol, plus petrol and flights; the percentage differs according to the item.

6 **Inheritance tax:** paid when someone dies, if their estate (home, possessions, savings, etc) is worth more than a certain amount — currently about £325,000. Spouses, charities, and community sports clubs are exempt.

7 **Capital gains tax:** paid on any profits you've made on any possessions or investments you sell that are worth more than £6000. It's not everything — cars, for example, are exempt — but jewellery, antiques art etc. all face this tax.

8 **Council tax:** a monthly or annual tax which is charged according to the property's value. Both renters and homeowners usually have to pay it, but there are discounts for people living alone, students, and disabled people. You can check your band on gov.uk to make sure you are not overpaying.

9 **Insurance premium tax:** an extra fee added to most insurance policies, like travel or car insurance.

WTF is a credit rating — and why should I care?

A credit rating — or credit score — is a grade that you're given (whether you know about it or not) based on your past dealings with money, stretching from store cards and mobile phone bills (as in, did you pay them on time?) to loans. Think of it as the GCSE you didn't study for — and the grade that probably matters more than any you did actually take.

You might wonder 'Why should I be bothered about what the banks think about me — I think they're a bunch of bastards?' Well, sadly, you need to care because that rating is then used by lenders or other financial services companies when they're deciding whether to give you the go-ahead for a credit card, loan, mortgage, or other financial service. So, if the rating was given in A-Level lingo, someone who had always paid off their monthly credit card, had steadily lived in one address, and had never missed a loan repayment, might get an A*, and be given uninhibited access to top mortgage deals (and receive generous terms). By contrast, someone who's been flaky with missing repayments, and/or had a few years without a fixed address (and no explanation for that), would be closer to an F … As in, F for "Fraid not, you can't have that mortgage.'

It's not as simple as 'yes' or 'no', though: when applying for a credit card or mortgage, someone with a good credit score is more likely to be offered a cheaper interest rate than someone with a bad one. It's not totally clear-cut: every lender follows a different policy for credit scoring, so someone who fails to meet one bank's criteria could still get credit from another.

But if you are being rejected, it's vital to find out why: look into your credit rating before making another application because blitzing loads of firms will trigger lots of credit searches, and that can be viewed negatively by lenders and put you on a downhill spiral. So, in the cases where it's not them (the bank), and it's you, what can you do?

INVESTIGATE YOUR CREDIT SCORE

Checking your credit score and making sure it's correct (or adding relevant explanations for any valid late payments) is quick and easy, and worthwhile because credit rating agencies make mistakes, and their screw-ups could cost you a lot of money. Check your credit score for free with an agency like Experian or Noddle, or on a free trial basis with Equifax.

They'll ask for basic information such as your address and current account provider, then will swiftly send your credit report over. Look through it for any missed payments or other problems — if you spot any mistakes (e.g. an unpaid bill that wasn't ever yours), send the credit agency proof such as a bank statement for the period, and that should lead to them removing it. You can also add notes to explain any blots on your payment history that were caused by a good reason (for example, if illness meant you fell behind on a loan repayment in the past); you'll need to send proof such as a doctor's note and ask for a 'notice of correction' to be added to your record.

HOW TO IMPROVE YOUR SCORE

A weird fact: having NO financial repayment history is almost as damaging as having a ropey one. So maybe you've never borrowed a penny, never had a credit card, or store card, or a mobile under your own name — you'd think your credit rating would be solid gold. Actually, agencies view non-borrowers with suspicion. So if you've got a glaringly empty record, you'll need to open one or more credit cards, and use them carefully for a few months while ALWAYS repaying the entire balance at the end of each month to build up your credit score.

Other general ways to boost your rating include registering on the electoral roll, installing a landline phone, and closing any unused bank accounts, mobile contracts, or store cards — having a large overall credit limit, even if it's unused, can be a big red flag to lenders.

Once you've done your credit rating spruce-up, time to find out if it's worked. Applying for credit cards to see if you're accepted (and at decent rates — exact figures depend on the Bank of England interest rate so shop around) is a good way to do this, but never apply on bank websites — you don't want to damage that newly buffed-up score! Instead, use the 'soft search' systems available via a comparison site, like TotallyMoney or MoneySavingExpert's credit card eligibility calculator, which let you know if you're likely to be approved for a deal, but don't besmirch your credit rating.

I don't intend to die soon … so do I need life insurance … or a will?

Ant and Dec have 'six-figure' life insurance policies against each other in the event one of them dies. Seriously. They've taken on board the fact that no one understands the existence of one without the other, or actually knows which one of them is which, and have taken out joint life cover so that if something were to happen, then the other one would get a payout.

However — it's pretty likely that you or I are not Ant, nor Dec. And, sadly, we're probably not worth millions of pounds either. If you're a 20- or 30-something with no plans to die anytime soon, you're probably thinking that life insurance is either one piece of expensive paper you don't need, or simply not considering it at all.

Whether or not that's okay depends on your circumstances — and how much you like to gamble. A *This Is Money* article recently revealed that, if you filled Wembley Stadium with 90,000 men aged 25–34, by the end of the year, 74 of them would be dead. To someone who's the sole earner in a family, life insurance — where you pay a regular premium and your loved ones are given an income to live on or a lump sum if you die — might well look worthwhile. It can be pretty cheap, just a few pounds a month, but in just one year, Britons claimed more than £1 billion on the most basic form of life insurance, according to trade body the Association of British Insurers. Most mortgage lenders also require a life insurance policy to be in place to repay the home loan in the event of the borrower's death.

However, if you're living alone, with no dependents, and a healthy lifestyle, you might think living by the spin of the roulette wheel and going for an uninsured life is fine for now.

If you do want to buy life insurance, the main things to consider are: how much cover you need (how much would you need to be paid out to your family if you died, to cover the mortgage or rent, or living expenses or childcare?), and what circumstances you want it to pay out in.

While we're thinking gloomy thoughts, writing a will is pretty much a good idea for everyone. Yes, the idea is about as uplifting as a Sunday spent listening to Coldplay's 'Fix You' on repeat, but currently over 60% of British adults haven't made a will, and this is why that's dumb:

If you've got any kind of savings, or a property, and especially if you've got kids or other dependents (even a pet), a will is vital — otherwise, your dependents' financial future could be screwed up, and your loved ones could end up having a big bust-up over your finances. It happens frequently — even to celebrities. Take Bob Marley, who had six children by different women, as well as three by his wife, Rita, and whose death at 36 — without a will — triggered huge fall-outs over his estimated $30 million legacy. Sure, we don't all have $30 million lying around, but a will does mean deciding who gets what: when Stieg Larsson, the author of *The Girl with the Dragon Tattoo*, died without leaving a will, his multi-million pound estate was inherited by his father, rather than his fiancée.

Wills can be cheap — theoretically you could scribble your will on a piece of loo roll, and as long as it was properly signed and witnessed it should be legally binding. But WH Smith or Amazon sell DIY will kits for just over a tenner. Using a template with standard sections and legal terms already included is easier and helps you ensure everything is signed, dated, and witnessed properly. Even with a kit, experts say you should only do a DIY will if everything is super simple — you want to leave everything to your husband or wife, for example. If you're co-habiting but not married, or have kids and the money will be put in trust etc., you should probably use a solicitor. The experts, who'll make you a watertight will, but are the priciest option, are often £300–£500. A cheaper will-writing service should cost around £150–£200, depending on the complexities and if you opt to use a lawyer. Or look out for Free Wills Month — usually in October each year — during which registered solicitors will help you to fill out your will paperwork for free, whilst encouraging you (although it's not required) to include a gift to one or more of a list of charities in your will in return.

The things you'll need to think about, however you make your will, are beneficiaries (who gets your cash, totally defunct CD collection etc.), maybe a plan for any small businesses you run, and which lucky person or people will be your executors. This is where it gets morbid and grown up; their responsibilities will include valuing assets and completing tax forms, and looking after any children's inheritance for the future. If you do have kids, you'll need to appoint guardians responsible for looking after any children under 18.

You'll need to update a will when you have any big life events such as getting married, buying a property, divorce, having kids, retiring, etc. Remember that if you have a child and are hoping for more, refer to 'children' instead of specific names in your will to save the need for an update. You'll need to tell your executor where to find your will — either in your home or with a solicitor or will-writing service — although they'll usually charge extra for this.

Insurance — travel, home, motor ... How can I spend the least possible money on the best possible cover?

Imagine spending a few hundred quid on a new gadget in the hope that you never, ever had to use it — weird concept, right? But that's what we do with insurance, buying it because the law makes us — car insurance if you want to drive on a public road, or building cover if you want a mortgage — or because the consequences of not buying it are a bit scary — as with health or life insurance.

But insurance fees are rising — as tax, healthcare, and other costs go up rapidly — so it's worth spending a bit of extra time researching the very best quote before shelling out. Here's how in five simple(ish) steps:

1. DON'T ACCEPT YOUR RENEWAL PRICE

Just letting last year's cover roll over at the price the insurer suggests is like *refusing to scoop up cash from the floor*. Crazy, right? If you're feeling lazy, just call up your provider and say you're switching because another firm has offered you the same deal for, say, £50 less — they'll normally match it, or at least go a bit lower. But for the full money-saving kapow, put your details into a bunch of comparison sites (going for MoneySupermarket, Confused, and GoCompare gives you a big range of providers). Then, check you've found the cheapest deal that matches your needs, but don't buy from the comparison site's link. Instead, use a cashback site.

2. IF YOU CAN AFFORD TO DO SO, BUY COVER IN ONE LUMP SUM, RATHER THAN IN MONTHLY PAYMENTS THAT WILL WORK OUT AS MORE ACROSS THE YEAR

3. FOR MOTOR INSURANCE, THINK ABOUT WHAT KIND OF COVER YOU NEED

Cover starts with very basic third-party insurance, which pays out for damage or injuries that you cause to someone else or their property in a car accident, but not for any damage to you or your car. If you've got an old banger and like to take a gamble, that could be one option. A little more generous is 'third-party, fire, and theft' insurance, which will pay out if your car is stolen, damaged, or burned by fire, as well as damage to third parties. Then there's comprehensive car insurance — the clue's in the name — which also covers damage to your own vehicle.

The best way to cut the price of car insurance is still the most basic: drive carefully. The more years of no-claims driving you notch up, the cheaper your cover will get. If you're a new driver, or have lost your no-claims discount (NCD) due to an accident, look at one of the insurers (such as Admiral, Elephant, and Diamond) that offer ten-month policies — they are viewed as the equivalent of one year's NCD. Another money-saving tip is to add a usually older, crash-free friend or relative driver to your policy. It's illegal to add them as the main driver if that's actually someone else (i.e. you), but you can add them to a policy as an extra driver even if they're not actually going to drive your car, and it often makes the overall cost of the policy lower.

4. FOR HOME INSURANCE, HAGGLE LIKE MAD

Because this is the cover that insurers love using to lure new customers in with — they reckon you just won't be arsed to switch in the future.

There are two types of home insurance:

1   Buildings insurance, which pays out for things affecting
    the bones of your home, like a fire, flooding, or subsidence.

2   Contents insurance, which covers the sofa/record
    collection/Nutribullet/everything inside.

If you've got a mortgage, you'll need buildings insurance as a legal obligation. But contents insurance is optional, for both renters and owners. If, however, you couldn't afford to cover the cost of replacing your valuables in the event of a burglary or other catastrophe, it's worth it. Shop around on comparison sites, ask for a cheaper renewal quote, and use cashback sites if you can. A lot of providers will offer a discount if you buy buildings and contents cover together. Try to avoid over-insuring: use a contents valuation calculator to work out the insured value of your possessions, but remember to separately name really valuable items, like an engagement ring or other jewellery, posh bike, laptop etc. Installing a burglar alarm and five-lever lock can also lower your quote.

5. FOR TRAVEL INSURANCE, OPT FOR AN ANNUAL POLICY IF YOU TAKE MORE THAN TWO TRIPS A YEAR, OR A SINGLE POLICY OTHERWISE

Experts say you should be seeing £1 million-plus medical cover on a policy, and if you're a big shopper, check that the baggage allowance covers the cost of your average suitcase.

Savings: if I stop splurging at ASOS/the pub and manage to get any, what should I do with them?

First thing? Don't shout about them. You'll immediately be volunteered to pay more than your share of rounds at the pub, until the question becomes void because the savings have evaporated.

But if you do have a bit of a nest egg, or you're working on one, maybe to be able to buy a pad one day, or splurge on a holiday, or to (yeah, we know it sounds a long way off) have an epic retirement, it's worth spending some time thinking about what your savings are actually doing. Are they languishing under your bed or in a stingy bank account where they are actually losing value due to inflation (the rate at which prices are rising, apologies for sounding like an economics A-Level textbook)? This question is especially important for millennials and younger people because the current state of the economy (let's be realistic here) means it's unlikely that anyone else, especially the state, is going to have much cash to help us in the future.

So, if you've got some savings, make them do some work — otherwise it's like that gym membership you take out every January and cancel every June (stop that habit too!) — you're chucking money down the drain.

But there's a problem: the economy being wobblier than a seven-year-old's front tooth means savings account interest rates are low. As in, 1% or lower, unless you do some serious homework. If it's lower than inflation — which most high-street bank account interest rates currently are — the value of your hard-earned money is being watered down fast. So what are your options for squirrelling away that cash?

1   **Savings accounts:** the safest, but usually least-lucrative
    option. Find the most generous interest-payer on a

comparison site like MoneySupermarket, and pick the account that works for your timings. The best deals usually come from 'fixed-term' accounts where your money is locked up for a set number of years — if that's okay for you, go for it, but remember to keep enough emergency cash aside with easy access. If you're putting aside a set amount each month, go for a regular saver account — they normally pay much higher interest rates. And weird-sounding, totally non-famous banks are often more generous than the high-street giants — just make sure they're registered under the Financial Services Compensation Scheme, a government-backed scheme that guarantees the first £85,000 of your savings for each registered bank or building society. If a lottery win means you have more cash than that and you want it in savings accounts, spread it out between several registered institutions to avoid losing out if a bank collapses.

2   **ISAs:** these special tax-free saving accounts are a top option if you pay tax in the UK. In a normal savings account, any interest you earn is liable to be taxed too — for every £1 of interest you earn, the taxman will take between 20% and 50%, depending on your earnings, although there is a tax-free allowance to get through first. You can avoid this with a special tax-free account, like an ISA. Each year, you can put around £20,000 in either a cash ISA account and/ or in an investment ISA that's a tax-free 'wrapper' around stocks and shares. If you don't use your annual allowance in one tax year, it disappears and can't be rolled over. There are also specialist ISAs like the Help to Buy ISA,

for those who have never bought a property before and are saving to do so. Savers can put in up to £1200 in the first month, and up to £200 each month after that. Then, when you're ready to put the cash towards a deposit on a first home, and if you've saved at least £1600 in the Help to Buy ISA, the government tops up the total by 25% — up to £3000 (which is payable to those who've saved up £12,000 or more in the account). The cash must be used on a property costing under £250,000 — or £450,000 in London. And on shared ownership properties the total value of the home, not just the stake you're buying, has to be under that threshold. You can't open a Help to Buy ISA and a conventional ISA in the same year (but you can retain old ISA accounts from previous years). The money can be withdrawn at any time, too — if, say, you decide to blow it on a round-the-world gap year rather than property, although you'd miss out on the bonus.

3 **Stocks and shares:** these can go really well or could crash and burn. Investing in the stock market is best for long-term savings — never invest money you will need in the next five or so years — and you should understand that, while the gains can be big, the losses can be total. If you know nothing about the markets, don't rely on a tip from some crazy friend. Your options are: you could gamble (only what you can afford to lose), you could steer clear, you could opt for professional advice, and/or you could reduce the risk by investing in a fund, a 'basket' of stocks and shares. Note that these, too, are still liable to the whims of the economy and a whole huge range of other

factors. The easiest way to actually buy stock is via sites like Hargreaves Lansdown, Interactive Investor and AJ Bell — but each has different fee structures, so shop around for the one that best fits your needs.

4   **Peer-to-peer lending:** the returns from these platforms (amongst the biggest are Zopa, Ratesetter, and Funding Circle) are usually more lucrative than cash. They work by savers handing over cash, which is then loaned, via the websites, to individuals or small businesses. There are better returns because the websites cut out the banks and face fewer overheads, but although the sites offer various guarantees, it's riskier than cash investments as you are lending money rather than saving it and your money is not protected by the Financial Services Compensation Scheme.

5   **Crowdfunding:** a.k.a. investing in start-ups in return for a share in future profits. This is one of the more fun ways to put your money to work — especially if you invest in a business that also pays out goodies, such as the street food stall that gives investors a free lunch once a month. But of course it's risky — half of new businesses aren't around after five years — so this isn't a good option for your life savings.

6   **Savings bonds:** saving bonds are a type of investment — where you're effectively 'lending' money to the institution (be it a bank, government, or corporation). In return, they agree to pay you back your original investment within an agreed period of time and with an agreed rate of interest. So bonds are like 'IOU' notes: the body offering the bond pays regular interest, but they have risks attached as the

value of your capital goes up and down with the value
of the bonds. When interest rates rise, the value of bonds
tends to fall, meaning investors can lose some or even all
of their money.

7   **Premium bonds:** they're backed by the government, cost
a quid each, you're guaranteed to get your money back,
but unless ERNIE picks out your number, your returns
are minimal. In fact, according to MoneySavingExpert,
if you lined up everyone with £1000 worth of premium
bonds in order of their year's winnings, you'd need to
walk past two-thirds of the line until you hit the first
winner — and they'd have received just a £25 cheque.
Still, you could win £1 million, and just that chance is
enough of a lure for some.

8   **Buy-to-let:** it might sound crazy when so many millennials
reckon they've been booted off the housing ladder by just
these investors, but it's an increasingly popular option for
people looking for better returns on their savings, even
if they can't afford their own place. There are growing
numbers of 20- and 30-somethings renting in London
and earning rent on cheaper properties bought up north
or elsewhere in the UK. On top of rental income, the value
of the property could rise, too — but you'll face special
tax bills, lots of admin, and the costs of maintaining the
property (either yourself or via a paid-for managing agent),
and the headache of finding tenants.

Millennials' money tips

'Set up a standing order into a savings account that comes out on the day you get paid. That way, you won't even notice it's gone. And set up one immediately when you get a pay rise, then you really don't miss it.'

'Shop around for a bank account. Some offer 5% interest up to £5000 (or similar). You literally make money while you're sleeping.'

'Keep your paperwork safe and filed correctly, especially anything to do with mortgage/finance. That way, when something goes wrong, you can actually find it in a couple of minutes, rather than hours.'

'Keep your current account balance low, just enough of a buffer. Move most of your money into better yielding savings accounts. Bonus point — when you see the low balance, it discourages impulse buys and makes you be more savvy to build the funds up again (when you do — move more out).'

'Never lend money that you can't afford to lose as it can cause rifts and make life awkward.'

'Stay away from store cards and credit cards — I learned the hard way many years ago.'

'Never ever impulse buy. If you see something you really like, think about it carefully, and if you still feel the same way about it after a week, then go ahead! Chances are you will have changed your mind and saved yourself loads of money.'

'Set up a budget and use it, every month. Include an emergency fund that you keep topped up when it has to be used. It's the best thing I ever did — stopped me getting into financial trouble when stuff happens, like the fridge packing up two weeks after the warranty expired.'

Making a budget: why it's not as boring as it sounds

Politicians use the Government's annual Budget as an opportunity to bicker endlessly while haphazardly calculating our nation's future. Your budget-making doesn't need to be like that.

These days, there are a bunch of apps which make it really easy to calculate your incomings — salary, extra freelance work etc. — and your outgoings — rent/mortgage, bills, shopping, food, and a bunch of stuff that's really easy to forget, like how much you spend on toiletries. You can use these, or go old school with a paper, pen, or Excel spreadsheet. But however you do it, making a budget is really important.

Why? Because living within your means will make it easier to save for the things you want, whether it's a round-the-world trip or a car — and it will give you a nest egg so if your job suddenly finishes or your ceiling collapses, you won't be utterly screwed.

Basically, spending an hour digging into your finances and working out a savings plan might not be the most fun thing in the world, but it could lead you to the most fun things in the world, because it'll give you the financial freedom to chase your dreams.

So that's the plus side to budget-making. Here's how to do it:

1. AT ITS MOST BASIC, A BUDGET IS JUST THE TOTAL OF ALL YOUR INCOME, MINUS ALL YOUR EXPENSES, TO SEE HOW MUCH EXTRA YOU HAVE — OR HOW MUCH DEBT YOU'RE GOING INTO

To make your budget, you'll need to get these figures, and the best way is to go through your bank statements. Once you have the details, you can plug them into an Excel spreadsheet or even just write them down the old-fashioned way. And remember, if most of your spending is pooled with your partner, you might want to work on a budget together.

Some new apps make the details easy for you:

- Mint shows you all your bank accounts' balances in one place, and breaks down where you've spent your money by organising your bank account debits into groups.
- Wally lets you take photos of your expenses to enter your spending, add your income details, set spending/saving targets, and track your cash.
- At Goodbudget, cash is digitally put into different 'envelopes' for different purposes, you can check the envelope balances (synced with your bank accounts), track expenses, and also sync between other people's devices,

so it's good for budgeting with a partner or housemates.

There's a free version or a £3.50-a-month souped-up version.

However or wherever you create your budget, you can then use it to set money goals, decide what to do with the extra cash, or work out how to tackle a regular shortfall.

A good general guide is the 50:30:20 rule, where fixed costs — rent/mortgage, bills that you can't cut out or avoid, like energy or mobile bills, insurance etc. — shouldn't exceed 50% of your incomings. Weekly expenses like food, entertainment, birthday presents etc. should take up no more than 30%, and, if possible, you should be aiming at putting the remaining 20% of your cash into a savings account.

2. IF YOU'VE FAILED WITH THE 'SAVE MORE £££' NEW YEAR'S RESOLUTION FOR THE PAST GAZILLION YEARS, TRY WRITING DOWN SPECIFIC WAYS THAT YOU PLAN TO SAVE TO STAY ON TRACK TO FOCUS YOUR SPENDING

Maybe it's not as sexy as a letter-pressed wall poster with a slogan for life, but having spare funds will probably make you pretty happy.

3. IF YOU STRUGGLE TO STAY ORGANISED WITH A BUNCH OF DIFFERENT BANK ACCOUNTS, BILLS, AND SPENDING ALERTS, TRY STREAMLINING THEM

Do you really still need that savings account at a bank in Wolverhampton that you opened aged 12? Do you need five credit cards?

4. IF YOU SCREW UP ON YOUR BUDGET AND ITS AIMS, THINK OF IT AS A HEALTHY EATING REGIME THAT YOU CAN GET BACK ON BOARD WITH

Just because you ate a whole packet of Jaffa Cakes on Saturday, no need to gorge again on Sunday. Same with money, don't follow up one blow-out bit of spending with a week of splurging, just forgive yourself and get back to the budget.

5. LOOK AT ANY BIG DISPARITIES

If you're spending more than you're earning, debt is an inevitable, depressing consequence unless you take action. You could do one of two things: boost your income (ask for a pay rise, go for higher-paying roles, build up a freelance portfolio in your spare time, clear your cupboards with a big sell-off on eBay, or make money in other ways in your spare time) or cut your costs. If you've got a weekly Ocado/Net-a-Porter/cocktails habit, trade down — spend less money shopping, stay in a few more nights each week, take a packed lunch to work etc.

Becoming a financial couple (don't expect cards'n'presents for this one)

… doesn't it sound romantic? But while money is always super-awkward to discuss, getting this chat out of the way early on is pretty important — not least because if it turns out your partner is a big spender who dismisses your urge to talk about Our Finances, while you've been saving for a deposit since you turned 12, then it doesn't bode well.

Most people reckon they become a 'financial couple' when

they move in together. Until then, it's easy to muddle along with one person buying one dinner, another shouting the cinema tickets, but once you're racking up bigger cumulative expenses, you need to have a conversation to work out what is your financial plan as a couple. Because there are lots of options:

'I THINK I ... WANT TO SHARE MY MONEY WITH YOU'

... are ten words that can, nowadays, mean considerably more than three other words that you might blurt out much earlier in a relationship. It's pretty easy to say 'I love you'; more challenging is the idea of sharing a bank account with your partner if you're not certain they have the same attitude to money as you, or buying something big and permenant together — especially a property. And while you might know the deepest, darkest secrets of your besties' sex lives and everything about their health, colleagues, career hopes, and family plans, finances often remain more secretive than certain presidential tax returns. Here are some of the main ways millennial couples share their cash:

1   **The total merger:** usually reserved for really serious couples, often married or in a civil partnership and/or co-owning property, who opt to pool all the money into one joint account. It makes it easier to pay household bills, and to balance the finances if one partner is earning a lot more and the other is studying, or staying home to raise kids, for example. On the downside, some people say this arrangement feels too claustrophobic — their spending holds no secrets — and if the relationship breaks up, it's messy.

Also, as a joint account holder, you have a legal obligation to the bank or building society: they can ask either one of you to pay off a debt on a joint account, so if your partner refused to pay, you could be asked to repay every penny.

2   **The mixed affair:** there's a joint account that both partners chuck a set amount of cash into on a regular basis for household bills, joint holidays etc., but each has separate accounts too — maybe for savings, or individual expenses. Can be a particularly good route for self-employed people, where it's useful to have a separate account for earnings, work expenses etc. for tax return admin. However, in a world where agreeing to delete Tinder is a Big Deal in a relationship, some couples reckon that keeping finances partly independent in this way doesn't feel like making a full commitment.

3   **Keeping things casual:** everything, from big bills to restaurant meals, is paid for on a casual basis — sometimes one person pays, other times the other does, and it's not really recorded. This mode works out for some relaxed couples, and means less paperwork, especially if one person takes charge of utility bills, while the other covers all food. But it can harbour resentment as both parties may think they're putting in more, and budgeting may be more difficult.

4   **The one financial whip-cracker:** one partner rules the financial roost, doing the bills, looking for the best deals, organising the finances, and the other just falls into line. Sometimes this situation comes about if one partner is a much higher earner, or if one has a history of being bad with money. This deal works for some couples, but watch

out — if the relationship doesn't work out well and you're the partner who is left in the dark, you could be led into trouble by the other's bad decision-making. Equally, if you made a questionable decision, you could be blamed. Which is never good for a happily-ever-after.

5 **The solo spenders:** separate bank accounts, separate spending plans, and separate savings — some couples like to keep things formal. Bills are paid 50:50, or one partner is responsible for one set, the other for the other; expensive purchases like furniture 'belong' to one person or the other. This is often the pattern early on in relationships, when a potential split is more likely and keeping things separate is simpler. Long-term, though, it can be more complicated, especially if incomes differ.

Once you've had a long chat, know about each other's existing finances (and you should cover *everything* from debts, credit cards, savings, to money plans for the future and any credit rating problems, to avoid surprises of the not-so-nice variety later — a friend discovered her fiancé had a debt problem only when they kept getting turned down for mortgages), then you should probably tackle a budget together. It doesn't have to take long or be all that dull. Especially if you do it together with a bottle of vino waiting as a reward.

Budgets are useful whether you're pooling your cash, keeping it separate, or opening a joint account to cover bills — you'll still need to know how much each partner is contributing, incomings, outgoings and any longer-term savings aims (like for a house, wedding, honeymoon, kids, etc.).

Then there are some practical decisions to make — where to deposit your money? What legal stopgaps should you put in place? Will bills be set up in both of your names? The latter can make it easier if one of you wants to contact a company about a complaint, for example, and could eliminate huge practical problems in the event that one person in the relationship dies, but it does mean you're jointly liable. Or will one person cover some bills, and the other be responsible for the rest?

You'll also need to think about your credit score. Because, like one partner's crappy dress sense dragging the other's image down, linking your finances to another person's (which can happen via a joint account, shared bills, or both being named cardholders on a credit card) unites your financial reputation. That means if your partner was to miss or delay a payment, or, worse, be declared bankrupt, then your own credit score could take a hit — making it tougher for you to secure a mortgage or other loan in the future, even if it's yonks after that relationship ended or you're trying to do so solo. So get your credit ratings checked out before becoming financially hitched — think of it like getting an STD check before first shacking up together: potentially embarrassing, but probably less painful.

Getting serious ...

The signs are all there — you've met their parents, gone Facebook official, you borrow their roll-on deodorant, don't care if they kiss you with dragon breath in the morning, and share a Netflix password — this relationship is Getting Serious. Maybe a property purchase, wedding bells, or kids are on the horizon

— your finances are likely to become more intertwined than the wires behind your TV, and though you think you're going to end up together, forever, in a happy-ever-after-situation, you really still need to think sensibly about protecting yourself and your money. The options are:

1 **If you're moving in together:** think about drawing up a 'cohabitation agreement' (also known as a 'living together agreement') if you're not planning on marriage or a civil partnership because couples who solely live together have very few legal rights if their relationship ends. Whatever Google or the office water cooler chat says, 'common law marriage' does not exist. These agreements therefore set out possessions you or your other half have bought or own, contributions you and they have made to the value of the home (including any major building work on the property), who pays what bills, and information about debts. Although DIY templates are available online, it can be a worthwhile investment to ask a solicitor to write one up because if the agreement is later needed in mediation or court, you'll need to be able to prove both parties were properly advised and backed the agreement when it was written up. Cohabitation agreements are, however, 'honourable agreements' — meaning not all clauses have to be enforced by the courts, although they can seriously cut down disagreements and smooth any break-up. If you are renting together, it is a good idea to have the tenancy agreement in both of your names.

2 **If you're moving into their home:** be aware that, if the house is only in one partner's name, then the other will

usually have no right to the proceeds from selling the house. That remains the case unless they can prove they contributed to the deposit, mortgage payments, or paying for major building works *because* it was agreed that doing so meant they owned a share of the house. If the property is not in your name, in the event of a break-up you may be lawfully kicked out. Equally, grim as it is to think about, if your partner dies — unless they have named you in their will — you might have no claim on the property, even though it's your home. (Unless you're married, in which case assets almost always pass directly to the surviving spouse.)

3   **If you're buying a property together:** you need to think hard — and take professional legal advice — about how to do so, especially if you're not married. The two main options — which a solicitor should explain in full — are to buy as 'joint tenants', or as 'tenants in common'.

4   **If marriage or a civil partnership is on the horizon:** you might want to shore up your personal financial position by taking out a pre-nuptial agreement. Seriously, pre-nups aren't just for the Kardashians of this world: it's a broad name for a legal document that will set out what you've agreed to retain or share before you pooled your resources. It might state, for example, that neither of you would try to claim a share of the other's family money, property, or business that they had before you got together, or set out that the flat that one of you bought before you met remains their own asset if you split up. Although pre-nups need to be drawn up by a solicitor, be aware that in England, Wales and Northern Ireland, they aren't fully legally binding

(they are in Scotland). The courts, however, take them into account in the event of a divorce, although they will want evidence that both parties took independent legal advice and were financially 'in the know' about each other's situations before signing.

If you or your partner own a business, think carefully before deciding whether the other partner will be involved. It sounds obvious, but if you're self-employed and your partner ends up supporting you in any way with it — whether by covering for you when you're ill or helping you do your invoicing — things can get complicated fast. A friend was invited by her boyfriend to move overseas with him and help him set up a new business. She worked like crazy on the project, and it was eventually a big success — but he still owned it 100%. Situations like this can lead to issues down the line ...

How to deal with massive income disparity between friends

It's becoming increasingly common: you and your buddy met at uni; she went on to become a software designer for a tech giant, earning £70,000 a year (AND getting that ridiculously Instagrammable free lunch every day), you really wanted to do journalism but now your job is writing — ugh, you hate the term, but — half the 'content' that's featured on her employer's site. For not much money. Then there's your neighbour who has almost a decade-worth of student loans from two degrees, who is struggling to make his start-up work, who's couch-surfing at his school-friend's who happened to go into banking and just earned a bonus bigger than your annual salary (you spotted a bank statement lying in the fruit bowl, and had to physically replace your eyes back in your head). Yet, you all go out for collective meals — meaning you end up getting indigestion halfway through due to worrying if having only a starter means you'll still be liable for a straightforward bill-split at the end, while Banker Neighbour goes for three courses …

How to stay friends when your salaries are whole-phone-number-streams-of-digits apart can be awkward. But income disparities are common, as some millennials pick between the high-paying corporate route, while others go for dream careers that involve long training spells, or a freelance life with more free time and a range of fulfilling work, but less dosh.

These differences can really give a friendship — or relationship — a kicking. The wealthier friend might worry about seeming condescending if they offer to pay for a meal, or buy a generous birthday present; the lower-earning friend doesn't want to feel like the One Who Says No to every chance to go out somewhere that might end up expensive, or feeling like a charity case. So what can you do?

Awkward, but you could use it as a 'true friend' test. When one of Lucy's colleagues went back to uni in her thirties, and moved back in with her parents to do so, she frankly explained to her friends that the dinner and drinks nights and cinema and theatre splurges were over for a few years: she'd love to meet us for walks, hot chocolate, free events etc. but she just couldn't afford her old level of entertaining and birthday presents. 'The good ones stuck around,' she explained, a few years later. 'But with some friends, even really old ones from school, it became apparent that without the whole atmosphere of a restaurant, or distraction of a film or cocktails, we didn't have that much in common any more. The friendships just died out.'

Talk about it. Explain to a high-rolling friend that you're cutting back at the moment, so instead of worrying through a pricey dinner about a possible bill-split at the end, collectively pick a restaurant from *Time Out*'s cheap eats list, or somewhere with a cheap fixed-price meal. And don't assume you will all split the bill equally — if one person has chosen to order less it might be because that's what they can afford right now.

Don't get too hung up on birthday presents — like the mum who loves her kid's splodgy drawing of her more than any extravagant gift, friends tend to be the same. An arty charity shop poster in a pound-shop frame, or tiny book collating things all your friends love, or a voucher to babysit/cook for a chum one night are all great, cheap options.

Don't shove it on a credit card in an attempt to keep up. It'll make you resentful in the long run, and cause potentially serious financial problems; it just isn't worth it.

If you're the higher-earning friend, you might feel like treating other friends now and then — just check they're okay with it before doing so, with a light-hearted comment like, 'I've just got paid, a colleague has two tickets for tonight's game, and I'm so up for doing something different — can I shout you a ticket as I don't want to go alone?' But don't try to get involved in friends' finances directly — shouldering loan payments, for example, or lending them cash — if it goes wrong it can ruin your friendship forever.

Should I care about paying off my student loan?

Maybe it's been an unwanted deduction from your pay packet for some time, or perhaps you've yet to hit the paying-back threshold and are worried about the extra interest. Or maybe you're still at uni racking up student debt and are scared about that huge number. Whatever your situation, debt can give anyone sleepless nights and costs money to deal with, so you might be wondering if you should try and pay it off ASAP. Or perhaps you're thinking that, given that it's the cheapest loan you'll probably ever be offered and it could even be wiped out one day, you shouldn't even care about repaying your student loan.

The final verdict on that depends on a few facts — like when you started uni and if you have other debts or savings. Students from England going to a university in England or the rest of the UK currently pay up to £9250 for tuition. Scottish students study for free in Scotland, but will pay up to £9000 in Wales and up to £9250 everywhere else. Welsh students pay up to £9000 in Wales and up to £9250 in the rest of the UK; Northern Irish students pay up to £4160 in Northern Ireland, up to £9000 in Wales and up to £9250 anywhere else in the UK. If you:

STARTED UNI AFTER 1 SEPTEMBER 2012:

You only start repaying your student loan when earning above £25,000 a year. If you hit that pay packet, you repay 9% of everything you earn above that figure; it comes off your salary automatically like an extra income tax. That continues for 30 years after graduation — and if you haven't repaid it by then, the rest (or even the whole) of the student loan is wiped out.

As a guide, someone earning £20,000 a year would repay nothing — they'd be under the £25,000 threshold. Someone earning £30,000 a year would repay £450 a year (9% of earnings above the £25,000 threshold). On a £35,000 salary it's £900 a year; on a £50,000 wage it's £2250 a year.

It's your responsibility to tell your employer (or HMRC, if you're self-employed) if you're earning more than £25,000 and no student loan deductions are automatically coming out of your pay — otherwise you could face hefty fines from the taxman.

So, is it worth chucking all your financial resources at repaying your student loan ASAP? If you've got other, more expensive loans, focus on paying them off first. Otherwise, use a student finance calculator to help you decide. If the analysis suggests you won't fully repay the student debt in 30 years, when it's eradicated, then overpaying it could be wasting your money. (Unless you feel a social duty to repay it — we're just talking cold, hard, cash here.) However, if your earnings mean you ARE likely to pay off your student debt in full, then doing it ASAP means you will save money on interest (see below) in the long term.

STARTED UNI BEFORE 1 SEPTEMBER 2012:

You'll start repaying your loan when earning more than £18,300 a year, (but be aware this figure is subject to change) at which point you'll be paying 9% of all earnings above that figure.

As an example, earning £22,000 a year will trigger £333 annual repayments; at £30,000, it's £1053 a year, at £50,000 it's £2853.

Again, the money is automatically taken from your pay

when you hit that threshold, so it's not left hanging around your bank account to tempt you.

And again it's your responsibility to tell your employer (or HMRC for the self-employed) if the loan isn't automatically coming out of your above-the-threshold salary.

The crucial difference here is the interest rate, which is set at inflation (the rate at which prices rise each year, which officials calculate by studying the cost of a basket of set items) or less. What that means is that the actual cost of the loan doesn't increase over time — in 20 years' time, it would buy the same value of holiday/food/clothes as it would today — even though the actual figure will be higher. The debt is also wiped out after a set time — 30 years for anyone who started uni between 2006 and 2011, although it's different for other dates and for Scots, so check your own circumstances: the MoneySavingExpert website has a useful student finance calculator.

So, is it worth chucking all your financial resources at repaying your student loan? If you've a pricey overdraft or credit card debt, tackle these first — they will cost you more. But beyond that, it's a direct choice. The amount of the debt might be increasing over time, but you won't feel a real impact on your pocket as the overall figure will pay for the same amount of stuff today as it did when you graduated. And leaving your debt ticking along in the background means that if you suddenly face a pay-cut, or lose your job, then the repayments will drop (or stop) too — and could disappear after 30 years.

Pensions. Just what?

If your boss starts talking about a workplace pension, you might hear one of two things: 1) Nothing, because the word itself and all the jargon around it is so boring you zoned out and started thinking about which sushi multipack is the best lunch option, or 2) Hang on a sec — agreeing to a pension means getting paid less now … just so I can have a souped-up mobility scooter when I'm old. Which I might not even get to be given the amount I'm boozing/sugar-gorging/not-going-to-the-gym at the moment. So what's the point?'

It's true — you've probably got a pay packet that's not quite giving you the lifestyle you dreamed of, and you're already seeing it eroded by student loan repayments, and you're finding that the tax cut from your salary is a whole lot more punishing than you thought, and you're struggling with a pricey rent bill or mortgage … So saying yes to a pension might seem about as appealing as repeatedly slamming your head in a fridge door. More than one in 10 workers have not started to save for a pension and won't start to do so until they are 46 years old, according to research by Prudential.

The word 'pension' just refers to a retirement plan which is topped up throughout your working life, usually squirrelled away into long-term investment funds by a specialist company, and which then turns into an income when you retire. But since the government doesn't want a few million destitute OAPs on its hands in a couple of decades' time, it's inducing more people to save for their retirement, partly by making employers enrol all their staff into a workplace pension scheme, called 'automatic enrolment'.

The upshot is, a lot of pensions are a bit like a 'buy one pack of Smarties, get two free' deal. You pay for one pack out of your salary, then your employer chips in for another, and the third is a gift from the government in the form of tax relief.

Under 'automatic enrolment', if you are earning above £10,000 a year, a minimum proportion (around 4% currently, but this will soon rise) of your earnings are invested by you, around 3% is added by your employer, and a little extra – currently around 1% is added as tax relief. But the figures can be higher if you choose, and a lot of workplaces match considerably higher payments. What that means is that, if your employer is paying into your pension scheme, then unless you've got huge debts to deal with and can't afford even a few extra pounds coming out of your salary, turning down a pension is a bit like rejecting a pay rise.

You don't have to tie up your pension with your workplace — a personal pension is another option. In any case, there are three main types of pension:

1 **State pension:** this is paid by the government to those who have made National Insurance contributions during their working life, or been credited with them while on certain benefits or raising children. It's currently up to around £125 a week. This could change by the time we're ripe for retirement though — pensions are a huge expense for the state. And the date for claiming it will likely get further off too — it's currently heading towards 68.

2 **'Defined benefit pensions':** these are becoming much rarer than they used to be, but are still paid to some employees

working in the public sector or big corporates. Here, the pension you get is based on how long you've been a part of the scheme and how much you earn, and provides a secure income for life, either based on your final salary in the role or an average of your pay while in the scheme.

3 **'Defined contribution pensions':** where your final retirement payments are based on cash put in by you and/ or your employer AND on investment returns during the scheme. Most personal pensions are this kind: you or your employer (if it's a workplace pension) pick a provider and make arrangements for your contributions to be paid in. You get the same tax relief (although there's more admin) and can choose where you want your contributions to be invested from a range of funds.

The date at which both of these latter two types of private pension can be withdrawn will depend on the rules of the pension scheme — it's currently usually around 55, but may be before for those retiring early due to ill health.

Some mortal thoughts: if you die before you can claim your pension, your beneficiaries (as set out in a will, or otherwise usually your spouse, parents, or children) will usually be paid it as a tax-free lump sum. It's more complicated, though, if the pension is worth more than the 'lifetime allowance' — currently set at around £1 million — or if you die aged 75 or older, in which case tax is involved. You can also nominate anyone — children, relatives, or even friends — to inherit your remaining pension fund in your will.

Pensions do mean a fair amount of admin. When moving

jobs, you can usually choose between sticking with a current pension plan and asking your employer to pay into that, rather than a new one, leaving that pension plan as it was and just starting another one at your new job, or keeping pots from different employers separate and combining them at a later date. It's 'tidier' to have all your pension funds in one place, but you'll need to think about any benefits you may be giving up under any new pension offered through a new employer.

If you're a freelancer, pensions might seem even more complicated as there's no one plonking the paperwork in front of you and saying, 'These are your options.' But it's still vital to think about retirement. Most self-employed people use a personal pension, where you can pick where you want your contributions to be invested from funds offered by the provider. How large a pension you build up depends on how much is paid in, how well your fund(s) perform, and the level of fees you pay. The Money Advice Service has a useful guide, which is linked in the back of this book.

Pensions aren't the only way people plan for retirement — some prefer to rely on cash savings, praying to some higher being, or hoping that a property investment will increase in value enough that downsizing releases enough cash to live a luxury retired life. There are other 'official' routes too, like:

The new 'LISA', or Lifetime ISA for the under-40s, where the government will add 25% to top up a maximum annual contribution of £4000 — so a gift of up to £1000 a year from the generous taxman. You can only access your cash if you use it to buy your first home, or turn 60, though. And this still isn't as generous as a pension that includes an employer's top-up.

(By the way, you're allowed to have a Help to Buy ISA and a LISA, but you can't get the first-time buyers' bonus on both.)

However you hope to live in your last decades/years of retirement (or otherwise — some millennials expect to be commuting while on zimmer frames, never actually being able to afford not to work), most people will need savings running into hundreds of thousands of pounds. So you need to do some planning. MoneySavingExpert has a useful calculator which can help with working out the sums.

How to compare the infinite comparables ...
(phone, internet, and energy bills)

When big websites have to shove dancing meerkats, twerking high-heeled blokes, and free cinema tickets in our faces to get us to even think about using them to switch telecoms, broadband, or energy supplier, you know it's not going to be the most fun process in the world.

But if you've been lax about switching anything from your gas and electricity provider to your mobile bill over the past few years, and just allowed the old, expired deal to roll over, there's almost certainly a cheaper option out there. Here's how to haggle down the costs of your ...

1   **Landline/internet:** there's lots of negotiating potential
    here. For a home phone/broadband package, you'll have
    to pay a standard landline fee — about £13 a month —
    then you can slap on the internet deal you want, as well
    as inclusive landline minutes if you don't exclusively use a

mobile. Shopping around, especially going beyond the big BT/Virgin Media names, can trigger big savings. Compare the options on SimplifyDigital and BroadbandChoices, always check if an offer is available via a cashback website, and check if your current provider will match any deal you've been offered — saves hassle and money.

2   **Mobiles phone:** cancelling a pricey mobile phone contract can feel tougher than breaking out of Guantanamo Bay. But recent research by uSwitch found that a quarter of us have never switched — and are wasting more than £170 a year as a result. If you're out of contract, use BillMonitor to work out how many minutes and how much data you actually need (most of us over-buy), then use that info to find the cheapest tariff (or pay as you go offer) on uSwitch or MoneySupermarket. Remember to nab cashback, too. And if you've found a good deal, often your provider will match — or better — it rather than lose you, so call up, say you're quitting, and wait to be put through to 'retentions' — the division of a mobile phone company that has the best deals around. Always recycle your old handset rather than leaving it lingering in your Stuff Drawer, too.

Another money-saving telecoms tip

If you're phoning abroad, from a mobile or landline, and can't do it from your office phone, try Skype, FaceTime, Google Hangouts, or a free Voip (online telephone provider) app like Viber. If you really need to call from a phone to another phone, search first for a cheap prefix to slash the cost via a site like NiftyList.

ENERGY

If we could heat our homes with the energy we give off getting pissed off about how much it costs to heat our homes, it would be a lot cheaper. But since we can't, and the average household's energy bill is now over £1200 a year, tackle your gas and electricity bills. Yes, it's annoying to deal with the paperwork of switching, the endless meter readings, and new direct debits. But that's exactly why the Big Six energy providers make such big profits. So put on some decent music, and spend half an hour saving money by doing some deal-hunting.

If you're tied into a fixed-term contract, it's usually not worth the penalty to move. Otherwise, if you've been lingering on a standard deal for some time, grab a recent bill — it will state your current supplier, tariff, and how much energy you're currently using, either in kilowatt hours (kWh) or as a monthly or quarterly spend. Tap this data into a site like CompareThe-Market or EnergyHelpline to find the cheapest option.

Dual-fuel tariffs, paid by direct debit, are usually cheapest. You might have to choose between a fixed-price deal (usually for a year or two; you'll be protected from price hikes, but if rates fall, you'll miss out), or a standard one. As ever, use a cashback site — which will pay you for joining some new tariffs — to top up your savings, but only if doing so gives you the cheapest deal. You'll need to note down meter readings on the date your providers are switched, but that's it.

Think green and you'll save money. On top of the fleece

onesie and extra jumpers you should wear all winter rather than ramping up the heating, find out if your energy provider will fit free loft and/or cavity wall insulation to stop heat loss (landlords will need to organise this if you are renting). Put silver foil behind radiators to reflect heat back into a room rather than out of the walls; use the washing machine at 30 degrees (it washes just as well, according to experts), and don't overfill the kettle, but do fill up dishwashers and washing machines before running them. Also, switch to eco-friendly light bulbs, and listen to Dad and turn them off when you're not in the room. All TVs, phone chargers, and other gadgets should be switched off at the wall, not left on standby, to save energy and money.

WATER

Unlike energy, you can't switch water provider. If you're not currently on a meter, check if it would be cheaper to switch to one using the calculator at the Consumer Council for Water website; providers install them for free. And try to use less of the wet stuff: the average shower uses about 15 litres fewer than a bath, for example. Water companies are also sending out freebie eco devices like flush-saving bags, and eco shower-heads, so ask yours if they're involved.

Credit cards and debt: getting out of it

Credit cards: they can be a calm drink at the boozer with friends, tiding you over until the end of the month when they're paid off in full, or they can be like that idiotic fourth shot you accepted at 3am on a regrettable Tuesday night out. Basically, if they're used carefully and responsibly, credit cards can give you lucrative spending rewards, help you avoid sticky financial situations like a bust car 36 hours before payday or a broken boiler, and protect you from fraudsters. But if your plastic habit gets out of control, it can lead to really expensive — and potentially life-ruining — debt. So, on that happy note, should you ever have a credit card? And what should you do if you're in trouble with one already?

Credit vs debit card — what's the difference?

When you use a debit card to pay for shopping or withdraw cash from an ATM, the money is automatically, and almost instantly, taken from your current account. So with a debit card, you must have enough money in your account (or an agreed overdraft) to cover the purchase. By contrast, a credit card isn't linked to your current account (so you can get one from a company quite separate from your bank). When you use it for spending, you're borrowing the funds (which you can do up to a pre-arranged limit) and will then pay for them at a later date. The cost of the purchase is added to your credit card account and you get a monthly statement every month, which you can choose to pay off in full with no interest, or pay a minimum amount set out by the provider, and repay the rest over a period of time. This usually incurs interest — so the quicker you pay off your balance, the less you'll pay for the privilege of borrowing.

What's the difference between standing orders and direct debits?

A standing order is a regular payment that you can set up with your bank to pay other people, companies, or organisations, or as a transfer to any other bank accounts in your own name. You can change or cancel the standing order whenever you like. A direct debit is another regular payment but it can only be set up by the organisation to which you're making the payment — such as a gym or charity.

WHY HAVE A CREDIT CARD?

It's the cheapest and easiest way to borrow money — up to a few thousand pounds — as long as you have a decent credit score. Banks spend millions each year advertising their '0 per cent' 'interest-free' deals, but only whisper — really, really quietly — in their small print that those offers are only available to those with sparkling financial records. So research a card's 'annual percentage rate', or APR, which is just banking jargon for how much borrowing money will cost in fees and interest. The average credit card APR is around 18%, but you can get this far lower if you successfully apply for one of the many interest-free deals (see overleaf). Just remember, ALWAYS pay back at least the minimum repayment each month, and if at all possible, pay back the total balance, as you'll otherwise be running up debts, which, whatever the interest level, will need to be paid back one day.

If you're diligent and a pro at hitting deadlines, credit cards can reward your shopping habit. Anyone who pays off the full balance each month should opt for a cashback card, which pays you back a percentage of annual spending — American Express and Capital One plus all the major banks offer these. Or look for one with freebies such as travel insurance — offered by Nationwide — or flights — as with Avios or Flybe cards. They usually have punishing interest rates, so they're only for those who can afford to pay the card off each month — setting up an automatic direct debit from your current account will avoid any defaults, as long as it's always topped up with enough funds. Some are fee-free; others impose annual charges, so you'll need to work out if the value of the rewards is worth more than the cost of the card.

The last major benefit of credit cards is their guarantee — under the Consumer Credit Act 1974, card providers have to pay out if you buy something that doesn't arrive — for example via an online retailer you've since realised is dodgy, or from a shop that goes into administration. Card providers only have to cough up if whatever you've bought costs over £100, and it only applies to credit, not debit, cards, so any pricey purchases are more safely bought on this kind of plastic.

How to complain

Okay, we all know how to moan (lesson one in toddler school, right? 'It's not faiiiiir …'). But knowing your consumer rights, and when and how to complain about a dodgy thing you've bought, or poor-quality service, is a pretty important part of being a grown-up. The biggest piece of legal protection you have is the Consumer Rights Act — it's more than a hundred pages long, and for detailed advice, check out *Which?*'s online guide. But a basic summary is:

- Anything you buy should be of satisfactory quality, fitting its description, do the job it promised to do, and last a reasonable amount of time.
- That means a hairdryer that only blows cold air out after two weeks should be refunded by the store (always go to the retailer, not the manufacturer, as your 'contract' is with the seller).
- But that doesn't mean a top you bought in a size medium can always be swapped for another — these details will be up to the shop to decide.
- With online purchases, the Consumer Contracts Regulations 2013 law means that you can usually cancel an order and get a refund — even if you've just changed your mind — within 14 days.
- The golden guidelines to a 'good complaint' are: know your rights, act as soon as you realise there's a problem, keep records of any communication, collect evidence, and stay calm and reasonable throughout.
- The Resolver site is helpful if you want to complain about your treatment by a shop, energy company, bank, or other kind of firm, setting out your consumer rights and guiding you to log your complaint in the right place.
- Be aware, too, that buying from private sellers, such as on online auctions, via social media marketplaces, or just from a neighbour, means far fewer rights than

when buying from a shop, and you could end up
hostage to their goodwill if something goes wrong
with a purchase.

WHAT ABOUT DEBTS?

If you've run up credit card debts, then you're not alone: shoppers put £339 million on plastic in just one month of 2017, and the total Britons owe on credit cards stands above £66 billion. But knowing you're part of a gang of debtors doesn't ease the stress. To tackle your debts, you'll need to work on your budget and cut your spending — you can start with the bills-savings tips above. But the first thing you can do is make sure you're paying the lowest possible interest rate.

Exactly how to do so will depend on your circumstances: if you've got multi-thousand-pound debt spread across various cards, you might be better off moving it to a low-interest personal loan. If you're less deeply into the red, taking advantage of banks' 0% interest cards might give you enough time to pay off your balances. There are lots of sources of expert, unbiased advice, so ignore the sharks plying their 'consolidation' deals on daytime TV and speak to an advisor at a charity such as National Debtline, which has a helpline and webchat, or Step Change, which offers the same but also has an online debt tool.

If you just need a short respite on interest payments to pay off your existing card debt, look for a '0% balance transfer', where you can move debt from another card or account; over the period that the offer is in place, you don't pay interest on the debt. The savings add up: someone with £2500 debt on a credit card charging 18%, repaying £100 a month, would pay almost £600 in interest and take two years and seven months to wipe out their debt. Whereas someone with an interest-free deal would spend zero on interest, and take two years and one month to repay their debt. But watch out, as lenders DO impose charges — usually 2–3% of the total debt — to open a 0% balance transfer deal. Usually this fee is much less than what you would be paying in interest, but check before proceeding.

All the main comparison sites let you compare credit cards according to length of deal, interest rates, and rewards. Remember to use any savings you're making on not paying interest to pay down more of your debt — the aim is to wipe it out completely before the deal comes to an end. Make sure you know when that is, too — and if you can't pay it off, try to switch to a new balance transfer to avoid being rolled onto the expensive standard interest rate.

A warning on borrowing — and who to turn to for debt and legal advice

Hire purchase, instalment plans, and deferred payments are all ways that you can buy now, pay later. They're the 'deals' that salesmen will try to ram down your throat (because, *kerching*, commission!). Sometimes they will be vital — for example, you might need hire purchase on a car if you need to travel for work and that's the only way you can afford it. And sometimes they will be fairly reasonable, with low interest rates. But often these kinds of payment plans have a catch — such as hefty interest rates, or repayment penalties, or the advertised low rates only apply to those with perfect credit ratings, when that might not be the case in your personal circumstances — so make sure you read all the small print before signing up.

The same is true with payday loans — short-term IOUs initially designed to tide people over until payday but now used by borrowers who want pricey football tickets, clothes, a new mobile etc., before they have the cash available. With a payday loan, the money is paid directly into your bank account, and you repay in full with interest and charges — usually a month later. But although the cost of these types of loans is capped by law, they still tend to work out very expensive. Think really hard before taking one out, and look into any viable alternatives, such as longer-term loans or interest-free credit cards.

Seek free debt advice from organisations such as Citizens Advice, Debt Advice Foundation, StepChange, PayPlan, or National Debtline.

For free legal advice, you may be eligible for legal aid depending on the kind of problem you are facing, and your financial circumstances. It's only offered to those facing serious issues, such as being at risk of homelessness or of abuse or serious harm, such as domestic violence: you can find out more on the government's website. For certain issues, solicitors at Law Centres offer free advice; they tend to specialise in employment, housing, immigration, debt, benefits, and discrimination cases, while Citizens Advice centres may be able to put you in touch with solicitors offering one-off, fixed-fee advice (say a 30-minute meeting for a pre-agreed fee). If you're a member of a trade union, you may have access to inclusive legal advice (not just on work issues), while Citizens Advice has more info on sources of Pro Bono (free) advice.

11 weird ways to make extra money

These aren't going to make you a millionaire, but they'll top up your earnings and you can do a lot of them in front of Netflix — paying off your subscription, if nothing else.

1. MYSTERY SHOPPING

Get paid anything from a few quid to as much as £100 for visiting and then reporting on the service at shops, spas, hotels, restaurants, and more — and get paid back your spending in-store too. Sites include MarketForceShopper, SecretSquirrel, GrassrootsMysteryShopping, and Maxim.

2. SURVEY-BUSTING

Answer questions, get paid. The cash is low — maybe as little as 50p per survey — but it adds up and can be done in front of the TV. Try ISay, GlobalTestMarket, and PopulusLive.

3. RENT YOUR STUFF

At RentMyItems you can hire out anything from a lawnmower, GoPro, or buggy to neighbours; at JustPark you can rent out your driveway to drivers (especially lucrative if you're near a station, sports event etc.); while at StoreMates you can turn your spare loft or cupboards into self-storage for neighbours.

4. SELL YOUR ~~CRAP~~ DESIRABLE POSSESSIONS ON EBAY

Pick a free listing day, or use Gumtree or Facebook selling groups for a fee-free option.

5. OFFLOAD YOUR GADGETS

Lots of specialist sites will buy your unwanted electrical goods — even phones with cracked screens and sat-navs that don't work. Check out recycling sites like MazumaMobile or EnviroFone. You enter the gadget's details, they'll offer you a price, and if you accept it then you send your device in and wait for a cash transfer.

6. FOCUS GROUPS

You have to get off your bum and go somewhere for these, but they pay anything up to £200 to quiz you in discussion groups about topics stretching from bank accounts to medicines. There are lots of local groups, or try SarosResearch, IndieField, and FocusForce.

7. SELL YOUR PHOTOS

Perfect snaps don't just have to go on Instagram. You can make money off them via photo banks like PicFair (set your own price), or iStock (receive a set royalty).

8. SIGN UP FOR CASHBACK

See page 107 for cashback website recommendations.

9. BE A FILM OR TV EXTRA

The money's not life-changing — between £60 and £100 a

day, usually — but it's something to brag about too … Until your big moment as 'background pedestrian' ends up on the cutting-room floor. To get gigs you can sign up with extras agencies — most charge, but it should be a low fee or come out of your first earnings. Make sure they're reputable and registered with the union BECTU.

10. SELL YOUR SKILLS

Amazing at writing birthday poems? Or drawing cartoons? Or translation? Open an Etsy shop, promote yourself on FiveSquids, PeoplePerHour, Freelancer, or StudentGems.

11. HUNT FOR LOST BOUNTY

We don't mean looking for treasure troves in the Caribbean Sea, but checking to see if there are any old childhood savings or premium bonds that you might have somehow forgotten about, or never known about. AtMyLostAccount, a site run by the trade groups the British Bankers' Association and the Building Societies Association and premium bond-operator National Savings & Investments, you can fill in your details and it will search for any funds in your name in one of 36 banks, all building societies, and NS&I records.

Financial SOS

Your salary only just covers your rent and you suddenly need emergency money to travel to see a sick relative. Or you've lost your job — out of the blue — and are at risk of being booted out of your home. Financial emergencies always come out of the blue, which is why it's a good idea to put a bit of cash away in an instant-access savings account, for emergencies (experts suggest trying to put away enough to cover three months' essential outgoings, including mortgage or rent, energy bills, and food). But if it's too late for that, what can you do? You may be eligible for benefits or a Budgeting Loan from the government, or, if you're waiting for a first benefit payment and have no cash, you could be able to apply for a short-term benefit advance or a Universal Credit Advance payment. The options will depend totally on your circumstances so it's best to find out more from the Money Advice Service, your local JobCentre Plus office, or a financial advice charity. The housing charity Shelter has lots of advice for those facing losing their home, including information on emergency housing from the council.

How to find a home

By now, you're nailing your health, you've got a job, and you can cook and clean like a pro, so you need somewhere to do one of the most fundamentally important things in life: relax. And while we wish we could tell you that finding a nice place to call home is as easy as checking into a hotel … we can't. But follow these steps and you'll be a lot closer to sorting your living situation — and making it a good one.

A guide to renting

The chances are, if you're a human and living in Britain, at some point you'll have to pay to live in a home someone else owns. And depressingly, by 'home' we really mean 'a room' (and, in some cases of renting meets *Harry Potter*, a 'cupboard under the stairs'). As things stand, the housing market isn't allowing young people to get onto the property ladder easily — unless they're seriously financially sorted — so it's important to be savvy from the start.

Renting — Kat's Story

'Take it from someone who knows — I've rented an all-in-one studio with a small partition wall between the loo and the head of the bed; a damp garden flat; a room in a shared house which fit ONLY a bed and a wardrobe (which was nice and cosy, actually); and an attic room in a family home which, when building work was going on, ended up covered in plaster every single day. And then, the holy grail — a room in a beautiful two-bedroom flat by the corner of a park, and at a not-extortionate price. But it took me six years of renting to get there, so here's how to find the goods, first time around.'

WHERE SHOULD YOU RENT AND WHAT CAN YOU AFFORD?

So, you've got a job and you're finally moving out of home (and we're not counting university, because mum and dad still did your laundry at Christmas). You want to share a nice place with like-minded people close to public transport, but when you start searching online you find hundreds of estate agents in the area and they all require your soul as a deposit. So how do you even start? Here's how to do the maths:

1   **Work out your monthly income:** this isn't your *gross income* (what you earn every month) but your *net income* — what actually hits your bank account once those annoying things like income tax, National Insurance, student loan repayments, and pension contributions have been taken out. Check your payslip, or there are loads of

websites that will calculate this for you; SalaryBot is very straightforward.

2   **Add up your monthly outgoings:** this is where, exactly, your money is going each month. Make a list of everything essential (or any fixed costs you can't live without), like your phone contract, gym membership, Netflix subscription, insurance, etc. Or just consult the budget you made when reading the last chapter!

3   **Then add on your travel costs:** this will vary depending on how far your workplace is from where you end up living, but tally up the cost of your monthly petrol, train tickets, or tube/bus pass. If you live in a big city with different travel zones like London, remember that it'll be more expensive to get to the city centre from Zone 4 than it would be to travel in from Zone 2, for example. Often the difference in cost balances out, with rental properties being cheaper the further away from the busiest/coolest areas of town.

4   **Don't forget your life:** you might be trying to get the biggest room for your buck, but if you can only afford to stay in and eat tinned soup, you'll probably end up hating it there. So, work out how much you think you're going to spend on food each week, the occasional night out, trips to the cinema, shopping etc.

5   **See what you've got left:** barely enough to afford a burrito? Revisit your essential and non-essential outgoings. Do you really need Sky Sports all year round? If not, cull it. Think you've got enough now? This is your magic number.

6   **Search within your budget:** now you've found out what you can afford, remember that it has to cover utility bills

like gas and electricity, water, council tax, and internet, as well as rent. What you end up spending on this will depend on where in the country you live, the size of the property, how many people you're sharing with, and how much they care about things like turning the plugs off. MoneySuperMarket have a home bill checker application on their website so you can see average prices in the area you're looking.

How to make things cheaper

Obviously, you want to save some cash. Here are some ways you *might* be able to do that:

Look at local council tax bands: council tax is an annual fee everyone in the UK has to pay that goes towards funding stuff in your local area like rubbish collection, keeping libraries going, and cleaning the streets. How much it costs is based on two things: where you live, and how much the property is worth. For example, in one south London borough, the 2017/18 rate of annual council tax for a band C property is £642.32. In the next borough over, Richmond, it's £1,456.48. Check your postcodes, people.

Consider a roommate: as in, an actual mate you'd share a bedroom with. It might not sound like how you'd like to start your independence, but plenty of places in more expensive cities offer rooms for two people sharing, with single beds.

Find room for negotiation: if you're thinking of moving into an already-established house share, the current tenants may have already shopped around for the best utility bill rates. But if you're taking on a whole property afresh — and as long as you'll be the ones paying the bills, not your landlord — it's worth getting savvy and finding providers with the best deals.

Become a property guardian: you live in old buildings such as care homes, police stations, church halls etc. which are unoccupied and where the owners want to avoid squatters or other issues that come from a building being unoccupied. The rent is usually around a quarter of market rents, but there are downsides (parties are banned, you can usually only stay a few months, and it might not be the lap of luxury). Agents organising these schemes include Camelot Europe, and Ad Hoc.

Consider an unconventional arrangement: like living with an elderly person who wants company, or with a family who you childmind for — these are usually arranged via agencies like HomeShare or community organisations such as churches, synagogues, mosques, local charities etc.

HOW TO FIND A PLACE TO LIVE AND PEOPLE TO LIVE WITH

Now you're armed with some numbers, you can start thinking about *where* to live. Tempting as it might be to settle on the area with the best pubs, it's worth considering:

- What your commute would look like (according to the Office for National Statistics, the average daily commute in 2015 was 57.1 minutes) — use a journey planner to work out how easy it would be to get from A to B.
- What you actually want in your local area. Do you live for the great outdoors or dream of a home in hipster heaven? Is it more important that you've got a gym down the road or 10+ places to have brunch?
- If you visit anywhere else very often. If your parents live on the south coast, and you're moving to London, perhaps don't set your heart on somewhere in the northernmost part of the city.

In happy news for Generation Rent, there's no shortage of places being let. But it won't be the same for every scenario; here are three of the most likely ones:

1. YOU WANT A ROOM IN AN EXISTING HOUSE SHARE

There are loads of websites that make finding options easy. SpareRoom, RightMove, EasyRoomate, and Gumtree are all reliable and have thousands of properties on their books at one time. They also offer a LOT of search options to help you narrow down preferences, like if you want to live with guys or girls, if smoking is ok, if pets are allowed, and so on.

There are sites with additional benefits, too; IdealFlatmate matches you with people on a personality basis, and London-Shared has starting prices that tend to be higher than most, but offers lovely furnished rooms with WiFi and free weekly cleaners included in your rental cost.

If you're looking in London or Manchester, SpareRoom also hosts SpeedFlatmating events where you can meet loads of people in one place. (These usually involve alcohol, so the chances of you getting an actual date out of it too are high. Win-win.)

If you'd rather live with people who you know — or know of — it's worth putting the feelers out amongst friends or colleagues to see if any of their mates need a new roommate. And you might find that your company or an industry organisation will have a message board where members can list available rooms.

2. YOU AND YOUR FRIENDS WANT TO FIND A PROPERTY TOGETHER

If there's a group of you looking to rent together, you can use the same websites as above, as well as online or shopfront estate agents to find entire properties. OpenRent specialises in lettings with private landlords, PurpleBricks has transparent fees and an easy-to-use app. It's a good idea to make sure everyone is aware of each other's budgets and requirements before you start looking, and establish some conditions before you move in to avoid drama later on: will you split the rent equally, or will it vary depending on the size of each bedroom? Will one person be responsible for all the rent and bills, or will the burden be shared?

3. YOU AREN'T SURE ABOUT LIVING WITH A BUNCH OF STRANGERS, BUT YOU CAN'T AFFORD TO LIVE ALONE

Slightly tricky, but not impossible. Here's where you might want to look into lodging in someone else's home. It's the same premise as taking a room in a house share, but as a lodger you live with the homeowner(s). This could be a family, a couple, a single person … anyone. In general, lodging tends to offer a bit more privacy because there's less onus on the renter to socialise with other tenants, and often you'll find a room which has an en-suite or more private space. Lodgings are usually advertised with 'live-in landlord' in the listing.

WHAT SHOULD YOU ASK AT YOUR FLATMATE 'INTERVIEW'?

Responding to an ad for a room and going along to see it is essentially a job interview, but to be someone's mate (or at the very least, an acquaintance). But you might spend so much time trying to prove you're *fun-but-also-respectful-while-baking-cakes-and-cleaning-up-after-everyone-because-I'm-just-like-that-ha-ha-ha* that you forget to ask about the people you might be living with for the foreseeable future.

So even if you've seen 17 flats already and think you've finally found the one, don't let your excitement about finally finding a room that comes with windows and doesn't smell like a bin distract you from asking questions about your potential flatmates, too. Here are some of the things you might want to ask about:

1 **Working hours:** if you do a regular 9–5 job, you might not be up for the early-morning wake-up call of someone who has just come in off a late shift in the early hours and decided to knock up a very noisy masterpiece in the kitchen while running a long cycle on the washing machine.
2 **Routine:** it might seem a bit much to ask people you've only just met what time they take a shower every day. But

if you're already talking about when they work, there's no harm in throwing in a 'So I bet you guys have your bathroom schedule nailed, right?' and see if a structured morning is their jam. It's better than a gladiatorial contest for the hot water every morning.

3   **How they organise housework:** is there a rota, do they have a system in place, or is it left pretty flexible? If you know which of those options you prefer, then find out how they currently handle the domestic labour.

4   **Neighbourhood:** if it's an area that's new to you, remember to ask your potential housemates if there are any local tips they can give you, and check how safe they feel walking around at night.

5   **How much they socialise:** some people think shared houses should be a friendship experience, where everyone's cooking together and hanging out at the weekends. Others are considerably less involved — you'll say hi in the kitchen when you're making your separate dinners, but not much else.

6   **What's getting watched on TV:** if you CANNOT STAND to be in the same room when *Love Island* is on or you're a dedicated Whovian, this is going to be important.Unless you plan on putting a telly in your bedroom or streaming stuff online the whole time, get an idea of their tastes now.

7   **What sports teams they support:** otherwise known as 'How much will it ruin their day and everyone else's if they lose?'. Some sporting allegiances can be more divisive than Brexit. And if you can find out which way they voted in the referendum, you're very good at this line of 'getting to know you'.

8 **Do they like to party:** and, more importantly, do they
like to party at home? Particularly important if you're
looking for a place that's calm and clean and quiet, and
hate the idea of strangers wandering into your room
after one too many lagers. Or if you are partial to a rager
yourself and are keen to find kindred spirits … It's harder
to ask someone you've just met if they dabble in anything
that doesn't come in a bottle. But if knowing whether
people you live with take drugs or keep them at home is
important to you, you've got nothing to lose by putting
yourself out there first. 'I've got to be honest, I'm not into
drugs. What about you?' is as good a conversation starter
as any.

Finding flatmates — Kat's story

'When I first started looking for a room in London, the most
nerve-wracking bit — not the fact that I was going into
strangers' houses, or pretending my finances were in control, or still finding the Tube really confusing — was trying to
get potential flatmates to actually *like* me.'

**YOU'VE GOT FIVE MINUTES TO LOOK AROUND: WHAT SHOULD BE
TOP OF YOUR CHECK LIST?**

Because the rental market waits for no one — you can find
yourself applying for a lease on the doorstep, while other
interested people are inside looking around — those precious

minutes when you get through the door are essential for finding out if your potential dream home is actually liveable.

As well as focusing on where you'll put all your trainers and how comfy the mattress is, there's a few essential things you should be looking out for. We asked Giles Barrett, a Senior Lettings Manager at Knight Frank, to give us a few tips about what to check when looking at rentals:

> 'Check the water pressure: turn the taps on or ask to turn on the shower.
>
> Check the quality of the blackout curtains/blinds in the bedroom.
>
> Check for rubbish bags outside, or general mess. It might be a sign of inconsiderate neighbours.
>
> Beware the closed curtain. Is it hiding a train track, a gas cylinder, or a building site?
>
> If there is strong smell of air freshener it is probably masking a deeper problem, like damp.'

And learn from those who have been there ...

'I moved into a flat without noticing that apart from an extension lead behind the fridge — which was next to the sink — there were no plug sockets in the kitchen. None.

I had to keep the kettle and toaster in the lounge and make smoothies on the floor by the sofa.'

'I went to see a room which seemed great from the description — four other young professional housemates, good-sized communal areas, walking distance to the Tube, and the rent wasn't going to put me below the poverty line. When I got there, I was shown to the back of the house and into a room the size of a shoe-box. It had no windows and contained the external back door! That was the one source of natural light for the room and the only access in and out of the shared garden. They offered it to me on the spot, but needless to say I didn't call them back.'

'I always check out the locks, as it's good to have newer ones. I once viewed a property that had been broken into so many times the lock was right at the bottom as the door had got so broken … that was a HUGE no.'

'One girl had a photo of herself on the wall. Just herself with no one else in the photo. That should have raised alarm bells. I wish it had!'

'I almost overlooked a room in a big, beautiful three-bedroom flat which was cheap for its excellent location — because it was right opposite one of the area's grimiest, and loudest, clubs. But then I realised that the bedroom on offer actually overlooked an empty car park on the other side, which was silent. Best nights' sleep I've ever had.'

'I've always been careful about sharing with single people who could be attracted to each other. Someone will always come home drunk looking for pizza and end up with penis, and you don't want to get caught in the middle!'

'The biggest turn-off when my housemate and I were looking for somewhere to live was that in a lot of places one bedroom was significantly bigger than the other. At the time, you might convince yourself that it's fine, but if you get the smaller room it might be a different story.'

'I always look at the bathrooms — I'd personally say you need one bathroom per two rooms (three at an absolute push). No one wants to be queuing for the bathroom in the early mornings.'

WHAT ARE THE HIDDEN COSTS OF RENTING AND ARE ANY NEGOTIABLE?

Ah, the fun bit! By which we obviously mean the least fun thing ever because the financial side of renting can feel like you're going out to eat at a nice restaurant, but even before you get there and look at the menu, you have to give them some money towards heating their ovens up, buying some new cutlery, and hiring someone to stand on the door and say you can come in.

The good news is the government is considering a lettings fee ban. While the details of how exactly this will impact the market aren't clear yet, it's a good sign that the unfair additional costs of renting a property will decrease.

Until then, there are some big things you should factor into your budget when you're preparing to rent somewhere. You're looking at:

1 **Holding deposit:** usually around £200–£500, according to Zoopla's 2017 guide. This is what you pay to take the property off the market. You'll get this money back once you've signed your rental agreement.

2 **Rent in advance:** usually one month's rent, paid before you move in.

3 **Deposit:** this can be anything from four weeks to two months' rent, and will be returned in full or in part when your tenancy comes to an end.

4 **Referencing fees:** this pays for checks on everyone who moves into the property, usually to ensure you're employed under the terms you say you are, and that you've been a decent tenant previously. Everyone moving in will have to pay for these individually, and you'll also have to pay for a guarantor's references to be taken out, if you have one.

5 **Other admin costs:** this could mean preparing the tenancy agreement, renewing a contract, or changing a house-sharer later down the line. Most estate agents will have fixed, non-negotiable fees for this, but it's always worth asking if they can bring the cost down.

6 **Inventory checking costs:** these are taken out when you move into and out of a property, and are usually shared 50:50 with the landlord.

7 **Unpaid rent:** if money bounces when it's debited from your account, you'll be charged. This is avoidable — make sure

you have set up a standing order with your bank and set a note in your diary just before you pay rent every month, to check you have the right funds there.

8 **Contents insurance:** any insurance your landlord holds won't apply to you, so you'll need to shop around for a good deal if you want to cover your belongings.

It's important to remember that these fees can differ hugely across estate agents. Some will charge a lot, others a lot less, but many will list them clearly on their websites. You should also check that estate agents are registered with a reputable regulatory body such as the National Association of Estate Agents or the Association of Residential Lettings Agents.

AGENCY VS PRIVATE LANDLORD; WHAT KIND OF LEASE IS NORMAL?

In day-to-day terms, whether you rent through an agency or through a private landlord will make little difference. But contractually, it might.

The most standard contract you'll come across is an Assured Shorthold Tenancy (AST), which means that your landlord doesn't live in the property with you. Usually these agreements are for six months or a year initially, and during that fixed term your landlord can't raise your rent.

You can also get an assured tenancy or regulated tenancy, which give you stronger rights. But they're less common in new tenancies, and you aren't likely to come across one if you're new to renting.

If you're a lodger, you may have an Excluded Tenancy Agreement. The main difference is that it's easier for you to be evicted than it would be with an AST. Some rental sites, like SpareRoom, provide their own basic contracts. It's an easy way for a private landlord to make a rental agreement formal, and is fairly standard.

If you aren't sure of your situation, Shelter have a handy tool that helps you check which type of tenancy agreement you have.

HOW TO TRANSLATE A RENTAL CONTRACT

You've finally found that liveable needle in a haystack of horrendous rentals and just want to kick back on your Ikea duvet and enjoy your personal 11.5 metres squared. But before you get the chance, you need to sign a contract. Here are the key things to look out for in that tenancy agreement:

Break clause: the earliest point that you can terminate your tenancy agreement. For example, if you're signing a one-year lease on a property, you could request a break clause that would allow you to terminate that agreement at any point after the first six months.

Deposit: the amount you pay to secure a property. This acts as your landlord's protection in case you cause any damages or expenses that need to be settled and paid for at the end of your tenancy. At the end of a tenancy, you are entitled to get your deposit back within 10 days of agreeing with your landlord how much will be returned to you.

Deposit protection scheme: this is where your deposit is held during your tenancy. All landlords renting out a property on an AST must put your money in one within 30 days of receiving it, and they're obliged to give you the details of where it's kept.

Further charges: anything other than your rent, or what is included in your rent. This could mean any or all of the following: council tax, TV licence, utility bills (gas, electricity, water), and telecommunications (phone, internet). Some properties may also come with a maintenance charge (for example, if there is a communal garden, manned reception, or security).

Guarantor: someone who 'guarantees' to pay your rent or any damages and expenses should you default. This only tends to be a requirement if you earn a low salary, are a student, or your employment is unstable. Usually this person needs to be a homeowner with a steady, long-term job — and they'll need to be ready and willing to vouch for you — so it's common to ask a parent or older family member.

Inventory and Schedule of Condition: a list of everything in the property when you moved in, and the condition it is in. Both you and your landlord will sign this list at the beginning of the tenancy, and it will be checked when you move out, to ensure everything is still there and in a suitable condition.

Permitted occupiers: the people allowed to live in the house.

References: these are taken out before a tenancy agreement is agreed, to prove that you earn enough to pay the rent every month (they may check with your employer) and having someone say you're a decent human being (usually a previous landlord).

Rights of access: this allows the landlord or agent access to the property if they need to repair or check something, and sets out how much notice they need to give you. You may also be asked to agree to regular inspections of the property.

Standing order: an agreement with your bank to pay your landlord or agent the agreed rental amount on the specified date every month.

Statutory repairing obligations: this sets out your landlord's responsibilities with regards to maintaining the condition of the property (and can vary, wildly).

Special clauses: this could be anything from a break clause to an agreement that you won't use pans of boiling oil to cook stuff (yes, really).

Quiet possession: the right for you to live in the property without unwanted disruption from the landlord or agent.

Term of tenancy: how long your tenancy agreement lasts for.

Termination: this sets out the terms under which you can end your tenancy. Usually, you must provide one or two months' notice. If you're renting a room in a shared house, it's worth checking whether it would be your responsibility to replace yourself if you decide to leave. If you terminate your contract early, your contract should also specify the conditions under which you can do that.

HOW TO GET COMPLAINTS RESPONDED TO WITHOUT BEING FOBBED OFF

Contacting the person in charge of your property can be as off-putting as asking your boss for a pay rise: necessary, a bit awkward, and likely to leave you feeling slightly unimportant afterwards. But, as Giles Barrett explains, estate agents don't want it to be like this any more than we do:

'I know that we are unpopular creatures, but I'm horrified to think we are intimidating. The first thing to establish is who is managing the property, the agent or the owner. For example, we are sometimes employed to find a tenant only. But more often than not, we are employed to find a tenant and manage throughout the tenancy. It is a good idea to establish this at the start so that you know who to turn to if or when things go wrong. If your agent doesn't respond then you should escalate the issue to senior management. If it is a landlord it can be trickier. With regards to withholding rent, you can only do so if your property is deemed 'uninhabitable'. That is not subjective (i.e. 'my water pressure is terrible'), it literally means uninhabitable (no water/heating).'

So what exactly counts as 'uninhabitable'? Essentially, anything that would make your home a hazard to the health or safety of someone living there — which can be assessed using the Health and Safety Standards for Rented Homes (Shelter have a good explainer online) — and could be an issue for the council's Environmental Health department.

KNOWING WHEN YOU'RE RESPONSIBLE FOR GETTING SOMETHING FIXED, AND WHEN IT'S YOUR LANDLORD'S JOB

In most tenancy agreements there will be a clause that sets out your landlord's and your own responsibilities for upkeep of the property. In general, though, it's the landlord who will have to take care of the major maintenance areas: we're talking structure (walls, roof, windows), plumbing and wiring, hot water and heating, and ensuring that the gas and electricity work safely.

As tempting as it might be to call them out when your oven bulb goes, or the outside drain is blocked with leaves, you're going to be responsible for minor issues like these. But what if you've got a problem that doesn't fall neatly into either category? The general rule of thumb is: if you've broken it, you need to fix it. Say you've dropped something heavy on the kitchen floor, and smashed a couple of tiles. Firstly — what on earth were you carrying that was THAT heavy? Secondly — you'll need to sort this one out. As it's something aesthetic, you're obliged to tell your landlord what's happened, and they may be able to recommend a handyman with good rates, or someone they have used before. If you're really lucky, they might even come around and fix the problem themselves.

But if you think your landlord isn't fixing something that IS their responsibility, keep a paper trail of when you've asked for the problem to be resolved, and a photographic record. It may come in handy when your tenancy ends and you're going through the casualties of your time there.

DOES ANYONE OUT THERE ACTUALLY KNOW WHAT CONSTITUTES FAIR WEAR AND TEAR?

There's another way to word this question, and it is: 'What can you get away with breaking in a property you don't own?' We all know that it's impossible to be an actual living person and leave a home in the exact state you found it in. Walls will get marked, floors will get scratched, paint will come off window panes, and, if you're really unlucky, your housemate will spill shoe polish all over the carpet. So, when does an accident become a headache? Giles Barrett explains:

'It's a subjective question, and depends which end of the telescope you're looking down. Let's take a non-property scenario. Imagine you drive your car into the back of someone at the traffic lights and cause a dent. As the offending party, it is in your interest to play the damage down as much as possible. As the party on the receiving end, it will be in your interests to highlight any damage as much as possible. It is the same when a landlord and tenant are discussing the return of a deposit. In an ideal situation, common sense is applied. For example, a minor scratch on a wall is not the same as My Little Pony transfer stickers left on one. Likewise, a slight fading of a patterned sofa is not the same as a red wine or milk stain.'

Still confused? Barrett has some reassuring advice: 'If a landlord and tenant really cannot agree, then a deposit service (like the Tenancy Deposit Scheme) will arbitrate and are, on the whole, tenant friendly.' He also recommends reading what the National Landlords Association have to say on it, on their website.

HOW TO SPLIT THE BILLS

Even if you're living with your best mates, the people who will rub your back when you're being sick and indulge your questionable choice in reality TV, the one thing that can drive a wedge between you like nothing else is money. Ultimately, you'll need to talk about who is paying for what at some point, and the easiest thing is to set some ground rules before anyone moves in. Here are some pointers to think about:

1   **The size of bedrooms:** it's unlikely you'll ever find a property that has rooms with the exact same dimensions. If the sizes are different enough for it to matter, you may want to agree to adjust your rent depending on the space each person gets.

2   **Room sharers:** are any of the bedrooms being shared by a couple? Said couple might want to split the rent and bills for that room neatly between them. But unless they're showering at the same time, and only plan on cooking joint meals and turning the lights on when they're in

a room together, that's not quite fair on the rest of the household.

3 **'Just visiting'**: by the same token, if a housemate asks for their friend/boyfriend/stranger they met on an escalator (true story) to stay for a few days, it's worth trying to find out exactly how long that might mean. Because it can be more awkward to bring up the idea of that person paying their way when you're a couple of weeks in and it's dawned on you that the visitor might actually be a new housemate.

4 **TV subscriptions**: is someone desperate for the sports channels when the rest of you couldn't give a toss? This kind of thing can bump your telly costs up by anything upwards of £20 a month. Decide as a group if it's something you really want to invest in — lest you find yourself paying for someone to watch footie — or worse, golf — non-stop every night.

5 **Working from home**: if a housemate is a freelancer or has a flexible work set-up, they're likely to use more electricity at home than anyone who goes out to an office all day. It might only be the lights on, their laptop plugged in, and brewing cups of tea — but in the winter, that might be having the central heating on all day, and even more cups of tea. And that will add up.

HOW TO STAY WARM WITHOUT PAYING TONS OF MONEY

About that central heating. Talk to anyone who rents for long enough, and they'll inevitably end up mentioning how many jumpers they own. Why? Because in most shared houses, when you want a bill to come down, the first thing to get switched off is the heating. But there are ways to maximise your warmth without wearing your entire wardrobe:

1 **Learn how to set your timer:** if you're not hooked up to a smart device like Hive, you'll likely have an old-fashioned timer that looks like the lock on a safe (and just as confusing). But it's very easy to set; search for 'set pin timer' on YouTube, and you'll find plenty of handy videos showing you exactly how to do it. Then choose, as a household, when to have the heating go on and off every day — and eliminate those passive-aggressive boiler takeovers.

2 **Stop letting heat out of your walls:** you can buy foil insulation (or make it yourself, by mounting a strip of tinfoil to cardboard) and put it behind your radiators so it sends the heat back into your home, not outside.

3 **Follow the breeze:** if you've got a draught, buy an excluder to block it out, or patch up the area with insulating tape (you can ask your landlord to do that).

4 **Use the furnishings:** closing curtains will help insulate a room, and a rug will stop heat travelling down through the floor.

5 **Keep the doors closed:** if there are rooms that lose heat quickly, close the doors to keep it in (and to stop the heat from other rooms travelling out that way).

WHOSE NAME GOES ON WHAT? DO YOU NEED A JOINT ACCOUNT?
If you're moving into an existing shared property, you may find that they already have a system for looking after utility bills.

In Kat's old flat, four people each looked after one bill each — gas and electricity, council tax, internet, and water — and every time a housemate changed, so would the name on that bill. Sounds simple enough, but the reality was like a monthly comedy skit of confusing calculations, passive-aggressive texts, and then one time they realised that one housemate hadn't been paying the council tax bill, resulting in a huge debt they all had to share.

But it doesn't have to be that way.

Here's how other people have done it:

'I rented a room in a property through SpareRoom, and the bills were inclusive of the lump sum we paid each month. We each paid the landlord a standing order, and he paid the bills for us. Easy.'

'My partner made more money than me when we first moved in together, so he paid £150 more rent/bills than I did. The feminist in me baulked a bit, but I would have been putting myself under too much pressure financially at that point to pay equal amounts. About a year in, I got a new job and a very nice salary bump which took us to around the same level and we decided to split it 50:50.'

'I've always tried to share whose name goes on what, as having your name on bills helps your credit rating. If you're the kind who looks after the pennies then it's easiest to just total everything up and split it evenly, however if a pound here or there won't keep you up at night, then it's fine to split things roughly. For me, as long as it roughly evens out, I don't mind if I'm over or underpaying slightly.'

'Me and my partner have always split the bills equally, with some of the bills in my name and the same number in his (but he has always paid about £100 more towards rent/mortgage, as he earns more money). We will be getting a joint account as soon as we have time to get to the bank together!'

'When I lived with housemates, rent was split equally unless a housemate had a much smaller room. And bills were always split equally too, with each housemate taking responsibility for a bill, i.e. one has council tax, one has gas and electric etc.'

'My partner and I split the bills on one joint card and manage half of them each. The same money goes into the account from both people each month. There's no surprises that way.'

'I have a joint bank account with my housemates. Bills come out at different times, so we worked out how much everything costs for the year, divided it by 12 months, and then by the number of people contributing to that bill. Everyone pays in their share at the beginning of each month, so there's transparency regarding how much people owe and what for, and we've always put everyone's name on each account. That way anyone can deal with an account, there's no onus on one person.'

'I live in a two-bed flat with a housemate, but share my room with my partner, so the rent and bills reflect this. Everyone had different opinions on how we should split things, but we were open and honest and made sure no one came away feeling like they'd got a bad deal.'

'There's often so much movement in a shared house that all taking a bill each works very well. When a person moved out, the new addition will take on that bill — it shares the responsibility and load.'

10 APPS EVERYONE SHARING A HOUSE/FLAT NEEDS

If you like your shared house to run like modern dating — offline, impersonal, and tucked safely behind a phone screen, apps will be your friend. In all seriousness, there are some really clever ways to get everyone doing their bit and paying their way, and it's a lot less awkward for a computer-generated program to tell your housemate to take the bin out than it is for you to bring it up over Tuesday night dinner.

1   **Acasa:** a simple way to split and pay for all of your household bills, Acasa also lets you set up who is paying how much for what, and when. It'll record everything (so you can stop pretending you don't know the answer to 'Oooh, Joe, I don't suppose you've paid me yet?') and to

streamline things even more, you can also get a quote and set up your energy and internet providers through the app, too.

2 **Bizzby:** a one-stop-shop for getting your house in order, Bizzby is a tool that'll find you any kind of household service you need in your area, from plumbers to handymen to cleaners. The app currently covers most of the UK, and is upfront about the call-out and service costs.

3 **BrightNest:** this is a handy place for finding tips to keep your house clean and ordered — and includes everything from how to find mould to sorting out pests. When you sign up, you can choose the kind of tips you want, including savvy, clean, green, healthy, handy, or creative. And each task card will explain why you should do it, how long it will take, how difficult it is and what you'll need.

4 **Chorma:** if splitting the household jobs up is your biggest issue, Chorma is an app that sorts that out, and that alone. You can designate tasks, make lists of stuff that anyone can volunteer for, and keep a record of who has been doing the most around the place.

5 **Our Home:** this is designed for families, but when you've seen your housemate eat three-day-old pizza in their pants while crying at *DIY SOS*, they're as good as. It lets you assign tasks (ok, chores), set a rota, and schedule reminders, so no one has an excuse for missing their household jobs. You can also add a grocery list, so if you share things like milk, washing powder, or cleaning products, everyone can see them on the list and swipe them off if they've picked them up while they're out.

6   **Monzo:** not just an app, but an actual functioning bank,
    this works exactly like your normal bank card in that you
    can still pay for things online and withdraw cash, but you
    can also send money directly to anyone else who has one
    without the faff of entering account numbers and sort
    codes to set them up as a payee. And you can record what
    you've paid them for, to help keep track. Good for bills,
    even better for impromptu takeaways that you put on
    your account.

7   **Sortly:** this is great if you're the kind of person who likes
    lists of lists, and labels every single thing they own. Sortly
    is basically an online inventory, so you can photograph
    and record things like valuables (for insurance), serial
    numbers (in case your microwave breaks), and if you're
    feeling very organised, you can use it when you move into
    a shared property. Document everything you moved in,
    and you'll know everything that's yours to take with you
    when you leave.

8   **Splitwise:** this is a free and easy-to-use app that helps
    you keep track of shared costs with friends, partners or
    housemates. You can easily keep a running tab of who
    owes what, and create groups as needed, which is great for
    planning trips, meals out, or splitting house stuff.

9   **White Noise:** if even your most extensive flatmate vetting
    has left you with night owls for neighbours, you may need to
    drown them out just to get some shut-eye. White Noise has
    40 different sounds, from rushing water and waves to air-
    conditioning units and a hoover (!), specifically designed to
    block out interruptions and have you falling easily into sleep.

10 **Wunderlist:** the clue is in the name; this is another one for
lists. But Wunderlist is big on collaboration; you can create
projects, assign tasks, upload and comment on documents,
and set due dates and notifications. If you're going through
any boring admin like renegotiating rent or arranging
for a handyman to visit, this is a good way to get your
housemates on the same page at the same time.

HOW DO YOU IMPROVE YOUR HOME (WHEN YOU'RE NOT ALLOWED TO)?

If you rent a property, the chances are that your contract
will be quite explicit about what you can and cannot do to
'improve' things. For most, this means you can't do much at all
'without the express written permission of the landlord' — and
that'll mean no holes in walls, no unsolicited paint jobs, that
kind of thing.

But don't let your tenancy agreement put you off entirely.
This stuff is usually subjective — for every landlord or estate
agent who takes a hard line with what you can and cannot
do, there'll be another who won't say no if you genuinely want
to improve things. Here's how to work your way round the
interiors obstacle course:

1 **Hanging pictures:** this is basically the hot-air-balloon-ride
of renting. Everyone wants to do it, but it can be a lot more
worry than it's worth. Sticking posters up with blu-tack
is an absolute no-no and shoving nails in walls is frowned
upon too. But if you have a picture rail, you can use picture
rail hooks and wire to hang frames (and make it look like

you live in a modern art gallery, which is nice). You can buy oversized prints and lean them against the wall for a cool look, or just ask your landlord if you can put stuff up. They'll probably tell you that you have to fill in all the holes when you leave, which isn't such a big deal, although you might have to paint over any Polyfilla, too.

2   **Fixtures and fittings:** are you desperate to up-cycle all the doors in the property with jazzy knobs from the local market? Let's be real, this is a 'nice-to-have', not a life necessity. But again, ask the question. If the answer is no and you are desperate for a new look, change them over but keep the old fittings safe, and switch them back in when you vacate the property.

3   **Painting:** if your lounge is a charming off-white colour that's more down to grub than a design choice and you want to fix it, ask if you can. It's unlikely that you'll be allowed to create a navy feature wall or do anything too outlandish, but you may be able to cover over it with neutrals.

4   **Light it up:** it's unlikely that you'll be able to change actual light fittings, but switching the lampshades won't break anything (unless you are really, really bad at changing lampshades). Remember to keep the old ones and put them back when you leave.

5   **Fully furnished:** if your property came complete with a battered old sofa that's been there since 1965, you can ask your landlord or agent to remove it when you move in. You'll likely have to buy a replacement, but it might be worth the cost. If there's furniture that's clearly not fit for purpose (Kat once moved in somewhere that had a divan

bed covered in mould), take pictures, raise the problem immediately, and get them to replace it. In a worst-case scenario, where something mildly offensive must stay, you can always get a throw that's big enough to cover it and disguise the thing.

6   **Go green**: struggling to find a way around decorating, but are desperate to make your place a home? Get thee to the garden centre. Most succulents are hard to kill and easy to look after, and you can perch them all over the place.

... AND HOW TO FIX IT WHEN YOU'VE IGNORED THE CONTRACT AND MADE A HOLE IN THE WALL

If you make changes to the property you are renting when you've signed a tenancy agreement saying you won't, you're going to be responsible for the fallout. While it's relatively easy to remove picture hooks and fill in the holes (and remember, you'll need to paint over the fillings, too), there's no guessing how much of a BAD THING this will be to your agent or landlord. So, if you're keen on playing things safe, just let them know before you do decide to change anything. They'll either say yes or no. If it's yes, get it in writing. It's up to you whether you play by the rules or not.

If you've done something bigger and bolder like stripped a carpet or got rid of some furniture without telling them and are slightly regretting it, it might be worth just confessing. Tell them you've been naughty, offer to make it right, and if that means getting in a handyman to help, run your choice of tradesman past them.

YOU'RE READY TO LIVE WITH YOUR OTHER HALF. CAN YOU MOVE THEM STRAIGHT IN?

So, you've found someone you want to share a bedroom with for the rest of time, congratulations! If this means you're moving into a home of your own together, happy house hunting. But if you want to move them into a property you already share with other people, you need to jump through a few ever-so-romantic hoops to make it happen.

First things first, check your tenancy agreement. Most will require that anyone who plans on living in the property — as opposed to just staying there for a short period of time — is added to the paperwork. Your landlord will need to give their written agreement, and it may mean your tenancy agreement needs to be redone entirely. And what does that mean? All together now — money! You'll likely be looking at a fee for the administration, but also for them to be referenced.

Some landlords may also ask for an additional deposit to be put down by the new tenant, but if you are already renting a whole property, it's more likely that the new tenant contributes towards the deposit which has already been paid by the other people living there.

The other option is trying to have your partner listed as a 'permitted occupier', which means that they won't be responsible for paying the rent or sorting any other important household stuff out. You would be responsible for them doing that stuff, so if your relationship breaks down, you might find yourself in a bit of a bind.

WHO CAN YOU GO TO IF YOUR LANDLORD/LETTING AGENT ISN'T LIVING UP TO THEIR END OF THE DEAL?

If you're in a difficult situation and need some external help, you don't *have* to just sit in your kitchen and cry while rain pours through the ceiling into saucepans on the floor. So, if you've really exhausted all methods of trying to get your landlord or agent's attention and help, here's who else you can try:

IF THE PROPERTY IS IN DISREPAIR

We know from the previously mentioned existential question that understanding wear and tear and responsibility for damages can be confusing. But it is clear that you can't stay somewhere that isn't liveable.

First things first — and this is important — no matter how much you want to dramatically roar 'I am withholding rent until this is fixed!', you can't. If you decide to hold back some of rent because your landlord isn't doing repairs on the property, you'll be in arrears, and could be evicted. However, you can go through a process to arrange for repairs to be done yourself. Shelter have an entire webpage dedicated to this process, which goes into it in more detail.

If the issue is something more unsettling and you genuinely think you're living in a property that's putting you or your housemates at risk, who are you gonna call? Environmental Health. Every local council has a department responsible for making sure anyone renting is living in conditions that won't harm them. They will look at problems in your home like damp and mould, pests, electrics or gas, and structural issues — a broken stairwell, for example. They will come out and inspect the property to assess whether work needs to be carried out.

To find them, search on your local council website or give them a call — for some, Environmental Health may come under a different name or department. It's worth bearing in mind that this is quite a serious step to take, so it's a good idea to let your landlord or agent know that you're planning to escalate the issue, and understand that the landlord may be able to evict you from the property instead of doing the repairs. If anything, it lets them know that you're serious about resolving the problem, which gives them a chance to sort it out before the council has to step in.

IF THE ISSUE IS FINANCIAL

In 2014, it became law that property managers and letting agents had to join one of three government redress schemes: the Property Ombudsman, the Property Redress Scheme, or the Ombudsman Services Property. These are free services which sort out disputes between tenants and agents, and they deal with issues like fees, hold-ups in processing rent, and inaccurate property descriptions.

To go down this route, you need to find out which scheme your letting agent is part of, and you must wait until eight weeks after your agent has sent a final response to you about the issue before you can complain to them. You might not be living happily ever after, but you may at least be able to recoup some of your money.

This is worth doing. Take it from Kat's friend, Christa, who found out that her dream home was not — surprise! — what it seemed:

What happened when I found out my flat had been illegally converted — Christa's story

'The first property I moved into with my partner was a basement flat in south London. You entered it down a precarious metal staircase, the bathroom was about 1 metre square, and the low ceilings were a nightmare, but we loved it. Three months into our tenancy, a surprise visit from the council resulted in us discovering it was also completely and utterly illegal. The landlord hadn't looked into planning permissions before extending into the basement of his four-storey house. We were told we had 28 days to move out. The estate agents who marketed and rented the flat effectively washed their hands of us and the situation, so after we'd found a new home we took them to the Ombudsman and won back all our fees, plus damages. It took us months but it was totally worth it.'

HOW TO GET YOUR DEPOSIT BACK

Remember that big lump sum of money you scrimped and saved to put down when you secured your rented property? Unless you've got cash pouring into your wallet you're probably going to want to see some of that again. Here's how to do it ...

If you started an Assured Shorthold Tenancy after 2007, your deposit will have gone into a tenancy deposit protection (TDP) scheme that's been backed by the government. This means your money is safeguarded and you'll get it back sharpish if you abide by the terms of your tenancy agreement and don't wreck the place. Your landlord has to issue you with a confirmation that your money has been put into the scheme within 30 days of you paying it.

At the end of a tenancy, your landlord must return your deposit within 10 days of you both agreeing the final sum to be paid back. But what if you can't agree? Your TDP will have a dispute resolution service, which is free. Both you and your landlord need to agree to use it, and you will need to provide evidence to back up your arguments, but if you do then they'll help resolve the issue.

So how do you avoid getting in a situation like that in the first place?

1 **Choose your housemates carefully:** if getting your money back at the end of the tenancy is of utmost importance to you, make sure the people you're living with respect the space as much as you do. Likewise, if you're looking for a party flat and aren't too bothered about cashback, live with people who want the same thing.

2 **Keep the place in good nick:** it might be stating the obvious, but number one on your priority list should very basic: maintaining the property you're renting. Unless they have extraordinarily high expectations, no reasonable landlord will expect to find a property in the precise condition they let it to you. But they will expect you to have lived in a clean, tidy, and responsible way — and if you can show you have, they may not find much reason to deduct money from your deposit.

3 **Update your landlord:** if you have damaged something

big and can't fix it, consider telling whoever you're renting from what's happened at an early stage. Honesty can go a long way to resolving a problem calmly later down the line.

4   **Keep note:** this might sound drastic, but if you do find yourself living with people who don't have the same kind of standards as you and they damage the property, it's worth keeping track of when it happened and who did it. Maybe do it privately. When it comes to checking out, you'll want to have your facts straight so that even if some of your deposit it deducted, it doesn't come out of your share.

A guide to buying

Most of us Brits are brought up with the mentality that home-ownership is the holy grail of being a Proper Grown-Up. It's seen as the road to wealth (because all property rises in value, forever, right?[4]). And it's that childhood image of you by your own fireside, or home bar, or reading nook, gazing around at all this space that really is yours …

But if you Google 'is it actually worth buying a house' you'll see some sharply contrasting views. '11 Reasons Why I Never Want To Own A House Again', writes one commentator sick of mortgage payments sucking up all her money. Then there's 'The Absolute Insanity Of Not Buying A House When You're Young' from someone analysing past property value

---

4   Wrong! Yes, general property prices have risen over time, and recent values have shot up faster than an estate agent's celebratory champagne cork, but arguably this means they're due for an adjustment. And there are always some properties that buck the trend, with dodgy structural problems, hidden area issues, or even a literal skeleton in the attic … (Houses where serious crimes took place can be seriously hard to sell, and that doesn't come up on the average solicitor's searches!)

trends. 'Buying A House Is For Suckers', goes another erudite first-page result. Put simply, there are pros and cons to property ownership — something Lucy's friend found out about when one of her walls collapsed when she tried to hang up a painting, and it turned out to be a structural problem which took months and thousands of pounds to fix.

So, have a think about those risks before spending another evening obsessing over house-porn …

WHY BUYING IS GREAT	WHY BUYING IS TERRIBLE
Your monthly mortgage repayments go towards buying your home, not making a landlord richer, and once they're paid off (sure, in a few decades' time), you can live rent free, and potentially make a profit.	Heavy upfront costs, like the deposit, stamp duty, and legal fees.
You won't have to ask someone permission to put up a shelf. Or a poster. Or to redecorate. Or rent out a room. You're the boss. And if you want to own a dog, or a rat, or a rattlesnake, you can (unless you're in a leasehold property that bans pets — check before snake-shopping!).	Your monthly mortgage costs are hostage to external forces — if the Bank of England raises interest rates and you don't have a fixed deal, your costs will rise. Meanwhile, your salary quite possibly won't.

You don't have to worry about being evicted because a landlord wants to sell up.	Buying a property can be like buying a puppy — they might turn out to be cute and well behaved, or they might have lots of future health problems and a running expense account at the vet. No matter how thorough a building survey is, unseen problems can arise with any property, and you're responsible for all repair costs.
Escalating rents in big cities mean mortgage payments can sometimes be cheaper than rents.	The buying and selling process is often stressful, and more drawn-out than you would believe.
	There are serious financial consequences if you fall behind on repayments — this is the main reason why buying a property is categorically different from buying something else, like a car. If you get into difficulty, you could face bankruptcy, or your home could be repossessed.

HOW DO YOU KNOW WHAT YOU CAN AFFORD?

You've decided to go for it, you want to clamber up the housing ladder. You've got a dream street in mind, a flat comes onto the market, you look at it online and the price looks crazy, valued at a figure that's a vast multiplier of salary — but then, so do all the prices. So how do you know what you can afford?

You'll need to think about a few things — your savings and how much of a deposit you can stump up; any funds coming in to help top that up, for example from family members; plus your earnings and how much you can afford to pay out of your salary. Be realistic in your planning and make sure to leave yourself enough to live on, plus, crucially, a bit extra — emergencies crop up, and however much you think owning your own place will make you satisfied forever, you're still going to want the odd holiday or meal out.

It might limit your buying options, but it's better to work out your realistic budget early on — otherwise you'll waste time (and heartache) viewing properties you can't afford, or even putting in offers that you then can't pursue. Doing the latter could give you a difficult-to-shed reputation for being unreliable amongst local agents.

As a starter to work out what kind of mortgage — and therefore property — you could be offered, use an online house-buying budget calculator such as the one offered by the Money Advice Service. But remember, no online form will be totally comprehensive. You need to factor in every possible expense in your life, from the expected council tax and utility bills in the new place, to your gym membership, meals out, supermarket expenses, haircuts, charity donations, holidays … Going through your credit card and current account expenditure for the past year can help.

These online calculators will then tell you how much a lender might be willing to lend you, what your monthly repayment costs would be at a range of interest rates, and how much you would have left over for monthly living costs. This is only a guide, though: banks and other mortgage lenders will base any offers on your personal circumstances, and interest rates will vary accordingly.

Crucially, in addition to working out your monthly budget limits, you will also need to work out all the upfront costs. This includes the deposit, stamp duty, legal fees, and mortgage costs. Usually, the larger the deposit as a percentage of the total price (a.k.a. the 'loan to value'), the better deal a lender will be prepared to offer you, because they're taking on less of a risk.

WHAT ARE THE MAIN HOUSE-BUYING COSTS?

It's easy to focus on the mortgage — especially as you might be paying it back for the next 25 years — and the deposit, since that's probably gobbled up all of your savings. But first-time buyers also face a bunch of upfront fees that can tot up to thousands. You'll need to factor in all of these when you work out your budget:

1 **The deposit:** the upfront cash paid when you buy a new home; lenders will demand at least 5% of the purchase price, more usually it's 10%–20% or more.

2 **Stamp duty:** tax paid on homes costing £125,001 or more. It's 2% on the portion from £125,001 to £250,000, 5% on the next £675,000, and then gets progressively higher up to 12%. But first-time buyers pay no stamp duty on the first £300,000 of any home costing up to £500,000. You can easily calculate a potential stamp duty bill online.

3 **Valuation fee:** charged by your mortgage lender for them to check whether the property is worth its agreed price.

The figure depends on the lender — and some offer 'sale'-type deals where it's free or cheap — and the property's value, but usually starts at £200 and can be as high as £2000. Despite the hefty cost, it's usually a fairly brief visit, perhaps even done via a drive past the property, and won't flag up any structural problems, so you're usually advised to also book a survey.

4 **Survey:** here, the fees depend on the size and price of the property, and the extensiveness of the survey you opt for — a basic 'home condition survey' might cost a few hundred pounds, where a full structural survey of a house can easily cost £1500+. This can be painful, especially if the survey reveals problems that mean you don't end up buying the property, but it's a really wise choice when you're probably buying the most expensive thing you'll ever own.

5 **Legal fees:** solicitors or conveyors generally charge between £900 and £2000 for legal work on a purchase; a particularly complex deal will cost more. They will also charge you £250–£300 for local council searches, which cover things like planning and environmental issues that could hit your home's value.

6 **Removal costs:** the price will depend on the scope of your stuff, whether you're moving from/to a ground-floor flat or a sixth-floor flat with a broken lift, and whether you opt for a removals team or just rent a van and do it yourself. Costs could stretch from £200–£500 for a two-bedroom flat move, to more or less for larger or smaller properties.

7 **Mortgage fees:** some mortgage companies charge a booking fee of between £100–£300, an arrangement fee

of up to £2000, as well as that mortgage valuation fee (see above).

8   **Maintenance and repairs:** the average buyer faces a moving-in repair bill of £5750, according to the Royal Institution of Chartered Surveyors.

Learn from those who have been there, done that ...

'We got our homebuyers' survey back, it included gems like: "The roof looks okay, but I'm not a roofer. Electrics look okay, but I'm not an electrician. Structure looks okay, but I'm not a builder ... etc. In summary, the survey felt like a scam — but I'm not a lawyer ... I found it really hard to know exactly what I was buying — and it was one enormous, important purchase for me.'

'I wish I'd known, before buying my flat, that people will lie and just don't care. After agreeing terms, receiving the contract and completing, we realised they'd taken the entire shed, which we'd planned to use for temporary storage. The shed was ours according to the contract, but it was too complicated and expensive to go after them.'

'My brother has just bought a house with his partner, despite being really clueless. I remember the day he called me to say he was outside a letting agents and was going in to get himself a mortgage. I responded that letting agencies didn't sell houses, they rented them. And, given they weren't a bank, they definitely didn't give out mortgages. Still, he went in ... It was a short visit. He was and still is amazed that he actually owns a house. If you're the same, make sure you have a good lawyer and mortgage advisor.'

'Use a mortgage advisor! It feels like an unnecessary cost when you first start looking, but mine got me a much better rate (and much more money) than I'd managed to find by myself, and when my mortgage offer got randomly rescinded the day before completion because my solicitors messed up, the advisor was worth her weight in gold running around getting everything sorted out. Also the mortgage guide on MoneySavingExpert is really helpful.'

'Make sure you get a proper survey done, and think carefully before taking on a property that has a lot of complications. A friend spent years saving up to buy a dream house in his hometown, despite the fact that he lives and works in London. His plan was to rent it out until he could move back there. He ended up buying a listed property that had previously been a shopfront and which came with a lovely new extension, but he neglected to get an independent survey done. As soon as he sealed the deal, he started to discover things that were seriously wrong with it: it was still listed as a commercial property so he couldn't rent it out, the listed status meant that any repairs cost an absolute fortune and required planning permission, and to cap it all off, the extension had been built illegally. The fact he didn't live in the town and had to travel down every weekend to try and sort it all out made things worse. It was the most stressful year of his life, but after taking legal advice and making the right applications he managed to get it sorted.'

HIDDEN COSTS OF HOMEOWNERSHIP

Oh yeah, you thought the depressing bills ended at completion, but they just keep coming in. They might be arriving on the doormat of your very own castle, sure, but they still need to be paid. Most are ones you have to pay anyway when renting — but remember, you will need to cover the below, plus all the usual living costs of grocery bills, commuting, life etc. on top of monthly mortgage costs.

1   **Energy and water bills:** you can reduce using the tips we gave earlier, but the average dual-fuel energy bill now tops £1100 in the UK, according to energy industry regulator Ofgem, while the average water bill is just under £400 say the water boards.

2   **Leasehold costs:** unless you own the freehold, you'll usually have to stump up for annual ground rent. This can be as little as £1 or as much as a few hundred pounds per year, plus possible service charges to the freeholder. If there are lots of common parts that require maintenance or a communal garden, the service charge will be higher.

3   **TV licence, broadband, cable, landline costs:** a lot will depend on whether you're buying services like subscription channels, streaming services, and high-speed

internet, but even basic packages plus a TV licence will easily top £600 a year.

4   **Buildings insurance:** required by a lender to protect a property from expensive and dangerous problems like fire, floods, and subsidence. Its sister, contents insurance, isn't obligatory but covers possessions. The average annual price for building and contents insurance is about £110, according to MoneySuperMarket, although the actual figure you'll pay depends on the size, security, and value of the home and possessions.

5   **Council tax:** the amount paid is based on where the property is and its valuation band. The average cost across the UK is £1600, but you can find out the specific figure by entering a property's postcode on the government website. Once you've moved in, bear in mind that it could be worth challenging your council tax rate: it was launched in a bit of a rush and most bands were decided by council staff driving up and down streets valuing homes from their cars. On the government website you will also be shown the bandings of neighbouring homes; if you spot similar-looking homes in a different band, yours could be wrong and can be appealed. Also, council tax bills assume two adults occupy the property as their main home, so if you're living alone you can apply for a 25% discount. Equally, any property exclusively inhabited by full-time students is exempt from council tax, and some recipients of benefits are eligible for discounts.

6   **Ongoing maintenance and building work:** when it comes to the total bill each year, your guess is as good as ours.

THIS IS ALL WAY TOO EXPENSIVE. WHAT ABOUT SHARED OWNERSHIP, HELP TO BUY, ALL THE THINGS POLITICIANS TALK ABOUT NON-STOP?

The soaring housing market has priced millions of millennials out — so a succession of governments have conjured up schemes aimed at giving young people a leg up onto the property ladder. But there are now so many, all with different demands and restrictions, that even the help has become confusing. So here's a guide. If ...

- You have a large enough income to make a mortgage payment each month, but are struggling to raise a deposit, then one of the Help to Buy schemes might work for you.
- You're looking for a new-build, and are under 40, then the Help to Buy or Starter Homes scheme could help.
- You only have a small deposit, then shared ownership, where you buy a share of between 25% and 75% in a property and pay rent on the remaining share, could be an option.

1   **Help to Buy:** if you're looking at a new-build, the 'Equity Loan' scheme sees the government lend you up to 20% of the cost of your home, interest-free for five years — so you'll only need a 5% cash deposit and a 75% mortgage to make up the rest. If you are buying in London, you can borrow up to 40% of the purchase price. So in the capital, for a £400,000 home, you would need a 5% deposit of £20,000, the government would stump up £160,000 (40%), and you'd need a £220,000 (55%) mortgage. The

scheme runs until 2021. The Help to Buy equity loan is interest-free for the first five years, after which, unless you've been able to pay the money back, you're charged an interest rate of 1.75% (this slowly increases each year in line with inflation plus 1%). These repayments will be on top of your ordinary mortgage repayments. Making part repayments to the equity loan, which is called 'staircasing', will mean lower costs when the interest-free period comes to an end after five years. You don't have to be a first-time buyer to be eligible for this scheme either.

2   **Starter Homes:** this new initiative will see 200,000 new-builds made available to first-time buyers under 40 at a discount of at least 20% off the market price — so they will be for sale for up to £250,000 outside London, and £450,000 in the capital.

3   **Shared ownership:** buying between a quarter and three-quarters of a property, and paying rent on the rest, is another option. Buyers can up their stake in the property when able to afford it. Eligibility differs in England, Ireland, Scotland, and Wales, but, as a guide, in England shared ownership is available to first-time buyers or those who once owned a home but now can't afford to do so, but you must have a household income under £80,000, or £90,000 in London. The scheme covers new-builds and homes being sold by another shared-owner. You'll need a specific shared ownership mortgage, which is offered by some but not all lenders, and you will need to afford all the usual house-buying costs, which won't be diminished just because you're not buying 100% of the property.

OKAY, I'VE FOUND THE ONE. NOW WHAT?

It's time to make an offer. When making your very first offer, you'll be super nervous, checking your phone, email, and signal every thirty seconds, and then be elated/devastated by the estate agent's eventual call. You might get lucky and have a quick 'Yes' and a smooth, speedy purchase process. But you'd be in the minority — Lucy ended up putting in more than 20 offers before having one accepted — for a flat she wasn't even sure about originally. In short, the property-buying system is convoluted and stressful. In England and Wales, offers are subject to contract, meaning either buyer or seller can walk away without penalty anytime up until the formal contract is signed and both parties have exchanged contracts. In Scotland, by contrast, both buyer and seller are legally bound much earlier in the process. But before you get to that, you have to actually put in the offer …

First, be realistic. Yes, negotiation is to be expected, but if you offer a massively reduced price, unless there are exceptional circumstances the agents might not take you seriously, and you could lose out to another bidder. Equally, if it's too high you'll end up feeling ripped off.

It's hard, but you need to try to think with your head, not your heart. You might love a property and fall asleep each night dreaming of how it will look filled with your furniture, but this is a huge amount of money, so you need to think rationally. Put it up against recently sold local, comparable properties: what did they go for? Look at how much is on the market in the neighbourhood to see if there's a glut, which will give you more bartering power, or very little about, meaning you could be competing with lots of would-be buyers.

Remember, however friendly they appear, the estate agent is acting for the seller. They want a sale to go ahead, and at the top price possible. They can't legally tell you how big any other offers were, or what the vendor is holding out for, but they may indicate if other bids were close to the asking price, or above it, or how much you'd have to move to get the nod. Common reasons for offering below-asking price include cheaper similar comparables, if the seller has a need for speed (e.g. you know they're desperate because they need to move before a new job, or a new baby, and think that will give you the upper hand), the property's poor state of repair, or if it's been lingering on the market for a while.

By contrast, if you know lots of potential buyers are swarming around the property, if there's a general shortage of availability and you urgently want to move, or you just really love the home and think it's fairly valued, you're more likely to offer asking price, or even above it.

You'll need to set out an offer in writing; indicating that it is 'subject to contract and survey', giving some explanation if your figure is above or below the asking price, presenting your details and your position as a buyer, and stating the offer is subject to its removal from the market. That last point is to cut your risk of being gazumped.

As an example:

Dear Estate Agent,

We have now inspected 1 House Road three times and would like to make an offer to buy it.

Given the building work required — including replacing the current roof and new guttering — and the recent lower sales prices of local comparables, we cannot go to asking price and would like to offer £XX, subject to contract, and survey, and to the property being taken off the market.

It will be a joint purchase and our details are:

Buyer One and Buyer Two, of XX current address.

We are first-time buyers with a substantial deposit and a mortgage agreement in principle agreed with Generous Bank Inc, and we are chain-free. We have only to give two months' notice on our current rental property and are therefore in a position to proceed quickly if our offer is accepted.

We look forward to hearing from you after you have obtained the vendor's instructions.

Yours,
Would-be buyers

Be aware, though, that buying a home rarely goes as smoothly as you'd like — your first offer may be rejected, you might have to go higher, or even pull out. An accepted offer could be rejected later down the line – house buying can be a long (and very stressful!) negotiation process.

House buying — Lucy's story

'When my boyfriend and I fell in love with a flat, put in an offer close to asking price, and sorted out a mortgage in principle,

I was already dreaming of how my furniture would look in its rooms and practically inviting my friends round to stay.

Next day, the offer was rejected, we couldn't go any higher, and it was another year before we finally had an offer accepted (on a totally different property miles away from that original one!) House buying in this country is complicated, time-consuming, and sometimes heart-breaking! You just have to get yourself the best professionals that you can, hope for the best, but don't expect a totally smooth process.'

I'M BUYING WITH SOMEONE ELSE. WHAT NOW?

Buying a new place with a partner (or friend, or sibling) is exciting — but also a tiny bit scary because there's always that thought of: what if it just doesn't work out and all of your finances are bound up more tightly than the mosh pit at a goth metal concert ... as Chris explains from his experience:

Breaking up is hard(er) to do ... if you have joint property — Chris' story

'In 2007, just before the financial crash, I was 25, working as a banker and desperate to get on the property ladder as prices kept rising. My girlfriend and I bought a two-bedroom flat in an "up-and-coming" part of east London. We didn't really think about an exit strategy at the time but verbally agreed on a 50:50 split of any profits above our initial contribution (I put down 90% of the deposit and stamp duty). I also agreed to pay an extra £300 per month towards the mortgage as I earned more. However, we didn't write anything down or speak to a lawyer — because, obviously, we didn't expect to break up.

But break up we did, early in 2010. It was amicable, and we agreed that my ex would be the one to move out. The flat was disappointingly still at exactly the same value as when we had bought it — but I agreed to stay, get a new mortgage and buy her out. Then it started to get a bit messy with disagreements over which estate agents' value to use, how to split the furniture (she wanted me to buy it all at original cost), and whether to split the early redemption fee on the original mortgage.

After months of stalemate, and a pathetically petty email exchange, we eventually compromised by using an average of two valuations. She took the furniture that she wanted and we split the mortgage fee evenly.

With hindsight, at the time of buying the flat we should have drawn up an official legal document and really thought about how it would play out if we did split up. It's an awkward conversation to have, as you don't want to think about breaking up with the person you love enough to buy a flat with, but relationships can turn sour and it would have saved us both a lot of time, energy, and money if we had.'

Unless you're married to your co-homeowner-to-be, you should take steps to protect yourself legally. There are the two main options, buying as:

Joint tenants, meaning you both own the property together. This is the usual option for married couples or those in a civil partnership, as if one owner dies, their share of the property automatically passes to the other owner. One individual can't leave part of the property to someone else in a will.

Tenants in common, meaning you all own a set stake in the property, but it doesn't have to be equal — so one could own 75%, the other 25%, for example. Usually used by friends or relatives who are buying together, as both or all tenants in common can sell their share of the property if they want to, and if one died, their share passes to whoever is named in the will or a next of kin.

Whichever method you use to buy, as joint property owners, you'll have equal rights to live in the property — however many times he/she leaves the loo roll holder empty or leaves approximately three drops of soup in the saucepan and doesn't wash it up 'because there's another meal in there'.

So, if you split up, or one person wants to sell and the other owners don't, and you haven't pre-planned this, you may have to go to court. Which is crazily stressful and expensive, and best avoided by asking a solicitor to draw up a 'just in case' legal agreement beforehand. This should set out under what circumstances the property will be sold; how much notice is required and what proportion of the sale price each person is entitled to; what happens if one person wants to keep the property; what happens if one of you loses your job, interest rates rise, or you can't cover the mortgage any more; and what will happen to all the other costs which need to be split: stamp duty, estate agent fees, mortgage fees, service charge, legal fees etc. Also, if either party is contributing a larger deposit or paying more monthly, this should be accounted for.

Be aware too that on a joint mortgage, which is normally restricted to just two people, you are both liable for the whole amount. So if one stops paying their share, the other is liable. This stuff is serious: you better really, really know (and, ideally, like) your co-buyer!

BUYING YOUR FIRST HOME — THE LINGO

You knew you'd need one helluva lot of money, a huge dose of patience, and a willingness to give up all your weekends to viewings in order to buy your first home — but a dictionary probably wasn't on your kit list. The house-buying jargon has become so complicated, though, that this A-Z glossary might come in handy:

Agreement in Principle: a mortgage lender's figure on how much they might lend you, based on the details you give them. It's not binding, but is vital to secure before you put in offers on properties, especially in a competitive market, as it shows sellers and agents that you've done your homework, and you're serious.

Annual Percentage Rate or APR: the interest plus fees that you'll be charged, each year.

Arrangement fee: the price usually charged by lenders for arranging your mortgage (nice of them, huh) — can range from a few hundred pounds to a few thousand. This can sometimes be added to your mortgage rather than paid up front — but doing so means you'll have to pay interest on it.

Asking price: negotiable figure for how much the seller wants to receive for their property.

Base rate: the interest rate set by the Bank of England, which is often used by mortgage lenders to set their own rates.

Broker: someone who charges a fee for independent mortgage advice. You don't have to use one, but they can help you secure a good deal (and succeed in getting a mortgage at all), and will provide guidance if you're confused by the process.

Building survey: when a qualified surveyor undertakes a thorough inspection and detailed breakdown of the property's condition, including its structure, any interior problems, necessary repairs, and maintenance advice. A full survey isn't obligatory, but is usually advised when spending such a significant amount of money on a new home.

Completion: when the property legally transfers to the buyer. This is the date where all inquiries must be answered, all forms signed, taxes (namely stamp duty) paid, mortgage organised, and purchase price transferred to the seller's solicitor. The buyer can then move in.

Conveyancing: the legal part of transferring ownership from one owner to another. For this, you'll need either a solicitor or a qualified conveyancer.

Discounted-rate mortgage: where the interest rate is a set amount less than the lender's standard variable rate (SVR, see below).

Early repayment charge: a penalty fee imposed for deciding to leave a mortgage deal during a specified period, usually the initial offer.

Exchange: the date when the buyers' and sellers' solicitors hand over contracts, the buyer pays a deposit (usually 10% of the agreed price), and the deal becomes legally binding. A buyer who pulls out after exchange is at risk of losing the deposit. A completion date is also agreed at the point of exchange, which is usually no more than four weeks' time.

Fixed-rate mortgage: when an interest rate is fixed for an agreed period of time, so you know exactly what your repayments will be, and are not affected by interest rate increases or decreases.

Freehold: owning the building and the land it stands on. As opposed to leasehold.

Gazumping: when an offer has been accepted on a property, but a different buyer then makes a higher offer, which the seller accepts. Unfortunately for buyers, this is completely legal before exchange of contracts.

Guarantor: when a third party (usually a parent or grandparent) legally agrees to meet the monthly mortgage repayments if the buyer is unable to.

Help to Buy: a government initiative that aims to help first-time buyers get on the property ladder.

Home report: contains details of the property, such as its condition, energy efficiency, and the property question-naire from the seller, with info like council tax banding and what fixtures and fittings are included in the sale.

Interest rates: the amount you pay your lender for borrowing money, shown as a percentage of the amount you borrow.

Leasehold: owning the building, but not the land it stands on, and only for a certain period (anything up to 999 years). It can be tougher to get a mortgage if there are fewer than 70 years left on the lease of the property you want to buy.

Loan to Value (LTV): the size of the money you're borrow-ing, compared to the value of your property. So example, if a home was valued at £300,000 and you had a mortgage of £240,000, the LTV is 80%. The lower your LTV, the better mortgage rate you'll get.

Monthly repayment: the amount you pay your mortgage lender each month, usually covering a percentage of your mortgage plus interest, apart from if you have a (rare) interest-only mortgage deal.

Mortgage: formal contract setting out money lent by a lender for the purposes of buying a property, which outlines the legal obligations of the borrower and the rights the lender has if the borrower fails to make a repayment.

Mortgage term: length of time the mortgage lasts — usually 25 years.

Negative equity: when the value of a home falls to a level that is below the amount remaining on its mortgage.

Offset mortgage: a special type of mortgage that links the balance of your savings and current account balances to the amount you've been lent. So if your savings account had £20,000 in it, for example, and your mortgage was £100,000 you would only pay interest on £80,000. Particularly useful for people with variable incomes, but who can't afford to 'lock away' cash as repaying a mortgage would do — the savings are still accessible to dip into if needed.

Payment holiday: a period (agreed with your lender) when you don't make repayments on your mortgage, although interest continues to build up during the time.

Remortgage: moving mortgage deals, without moving house. Usually to save money on a cheaper deal, to change to a different type of mortgage, or to release cash from the property.

Service charge: fee paid to a managing agent for the maintenance of a leasehold property.

Shared ownership: buying a share of a property (usually 25%–75%) and paying rent on the remaining share.

Stamp Duty Land Tax: a.k.a. SDLT or just stamp duty — a tax on property (or land) purchases worth over £125,000. The amount you need to pay increases as the purchase price of the home goes up.

Standard variable rate (SVR): an interest rate set by a lender, that they can vary at any time. When a fixed or tracker deal ends, the mortgage usually rolls over to an SVR deal.

Standard valuation: a very brief version of a survey, which lenders will insist is carried out on a property before they will pay out on a mortgage. The property will be inspected and any obvious major defects named, but it's far less thorough than a building survey.

Tracker mortgage: where the interest rate moves directly in line with another rate (usually the Bank of England's base rate) over a certain period of years. So if the Base rate rose 0.5%, the monthly mortgage payment will go up too, either by the same amount of by a pre-set amount (if the tracker was, for example, 'base rate plus 1%', it would go up by 1.5%).

Home security

When you've spent what feels like your entire life saving enough to own a home, you should definitely spend a few hours (and pounds) thinking about how to keep it safe from burglars. The police warn that homes with no security measures in place are five times more likely to be burgled than those with simple security measures. Some things to consider include:

- Good window locks and strong deadlocks, used every time you leave the house, even if just for a few minutes or in the garden.
- Never keep keys near any doors or windows, and keep them out of sight.
- Install a visible burglar alarm and motion-sensor outside lighting.
- Get to know your neighbours and let trusted ones know if/when you're away.
- Leave lights (and radios) on time-switches to make your house look occupied.
- Make sure bikes are secure — lock them to an immoveable object if they're in a shed or garage.
- Mark your valuables (laptop, phone, bikes etc.) with

your postcode and house number and register it on the Immobilise website .

- Join (or form) any local Neighbourhood Watch schemes.
- Store valuables like jewellery and passports in a secured safe.
- Never open the door unless you're sure who's there.
- And never post holiday snaps on Instagram or other social networks until you're back — burglars can stalk these sites to look for empty homes.

White goods

You need a washing machine, you expect to google 'washing machine', look at a few, and buy one, but then you discover this whole VORTEX of crazy washing machine advice and options and brands and prices and warranties and end up wondering if it'd be simpler just to become a nudist and eliminate the need for clean clothes?

Well, maybe not quite, but there are a huge number of options when buying white goods — the lingo for any large electrical device for the home. Generally the rule is 'you get what you pay for' — more established, European brands may have their own customer service for repairs, for example, while cheaper Asian brands might rely on third-party engineers; pricier models will usually do more, and have longer guarantees. But other things to consider include how repairable the item is, what the brand's aftersales service is like, what features are included, price, and whether you need 'top of the range' for something you're planning on keeping for decades or a budget option is better.

Consider registering with *Which?* — it often runs £1 trial offers — as it has long reports from detailed tests on hundreds of white goods, including 'best buy' options.

WARRANTIES AND GUARANTEES

Sales people will fling all kind of jargon at you in their bid to hit a commission bonus — so look into the details of any 'warranties' or 'guarantees' they're hurling around. A guarantee is usually free, offered by the manufacturer, who is basically promising that if the quality of its product or service fails then it will fix or replace them during the period of the guarantee. Warranties usually come at an extra cost, effectively involving you insuring yourself against future problems — they tend to last longer. Neither cover basic 'wear and tear' or clear faults on your part (if you drop your camera down the loo, no one's going to pay up to fix it apart from you), but both are on top of your basic consumer rights.

Guarantees last varying amounts of time (the standard is one year) and you'll sometimes need to 'activate' them by registering your details on a card when you purchase the item and sending it off (or via an online form). To make a claim, you'll need to read through the paperwork (on the receipt, or in a separate leaflet or online) to discover if the fault is covered and what you're entitled to, such as a repair, replacement, or your money back. You'll usually need a receipt, the claim will need to fall into the period covered by the guarantee, and you may need to pay postage costs.

With a warranty, you'll need to consider whether the cost is worthwhile before shelling out. As a consumer, you can utilise your right to a 'cooling off' period. So if, for example, you bought an extended warranty at the same time as an electrical good, and that warranty lasts at least 12 months, you have the right to cancel it within the first 45 days (as long as you haven't made a claim).

WE'RE GOING ON A HOUSE HUNT ... 19 THINGS TO LOOK FOR ON A VIEWING (AND QS TO QUIZ THE AGENT/SELLER)

1   Get to the property a bit early, so you can look at the outside before the agent intrudes. What's the transport like? Is there a station nearby? Parking? Any big office/school/industrial buildings nearby that could be disruptive? Be aware of the time you're there — if it's 3pm on a Saturday, it might be quieter than 9am on a Monday morning.

2   Walk around the neighbourhood. Do other properties in the street look in good nick? Is 'yours' the best or the worst in the road? Is there somewhere nice to go for a pint, to pick up a pint of milk, to have something to eat? Has there been any recent flooding?

3   If you spot any neighbours out and about, try to grill them! Ask them what the road is like, any downsides, any property gossip about the one you're interested in, any

neighbourly disputes, and any recent works carried out. Approaching a stranger isn't a very British thing to do, but most people are more than happy to chat about their neighbourhood. You can start by simply asking 'Do you like living here?'

4   Once you're inside, reverse the estate agent tricks. You might find all the lights are switched on, music is tinkling away, coffee is brewing, and a cake is baking. Okay, you can't turn the oven off, but don't get duped — is the music covering up rattling trains or noisy traffic? Is the heating on but it still feels chilly? You won't live in a house with all the lights on all the time, so dim them to check the natural lighting.

5   Don't get distracted by a beautiful rug or cool Scandi furniture — that'll all be going in the removals vans. Instead, scrutinise the ceilings, windows, and walls for any signs of damp patches, leaks, mould, and check windows for rotting frames or condensation — run a finger along the glass — as this could show poor insulation.

6   Look at the size of the rooms. If the furniture is tiny, would yours fit, or make the rooms look really squashed? If you're thinking of renting out a room, is the communal space big enough, and is the layout conducive? For example, if there is only one en-suite bathroom.

7   Does your phone work? Sounds silly but unless you're planning a permanent digital detox, check to see if your phone and a friend's phone on another network works. And ask about the internet connection, as some areas are served with better quality internet than others.

8   Do some amateur surveying: turn on a tap to see if the hot

water works and test the strength of the water pressure, check for any big cracks in the wall, look to see if any gutters are cracked or leaking outside, check if the brickwork is in good condition or needs repainting or repointing — the latter is needed to tackle crumbly grouting. These might not be reasons to walk away from buying the property, but could give you reasons to question the price.

9 Look out for weird paint jobs or furniture placement. If a patch of wall has been repainted, for example, the seller could be trying to hide a damp problem. If a rug is in an odd place, is it hiding a problem with the flooring?

10 If there's a garden, does it fit your needs? A lawn and flowerbeds look lovely, but are high-maintenance, so make sure you're up for it; an ornamental pond might not be ideal if you're thinking of having kids.

11 Is there enough storage space to sequester your entire retro Nintendo collection, all your trainers, and the childhood stuff your parents are probably going to insist your remove from your old bedroom now?

12 If the central heating is on, use it as an opportunity to check that it works — are all the radiators hot? How old is the boiler?

13 Quiz the agent and/or owner about what's included — are any appliances, furnishings etc. being left behind? It could save you a lot of cash if so.

14 Ask the agent what the level of interest has been like — how many viewings they've done, have any offers come in yet, what's the seller's position — are they ready to move or are they in a chain?

15 If the property is leasehold, how long is left on the lease and are there any restrictive conditions, like not being able to have wooden floors or own pets?

16 You might not be thinking about it now, when all your money will be swallowed up by the purchase, but look at whether the property has 'potential' — can it be extended? Remodelled? Loft conversion? They can all boost the value of a property, and even if you sell it on one day without doing any works, it can make it more desirable. Check if neighbouring properties have extended or converted lofts or garages etc. — if so, you'd be more likely to get planning permission.

17 If the seller is around, ask them as much as you can face-to-face — it's harder for them to lie! Why are they leaving, what's the best and worst thing about the property, and the area? How often has maintenance work, things like external painting, been carried out? How much are utility bills? What work realistically needs to be carried out in the next year or so?

18 One for the agent, unless you're bold enough to ask the vendor, but is there room for manoeuvre on the price? A ready agreement to negotiate might ring alarm bells about why the seller is desperate to get shot of it — and equally a steadfast 'No' might mean it will be over your budget.

19 If you're interested, book more viewings — at different times of day, if possible, to find out how the light, traffic, and noise levels change.

Congratulations ...
you're an adult!

We said at the start that there wasn't one big moment that made either of us feel we were suddenly 'adults'. There were lots of them (and half the time we still feel like kids in grown-up clothes. Or child-sized shoes when it comes to Lucy).

But if the process of interviewing the hundreds of people who helped with the advice and embarrassing admissions in this book taught us anything, it was that we're not alone in maturing slower than a chunk of cheddar.

The truth is, adulthood doesn't happen overnight. You might have passed your driving test, but still not know how to put the washing machine on a spin cycle. You might own a house, but find asking for a pay rise impossible. No one is born knowing how to do all this stuff; and, actually, half the experience is learning it.

We hope, armed with this book, you'll find being an adult less confusing, a lot clearer, and maybe even — who knows! — fun.

Good luck.

Final adulting words of wisdom

'Mostly, people won't get upset if you rearrange appointments or plans, especially if you do so in plenty of time. So don't say yes to things you don't want to do, or put off rearranging, because you're worried about their reaction. Also, you're not at school any more; as an adult, strangers will usually give you the benefit of the doubt at least once, so use that, and use it wisely and justifiably, and don't squander it.'

'No matter how perfect others appear to be, every relationship has its issues and there is no such thing as the perfect couple or parent. Some people are just better at faking it than others and social media helps the fakers fake it! Be kind to others, as you never know what secret battles they are facing that may be making them tricky customers or friends.'

'Get pyjamas that look like exercise clothes ... Then when you roll out of bed to do chores/shopping/the school run everyone else will think you are off to a class not straight back to bed!'

'Don't take what others think of you too seriously — it will only lead to spending too much time looking to please others and not enough time living your life ... above all, just do what makes you happy.'

'Getting old is inevitable, but growing up is optional —
I have learned "how to behave in public" but you are never
too old to have fun ...'

'Something that has helped me is to always remember to
take some time for yourself. With everything going on —
work, relationships, life in general — sometimes you forget
to rest! Remember to set aside some time every week for
a hot bath, a good book, or even a nice quiet walk somewhere you love. It helps to improve your mental health and
make sure you are happy.'

'Don't worry too much about friends that you lose touch
with, there's a reason they aren't in your life any more and
you will always meet new people and new friends throughout your life.'

'Before leaving the house always check the bottom of your
jeans for yesterday's pants ...'

'Reward yourself to make you happier ... Shit day at work?
Survived a big interview? Got grilled at a meeting? Reward
yourself! Whether your reward is raiding your Champion
Sweets stash or cooking your favourite dinner, rewards are
there to help give some positivity when you can't see it in
amongst the task you're doing.'

'Don't let the fear of what others might think stop you
from being yourself and doing the things you want to do.

Research has shown that a common end-of-life regret people have is having lived their life according to others' expectations rather than a life true to themselves.'

'When in doubt, look for an adultier adult, someone who is more successful at adulting than you.'

'Learn to value yourself more and realise when people are taking advantage of you, to be a kind person but always be aware of what is happening; it is okay to say no.'

'Adulting tip: no one else has it all figured out either! Some people are just better at faking it on social media. Relax. You're doing fine.'

'Be kind to everyone you meet and surround yourself with those type of people, too. Life will be much happier for you.'

'Don't say "yes" if you want to say "NO!" Whether that's NO to going out with the girls when all you really want to do is to stay in and have a quiet night, or NO to putting more responsibility on your shoulders.'

'Make a list of goals you want to achieve in life, and re-evaluate it every few months.'

'When you get clothes out of the washing machine, stretch them and smooth them out before hanging them to dry, it helps reduce creases and reduces the need for ironing!'

'Let yourself off the hook! Have a lie-in or spend all day in your pyjamas at the weekend, relax. You'll be a better adult.'

'Always keep vinegar in the house! It is useful for a multitude of sins, from putting on your chips to cleaning windows, and removing stains from fabric or embarrassing odours from carpets.'

'My adulting tip — live in the now, stop telling yourself that you'll be happy when you have more money, your own house, a new car etc. etc. or you'll always be waiting on happiness rather than enjoying the moment.'

'Plan ahead and book days out online in advance — it's nice to have something to look forward to and usually works out cheaper, too.'

'Remember everyone else is just winging it!'

Useful links

Chapter 1: Food and scoffing

Use-by dates info: food.gov.uk/science/microbiology/
use-by-and-best-before-dates

Find the best quality supermarket own-brands foods:
supermarketownbrandguide.co.uk

Leftover ideas: lovefoodhatewaste.com, supercook.com

Comparison website for supermarket food costs:
mysupermarket.com

Supermarket deal-flagging websites: fixtureferrets.co.uk,
hotukdeals.com

Cheap food that's beyond/nearly beyond its best-before
date: approvedfood.co.uk

Alcohol deals: quaffersoffers.co.uk

Eat your neighbours' surplus food: olioex.com

Nab restaurants' unsold food for less: toogoodtogo.co.uk

Chapter 2: Cleaning

Washing machine usage tips: persil.com/uk/laundry/laundry-tips/washing-tips.html

Cleaning and tidying site: unfuckyourhabitat.com

Home cleaning help: goodhousekeeping.co.uk/institute/household-advice?a=7901

Chapter 3: Physical and mental health

REGISTERING WITH A MEDICAL PROVIDER

Find a GP: nhs.uk/Service-Search/GP/LocationSearch/4

Find a dentist: nhs.uk/Service-Search/Dentists/LocationSearch/3

Find a sexual health clinic: nhs.uk/service-search/sexual-health-information-and-support/locationsearch/734

Find a therapist: nhs.uk/Service-Search

CONTACTING THE NHS

NHS Customer Contact Centre: england.nhs.uk/contact-us

NHS out of hours services: nhs.uk/NHSEngland/AboutNHSservices/doctors/Pages/out-of-hours-services-old.aspx

NHS 111: england.nhs.uk/urgent-emergency-care/nhs-111

OTHER USEFUL NHS LINKS

Dental charges: nhs.uk/common-health-questions/dental-health/how-much-will-i-pay-for-nhs-dental-treatment/

Low-income scheme: nhsbsa.nhs.uk/nhs-low-income-scheme

Prescription costs: nhs.uk/NHSEngland/Healthcosts/
Pages/Prescriptioncosts.aspx

Live Well diet advice: nhs.uk/Livewell/weight-loss-guide/
Pages/calorie-counting.aspx

Live Well exercise advice: nhs.uk/Livewell/fitness/pages/
physical-activity-guidelines-for-adults.aspx

Live Well insomnia advice: www.nhs.uk/Livewell/
insomnia

MENTAL HEALTH

NHS mental-health services: nhs.uk/NHSEngland/
AboutNHSservices/mental-health-services-explained

Types of therapy available: nhs.uk/conditions/
stress-anxiety-depression/types-of-therapy

Accessing NHS mental-health services: nhs.uk/
NHSEngland/AboutNHSservices/mental-health-services-
explained/Pages/accessing%20services.aspx

NHS online mental-health services: nhs.uk/Conditions/
online-mental-health-services/Pages/introduction.aspx

**British Association for Counselling & Psychotherapy
(BACP):** itsgoodtotalk.org.uk

MIND urgent help: mind.org.uk/need-urgent-help

MIND action plans: mind.org.uk/workplace/
mental-health-at-work/taking-care-of-your-staff/
employer-resources/wellness-action-plan-download/

The Samaritans: samaritans.org

Time to Change: time-to-change.org.uk

Disability under the Equality Act 2010: gov.uk/
definition-of-disability-under-equality-act-2010

HEALTH APPS

Couch to 5k: nhs.uk/Tools/Pages/couch-to-5k.aspx

Sleepio: sleepio.com

ONLINE MENTAL-HEALTH SERVICES

Silvercloud: apps.beta.nhs.uk/silvercloud

Big White Wall: bigwhitewall.com

Fear Fighter: fearfighter.cbtprogram.com

Ieso: iesohealth.com/en-gb

OTHER USEFUL LINKS

First Aid: sja.org.uk

Fit notes: nhs.uk/chq/Pages/1062.aspx?CategoryID=87

Statutory sick pay: gov.uk/statutory-sick-pay

Terrence Higgins Trust: tht.org.uk

Chapter 4: DIY SOS

Useful advice and how-tos: http://www.diy.com/ideas-advice/1.hroot

Energy saving advice: energysavingtrust.co.uk

Gas Safe Register: gassaferegister.co.uk, 0800 111 999

DIY advice: diydoctor.org.uk

Handyman tips and advice: diydoctor.org.uk, ultimatehandyman.co.uk

Tradesman recommendation websites: ratedpeople.com, myhammer.co.uk

Chapter 5: Trains, planes, and automobiles

CARS

Driving test info: https://www.gov.uk/learn-to-drive-a-car

Practice theory tests: https://www.gov.uk/take-practice-theory-test

Cheap passport photos: Paspic.com

Car clubs: ZipCar.co.uk, EnterpriseCarClub.co.uk

Lift-share sites: BlaBlaCar.co.uk, liftshare.com

Cheap fuel: petrolprices.com

Car data: Whatcar.co.uk, Carbuyer.co.uk, HonestJohn.co.uk, Parkers.co.uk

Second-hand car's background: hpicheck.com

Cheaper parking: parkopedia.com, justpark.com, holidayextras.co.uk

Car maintenance: youtube.com/user/DIYautotech, youtube.com/user/ehowauto/playlists, youtube.com/expertvillage

Car hire excess-protection policies: protectyourbubble.com, questor-insurance.co.uk, carhireexcess.com

Highway Code: gov.uk/browse/driving/highway-code-road-safety

Road safety tips: brake.org.uk

Car tax bands: gov.uk/vehicle-tax-rate-tables

Car fuel stats: carfueldata.direct.gov.uk/

Car servicing info: rac.co.uk/car-care/car-service

Car comparison site: parkers.co.uk/cars/reviews/compare-cars/

Search car parts prices: autopartstrader.co.uk/carparts

USEFUL LINKS

TRAINS

Journey-splitting: splityourticket.co.uk

Plan train journeys in advance: nationalrail.co.uk/times_fares/booking_horizons.html

Cheap ticket alerts: thetrainline.com/ticketalert

Train fare comparison: thetrainline.com (But cheaper to book direct with the operator, as doing so means avoiding fees.)

Railcards: railcard.co.uk

Train journey refunds: trainrefunds.co.uk

Tube journey refunds in London: tfl.gov.uk/fares-and-payments/refunds-and-replacements

Cheapest fare finder: ojp.nationalrail.co.uk/service/farefinder/search

BIKES AND WALKING

Government tax-efficient bike-buying scheme: cyclescheme.co.uk/getting-a-bike

Subsidised cycling training (in some areas): cycletraining.co.uk

Bike maintenance guides: britishcycling.org.uk/knowledge/bike-kit/maintenance

Walk (find the most direct or enjoyable routes): walkit.com, google.co.uk/maps

FLIGHTS

Comparison sites: Kayak.co.uk, Skyscanner.com, Momondo.co.uk

Charter flights: charterflights.co.uk, flightsdirect.com, travelsupermarket.com

'Fly Everywhere' option: skyscanner.net/news/
skyscanner-tips-and-tools-everywhere-search

European Health Insurance Card: ehic.org.uk

'Secret hotel rooms': hotwire.com, lastminute.com/hotels/
top-secret.html (Top tip: use secrethotelsrevealed.co.uk to
identify.)

Chapter 6: Work

GENERAL EMPLOYMENT

Salary checkers: linkedin.com/salary, glassdoor.
co.uk/Salaries, indeed.co.uk/salaries, totaljobs.com/
salary-checker/salary-calculator

Prospects CV advice: prospects.ac.uk/careers-advice/
cvs-and-cover-letters

TYPES OF JOBS

Glassdoor: glassdoor.co.uk

Prospects: prospects.ac.uk/job-profiles, prospects.ac.uk/
planner

UCAS: ucas.com/ucas/after-gcses/find-career-ideas/
explore-jobs

The Book of Jobs by **Lucy Tobin:** www.quercusbooks.
co.uk/books/detail.page?isbn=9781784291341

JOB FAIRS AND EVENTS

Prospects: prospects.ac.uk/events

TheJobFairs: thejobfairs.co.uk

Creative Access: creativeaccess.org.uk/news-and-events

WORK EXPERIENCE AND TRAINING

Placements and internships: Milkround.com, Studentjob.
co.uk, Ratemyplacement.co.uk
Traineeships: gov.uk/find-traineeship
Apprenticeships: gov.uk/apply-apprenticeship
Networking: eventbrite.co.uk, meetup.com

EMPLOYMENT RIGHTS

Intern rights: gov.uk/employment-rights-for-interns,
www.gov.uk/guidance/national-minimum-wage-work-
experience-and-internships#what-counts-as-an-internship
Volunteer pay and expenses: gov.uk/volunteering/
pay-and-expenses
National Minimum Wage: gov.uk/
national-minimum-wage-rates
Benefits: gov.uk/benefits-calculators
Workplace bullying: gov.uk/
workplace-bullying-and-harassment,
citizensadvice.org.uk/work/discrimination-at-work/
what-are-the-different-types-of-discrimination/harassment-
at-work, acas.org.uk, mind.org.uk/information-support/
tips-for-everyday-living/work/workplace-relations
Disability discrimination: citizensadvice.org.uk/law-
and-courts/discrimination/protected-characteristics/
disability-discrimination/
Redundancy: worksmart.org.uk/work-rights/
losing-your-job/redundancy/i-have-been-made-redundant-
what-payment-am-i-entitled
Finding a union: worksmart.org.uk/tools/union-finder

SELF-EMPLOYMENT — GETTING SET UP

Going self-employed: simplybusiness.co.uk

Becoming a sole trader: gov.uk/set-up-sole-trader

Becoming a limited company: gov.uk/
limited-company-formation

Companies House: gov.uk/government/organisations/
companies-house

Finding an accountant: unbiased.co.uk

SELF-EMPLOYMENT — HANDLING YOUR INCOME

Late payments: gov.uk/late-commercial-payments-
interest-debt-recovery

Self-assessment ready reckoner: gov.uk/self-assessment-
ready-reckoner

Paying your student loan: gov.uk/guidance/tell-hmrc-
about-a-student-loan-in-your-tax-return, www.slc.co.uk

Invoicing: gov.uk/invoicing-and-taking-payment-from-
customers/invoices-what-they-must-include

Sample invoices: crunch.co.uk/knowledge/invoice-templates

Self-employment business tax: gov.uk/topic/business-tax/
self-employed

Corporation tax: gov.uk/corporation-tax

Expenses: gov.uk/simpler-income-tax-simplified-expenses

STARTING YOUR OWN BUSINESS

Business plans: princes-trust.org.uk/
help-for-young-people/tools-resources

Chapter 7: Life admin (a.k.a. THAT DRAWER)

ONLINE SECURITY

Password generator: identitysafe.norton.com/
password-generator

Back-up services: dropbox.com, drive.google.com, icloud.
com, sharefile.com

APPS TO HELP YOU GET ORGANISED

(Available for iPhones at apple.com/uk/ios/app-store,
Android at play.google.com/store/apps, Windows at
microsoft.com/store/apps)

Evernote for to-do lists: evernote.com

Loyalive for loyalty cards: loyalive.com

IFTTT to help remember things: ifttt.com

Unroll.me for inbox organising: unroll.me

Citymapper to not get lost: citymapper.com

Redlaser to find cheap deals: redlaser.en.softonic.com

Spending tracker for budgeting: goodbudget.com

Calm to distress: calm.com

FEEL-GOOD IDEAS

Good gym: goodgym.org

Casserole club: casseroleclub.com

Befriend someone elderly: fote.org.uk, contact-the-elderly.
org.uk/become-a-volunteer/how-it-works

Governor roles: inspiringgovernance.org

Volunteer role databases: vinspired.com/volunteer,
reachvolunteering.org.uk, do-it.org

Chapter 8: Etiquette and emotional intelligence

GIFTS FOR NEW PARENTS

Don't Buy Her Flowers: dontbuyherflowers.com

Birchbox: birchbox.co.uk

Molly Maid vouchers: mollymaid.co.uk/
molly-maid-gift-vouchers

MAKING FRIENDS

Bumble BFF: thebeehive.bumble.com/bumble-bff

MeetUp: www.meetup.com

City Socializer: citysocializer.com

HELP WITH DIFFICULT PARENTS

My Horrid Parent: myhorridparent.com/resources

BRITISH ETIQUETTE

Debretts: debretts.com

ABUSIVE RELATIONSHIPS

Refuge: www.refuge.org.uk

Women's Aid: womensaid.org.uk

Chapter 9: Money, money, money

If in doubt, look at moneysavingexpert.com

TELECOMS

Compare mobile tariffs: billmonitor.com,
moneysupermarket.com

Alternatives to pricey phone numbers: saynoto0870.com

Cheap phone abroad access codes: niftylist.co.uk/calls

Broadband comparison: simplifydigital.co.uk; broadband-choices.co.uk, uswitch.com; moneysupermarket.com

ENERGY AND WATER

Energy: comparethemarket.com, energyhelpline.com

Water meter check: ccwater.org.uk

FINANCIAL CHECKS

Check your credit score for free: experian.co.uk, noddle.co.uk, equifax.co.uk (free trial — don't forget to cancel)

Shares: hl.co.uk, .iii.co.uk, youinvest.co.uk, stockopedia.com

Financial Services Compensation Scheme: fscs.org.uk

BUDGET APPS

Mint: mint.com

Wally: Wally.me

GoodBudget: Goodbudget.com

CONSUMER RIGHTS INFO

Which: https://www.which.co.uk/consumer-rights/shopping

PENSIONS

State pension info: gov.uk/browse/working/state-pension, gov.uk/workplace-pensions

Pension guide: moneyadviceservice.org.uk/en/articles/pension-information-guide-to-the-basic-facts

Advice: pensionsadvisoryservice.org.uk

Citizens advice on pensions: citizensadvice.org.uk/
debt-and-money/pensions

Retirement planning tips: ageuk.org.uk/
information-advice/money-legal/pensions

CREDIT CARDS AND SPENDING

'Soft search' credit card comparison: TotallyMoney.com,
moneysupermarket.com/credit-cards

Cashback credit cards: moneysavingexpert.com/
credit-cards/cashback-credit-cards

Eligibility: moneysavingexpert.com/eligibility/credit-cards

INSURANCE

Insurance comparison sites: moneysupermarket.com,
confused.com, gocompare.com

Home contents insurance calculator:
confused.com/home-insurance/guides/
how-to-calculate-your-home-contents

Advice and tips on insurance: moneyadviceservice.org.uk/
insurance

SAVINGS

Savings deals: moneynet.co.uk, moneyfacts.co.uk

Peer-to-peer lending: zopa.com, ratesetter.com,
fundingcircle.com

Premium bonds: nsandi.com/premium-bonds

Premium bonds chance calculator: moneysavingexpert.
com/savings/premium-bonds-calculator

ISAs: https://www.gov.uk/individual-savings-accounts/
how-isas-work

STUDENT FINANCE

Student loan info: gov.uk/student-finance,
moneysavingexpert.com/students/student-finance-calculator

DEBT ADVICE

National debtline: nationaldebtline.org

My Money Steps: mymoneysteps.org

Step Change: stepchange.org

Citizens Advice: citizensadvice.org.uk

Debt Advice Foundation: debtadvicefoundation.org

PayPlan: payplan.com

LEGAL ADVICE

Legal aid: www.gov.uk/legal-aid

Law Centres: lawcentres.org.uk

Citizens Advice: citizensadvice.org.uk/law-
and-courts/legal-system/taking-legal-action/
help-with-legal-costs-free-or-affordable-help/

Free wills: freewillsmonth.org.uk

SHOPPING

Price comparison sites: Kelkoo.co.uk, pricerunner.co.uk,
google.co.uk/shopping

Cashback: topcashback.co.uk, quidco.com

Voucher sites: vouchercodes.co.uk, hotukdeals.com/
discountvouchers

Amazon discounts: zeezaw.co.uk,uk.camelcamelcamel.com/
eBay discounts: fatfingers.co.uk, and 'sniper'
auctionstealer.co.uk

MONEY-MAKING SOURCES

Mystery shopping: secretsquirrel.com,
grassrootsmysteryshopping.com, retail-maxim.co.uk
Survey filling-in: i-say.com, globaltestmarket.co.uk,
populuslive.com
Rent your stuff: rentmyitems.com, justpark.com,
storemates.co.uk
Sell your stuff: gumtree.co.uk, ebay.co.uk, facebook.com/
marketplace, Shpock.com
Gadget recycling: mazumamobile.com, Envirofone.com
Focus groups: sarosresearch.com
Sell your photos: picfair.com (set your own price),
istockphoto.com (receive a set royalty)
Sell your skills: etsy.com, fivesquid.co.uk, peopleperhour.
com, freelancer.com, studentgems.com
Hunt for lost savings: mylostaccount.org.uk,
thepensionservice.gov.uk

CONSUMER ADVICE

Advice for complaints and claims: Resolver.co.uk
Money-saving tips: moneysavingexpert.com
Benefits advice: citizensadvice.org.uk/benefits
Trading Standards: tradingstandards.uk
Financial Ombudsman Service: financial-ombudsman.org.uk
Advice Guide (from Citizens Advice): adviceguide.org.uk

Retirement advice: direct.gov.uk/en/
Pensionsandretirementplanning/index.htm,
pensionsadvisoryservice.org.uk/

Chapter 10: How to find a home

AFFORDABILITY

Salary calculator: salarybot.co.uk
Home bill checker: moneysupermarket.com/
home-bill-checker/
Council tax bands: gov.uk/council-tax-bands

FINDING SOMEWHERE TO LIVE

Property guardians: uk.cameloteurope.com,
adhocproperty.co.uk, homeshareuk.org
House shares: spareroom.co.uk, rightmove.co.uk,
easyroomate.com, gumtree.co.uk, idealflatmate.com,
londonshared.co.uk, openrent.co.uk, purplebricks.co.uk

THE LEGAL STUFF

Rental fees: zoopla.co.uk/discover/renting/rental-
fees/, citizensadvice.org.uk/housing/renting-a-home/
tenancy-agreements/#h-what-is-a-tenancy-agreement
Tenancy checker: england.shelter.org.uk/get_advice/
downloads_and_tools/tenancy_checker
Health and safety in rented homes: england.
shelter.org.uk/housing_advice/repairs/health_
and_safety_standards_for_rented_homes_hhsrs,
england.shelter.org.uk/housing_advice/repairs/

how_to_complain_about_an_unsafe_home

Fair wear and tear: landlords.org.uk/news-campaigns/news/what-fair-wear-and-tear

HOUSE-SHARE APPS

Acasa: helloacasa.com

Bizzby: bizzby.com

BrightNest: brightnest.com

Chorma: www.chorma.com

Our Home App: ourhomeapp.com

Monzo: monzo.com

Sortly: sortly.com

Splitwise: splitwise.com

White Noise: tmsoft.com/white-noise

Wunderlist: wunderlist.com

OTHER RESOURCES

Repairing a home: england.shelter.org.uk/housing_advice/repairs/doing_the_repairs_if_your_landlord_wont

Property Ombudsman Scheme: tpos.co.uk

Property Redress Scheme: theprs.co.uk

Ombudsman services: ombudsman-services.org/sectors/property

Shelter for housing advice: shelter.org.uk

AT HOME — BUYING, RENTING, LOOKING AFTER IT

Home Insurance value calculator: abi.bcis.co.uk/#calculation

Buying calculator: moneyadviceservice.org.uk/en/tools/

house-buying/mortgage-affordability-calculator

Stamp duty calculator: gov.uk/guidance/
hmrc-tools-and-calculators#stamp-duty-land-tax-sdlt

Council tax info: gov.uk/council-tax-bands **and appeals:**
gov.uk/council-tax-appeals/challenge-your-band

Help to Buy: helptobuy.gov.uk

Shared ownership: helptobuy.gov.uk/shared-ownership/

Home security: immobilise.com

Neighbourhood watch: ourwatch.org.uk

Reclaim council tax: the Valuation Office Agency's
website voa.gov.uk

Eco-efficient homes advice: energysavingtrust.org.uk/
home-energy-efficiency/home-improvements

Acknowledgements

Lucy:

After a meeting in the *Women's Hour* green room, Sarah Braybrooke, I was pretty amazed that you reckoned I was, à la *Rugrats*, All Growed Up enough to co-write this book. But I'm thankful that you did. And very glad, too, for your literary matchmaking with Kat. From getting stuck in woodland mud to 3am WhatsApps, Ms Poole, you've been the co-author of dreams … to the extent that I've overlooked my 'no friends with Hotmail addresses' rule for you.

Thank you, Molly Slight, for owning 84 Bugattis and *still* working hard on our MS (I'd definitely have retired …), and to Philip Gwyn Jones for all your help and wise words.

Mum and Dad thanks for all the babysitting whilst I scribbled away – and for teaching me how to be the adult I suppose I must admit I am.

Thanks, too, to all the friends and family who've made me laugh with embarrassing stories you'd never before shared but are now immortalised in these pages … Your secrets are safe with us.

Kat:

This book wouldn't have happened without Sarah Braybrooke at Scribe; thank you for letting me write so honestly about what adulthood, so far, has been like for me, and introducing me to my co-author and friend for life, Lucy Tobin. It has been such a treat to write with you, Lucy — I genuinely never expected to work with someone I love hanging out with, too.

Thank you to Molly Slight who helped turn our words into the book you're holding now, and to Philip Gwyn Jones for supporting this project from the very beginning. Anna Fielding, thank you for showing me such kindness and encouragement. To everyone who shared personal stories, lessons, and professional insight that makes this book what it is — I am eternally grateful.

Mum, Dad, and Johnny, thank you for cheering me on, even when you didn't have a clue where I was going next. And to the amazing women who have been there through the ups and downs and the what-do-I-do-nows, your friendships (and the stories that go with them) are proof that some of the best things in life really do happen when you're an adult. Amy, Becci, Christa, Hannah, and Ally, thank you.

Index